ILLUSTRATED COMPUTER DICTIONARY FOR DUMMIES®

3RD EDITION

COMPUTER BOOK SERIES FROM IDG

References for the Rest of Us!®

Are you intimidated and confused by computers? Do you find that traditional manuals are overloaded with technical details you'll never use? Do your friends and family always call you to fix simple problems on their PCs? Then the *...For Dummies*® computer book series from IDG Books Worldwide is for you.

...For Dummies books are written for those frustrated computer users who know they aren't really dumb but find that PC hardware, software, and indeed the unique vocabulary of computing make them feel helpless. *...For Dummies* books use a lighthearted approach, a down-to-earth style, and even cartoons and humorous icons to diffuse computer novices' fears and build their confidence. Lighthearted but not lightweight, these books are a perfect survival guide for anyone forced to use a computer.

> *"I like my copy so much I told friends; now they bought copies."*
>
> **Irene C., Orwell, Ohio**

> *"Quick, concise, nontechnical, and humorous."*
>
> **Jay A., Elburn, Illinois**

> *"Thanks, I needed this book. Now I can sleep at night."*
>
> **Robin F., British Columbia, Canada**

Already, millions of satisfied readers agree. They have made *...For Dummies* books the #1 introductory level computer book series and have written asking for more. So, if you're looking for the most fun and easy way to learn about computers, look to *...For Dummies* books to give you a helping hand.

IDG BOOKS WORLDWIDE

5/97

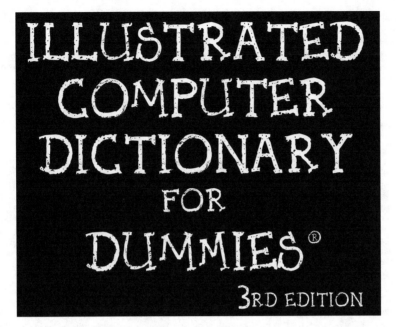

ILLUSTRATED COMPUTER DICTIONARY FOR DUMMIES®

3RD EDITION

by Dan and Sandy Gookin

IDG Books Worldwide, Inc.
An International Data Group Company

Foster City, CA ♦ Chicago, IL ♦ Indianapolis, IN ♦ Southlake, TX

Illustrated Computer Dictionary For Dummies® 3rd Edition

Published by
IDG Books Worldwide, Inc.
An International Data Group Company
919 E. Hillsdale Blvd.
Suite 400
Foster City, CA 94404
www.idgbooks.com (IDG Books Worldwide Web site)
www.dummies.com (Dummies Press Web site)

Library of Congress Catalog Card No.: 97-81225

ISBN: 0-7645-0143-7

Printed in the United States of America

10 9 8 7 6 5 4 3 2

3E/QX/QR/ZY/IN

Distributed in the United States by IDG Books Worldwide, Inc.

Distributed by Macmillan Canada for Canada; by Transworld Publishers Limited in the United Kingdom; by IDG Norge Books for Norway; by IDG Sweden Books for Sweden; by Woodslane Pty. Ltd. for Australia; by Woodslane Enterprises Ltd. for New Zealand; by Longman Singapore Publishers Ltd. for Singapore, Malaysia, Thailand, and Indonesia; by Simron Pty. Ltd. for South Africa; by Toppan Company Ltd. for Japan; by Distribuidora Cuspide for Argentina; by Livraria Cultura for Brazil; by Ediciencia S.A. for Ecuador; by Addison-Wesley Publishing Company for Korea; by Ediciones ZETA S.C.R. Ltda. for Peru; by WS Computer Publishing Corporation, Inc., for the Philippines; by Unalis Corporation for Taiwan; by Contemporanea de Ediciones for Venezuela; by Computer Book & Magazine Store for Puerto Rico; by Express Computer Distributors for the Caribbean and West Indies. Authorized Sales Agent: Anthony Rudkin Associates for the Middle East and North Africa.

For general information on IDG Books Worldwide's books in the U.S., please call our Consumer Customer Service department at 800-762-2974. For reseller information, including discounts and premium sales, please call our Reseller Customer Service department at 800-434-3422.

For information on where to purchase IDG Books Worldwide's books outside the U.S., please contact our International Sales department at 415-655-3200 or fax 415-655-3295.

For information on foreign language translations, please contact our Foreign & Subsidiary Rights department at 415-655-3021 or fax 415-655-3281.

For sales inquiries and special prices for bulk quantities, please contact our Sales department at 415-655-3200 or write to the address above.

For information on using IDG Books Worldwide's books in the classroom or for ordering examination copies, please contact our Educational Sales department at 800-434-2086 or fax 817-251-8174.

For press review copies, author interviews, or other publicity information, please contact our Public Relations department at 415-655-3000 or fax 415-655-3299.

For authorization to photocopy items for corporate, personal, or educational use, please contact Copyright Clearance Center, 222 Rosewood Drive, Danvers, MA 01923, or fax 508-750-4470.

is a trademark under exclusive license to IDG Books Worldwide, Inc., from International Data Group, Inc.

About the Authors

Dan Gookin is as close to a household name as it gets in the computer book industry. Dan is not only a wonderful writer, but also a computer "guru" whose job is to remind everyone that computers are not to be taken too seriously.

Dan has written over 60 books on computers, including the original ...*For Dummies* book, *DOS For Dummies.* Dan's most recent titles include the best-selling *PCs For Dummies,* 4th Edition, *Word 97 For Windows For Dummies,* and *Discover Windows 95.* Dan holds a degree in Communications-Visual Arts (okay, let's be honest: Art!) from University of California-San Diego and currently lives with his wife and four sons in the rustic and untamed state known as Idaho.

Sandra Hardin Gookin has an amazing ability to make difficult tasks easy to understand. This comes, in part, from her Speech Communications degree from Oklahoma State University, but mainly from having to communicate with her five boys (four children + one husband, Dan). Sandra works with Dan to make computer terms easy for you to understand. If she can understand them, you will too. Sandra's other books include *Parenting For Dummies* and *Discover Windows 95.*

ABOUT IDG BOOKS WORLDWIDE

Welcome to the world of IDG Books Worldwide.

IDG Books Worldwide, Inc., is a subsidiary of International Data Group, the world's largest publisher of computer-related information and the leading global provider of information services on information technology. IDG was founded more than 25 years ago and now employs more than 8,500 people worldwide. IDG publishes more than 275 computer publications in over 75 countries (see listing below). More than 60 million people read one or more IDG publications each month.

Launched in 1990, IDG Books Worldwide is today the #1 publisher of best-selling computer books in the United States. We are proud to have received eight awards from the Computer Press Association in recognition of editorial excellence and three from *Computer Currents'* First Annual Readers' Choice Awards. Our best-selling *...For Dummies*® series has more than 30 million copies in print with translations in 30 languages. IDG Books Worldwide, through a joint venture with IDG's Hi-Tech Beijing, became the first U.S. publisher to publish a computer book in the People's Republic of China. In record time, IDG Books Worldwide has become the first choice for millions of readers around the world who want to learn how to better manage their businesses.

Our mission is simple: Every one of our books is designed to bring extra value and skill-building instructions to the reader. Our books are written by experts who understand and care about our readers. The knowledge base of our editorial staff comes from years of experience in publishing, education, and journalism — experience we use to produce books for the '90s. In short, we care about books, so we attract the best people. We devote special attention to details such as audience, interior design, use of icons, and illustrations. And because we use an efficient process of authoring, editing, and desktop publishing our books electronically, we can spend more time ensuring superior content and spend less time on the technicalities of making books.

You can count on our commitment to deliver high-quality books at competitive prices on topics you want to read about. At IDG Books Worldwide, we continue in the IDG tradition of delivering quality for more than 25 years. You'll find no better book on a subject than one from IDG Books Worldwide.

John Kilcullen
CEO
IDG Books Worldwide, Inc.

Steven Berkowitz
President and Publisher
IDG Books Worldwide, Inc.

Eighth Annual Computer Press Awards ≥1992

WINNER
Ninth Annual Computer Press Awards ≥1993

WINNER
Tenth Annual Computer Press Awards ≥1994

WINNER
Eleventh Annual Computer Press Awards ≥1995

IDG Books Worldwide, Inc., is a subsidiary of International Data Group, the world's largest publisher of computer-related information and the leading global provider of information services on information technology. International Data Group publishes over 275 computer publications in over 75 countries. Sixty million people read one or more International Data Group publications each month. International Data Group's publications include: **ARGENTINA:** Buyer's Guide, Computerworld Argentina, PC World Argentina; **AUSTRALIA:** Australian Macworld, Australian PC World, Australian Reseller News, Computerworld, IT Casebook, Network World, Publish, Webmaster; **AUSTRIA:** Computerwelt Osterreich, Networks Austria, PC Tip Austria; **BANGLADESH:** PC World Bangladesh; **BELARUS:** PC World Belarus; **BELGIUM:** Data News; **BRAZIL:** Annuário de Informática, Computerworld, Connections, Macworld, PC Player, PC World, Publish, Reseller News, Supergamepower; **BULGARIA:** Computerworld Bulgaria, Network World Bulgaria, PC & MacWorld Bulgaria; **CANADA:** CIO Canada, Client/Server World, ComputerWorld Canada, InfoWorld Canada, NetworkWorld Canada, WebWorld; **CHILE:** Computerworld Chile, PC World Chile; **COLOMBIA:** Computerworld Colombia, PC World Colombia; **COSTA RICA:** PC World Centro America; **THE CZECH AND SLOVAK REPUBLICS:** Computerworld Czechoslovakia, Macworld Czech Republic, PC World Czechoslovakia; **DENMARK:** Communications World Danmark, Computerworld Danmark, Macworld Danmark, PC World Danmark, Techworld Denmark; **DOMINICAN REPUBLIC:** PC World Republica Dominicana; **ECUADOR:** PC World Ecuador; **EGYPT:** Computerworld Middle East, PC World Middle East; **EL SALVADOR:** PC World Centro America; **FINLAND:** MikroPC, Tietoverkko, Tietoviikko; **FRANCE:** Distributique, Hebdo, Info PC, Le Monde Informatique, Macworld, Reseaux & Telecoms, WebMaster France; **GERMANY:** Computer Partner, Computerwoche, Computerwoche Extra, Computerwoche FOCUS, Global Online, Macwelt, PC Welt; **GREECE:** Amiga Computing, GamePro Greece, Multimedia World; **GUATEMALA:** PC World Centro America; **HONDURAS:** PC World Centro America; **HONG KONG:** Computerworld Hong Kong, PC World Hong Kong, Publish in Asia; **HUNGARY:** ABCD CD-ROM, Computerworld Szamitastechnika, Internetto online Magazine, PC World Hungary, PC-X Magazin Hungary; **ICELAND:** Tolvuheimur PC World Island; **INDIA:** Information Communications World, Information Systems Computerworld, PC World India, Publish in Asia; **INDONESIA:** InfoKomputer PC World, Komputek Computerworld, Publish in Asia; **IRELAND:** ComputerScope, PC Live!; **ISRAEL:** Macworld Israel, People & Computers/Computerworld; **ITALY:** Computerworld Italia, Macworld Italia, Networking Italia, PC World Italia; **JAPAN:** DTP World, Macworld Japan, Nikkei Personal Computing, OS/2 World Japan, SunWorld Japan, Windows NT World, Windows World Japan; **KENYA:** PC World East African; **KOREA:** Hi-Tech Information, Macworld Korea, PC World Korea; **MACEDONIA:** PC World Macedonia; **MALAYSIA:** Computerworld Malaysia, PC World Malaysia, Publish in Asia; **MALTA:** PC World Malta; **MEXICO:** Computerworld Mexico, PC World Mexico; **MYANMAR:** PC World Myanmar; **NETHERLANDS:** Computer! Totaal, LAN Internetworking Magazine, LAN World Buyers Guide, Macworld Netherlands, Net, WebWereld; **NEW ZEALAND:** Absolute Beginners Guide and Plain & Simple Series, Computer Buyer, Computer Industry Directory, Computerworld New Zealand, MTB, Network World, PC World New Zealand; **NICARAGUA:** PC World Centro America; **NORWAY:** Computerworld Norge, CW Rapport, Datamagasinet, Financial Rapport, Kursguide Norge, Macworld Norge, Multimediaworld Norge, PC World Ekspress Norge, PC World Nettverk, PC World Norge, PC World ProduktGuide Norge; **PAKISTAN:** Computerworld Pakistan; **PANAMA:** PC World Panama; **PEOPLE'S REPUBLIC OF CHINA:** China Computer Users, China Computerworld, China InfoWorld, China Telecom World Weekly, Computer & Communication, Electronic Design China, Electronics Today, Electronics Weekly, Game Software, PC World China, Popular Computer Week, Software Weekly, Software World, Telecom World; **PERU:** Computerworld Peru, PC World Profesional Peru, PC World SoHo Peru; **PHILIPPINES:** Click!, Computerworld Philippines, PC World Philippines, Publish in Asia; **POLAND:** Computerworld Poland, Computerworld Special Report Poland, Cyber, Macworld Poland, Networld Poland, PC World Komputer; **PORTUGAL:** Cerebro/PC World, Computerworld/Correio Informático, Dealer World Portugal, Mac*In/PC*In Portugal, Multimedia World; **PUERTO RICO:** PC World Puerto Rico; **ROMANIA:** Computerworld Romania, PC World Romania, Telecom Romania; **RUSSIA:** Computerworld Russia, Mir PK, Publish, Seti; **SINGAPORE:** Computerworld Singapore, PC World Singapore, Publish in Asia; **SLOVENIA:** Monitor; **SOUTH AFRICA:** Computing SA, Network World SA, Software World SA; **SPAIN:** Communicaciones World España, Computerworld España, Dealer World España, Macworld España, PC World España; **SRI LANKA:** Infolink PC World; **SWEDEN:** CAP&Design, Computer Sweden, Corporate Computing Sweden, Internetworld Sweden, it.branschen, Macworld Sweden, MaxiData Sweden, MikroDatorn, Natverk & Kommunikation, PC World Sweden, PCaktiv, Windows World Sweden; **SWITZERLAND:** Computerworld Schweiz, Macworld Schweiz, PCtip; **TAIWAN:** Computerworld Taiwan, Macworld Taiwan, NEW ViSiON/Publish, PC World Taiwan, Windows World Taiwan; **THAILAND:** Publish in Asia, Thai Computerworld; **TURKEY:** Computerworld Turkiye, Macworld Turkiye, Network World Turkiye, PC World Turkiye; **UKRAINE:** Computerworld Kiev, Multimedia World Ukraine, PC World Ukraine; **UNITED KINGDOM:** Acorn User UK, Amiga Action UK, Amiga Computing UK, Apple Talk UK, Computing, Macworld, Parents and Computers UK, PC Advisor, PC Home, PSX Pro, The WEB; **UNITED STATES:** Cable in the Classroom, CIO Magazine, Computerworld, DOS World, Federal Computer Week, GamePro Magazine, InfoWorld, I-Way, Macworld, Network World, PC Games, PC World, Publish, Video Event, THE WEB Magazine, and WebMaster; online webzines: JavaWorld, NetscapeWorld, and SunWorld Online; **URUGUAY:** InfoWorld Uruguay; **VENEZUELA:** Computerworld Venezuela, PC World Venezuela; and **VIETNAM:** PC World Vietnam.   3/24/97

Authors' Acknowledgments

I would like to extend special thanks to the following folks who helped make this dictionary happen. First, thanks to my co-author for the first two editions, Wally Wang, as well as to Chris Van Buren, who helped with the first edition. Thanks also go to this book's original editor, Laurie Smith. And I'd also like to thank Drew Moore, who did the artwork for editions one and two. Gratis to Kevin Spencer for looking up some of the words no one could find anywhere. Thanks to all the other people who wrote computer dictionaries from which we stole words we never really use. And, as usual, thanks to the IDG Books staff for doing such a blasted fine job with everything.

No one named "Webster" was involved with this project. No meat products (or meat by-products) were consumed while typing the text of this book.

Dan Gookin

Publisher's Acknowledgments

We're proud of this book; please register your comments through our IDG Books Worldwide Online Registration Form, located at http://my2cents.dummies.com.

Some of the people who helped bring this book to market include the following:

Acquisitions, Development, and Editorial

Project Editors: Rev Mengle, Tim Gallan

Acquisitions Editor: Michael Kelly

Associate Permissions Editor: Heather Dismore

Copy Editors: Christine Meloy Beck, Rebecca Whitney

Technical Editor: Allen L. Wyatt

Editorial Manager: Leah P. Cameron

Editorial Assistant: Paul E. Kuzmic

Production

Project Coordinator: Regina Snyder

Layout and Graphics: Lou Boudreau, Angela F. Hunckler, Jane E. Martin, Drew R. Moore, Brent Savage, Janet Seib, Michael A. Sullivan

Proofreaders: Betty Kish, Christine Berman, Nancy Price, Rebecca Senninger, Janet Withers

Special Help: Elizabeth Netedu Kuball, Copy Editor; Donna Love, Editorial Assistant; Stephanie Koutek, Proof Editor

General and Administrative

IDG Books Worldwide, Inc.: John Kilcullen, CEO; Steven Berkowitz, President and Publisher

IDG Books Technology Publishing: Brenda McLaughlin, Senior Vice President and Group Publisher

Dummies Technology Press and Dummies Editorial: Diane Graves Steele, Vice President and Associate Publisher; Mary Bednarek, Acquisitions and Product Development Director; Kristin A. Cocks, Editorial Director

Dummies Trade Press: Kathleen A. Welton, Vice President and Publisher; Kevin Thornton, Acquisitions Manager; Maureen F. Kelly, Editorial Coordinator

IDG Books Production for Dummies Press: Beth Jenkins, Production Director; Cindy L. Phipps, Manager of Project Coordination, Production Proofreading, and Indexing; Kathie S. Schutte, Supervisor of Page Layout; Shelley Lea, Supervisor of Graphics and Design; Debbie J. Gates, Production Systems Specialist; Robert Springer, Supervisor of Proofreading; Debbie Stailey, Special Projects Coordinator; Tony Augsburger, Supervisor of Reprints and Bluelines; Leslie Popplewell, Media Archive Coordinator

Dummies Packaging and Book Design: Patti Crane, Packaging Specialist; Lance Kayser, Packaging Assistant; Kavish + Kavish, Cover Design

♦

The publisher would like to give special thanks to Patrick J. McGovern, without whom this book would not have been possible.

♦

Contents at a Glance

Introduction

H ere it is, the *Illustrated Computer Dictionary For Dummies,* 3rd Edition, your shield in the constant word battle that takes place between the nerds, geeks, technoweenies, and people like us who have to put up with the jargon. I've scoured the magazines and manuals. I've hung out at seminars and snuck into corporate BBQs. I've hunted down words in dark programmers' dungeons, listened to taped conversations of bigwigs talking in acronym-speak. I've been to Microsoft and read the bathroom stall walls. I've even made up a few words myself. The end result is this light-hearted approach to understanding computer terms and — if you dare — finding out how to incorporate such terms into your everyday conversation.

The Logical Approach

After long periods of careful thought, this book is laid out in alphabetic format and, further, to alphabetize all the words for your referencing needs. Symbols ("@#$%^&*!") and numbers (0-9) are listed first in their own chapter. But after that, it's A to Z — with all the letters in between in proper order. (I'm assuming you know the alphabet here, sung to the tune of *Twinkle Twinkle* in case you forget; ask any 6-year-old.)

Each chapter starts off with a graphical depiction of the letter (or random things for the symbols). You see the letter and then boxes describing the letter: Nerd Info, Braille, Alien Alphabet, Semaphores, American Sign Language, and Morse Code.

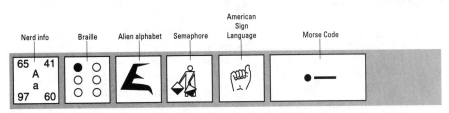

The Nerd Info box contains the ASCII code values for each letter in the four corners: decimal values on the left and hexadecimal values on the right. Uppercase letters are shown at the top; lowercase on the bottom. This stuff is for true computer nerds only, but it looks cool so I include it anyway.

The words are presented in the following format. First comes the word itself, then a pronunciation guide, followed by the word's meaning or a definition, and optionally sample usage:

> **dictionary** (dik-shun-aeree) A book that contains a list of words, their pronunciations, and meanings. When you don't know what a word means, you look it up in a dictionary. When you want to be sure you're using a word properly, you look it up in the dictionary. When you're losing an argument and need some random, though professional-sounding source to quote, you use the dictionary. "My kid keeps asking me what words mean, so I tell him to 'look it up in the *dictionary*,' since I'm too embarrassed to admit I don't know what the words mean myself."

Icons Used in This Book

As you are reading, you'll occasionally see an icon or two next to a word. The icon indicates that at least one of the definitions relates to one of the following:

An Internet or online term.

A term having to do with the Windows operating system.

A Macintosh computer term, just to make the Mac folks happy.

Philosophical Stuff

The purpose behind this dictionary is to both enlighten and inform. To add flavor, I toss in some entertainment value as well. Computers are always thought of as these big, frowning, cold, serious devices of torment — like nuns in a Catholic school. The truth is, they aren't. And nuns really aren't big and frowning either! Instead, computers have a vast potential for humor and enjoyment, as I'm sure nuns do, too! This book presents technical information with that attitude in the hopes that you will understand it better. And if not that, then at least you're able to tolerate the terminology with a modicum of levity.

@, #, 1, 2, 3

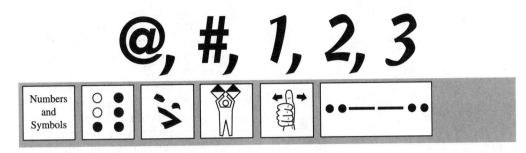

! *(exclamation point or bang)*
1. Used at the end of a sentence to denote excitement: "Your wife is here!" Or maybe surprise, "My heart!" In Spanish, a preceding exclamation point pre-alerts a reader to the excitement level of the sentence: "¡Su esposa esta aqui!" Y "¡Mi corazon!" 2. In the C programming language, the ! is used to mean *not,* as shown in this example:

```
!TRUE = FALSE
```

This line means, "Not true is the same thing as false," which is almost a universal truth anywhere except in Washington, D.C. 3. In the old USENET electronic-mail system, ! was called a *bang,* and it was used in someone's electronic address — like a highly effective zip code. For example:

```
crash!dang
```

This line may have been the electronic address of dang (Dan Gookin) on the crash system. The address is "crash, bang, dang." (It's no longer a valid address on the Internet.)

Did you ever notice that all the sentences in *Mad* magazine end in either an exclamation point or a question mark?

!= *(not equal)* Not equal. A combination of the ! (not) and = (equal) signs, often used in making a mathematical comparison, such as in the C language. "Watching baseball on TV is just != to being at the ballpark." See also $<, >$.

" *(double quote)* Often used to "hug" text, in what's called a *string* of text. For example:

> "The pastry was dry, and the coffee tasted like it had been strained through a dirty gym sock."

Although the text between the quotes is the "string," the quotes themselves are not.

*(pound, number,* or *tick-tack-toe)*
1. The pound symbol, above the 3 on American keyboards. Used in written language to represent numbers or items: "All right, Becky, you chose #3, Medical Instruments I've Found on the Beach." 2. In some versions of UNIX, the # is the system prompt:

```
# rm /usr/*
```

3. The # symbol also has appeal as a nice, solid character. Some people use it decoratively or to produce crude graphics:

@

```
######
#      #
#  #  #  #
#      #
#  ####  #
#  ##   #
#      #
######
```

4. On British keyboards, the # symbol is replaced by £, which really means *pound.* (A # is called the *hash* character in English English.)

$ *(dollar sign* or *string* or *hex)* **1.** Used in a number of ways, most of which have to do with money. When it's followed by a number, as in $1,000,000, the dollar sign means, obviously, one million dollars, big bucks, moola. **2.** In the BASIC programming language, a dollar sign is used to identify a *string,* or text variable. FIRST$ is a variable named FIRST that holds a string value. It's pronounced "first-string," by the way; not "first-SS" or "first-dollar sign." **3.** Some programming languages use the dollar sign to denote a *hexadecimal* (base 16) number. For example, $14 is the hexadecimal value 14 (20 decimal). $A1 is the hexadecimal value A1 (161 decimal). In this usage, the $ is pronounced "hex." $A1 is "hex-A-one." **4.** In MS-DOS, the dollar sign is used as a meta character to insert exciting items into the DOS prompt:

```
prompt $p$g
```

In the preceding line, the $P inserts the current path into the DOS prompt, and $G inserts the greater-than (>) character.

% *(percent sign)* **1.** Sometimes represents a percentage value: 15% means 15 percent or 15 parts of 100 or .15 or a value that's considered fairly good for weather forecasters and economists. The percent sign also plays numerous roles in various programming languages. **2.** In BASIC, the percent sign denotes an integer variable: ITEM% is an integer variable named ITEM. You don't pronounce the %. **3.** In the C programming language, the % is used as the *modulus* operator (which figures out the remainder when one number is divided by another). It's also used to format output with the `printf` function.

& *(am-per-sand)* **1.** Correctly called an ampersand. *Ampers* comes from the ancient Vulcan word for "this squiggly symbol means," and *and* means "and." **2.** Commonly used to represent *and,* as in "such & such" or "Baby want some c&y?," or, more accurately, "Sterling, Worbletyme & Grockmeister." Most purists reject this form, preferring to spell out the letters a-n-d. **3.** In computer programming, & sometimes represents a "logical AND," as shown in this example:

```
IF(NUMBER=1 & LETTER=A) THEN
"We're at the beginning."
```

4. In the C programming language, two ampersands are used to make a logical AND operation — &&.

' *(apostrophe* or *tick* or *single quote)* **1.** In English, marks the possessive, as in "Bill's deficit." **2.** Pairs are used to double-quote text, often with the accent grave (backward apostrophe, or `):

"This is less serious than we thought."

3. In the BASIC programming language, the apostrophe at the beginning of a line marks a comment.

( ) *(parentheses or parens)* 1. Parentheses are used in programming to group things together. Usually used in long mathematical operations; what appears between the parentheses is figured out first. 2. Most programming languages use parentheses to group together options and "arguments" for certain commands and keywords. 3. A single parenthesis is called a *paren*. When someone says "left paren," he's referring to the (character. The right paren is the). This stuff comes in handy when you're reading computer typing instructions over the phone.

(C) *(copyright symbol)* 1. Many software packages use a big *C* in parentheses to represent the © (copyright) symbol because the © isn't on most keyboards. Likewise, you may see (TM) to represent a trademark. 2. In most Microsoft Office applications, you can produce the copyright symbol by pressing Ctrl+Alt+C on your keyboard; pressing Ctrl+Atl+T produces the trademark symbol.

* *(asterisk or star or splat)* 1. In most computer programming languages and spreadsheets, the asterisk serves as the multiplication symbol, probably because the × symbol does not appear on the keyboard and a little *x* just doesn't cut it. 2. In some operating systems, the asterisk serves as a wildcard character representing a group of letters in a filename. The asterisk is pronounced "star" in this case: *.* is "star-dot-star." 3. In e-mail and other plain-text communications, the asterisk is used in a decorative fashion. Occasionally, it adds emphasis when neither italics nor bold type is available:

```
I was so *embarrassed*.
```

4. The asterisk may be used as a form of self-censorship in sending an e-mail message:

```
Eat **** and die!
```

5. Nathan Hale did not say, "I regret that I have but one asterisk for my country." 6. Other names for * include *dingbat* and *splat*. *Splat* is from the final result of dropping something mushy from a high altitude. The resulting spot looks like this:

+ *(plus)* 1. The addition symbol. Be grateful that this symbol is on your keyboard, lest you be forced to use the letter *T* or something equally obnoxious to represent addition:

```
2 + 2 = 5
```

2. The plus sign may also be used to connect two items, as shown in this example:

```
COPY A.DOC+B.DOC AB.DOC
```

@

In DOS, this command glues the file B.DOC to the end of the file A.DOC, creating a new file, AB.DOC. This process is known as *concatenation,* which is translated literally as "sticking two cats together," though the more common "sticking two things together" is generally accepted. See *concatenation* for the details and pronunciation.

– (minus sign or hyphen) 1. The minus sign is used in various corners of computer mathdom, primarily as the minus sign:

```
4 - 2 = 2
```

It's also used to identify a negative number:

```
-5
```

2. The hyphen is the minus sign's evil twin, which is the same character except that it's used with words, as in Mary-Frances. 3. Two hyphens can be used together in text to denote a clause or parenthetical element - - like this! 4. In typographical terms, you can use hyphens, en dashes, and em dashes, which are each used in different circumstances. The hyphen is the smallest one of the three. An *en dash* is a dash character, with the same width as the letter *n.* The *em dash* is a longer dash, with the same width as the letter *m.* This stuff is all typographical trivia that makes only finicky editors happy.

. (period or dot) 1. Used in text to mark the end of a sentence. 2. In math, the period is used to mark the decimal portion of a number: 3.141. In that case, it's pronounced "point," as in "three point one four one." 3. In some countries, a period is used to separate the hundreds from thousands or thousands from ten thousands: 1.000 is one thousand. (In these weird places, the comma is used as the decimal point. Strange.) 4. In some operating systems, a period is used to separate a filename from its extension. 5. A hockey game has three periods. 6. A period is used to separate elements in an Internet address. In this case, the period is pronounced "dot," as in:

```
www.dummies.com
```

which is pronounced "Dub-ohl-yoo dub-ohl-yoo dub-ohl-yoo dot duh-meez dot kom."

/ (slash or division symbol) 1. The forward-slash character is used in text to separate items: on/off, up/down, and so on. 2. In computer math, the / symbol is used for division because the ÷ character isn't available on most keyboards. So, 15/3 means "15 divided by 3." 3. This symbol has a host of names associated with it. In addition to hearing it called *slash* and *division symbol,* you may hear it as *forward slash, solidus, stroke, virgule, and the forward-pointing thing under the question-mark key.*

: (koh-lon) 1. In most PC operating systems, a colon is used after a disk drive letter, such as in the C: drive to refer to your hard drive, and after device names, such

General Colin Powell.

as in PRN: to refer to the printer. 2. In C programming, the colon is sometimes used, such as when you're declaring structure templates for bit fields. 3. Humans use the colon to digest food.

 :-) *(smile or smiley)* Electronic-mail method of showing a smile. (To see the smile, put your head on your left shoulder.) It implies that the tone of the message is happy. This technique is necessary in many cases when a tongue-in-cheek message can easily be misunderstood. "No, I don't think that you're a geek. You have no fashion sense, but you're not a geek. :-)"

 :-(*(frown)* Electronic-mail method of showing a frown, as in sadness. The opposite of :-).

:-* *(kiss)* Electronic-mail method of showing a kiss, as in physical contact, lips meeting. Do not use casually.

; *(semicolon)* Used in some Windows files and in the DOS CONFIG.SYS file, as a symbol to show that a line of text is a comment and not some command:

```
;This line will be ignored: The
computer is afraid of it!
```

;-) *(wink)* Electronic-mail method of showing a wink, as you would do in a verbal conversation. See also *:-)*.

< *(less than)* 1. Used in most computer programming languages to compare two values and test to see whether one is less than another. 2. Some operating systems use the less-than symbol to redirect input to a device.

<= *(less than or equal to)* The less-than symbol can be combined with the equal sign to compare two values in a test. The test passes if the first value is less than or equal to the second, as shown in this example:

```
9 <= 10 is true
10 <= 10 is true
10 <= 9 is false
Hollywood <= "real life" is
always true
```

< > *(not equal to* or *angle brackets)* 1. In some programming languages, the < > symbol set is used to test whether two values are not equal to each other. It's pronounced "not equal to." 2. Angle brackets are sometimes used when straight-edged people tire of parentheses. No rhyme, reason, or rule exists for when to use these things. 3. Angle brackets may also enclose emphasized text in e-mail messages. "Tomorrow, I'm turning <gasp> 30 years old!"

= *(equal sign)* 1. Used to denote equality or that something is equal to something else. For example, TASTES GOOD = CALORIES. 2. In most programming languages,

How the equal sign equates two items.

the equal sign is used for assigning a value to a variable.

== *(double equal sign* or *is equal to)* 1. Used in some instances to denote that two things are equal. 2. In the C programming language, the double equal sign is used for comparing two values.

> *(greater than* or *quote* or *redirected output)* 1. The greater-than symbol in math. For example:

```
Feelings > Honesty
```

Many computer nerds are still trying to figure out the preceding relationship. 2. Commonly used in electronic mail when you're quoting what someone has just written to you:

```
You wrote:
>Your mother dresses you funny.

And you wonder why I don't
write you anymore?
```

Other characters can be used to quote text, though > is most common. 3. Used in some operating systems to redirect output to a file or some other device.

>> *(append)* There is really no way to pronounce any of these symbols, though "ugh-ugh" is often used. Some say "double greater-than." Others may just say "append," which is what these characters do in DOS.

```
TYPE SIGNATUR.TXT >>
LETTER.DOC
```

The preceding DOS command takes the information in the file SIGNATUR.TXT and sticks it on the end of the file LETTER.DOC. Note that this trick works only with text files, not with documents created with a word processor or other formatted documents. 2. The bit-wise shift-left command in the C language — something completely nerdy that needs no additional explanation here. 3. In some European languages, these characters are used as quotes, though they're doubled up:

>>Jacques! The quiche is ruined!

>= *(greater than or equal to)* Used to compare two values in a test (as in a database query, for example). The test passes if the first value is greater than or equal to the second value, as shown in this example:

```
10 >= 9 is true
10 >= 10 is true
10 >= 11 is false
good >= evil — we hope is true
```

? *(question mark)* 1. The question mark sits at the end of a sentence when the sentence is a question? Sure, it does! 2. Used in some operating systems as a "wildcard" character, a placeholder for other characters to be matched in a search. 3. In BASIC, the ? can be used as an abbreviation for the PRINT command.

@ *(at sign)* 1. An abbreviation for "at," as in "Meet Jon @ 7 p.m. for secret rendezvous."

2. Used in Internet mail addresses to identify the domain, as shown in this example:

```
dang@idgbooks.com
```

which is the address of *dang* (Dan Gookin) "at" *idgbooks* (dot) *com,* which is the domain. 3. Like the * and # symbols, the @ has a variety of other terms used to describe it. You may encounter *about, strudel, rose, cabbage,* and others.

[] *(square brackets* or *brackets)*
1. Parentheses that just never really caught on. Mostly, square brackets are used to describe options for a command, as shown in this example:

```
spin [/fast] [/backward]
```

The brackets mean that the items enclosed within them are optional. 2. Brackets are used in various programming languages in different ways. In C, they contain array element numbers; in assembly language, they reference memory locations; and so on.

**** *(backslash)* 1. The symbol used in MS-DOS to separate directories and filenames, as in C:\WINDOWS\SYSTEM or A:\PASCAL. Don't goof up the backslash key with the forward slash (/). 2. A backslash is used in various programming languages for various purposes too various to mention here.

^ *(caret* or *hat* or *control)* 1. The wee little symbol above the 6 key on most keyboards. Used in foreign languages to accent certain letters, the caret symbol also has a variety of computer purposes. 2. Used as an abbreviation for *control,* which refers to the ASCII control characters as well as to key combinations on your keyboard. So, Ctrl+S can also be written as ^S (pronounced "control-S"). You may even see ^S appear on a menu as a

command's shortcut key. 3. The symbol is used in many programming languages for a variety of purposes. In BASIC, ^ is used as a mathematical operator for "raise to the power of." 2^4 means 2 to the fourth power. In C, ^ is used as a bit-wise exclusive OR operator.

_ *(underline* or *underscore)* 1. The underline is often used as a replacement for a space when the space is not allowed — for example, FILE_NAME rather than FILE NAME. 2. Used to emphasize words in e-mail messages in which text can't be underlined:

```
Now you're _really_ fired!
```

3. Unlike with a typewriter, you can't backspace and press the underline key to underline your text on a computer screen. It just doesn't work that way.

` *(accent grave)* 1. A backward apostrophe, most often used for simulating double quotes, as in this example:

```
``Oui, oui. It is a sauce we
make from grease and flour.''
```

Normal apostrophes end the quote, and the accent grave (located in the upper-left corner of your keyboard) starts the quote. 2. The hardest part about dealing with this doodad is how to pronounce it. Is it "grave," as in serious or a place where dead bodies go to relax? Or is it gravé, as in the way a French person would say gravy? 3. Used to accent letters in some foreign languages. To accent a letter in a Microsoft Office application, press Ctrl+` and then the letter you want accented.

{} *(curly brackets* or *curly braces)* 1. An alternative form of parentheses, most often found in C language programs. Curly brackets are used to "hold" various items in a program, items that belong to certain parts of the program or carry out specific functions. 2. Often used when someone gets tired of plain ol' parentheses.

| *(vertical bar* or *pipe)* 1. Many programming languages use the pipe symbol as the logical OR mathematical operator. It's pronounced "or," as in:

```
SIX-OF-ONE | HALF-A-DOZEN-OF-
THE-OTHER
```

2. In the C programming language, the pipe is used as a bit-wise logical OR. Two pipe symbols, | |, are used as the logical OR for comparing two values. 3. In some operating systems, the pipe is used to send ("pipe") output through a filter, such as in a sorting program. The filter modifies the output.

~ *(tilde)* 1. Pronounced *till-day* or *till-dee*. 2. Used as an accent character in some languages: For example, *año* means *year* in Spanish. To produce that character in a Microsoft Office application, press Ctrl+~ (which is Ctrl+Shift+`) and then the N key. 3. Some programming languages may use ~ to mean *not*. See *!,* the *exclamation point.* 4. In the C language, the tilde is the one's complement operator. 5. In Australia, the national anthem is *Waltzing Ma~.*

0 *(zeer-oh)* The symbol for the number zero, which shouldn't be confused with a capital letter *O;* they may have been the same thing on old typewriter keyboards, but not on a computer. Sometimes, a zero has a diagonal line through it, just to drive home that it is a zero and not a big O.

101-key keyboard *(won-oh-won-kee kee-bord)* A keyboard that has four distinct parts: a typewriter keyboard, cursor keypad, numeric keypad, and row of function keys. "Bob's

A 101-key keyboard.

the doubting type. He counted every little key on his keyboard and was, in fact, quite pleased to find 101 of them."

10000 bug *(ten-thow-zund buhg)* A problem with computers in the year 10000 when people are forced to deal with the fact that programmers of the late 1990s fixed the 2000 bug but did not anticipate the rollover from the year 9999 to the year 10000. See also *2000 bug.*

1-2-3 *(won-too-three)* A spreadsheet program. See *Lotus 1-2-3.*

16-bit *(siks-teen-bit)* Referring to something that works with computer information 16 bits at a time. Twice as efficient as 8-bit stuff and half as efficient as 32-bit thingies. "A *16-bit* version of a 2-bit shave and a haircut would probably result in a trip to the infirmary."

2000 bug *(too-thow-zund buhg)* The common name given to the limitation of older computers and software programs to deal with the change from 1999 to the year 2000. To save space in older computers with limited memory, programmers often took shortcuts. One of them was storing the current year as a two-digit number. On New Year's Eve 1999, which is stored as 99 in a computer, the year rolls over to 00, which is interpreted as the year 1900 in all those computers. Massive amounts of money are being spent to fix the programs. Hopefully, the world won't shut down when the year 2000 arrives. See also *10000 bug.*

2-bit *(too-bit)* 1. Something cheap, insignificant, or not worthy of attention, such as some people you may know. 2. Twenty-five cents. "Your opinion and *2 bits* will get you an extra shot of espresso in your latté."

286 *(two-ay-tee-siks)* Nickname for the 80286 microprocessor, used in the IBM AT class of computers. Successor to the old 8088 PCs and supplanted by the 386 family of PCs.

2X *(two-eks)* See *double-speed drive.*

3-D *(three-dee)* Abbreviation for *three-dimensional.* "Linus, it's hard to tell whether the board enjoyed your *3-D* presentation with half their faces buried in motion-sickness bags."

3-D mouse *(three-dee mows)* A mouse (pointing device) that moves up and down in addition to back and forth and left and right. Typically used with three-dimensional software.

32-bit *(thur-tee-too-bit)* A computer something-or-other that works with 32-bit chunks of information. Pentium-type PCs have 32-bit microprocessors. "A *32-bit* computer is to a 16-bit

computer as an 8-cylinder car is to a 4-cylinder model."

386 *(three-ay-tee-siks)* Abbreviation for the 80386 family of microprocessors, which includes the 80386, 80386DX, and so on. "Believe it or not, *386* computers were once thought of as so fast that only nerdy scientists would use them. Now, good luck trying to get a seven-year-old not to sneer at one."

404 Error *(for-oh-for ayr-or)* A Web browser message telling you that the Web page you tried to load can't be found. See *Web browser, World Wide Web.*

486 *(for-ay-tee-siks)* Abbreviation for the 80486 family of microprocessors. Also known as the i486, 486DX, 486DX2, 486DX4, 486SL, 486SLC, and maybe even the 486SX. At one time, all this meant something. Today, it's something nerds debate over lunch.

4X *(for-eks)* See *quad-speed drive.*

640K limit *(siks-for-tee-kay lim-it)* The design limitation restriction on all IBM-compatible computers that restricts them to using a maximum of 640K of conventional memory. "In 1981, *640K* was a ton of memory, so the 640K limit was thought to be unbreakable. Today, Windows breaks it with a wiggle of its pinky toe."

6502 *(siks-tee-fiev-oh-too)* The family of microprocessors used in the original Apple computers. Eventually, the 6502 was replaced by the 65C02 and then by the 65C16 in the Apple IIgs computer, the last of the mighty Apple II line.

@

68000 *(siks-tee-ayt-thou-zend)* Refers to the family of microprocessors used in Macintosh computers. Motorola makes them.

680x0 *(siks-tee-ayt-oh-eks-oh)* Abbreviation to indicate the Motorola 68000 family of processors, including the 68000, 68020, 68030, 68040, and whatever's next. "All Macintosh computers use the *680x0* processor. The bigger the number *x,* the more you paid for your Mac."

68881 *(siks-tee-ayt-ayt-ay-tee-one)* The math coprocessor used in the 68000 processor.

6X *(siks-eks)* Six times as fast as the original CD-ROM drive speed. Used to impress computer buyers with how fast their CD-ROM drives are.

8-bit *(ayt-bit)* Refers to a computer-something that works with information in 8-bit chunks. "Today, *8-bit* computers are about as impressive as the Yugo."

80286 *(ay-tee-too-ay-tee-siks)* Numeric designation for the processor used in the IBM AT family of computers. "The *80286* isn't used in computers today, though some government devices, such as nuclear power plants and the space shuttle, still use them."

80386, 80386DX *(ay-tee-three-ay-tee-siks; -dee-eks)* The first 32-bit microprocessor used in IBM-compatible computers. 80386DX is the official designation, though most folks would say 80386, or just 386. "The minimum requirement to run Windows is a *80386* processor. Yeah, right. That's like saying that the minimum requirement to get into Harvard is a spinal cord."

80386SX *(ay-tee-three-ay-tee-siks es eks)* A low-cost and slower version of the 80386DX processor. Like the 80386DX, this processor can process 32 bits of data at any given time, although it can transfer only 16 bits of data at a time.

80387 *(ay-tee-three-ay-tee-sev-en)* The math coprocessor designed to work with the 80386DX, 80386SX, and 80386SL processors. "Plugging a *80387* math coprocessor into a 80386 computer is like strapping a calculator to its belt."

80486, 80486DX *(ay-tee-for-ay-tee-siks; -dee-eks)* Numeric designation for the processors used in many IBM-compatible computers; the successor to the 386 line. The 80486DX is its official name, though many people use 80486, 486, or i486 because they think that it makes them sound cool.

80486SX *(ay-tee-for-ay-tee-siks es eks)* Low-cost and slower version of the 80486DX processor. The main difference is that this processor lacks the math coprocessor capabilities of the 80486DX. Now found only on cheap clones at the bottom of illegal landfills.

80586 *(ay-tee-fiev-ay-tee-siks)* The unofficial designation for the Pentium processor. The main reason Intel chose not to name this microprocessor the 80586 is that no one can trademark a number. So Intel came up with a trademarkable name (Pentium) instead. "Even though the chip is officially called Pentium, you still hear the die-hard geeks referring to it as a *586.*"

8086 *(ay-tee-ay-tee-siks)* A 16-bit processor used in some early IBM-compatible computers — most notably, the first Compaqs.

8087 *(ay-tee-ay-tee-sev-en)* The math coprocessor designed to work with the 8088 and 8086 processors.

8088 *(ay-tee-ay-tee-ayt)* The first processor used in the IBM PC. Although it's a 16-bit processor, it can transfer only eight bits of data at any given time, kind of like having only one door rather than two on a city bus. "Knowing that the first IBM PC used an *8088* microprocessor is as trivial as knowing the name of the guy who drives the Zamboni at a hockey game."

80x86 *(ay-tee-eks-ay-tee-siks)* An older designation referring to the entire Intel family of microprocessors, from the ancient 8088 to the Pentium. Replaced by x86. See *x86*. "Dave thinks that he's being clever when he refers to all *80x86* processors as 6,880 processors. (Only those who know that 80 multiplied by 86 is 6,880 will get this one.)"

8.3 filename *(ayt dot three fiel-naym)* The old MS-DOS filename law: Filenames are restricted to eight characters followed by an optional period and as many as three additional characters as an "extension."

83-key keyboard *(ay-tee-three-kee kee-bord)* The name of the original IBM PC keyboard, which had (ironically) 83 keys. Unlike today's 101-key keyboards, the numeric keypad was scrunched up next to the main typewriter keys. It had no separate cursor keys, and all the function keys (F1 through F10) were arranged in two columns down the left side of the keyboard. It made a nifty *clacky* sound.

84 Lumber *(ay-tee-for lum-ber)* The name of a lumber company. This term has nothing to do with computers — I just remember it from my childhood.

8514 *(ay-tee-fiev-for-teen)* A graphics standard for the PC, similar to Super VGA. See *Super VGA*.

86 *(ay-tee-siks)* Bar and restaurant lingo meaning that something is out of stock or no good. Can refer to any part or item that no longer serves a purpose or should be eliminated. "Whew! Those shellfish are *86!*"

@

@

A

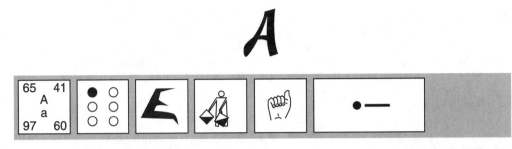

A: *(ay-co-len)* The primary floppy disk drive. On a PC, the first disk checked for a copy of the operating system startup instructions. Often pronounced without the "colon" part, as in, "I looked in my *A* drive to see why the disk wouldn't go in and lo and behold, there was a sandwich shoved in there. Yeah, I have kids."

aardvark *(ard-vark)* One of the first words listed in good dictionaries. Comes from the old Afrikaans phrase meaning "earth pig," which refers to a nocturnal mammal known to burrow its way through African

Not an aardvark.

terrain, eating termites and dragging its big floppy ears, long ugly tongue, and heavy tail. "The dictionary Gods will curse you if you leave *aardvark* out of any dictionary you write."

abacus *(ab-a-kus)* A handheld tablet used for making mathematical computations. The abacus uses beads and your fingers to quickly figure out addition, multiplication, subtraction, and division. It does this stuff quite accurately, faster than most people can use a calculator, and its batteries last a lifetime.

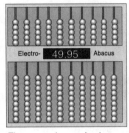

The new, electronic abacus.

abandon *(uh-ban-dun)* To clear the work from your computer screen without saving it. Basically, the work is lost, never to return.

ABC *(ay bee see)* Abbreviation for *Atanasoff-Berry Computer,* a device that was a precursor to the ENIAC and, therefore, is sometimes considered to be the first electronic digital computer. The ABC was created by Professor John Atanasoff and student Clifford Berry at Iowa State University in the early 1940s.

abort *(uh-bort)* To stop something before it's too late, such as a program running out of control or a nuclear missile careening toward Moscow. Popular methods include frantically hitting Esc, Ctrl-C, or the Break key. Rent the movie *WarGames* and you'll see what I mean.

Abort, Retry, Fail? *(uh-bort, ree-tri, fay-el)* The cryptic message DOS displays when it can't figure out what to do next. Type **A** to cancel. If you can fix the problem, such as placing a floppy disk in drive A, then type **R** for Retry. Don't bother with Fail. (In some versions of DOS, the message is "Abort, Retry, Fail, Ignore?")

About box *(uh-bowt boks)* A tiny little window that appears in the middle of the screen, displaying the program's name, version number, and anything else the programmers thought the general public might want to know. For an example, see the "About Program Manager" option under the Help menu in Windows. "Ever wonder why the *About box* never tells you what the program is supposed to accomplish? I suppose that should be the What's-it-all-About box."

abs *(abs)* 1. An abbreviation for *ABSolute value.* 2. Abs is a command used in many programming languages and spreadsheet programs that calculates the absolute value of a number – never negative, always positive. "If your spreadsheet shows a tax balance of –$12,500, quickly calculate the *abs* value, and you'll wind up with a refund instead of owing money."

The absolute value of 4.

absolute address *(ab-so-loot uh-dress)* See *address.*

absolute reference *(ab-so-loot ref-er-rens)* A term used in spreadsheets that tells a formula to use a specific cell or group of cells. If you copy or move the formula from one cell to another at a later date, the formula still uses the specific cell reference defined earlier. "An *absolute reference* is something you have to specifically demand if you want to make sure your spreadsheet formulas don't get all screwed up."

AC *(ay see)* Abbreviation for *Alternating Current.* See also *DC.* "The power that comes out of the wall socket is *AC.* Computers, and most other devices, use DC. A device called a transformer converts the two, keeping everyone happy."

Accelerated Graphics Port *(ak-sel-ur-ay-ted graf-iks port)* A graphics standard for displaying 3-D images.

accelerated video adapter *(ak-sel-er-ate-ed vi-dee-oh ah-dap-ter)* A special piece of video hardware that makes graphics work faster. "No, Officer, I wasn't speeding. It just looks that way because I have an *accelerated video adapter* attached to my car."

accelerator *(ak-sel-er-ate-er)* 1. A piece of hardware or software that makes some other (typically slow and pokey) device in the computer work faster. 2. Another term for shortcut keys. An accelerator enables you to do the same function as with a mouse, except by using a key or a combination of keys.

accelerator board *(ak-sel-er-ate-er bord)* A special circuit board that plugs into a computer and makes it or one of its parts run faster. Accelerator boards usually contain a faster processor that replaces or supplements the computer's existing processor. See also *processor.* "Too bad they don't make *accelerator boards* for commercials on the TV."

access *(ak-sess)* The ability to get into something or to locate something. Access is used in respect to disks, records, files, and network entry procedures.

access arm *(ak-sess arm)* The arm that holds the head that reads and writes the information on the disk in a disk drive. "Oh, the read-write head is connected to the . . . access arm! And the access arm is connected to the . . . access shoulder! And that is the way of the Lord!"

The access arm both reads and writes information.

access code *(ak-sess kohd)* Also known as the *user name* or *ID* and the *password* on a network or online service. "The workers started gathering weapons in hopes that it would inspire Marcia to remember the *access code* for the payroll system."

access number *(ak-sess number)* The telephone number used by subscribers to get into their online service.

access time *(ak-sess tiem)* The way that a hard drive's speed is measured.

Each hard drive has a different access time, measured in milliseconds (ms). The fewer the milliseconds, the faster the hard drive. "A good, fast hard disk has an *access time* of 8 milliseconds. Steve, on the other hand, has an *access time* of about 48 hours."

accessory *(ak-sess-oh-ree)* The little extra doohickeys used with your computer. See also *peripheral.* "I want to do my whole computer lab in pink *accessories.*"

account *(uh-cownt)* Your presence on a computer system. Typically everyone at a large corporation, university, or secret evil government installation has his own account on the computer system. If you subscribe to an Internet service provider, then you have an account on its system. "Matt has no social life; his computer *account* is overdrawn."

accounting package *(uh-cown-teen pak-adj)* Software that keeps track of business expenses and other accounting nonsense.

accumulator *(uh-kyoom-yoo-lay-tor)* 1. A microprocessor register that holds values or results of some operation. Typically this is the A or AX register. 2. One who accumulates. "Bill is an *accumulator* of money."

ACK *(ack,* like you're choking) 1. Abbreviation for *acknowledge,* ASCII code 6, produced by the Ctrl+F keyboard combination. 2. In some areas of computer communications, the ACK code is sent by one computer to acknowledge the proper receipt of information from another computer. See also *NAK, ASCII.*

acoustic coupler *(ah-koo-stik cup-ler)* An old-style modem device that works by shoving

Old-style acoustic coupler modem.

the handset of a telephone into two rubber cups. This kind of nonsense was necessary in the old days, before the breakup of AT&T, when phones were directly wired into the wall and you really didn't have a phone jack into which you could plug a modem. Acoustic couplers are still widely used in foreign countries and for laptops when access to a phone jack is restricted. Hollywood loves them as well, because they're more obvious ("Look, Shirley! The computer is 'talking' on the phone!") than dull-old modem boxes. "Did you hear? Madonna's gone high-tech. She's replaced her cone bra with a pair of *acoustic couplers.*"

ACPI *(aye see pee eye)* Acronym for *Advanced Configuration and Power Interface.* A way to manage power consumption in a computer system, as well as household devices and other office equipment. On a computer, ACPI allows you to turn off some devices while keeping the rest of the computer running. "Marge must have her *ACPI* on; she's talking but I think her brain is asleep."

Acrobat files *(ak-row-bat fi-els)* A type of file format commonly used to store

documents on the Internet. Acrobat (the program) works like an online fax machine. The files look the same on both the viewer's screen and the sender's screen. You need to obtain an Acrobat reader to view the files.

acronym *(ak-ro-nim)* A word created by taking letters from two or more words to create a new word. Examples are BASIC, FORTRAN, and DOS. "I hear the Pentagon allocates $75,000 each year to a committee designed to conjure up useless *acronyms.* What do they know? The computer industry does it every year for free!"

active *(ak-tiv)* A common computer word that refers to something that is the current focus of attention.

active area *(ak-tiv ayr-ee-uh)* A region of the screen or window that is accepting input or some other type of stimulation (but not singing) from the user.

active cell *(ak-tiv sell)* The cell in a spreadsheet that is selected or highlighted.

active configuration *(ak-tiv con-fig-yoor-aye-shun)* 1. The current configuration, typically when several different types of configurations are available. 2. The factory configuration. See *default.*

Active Desktop *(ak-tiv desk-tohp)* A feature of Windows 98 that allows an application, such as a Web browser, to take over the desktop; the application appears as the desktop instead of some background pattern or graphic.

active file *(ak-tiv fi-el)* The file or document currently being created, edited, or manipulated somehow by the operating system or a specific application.

active light *(ak-tiv lite)* A teensy light on some computer device that lets you know something is alive and ticking (or dead and annoying).

active matrix *(ak-tiv may-triks)* A type of color display found on many laptops. An active matrix display uses transistors to control the screen. If you were an engineer, you'd be impressed by this and nod your head accordingly. "My new KneeCap 150 laptop uses the superior *active matrix* display, so I can see crisp color graphics of a parrot at 39,000 feet."

active window *(ak-tiv win-dow)* The window on the screen that's currently in use. If two or more windows appear on the screen, the active window usually appears brighter around the edges. See also *window*. "It's the goal of every window on the screen to become the *active window*."

Ada *(Ay-duh)* 1. A structured programming language that was supposed to be the standard language for all defense-related programming work. Naturally, hardly anyone uses it, although U.S. taxpayers

Not the Countess of Lovelace.

supported all its development. 2. Ada Byron, the Countess of Lovelace, who is generally credited with writing the first computer program for a mechanical loom machine that Charles Babbage designed. She was Lord Byron's niece. Ada (the programming language) is named after her. "I'm sure the Countess of Lovelace would be pleased with the fact that a program written in her name is used to fire missiles from nuclear-powered aircraft carriers."

Adam West *(ad-um west)* The star of the *Batman* TV series that appeared during the '60s. "There just is no other Batman than *Adam West.*"

adapter *(uh-dap-ter)* 1. Another name for an expansion card. Typically, a piece of hardware that plugs into your computer's innards (into an expansion slot). Unlike an expansion card, which may just expand the computer's features, the adapter is used to communicate with an external device, like a hard drive, monitor, or some other doohickey. 2. A simple connector, designed to hook up two plugs of different types. "Earl is convinced that he can use his computer to help him garden. He's currently looking for a weed-whacker *adapter.*"

add-on *(add-on)* Anything that is added to a computer to enhance or increase its capabilities. Costs money.

add-on program *(add-on pro-gram)* A program that works with and enhances the features of another program. "The original Lotus 1-2-3 was terribly popular despite its somewhat limited abilities. To fill in the gaps, enterprising individuals

A

created *add-on* programs to boost 1-2-3's features."

 address *(uh-dress)* 1. A memory location. The value is often displayed in hexadecimal (base 16), mostly just to keep anyone but official PC Postal Employees from finding anything in memory. Every-thing stored in your computer's memory has a specific *address*. 2. The location of an item in a spreadsheet. Cells in a spreadsheet have a row and column address. "The *address* of the first cell in a spreadsheet is A1. That's also the name of my favorite steak sauce." 3. The location of something on the Internet. This may be an electronic mail address or a Web page address. "You want my *address?* Which one do you want? You have three to choose from: e-mail, Web page, or my *address* in the IRS computer's memory banks."

address book *(uh-dress book)* A place to store your elec-tronic mail names and ad-dresses. "My *address book* is filled with all the most popular geeks, thanks to online dating."

admin *(add-min)* The computer account for the person or people who actually run the computer system. "When you need to complain, send mail to *admin*. Include a bribe and you get help faster"

ADSL *(aye dee ess el)* Acronym for *Asymmetric Digital Sub-scriber Line,* a new type of fast online communications that allows top speeds without new wiring. Designed to replace ISDN. See also *ISDN.*

afk *(aye eff kay)* Acronym for *away from keyboard.* Used during Internet chat groups when someone leaves the computer.

```
Ok Jon, we'll meet in Hawaii for
that secret rendezvous
(afk)
Sorry, I had to go put some more
medicine on this huge fever
blister I have on lip.
```

agent *(ay-jent)* An automated pro-gram. A program or utility that carries out specific tasks at specific times or when certain conditions are met. For example, an agent may inform you that your disk drive is getting perilously full. "I have an *agent* that doesn't tell me anything. It must be a secret agent."

AGP *(ay jee pee)* Acronym for *Accel-erated Graphics Port.* See *Accelerated Graphics Port.*

AI *(aye eye)* See *artificial intelligence.*

air vents *(ayer vintz)* Holes or slits found on the console panel of your computer. Like any other motor, your computer has to breathe.

alarm *(uh-larm)* 1. An audible or visual warning that something has gone wrong. 2. A reminder found in calendar programs.

alert box *(uh-lert boks)* A graphical box or window that displays a mes-sage or warning.

ALGOL *(al-gall)* 1. Acronym for *ALGOrithmic Language.* ALGOL was one of the first programming languages to encourage structured programming. Pascal is a direct descendent of

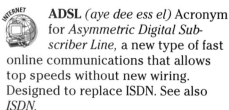

ALGOL. 2. Has nothing to do with Al Gore. "When Betty told her parents she programmed *ALGOL,* they thought she was working for the Clinton Administration."

algorithm *(al-gor-rithm)* 1. A step-by-step set of instructions that accomplishes some common programming task in a simple, yet dignified, manner. 2. The pace at which Al Gore does the *Macarena.*

Has he got rhythm, or is he just A-flat?

alias *(ay-lee-ess)* 1. A code or symbol representing something else. 2. A reference to a file that may look like it's right there in front of you, but could be anywhere. An alias makes it easy to find common files but doesn't require all the disk space a full-on copy would. Think of alias files as Elvis impersonators that can appear everywhere you look. "The FBI is having trouble finding its word processing documents. Experts assume the files are using *aliases,* and when those aliases are known, the files should be easy to locate."

aliasing *(ay-lee-ess-ing)* The ugly-looking jagged or stair-stepped appearance of diagonal lines in computer graphic images. Sometimes referred to as "the jaggies." "Trying to draw diagonal lines on a computer is about as easy as drawing circles on an Etch-A-Sketch. Whenever you draw a diagonal line, you get *aliasing,* which makes your straight line look like the kind of staircase a 7-year-old would build."

alignment *(uh-lien-mint)* 1. A hard disk's drive head's ability to read and write information without error. 2. Text's relationship to the left and right margins, as in "centered," "left-justified," and so forth. "Shirley is so cute. She tried to adjust the *alignment* of text in her word processor by tilting the monitor." 3. The arrangement of graphics; how the graphics line up to each other: centered, to the left, right, top, or bottom.

allocate *(al-oh-kayt)* The process of dividing a computer's resources. "In the Bible, Matthew 14:15 describes how Jesus *allocated* two fish and five loaves of bread between 5,000+ people. Now if only he could come back and allocate our two Pentiums and one laser printer between 10 people in the office."

alpha geek *(al-fuh geek)* The lead nerd at your company. The guy who usually makes all the computer decisions, whether

A typical alpha geek.

that's really his job or not. Could also be a she. "He" is used here because it's the third-person gender neutral in English. No sexist statement intended. To wit: "Mary is our *alpha geek.* Tell her about the toast in the CD-ROM drive."

alpha test *(al-fuh test)* The initial testing of a new program, usually conducted by the programmers and

A

their trusted friends. Alpha test programs usually don't work correctly. "Before Microsoft released Windows 95, they ran it through an *alpha test* of their own employees. After they found the first few bugs, they released the program into beta test so that everyone else could find those same mistakes, too."

alphanumeric characters *(al-fuh-noo-mar-ik kar-ik-ters)* Letters and numbers. Not symbols. Not punctuation marks, diacritics, or dingbats. And something like " ïÔø" is way-out.

Alt *(alt,* like *halt* without the *h)* A special type of shift key on computer keyboards. Often used in combination with other keys to give commands to the computer. Common commands are Alt+S to save a file and Alt+P to print something. "In some programs, you press *Alt*+R to redo something. In other programs, you press *Alt*+R to replace. And in outer space, *Altair* is a star in the constellation Aquila."

Altair *(alt-ayr,* not *al-tar)* 1. The name of one of the first personal computers available. 2. A star in the constellation Aquila. (See preceding Alt+R joke.) 3. Home of the Krell.

 **AltaVista** *(al-ta vih-sta)* 1. One of the many search engines on the Internet. It's foreign: "Vista" means *to see* and "Alta" is a contraction of the Italian *Alotta.* 2. www.digital.altavista.com

alternating current *(al-ter-nat-ing ker-ent)* The type of electricity used in America. Often abbreviated as *AC.*

Alternating current changes polarity a given number of times a second, referred to as *Hertz.* It sounds screwy, but it allows electricity to flow farther than direct current (DC). Your computer, and most electronic devices, must convert AC power to DC to run properly.

The place where you get alternating current.

 **America Online** *(uh-mayr-ik-uh on-lien)* A national dial-in computer service (abbreviated AOL) where you, your computer, and a modem can do all sorts of interesting things much cheaper than you can on CompuServe. America Online is quite popular and a nifty way to try out the Internet without a huge investment in software. "If *America Online* went to Europe, would it still be *America Online,* or would it be called Europe Online? Or maybe America in Europe Online?"

Amiga *(uh-mee-ga)* The name of the most technologically advanced, inexpensive personal computer on the market. Of course it flopped.

amp *(amp)* 1. Abbreviation for *AMPere,* which is a unit for measuring the strength of an electric current. "Volts, smolts. It's the *amps* that will kill you." 2. A device connected to your computer speakers that allows everyone in the neighborhood to know when you're zapping aliens with your turbo thruster rifle.

ampersand *(am-per-sand)* The way you pronounce &. See &.

analog *(an-a-log)* The opposite of digital. Analog values are not absolute values; they are immeasurable or constantly changing. For example, an analog clock has a dial and hands that sweep around. A digital clock displays numbers and only changes on the minute. See also *digital.* "Computers are *digital,* which means they understand On and Off, Yes and No. People are analog because they understand Yes, No, I dunno, who cares?, why are you asking me this?, maybe, and we'll see."

analog modem *(an-a-log mo-dum)* The traditional type of modem. Modems are analog because they take digital information from the computer and convert it into sounds that can travel over phone lines. Of course, today the phone company takes the sounds and converts them into digital information to make the transfer more efficient. See also *digital modem.*

analog to digital port *(an-a-log to di-ji-tul port)* Also known as "A-to-D port," it's another term for the computer's joystick port. It's the way the computer reads movement of the joystick. "I suppose they called it *analog to digital port* because scientists in white lab coats would look silly working on a joystick port."

AND *(and)* 1. A logical operation comparing two bits. The result of the operation is based on the value of the two bits, in this case whether they are

AND

1 AND 1	=	1
1 AND 0	=	0
0 AND 1	=	0
0 AND 0	=	1

How the AND operation works.

the same or different (see chart). If both bits are the same (both 1 or both 0), the result is TRUE or 1. Otherwise, the result is FALSE or zero. 2. The programming command that performs the logical AND operation.

andama *(end-um-ah)* A fill-in word when you're trying to think of something else to say, or really don't have anything of importance to say. From the vulgar Latin *etama,* which means exactly the same thing. "This girl in my school has this really big mole on her lip, *andama* I, uh, can't seem to keep from staring at it during class, *andama,* and now all the other kids keep looking at it, too."

animation *(an-uh-may-shen)* To use your $3,000 computer to create Saturday-morning-style animated cartoons. Creating the appearance of movement of drawn objects. See also *Mickey Mouse.* "Our spreadsheet uses *animation* to help illustrate the declining sales of our competitors. Alas, we don't have the sound hooked up, so when the graph slams into zero, George makes an audible thud noise."

A floppy disk containing a computer animation.

annotation *(an-oh-tay-shen)* A note inserted into a document, used mostly when two or more people are working on the same thing and need to exchange notes. Annotations don't print with the rest of the text and are usually visible only by using special commands.

A

A

 anonymity *(an-on-im-it-ee)*
The concealment of the
identity of a person posting a
message to a newsgroup. The ability
to post a message or send e-mail
without the recipient knowing who
sent it. "It's much easier to have an
outrageous opinion when you have
anonymity."

ANSI *(an-see)* 1. Abbreviation for
American National Standards Institute,
an organization that defines standards for different industries that
most people ignore anyway. 2. Specific rules that govern the way programming languages are supposed to
work. 3. Commands that control how
information is displayed on a computer screen (largely ignored). 4. A
type of graphics used by text-based
BBS systems. 5. How kids get when
they've been riding in the car too
long. ("Kids get ANSI.")

ANSI bomb *(an-see bom)* A devious
sequence of ANSI commands that
actually types a deadly DOS command on your computer. Setting up
an ANSI bomb can be done in a
number of ways, none of which I'd
like to write about in any detail here.
Leave it to say that when such a
string of ANSI commands appears on
your screen, there's little you can do
to stop it except to immediately shut
off your computer.

ANSI C *(an-see cee,* or *Aunt C C)* A
standard definition for the C programming language as defined by the
American National Standards Institute. Nearly every C compiler tries to
follow the ANSI C standard as closely

as possible, and then they add
enhancements that pretty much
destroy the whole purpose of a
standard in the first place.

ANSI character set *(an-see kar-ak-ter
set)* A standard set of characters used
by a computer. The ANSI character
set includes ordinary letters and
numbers plus strange little symbols
such as foreign language symbols,
smiley faces, and lines and boxes.
"Linda is a collector. All she needs is
the evil Dr. Modulus statuette, and her
ANSI character set will be complete."

ANSI graphics *(an-see gra-fiks)*
Special characters that create simple
graphics such as lines, boxes, and
colors. Often used by text-only BBSs.
See *BBS.* "Earl spent months working
with *ANSI graphics* to make his screen
look colorful and exciting. Alas, he
didn't impress the user group because
by the time he was ready to show us
all, we'd switched over to Windows."

ANSI screen control codes *(an-see
skreen kon-troll kodz)* Yet another
standard that specifies a series of
characters that clears computer
screens. They work through the
ANSI.SYS device driver in the
CONFIG.SYS file under DOS. Windows
has rendered these codes moot.
"Using *ANSI screen control codes*
today is about as common as finding
a vertical hold knob on a TV set."

answer only modem *(an-sir own-lee
mo-dum)* A modem that can answer
calls but not initiate them.

answer/originate modem *(an-sir or-
idj-uh-nayt mo-dum)* A modem that can

answer and initiate calls. Most modems are answer/originate, which makes the term about as useful as *round car tire.*

answer mode *(an-ser mowd)* The state of a modem when it's ready to receive calls from other computers. In this mode, the modem picks up the phone whenever it rings. Normally modems are not in this mode; they're in originate mode. See *originate.* "At the start of the press conference, the senator will read a brief statement, then he will switch into *answer mode.*"

antiglare screen *(an-tee-glayr skreen)* A device to put over your computer monitor that cuts the glare from indoor lighting or from the outside sun. Basically, it keeps you from squinting and getting eye strain. Most anti-glare gizmos are nothing more than a rack containing a stretched piece of nylon; beige or black, no taupe.

antivirus *(ant-ee-vi-rus)* A type of program (utility software) that scans your system and detects viruses or other evil programs. Antivirus software may also remove the infection, deleting it from your hard drive, and it may also actively protect your PC from infection. It all depends on how much you want to be bothered by antivirus software and how much you put your PC at risk. "It's a good idea to run *antivirus* software on your computer, especially if you're using a lot of diskettes that others use or if you download software from questionable sources."

any key *(an-ee kee)* Any key on your keyboard. Programmers use the term *any key* to try to make things easier on you, when they actually want you to use the Enter key or the spacebar. In their twisted little minds they think, "Hey, I'll just tell them they can press *any key* to continue, which allows them the freedom to press any key they like." In practice, it leads to frustration and eternal hunting for a key labeled *Any.*

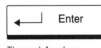

The real Any key.

AOL *(Ay oh el)* 1. Acronym for America Online. See *America Online.* 2. Often followed by the word "crashed" or the idiomatic "is lame."

API *(ay pee eye)* 1. Acronym for *Application Program Interface,* which is yet another scheme that's supposed to make computers easier than they really are. API defines a standard way that programs work with pull-down menus, dialog boxes, and windows. Microsoft Windows, OS/2, and the Macintosh are examples of API in action. 2. Another rule no one really follows.

append *(ap-end)* To stick one thing on to the end of another thing. When you append a file, you stick one file on the end of another, making one large file. "Bertha almost gave our system administrator a heart attack. He asked her to *append* one file to another, explained what it meant, and then later caught her gluing two disks together."

A

Apple II *(ap-ol too)* One of the first personal computers that actually did something useful. After introducing the Apple II, Apple released enhanced models called the Apple IIe, Apple IIc, and finally the Apple IIGS. Finally, Apple decided to drop the whole Apple II family altogether and focus on selling Macintoshes. "I asked Wayne why he looked so pale. He said he saw the same *Apple IIe* he bought in 1983 for $2,500 at a garage sale and they were asking $20 for it."

Apple III *(ap-ol three)* A computer that was supposed to replace the Apple II but wound up being ignored by the general public. After turning into a public embarrassment to Apple, the Apple III quietly disappeared and can now be found in landfills all across America. "Betcha didn't know that Apple will not name any product with a 'three' in it because of the bad luck associated with the old *Apple III* computer."

 Apple Computer, Inc. *(ap-ol kom-pyoo-ter ink)* The makers of the Apple II series, the Macintosh series, and several other products. Based in Cupertino, California. Steve Jobs and Steve Wozniak, who had been teen-age friends, founded the company in a family garage in Silicon Valley. Eventually Apple Computer grew into a billion-dollar empire. But they never realized that what they were selling was *software* and not *hardware,* so the company eventually lost its status as a computer pioneer.

 Apple Desktop Bus *(ap-ol desk-top bus)* Sometimes abbreviated as *ADB,* the Apple Desktop Bus defines an interface standard for connecting keyboards, mice, trackballs, and other input devices to Apple Macintosh computers.

Lots of things can be connected to the Apple Desktop Bus.

 Apple Extended Keyboard *(ap-ol eks-tend-ed kee-bord)* A 105-key keyboard that works with the Macintosh SE, Macintosh II, and Apple IIGS computers.

Apple key *(ap-ol kee)* A key on an Apple keyboard that has the outline of the Apple logo. This key is similar to the Control key on an IBM computer.

Apple menu *(ap-ol men-yoo)* The tiny little apple (with a bite taken out of it) that appears in the far-left corner of the menu bar in Macintosh computers. Clicking on the Apple menu displays desk accessories and other programs. "Herb was crushed not to find any cobbler in the *Apple menu.*"

AppleShare *(ap-ol shayr)* A network operating system developed by Apple to work with Macintosh computers.

 applet *(ap-let)* 1. A mini-application, typically the ones that come with Windows, such as Paint or WordPad. 2. Any small program designed to do a specific task (hence *applet* as opposed to *application*). 3. A small Java program that Java-happy Web browsers can run on the Internet.

AppleTalk (*ap-ol tok*) A local area network standard developed by Apple to hook Macintosh and IBM PC computers together. Every Macintosh computer has an AppleTalk port built in (the same can't be said for IBM computers). AppleTalk is an inexpensive way to create a network, but it tends to be slower than other types of networks. See also *network*.

application (*ap-li-ka-shen*) Another name for a program such as a word processor, spreadsheet, or database. Application implies work getting done or using something to meet an end. The word *program* is too robotic for most people.

application icon (*ap-li-ka-shen ie-kon*) A tiny graphic symbol that represents a program. Double-clicking the mouse pointer on the graphic symbol opens the program.

ARC (*ark*) The name of a popular data compression program that takes multiple files and smashes them into a single, smaller one. Once used heavily on IBM computers, the ARC file standard has been replaced by the ZIP standard. "*ARC* is short for *archive,* which is where you want to keep something. ARK, on the other hand, is short for Arkansas. Don't put your documents there; someone may shred them."

Archie (*arch-ee*) A program designed to find files (archives) on the Internet. Archie was text-based and although it can still be accessed, it has been replaced by various search engines on the World Wide Web. See also *search engine.*

architecture (*ark-uh-tek-chur*) 1. The particular (and arbitrary) way computer equipment is designed. Similar computers, such as IBM PCs and clones, are said to have the same

Roman architecture.

architecture. 2. Refers to the design of a communication system, as in "network architecture." See also *open architecture.* "Paul is taking a class on computer architecture. They're starting with the early cage-look and moving up into the neo-classic, fawn-white structures."

archive (*ar-kiev*) A place where important files are stored. Often this place is where you can never find the files again.

archive bit (*ar-kiev bit*) A bit that is used by a backup program to determine whether the file has been backed up.

argument (*arg-yoo-mint*) A value given to a program. Most often used in programming. "The main program needs to give two arguments to the subprogram so that it can work properly. After the subprogram gets these two arguments, it can plot the next most likely sighting of Elvis, Bigfoot, and the Loch Ness Monster."

A

ARP *(ay ar pee)* Acronym for *Address Resolution Protocol,* the method by which Internet addresses are found. Techy stuff. ARP is what takes a cryptic-looking number and translates it into a Web page somewhere in the known universe.

ARPAnet *(ar-pa-net)* Acronym for *Advanced Research Projects Agency network,* nationwide computer network created by the Department of Defense to link research institutions and universities together. ARPANET was merged with several other networks to create the Internet.

array *(uh-ray)* A collection of similar information, such as a list of numbers, codes, text, or other items. All the items are usually of the same type. Each item in the array is an element. For example, an array may contain a list of blow-gun poisons used by various Amazon tribes. The array could be called the *sting-array,* and each item in the array would be referenced by a unique element number.

arrow keys *(aer-ow keez)* Special keys on the keyboard that move the cursor up, down, left, or right. Not surprisingly, the arrow keys have little arrows on

Squiggly lines.

them. They're also referred to as *cursor keys.* "Bill just quit tech support. He told a lady to press the up-arrow key and she shot back at him that there were 12 arrows on her keyboard, five of which pointed up."

artificial intelligence *(ar-tuh-fish-al in-tel-uh-jentz)* The fascinating science of making computers as smart as human beings (which may be a step backward in some cases). Recently, the art of inserting Artificial Intelligence into computers has become nothing more than making a program do what you want it to do. "Bob's been working on that *Artificial Intelligence* program for years. He says that soon he'll make computers just as smart as he is. This prospect worries me because I just saw him back his car over a fire hydrant."

ascender *(uh-sen-der)* The part of a lowercase letter that extends upward and rises above the x-height. The letters *t* and *h* have ascenders. The letters *s, u,* and *n* do not. "Letters with *ascenders* go to heaven when they're deleted; letters with descenders suffer an eternity in word processing purgatory."

ascending order *(uh-sen-ding or-der)* To arrange information from lowest to highest. "Hopefully the air traffic controller arranges the airplanes to take off in *ascending order.*"

ASCII *(ass-kee; not ask-too)* 1. An acronym that stands for *American Standard Code for Information Interchange.* ASCII defines a standard way for representing characters on computers. This is handy because computers that recognize ASCII can share files that contain only ASCII characters. See also *Unicode.* 2. A plain, boring text file. ASCII files contain no formatting or other information, just letters, numbers, and punctuation symbols. "A file composed of *ASCII* characters is about as exciting as gum without any flavor." 3. Character codes zero through 127. See *ASCII codes.*

ASCII Code Table for ASCII Words

Code	Character	Keyboard	Name
0	^@	Ctrl+@	NULL
1	^A	Ctrl+A	SOH, start of header
2	^B	Ctrl+B	STX, start of text
3	^C	Ctrl+C	ETX, end of text
4	^D	Ctrl+D	EOT, end of transmission
5	^E	Ctrl+E	ENQ, enquire or "Here is . . ."
6	^F	Ctrl+F	ACK, acknowledge
7	^G	Ctrl+G	BELL (goes "ding")
8	^H	Ctrl+H, Backspace	BS, backspace
9	^I	Ctrl+I, Tab	TAB, tab key
10	^J	Ctrl+J	LF, line feed
11	^K	Ctrl+K	VT, vertical tab key
12	^L	Ctrl+L	FF, form feed
13	^M	Ctrl+M, Enter	CR, carriage return
14	^N	Ctrl+N	SO, shift out
15	^O	Ctrl+O	SI, shift in
16	^P	Ctrl+P	DLE, data link escape
17	^Q	Ctrl+Q	DC1, device control one
18	^R	Ctrl+R	DC2, device control two
19	^S	Ctrl+S	DC3, device control three
20	^T	Ctrl+T	DC4, device control four
21	^U	Ctrl+U	NAK, negative acknowledge
22	^V	Ctrl+V	SYN, synchronize
23	^W	Ctrl+W	ETB, end transmission block

Code	Character	Keyboard	Name
24	^X	Ctrl+X	CAN, cancel
25	^Y	Ctrl+Y	EM, end message
26	^Z	Ctrl+Z	SUB, substitute
27	^[	Ctrl+[, Esc	ESC, escape

Code	Character	Keyboard	Name
28	^\	Ctrl+\	FS, form separator
29	^]	Ctrl+]	GS, group separator
30	^^	Ctrl+^	RS, record separator
31	^_	Ctrl+_	VS, version separator

Code	Character	Code	Character	Code	Character
32	[space]	64	@	96	'
33	!	65	A	97	a
34	"	66	B	98	b
35	#	67	C	99	c
36	$	68	D	100	d
37	%	69	E	101	e
38	&	70	F	102	f
39	'	71	G	103	g
40	(	72	H	104	h
41	)	73	I	105	i
42	*	74	J	106	j
43	+	75	K	107	k
44	,	76	L	108	l
45	-	77	M	109	m
46	.	78	N	110	n
47	/	79	O	111	o
48	0	80	P	112	p
49	1	81	Q	113	q
50	2	82	R	114	r
51	3	83	S	115	s
52	4	84	T	116	t
53	5	85	U	117	u
54	6	86	V	118	v
55	7	87	W	119	w
56	8	88	X	120	x
57	9	89	Y	121	y
58	:	90	Z	122	z
59	;	91	[	123	{
60	<	92	\	124		
61	=	93	]	125	}
62	>	94	^	126	~
63	?	95	_	127	[delete]

A

ASCII codes *(ass-kee kodz)* Code numbers from zero through 127 that are assigned to characters, as well as special codes. The codes are divided into four types: control codes, symbols, uppercase letters, and lowercase letters.

ASCII file *(ass-kee fi-el)* 1. A file that contains only ASCII characters. Often this kind of file is used when exchanging information between two word processors that don't read each other's formats. Also, some system files, such as CONFIG.SYS, must be in the ASCII (or plain text) format. 2. Another term for any of the following: text file, plain text file, DOS text file, unformatted document, or text-only.

Ashton-Tate *(ash-ton tayt)* The company that developed the dBASE series of programs. See *dBASE*. At one time they were one of the "Big Three" software developers; back in the early 1980s it was VisiCorp, who did the VisiCalc spreadsheet; MicroPro, who did WordStar; and Ashton-Tate, with dBASE. Today their building in Silicon Valley is a waterbed store. The founder was Charles Tate. Ashton was the name of the parrot in the lobby.

aspect ratio *(ass-pekt ray-she-o)* The ratio of the horizontal dimension of an object to its vertical dimension. A term used in graphics. "Movie buffs will tell you that most films are shot with a 3x4 *aspect ratio*. And if you take the screen and mentally turn it sideways into the theater, that marks the ideal row for viewing the picture." (This sounds impressive, but I just made it up.)

assembler *(ah-sem-bler)* A special program used to convert programs written in assembly language into machine code that the computer can understand. Not to be confused with *assembly language,* which is the type of programming language an assembler assembles.

assembly language *(ah-sem-blee lang-gwij)* A type of programming language that directly manipulates the computer's microprocessor. Assembly language programs are usually longer and harder to read than programs written in C or BASIC. On the other hand, assembly language programs run faster and take up less disk space than similar programs written in other languages.

asterisk *(ass-ter-isk)* The * symbol on the keyboard. See *.

asynchronous *(ay-sink-ron-us)* 1. Any process that isn't synchronized. Often used when sending or receiving data through a phone line. Most likely a term you'll never use in your life, but it can make you sound knowledgeable around other computer geeks. 2. The opposite of synchronous. See *synchronous.*

AT *(ay-tee)* 1. An acronym (like you were expecting somebody's initials?) for *Advanced Technology.* "In the computer biz, it's risky naming anything new *AT* because all advanced technology is outdated in 18 months anyway. 2. A type of computer compatible with the original IBM PC AT. Though that computer sported an 80286 microprocessor, most of today's systems are said to use the same design (or *architecture*) as the original AT. 3. The name of a set of modem commands originated on the Hayes micromodem. They used to call them Hayes-compatible modems, but now they claim them to be AT-command compatible. The AT is short for "attention!"

AT&T *(ay tee and tee)* 1. An acronym that stands for *American Telephone and Telegraph.* Once a feared competitor for IBM, AT&T never really hit it big selling computer hardware. Today AT&T concentrates on communications systems and offers the national Internet service, AT&T WorldNet. 2. The original developers of the UNIX operating system.

ATM *(ay tee em)* 1. Acronym for *Asynchronous Transfer Mode,* a method of sending audio, visual, and computer data over one line without getting anything confused or melting any telephone poles. 2. An acronym for a friendly robot that dispenses money. In this case, the acronym stands for *Automated Teller Machine.*

 attaching files *(uh-tach-ing fi-els)* To send a file through e-mail or to post a file to a newsgroup. Text files are attached as text. Binary files (programs, sound files, images, and so on) are converted into a special text

Phil loves to attach files.

format by using a file encoder. The e-mail program is generally responsible for encoding and decoding the files.

audio *(aw-dee-oh)* 1. Relating to sound. "A computer with *audio* capability can annoy your ears as well as your eyes." 2. Sound technology. A computer component that deals with sound.

audiovisual *(aw-dee-o-viz-yoo-al)* Relating to both sight and sound.

`AUTOEXEC.BAT` *(aw-toh-eks-ek dot bat)* A file containing commands that run each time DOS or Windows starts. See *batch file.* Short for *AUTO EXECutable BATch file.* No longer required by Windows 95, though included for compatibility reasons.

 autoresponders *(aw-toh-ree-spond-ers)* An e-mail address that sends a canned response to any e-mail it receives. Also known as autoreply, mailbot, and e-mailbot. "The White House uses autoresponders to people who send them e-mail. Basically, their autoresponder says thanks for writing, but we're not going to read your message."

AUX *(oks)* The first serial port on a PC, also known as COM1. AUX is short for *AUXiliary port.* "Old Farmer Vern gave up computing altogether. The toll-free phone support guy told him to plug his modem into the *AUX* port. Darn beast nearly hooved him to death."

Avogadro's Number (*av-o-god-rowz num-ber*) 1. 6.0225×10^{23}. 2. A very large number. 3. A constant value used by scientists that represents something so important that they decided to name it after the guy who discovered it. "I'm tired of calling up girls who turn me down for dates. Give me *Avogadro's Number,* and maybe I can talk physics to him or something." 4. Rumor has it that if you dial *Avogadro's Number* backward, you can hear demonic messages.

Some guy, probably not Avogadro.

axis (*aks-iss*) An imaginary line drawn through the center of something. In computer graphics, the X-axis runs horizontally, left to right. The Y-axis runs vertically, up and down. "The world tilts on its *axis*, about 23 degrees. At 212 degrees, water boils."

A

B

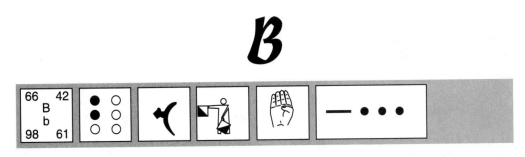

B: *(bee koh-lon)* The drive letter given to the (optional) second floppy-disk drive on a PC.

back button
(bak but-en)
1. A graphical button in Web browser software used to return to the previously visited Web page. "I go to the Chiropractic Web page just by pushing my *back button.*" 2. A place on your back that you have your spouse press and it makes you go "Ahhh!"

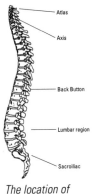

The location of the Back Button on your spine.

back door *(bak door)* A secret way of getting into a program that usually only the original programmer knows about (such as a secret password). It sounds sneaky, but it allows programmers to update software with a minimum of hassle. It is not a bug or virus.

back panel *(bak pan-el)* The panel at the rear of the computer. Most of the connections to power and the peripherals are made at the back panel. "Yup, those guys who design computers are smart. They put all the cable connections on the *back panel* so they'd be inconvenient to everyone."

background *(bak-grownd)* 1. A multitasking term; when an operating system runs a program (or *task*) that you're not currently working with or have visible on the screen. See *multitasking, active window.* "Though you can run two or more programs at the same time, you can use only one program at a time. All other programs run in the *background,* like extras in a Godzilla movie." 2. Another term for desktop wallpaper, the graphic design or image you see while using an operating system like Windows. See *wallpaper.*

background noise *(bak-grownd noyz)* Any interference on a telephone line, usually electrical static. Background noise often causes random or "garbage" characters to appear and can disconnect you if the noise is loud enough.

Africa.

backlit *(bak-lit)* A screen illuminated with additional lighting from behind. Often used to highlight LCD screens found on older laptop computers. "Harry is so cheap. He saved himself $50 by not getting a *backlit* laptop, thinking he could just hold a flashlight behind the lid to accomplish the same thing."

backslash key *(bak-slash kee)* The key with the \ symbol on it, often found above the Enter key on most keyboards. See \. "Over the phone, you might say: 'Type CD *backslash* DOS and press the Enter key.' But the person you're talking to types this:

```
Seedy back slash doss and press
the inner key
```

backspace *(bak-spays)* 1. The key on the keyboard that has the word *Backspace* or a left-pointing arrow on it. 2. The act of pressing the Backspace key, which deletes something. In a word processor, the Backspace key erases the character to the left of the cursor (like a little PacMan). "Too bad they don't have a *Backspace* key to take back things you shouldn't have said."

backtracking *(bak-trak-ing)* A system to try to find a problem in a program. You try one solution, and if it doesn't work, you go back and try another one.

backup *(bak-up)* 1. A safety copy of a file made in case the original file is unintentionally changed or destroyed. "Hey Jefferson! Houser just erased our Christmas bonus file. Where's that *backup* you made yesterday? You did make a *backup*, didn't you? Jefferson, how come you don't look so good?" 2. The copy of the file itself. 3. The process of creating a backup file or a backup of every file in the computer system. 4. The MS-DOS command that performed the backup operation. 5. The name of any program that backs up files.

backward compatible *(bak-werd cumpat-uh-bul)* When software written for an earlier version of a microprocessor works on a later model. Can also refer to files for a specific application. If the program can still read files generated by an older version, it's said to be backward compatible.

bad *(bad)* A prefix used to refer to something as no longer good or unable to perform its job. For example, "bad sectors" on a disk drive refer to an area so damaged by meteor showers as to be unable to store any information. It does not refer to the moral disposition of any software or hardware.

BAK *(bak)* A three-letter file extension given to backup files, especially the ones created automatically by some applications (such as some word processors). The backup file name looks like this: `memo.BAK`.

 balloon help *(buh-loon help)* 1. Starting with System 7 on the Macintosh, Apple introduced *balloon help*, which provides little windows of helpful information on the screen. Balloon help gets its name because the windows it displays look like the speaking balloons seen in comic strips. "*Balloon help* just displays a little bit of help, unlike the normal Help menu that displays gobs of information you can't use or understand."

A different kind of balloon help.

bandwidth *(band-width)*
1. A measurement of a signal, typically done in hertz. For example, the speed at which the information is sent from the computer to the monitor. 2. A disparaging term in e-mail or on newsgroups referring to a useless message or a message with little information as a "waste of *bandwidth*." 3. Bandwidth is not how much space a musical groups takes up while on stage.

bank switching *(bank switch-ing)* 1. A way of quickly switching between two different groups of memory chips, giving the illusion that it's all the same memory. Bank switching is used to overcome built-in hardware limitations. For example, PCs in the '80s used bank switching to provide more memory. See *Expanded memory*. 2. What Wells Fargo is trying to get BankAmerica customers to do, and vice-versa.

bar code *(bar kohd)* 1. A pattern of narrow and wide black and white strips. The strips represent numbers or codes that are read by a scanning device. This provides a much faster method of product and inventory identification than relying on hourly employees with optional reading skills. 2. "Whaddya having?" "Whaddya got?" "Whiskey." "I think I'll have a whiskey then."

78083 128169.

base *(bays)* The number of digits used in a counting system. Base 10 uses ten digits, base 2 (binary) uses two, and base 16 (hexadecimal) uses sixteen. "Most people use *base* 10 because we have five fingers on each hand. My cat has only four toes on each paw, so he must count using *base* 8 (or *base* 16 if he uses his back paws, too)."

BASIC *(bay-sik)* 1. Acronym for *Beginner's All-purpose Symbolic Instruction Code,* it's a programming language specifically designed to make programming easier. Developed at Dartmouth in the late '60s/early '70s. Early PCs and versions of DOS came with a version of the BASIC programming language because most early PC buyers would write their own programs for the thing – kind of like carving your own set of golf clubs before playing each day. 2. Used disparagingly; although BASIC is easy to use, many programmers look down on it as a "toy" language. Early versions of BASIC lacked the ability to create cool programs that would wipe out your hard disk or blow up your modem. Newer versions of BASIC now offer such features, but BASIC no longer has the popularity it once did, being replaced by the C programming language.

BAT *(bat)* The file extension identifying batch files. See *batch file,* which just happens to be the next word.

batch file *(batch fiel)* 1. A special text file that contains lists of operating system commands and special instructions. Running the batch file causes the computer to follow all the instructions. 2. In DOS, any file that

B

ends with the BAT extension. Batch files are essentially text files, though the text in the files are DOS commands and special batch file programming instructions. "I'm sorry you misunderstood me; I said that HILLARY should be a *batch file.*"

Batman *(bat-man)* A popular comic book character who dresses like a bat and goes around doing good deeds in crime-ridden Gotham City. "I like *Batman* because he's the only superhero who isn't radiated or mutated in some way. He just has a lot of cool gadgets." See *Adam West.*

battery backup *(bat-er-ee bak-up)* 1. A battery that's ready to supply electricity the moment a power outage occurs. See also *UPS.* 2. The battery inside your PC that keeps track of the current time and other configuration information even when Mr. Computer is unplugged.

A backup battery.

baud *(bod)* 1. The rate of signal changes when transmitting data, such as over a modem. Named after French engineer J. M. E. Baudot. Commonly, and incorrectly, confused with bits per second (bps) when measuring modem speed. See *bits per second.* 2. Because it rhymes with *bod* (short for body), *baud* is often the source of much lame computer humor: "Peter tried to pick up that cute girl in the computer science class using his modem. She slapped him, though, after he asked her what her *baud* rate was."

bay *(bay)* 1. A compartment inside the computer console designed for system expansion. 2. The compartment inside a computer console into which you place a disk drive.

BBS *(bee bee ess)* Acronym for *Bulletin Board System,* a computer and modem that others can dial into and copy files, leave messages, and share information. Most are privately run, though many major developers and manufacturers have their own BBSs for users desiring technical information or updates. The World Wide Web is quickly replacing the BBS for this type of information exchange. "Most *BBS* systems have more BS than B."

BBSs *(bee bee ess ess)* Plural of BBS; bulletin board systems.

BCD *(bee see dee)* Acronym for *Binary Coded Decimal,* which is a technique that programs use to ensure accuracy for financial calculations. "Most spreadsheets use *BCD* so that rounding errors won't mess up your calculations. My accountant should try *BCD* sometime. . . ."

beach ball pointer *(beech bal poyn-ter)* A mouse pointer that appears to let you know that the computer is actually doing something although nothing seems to be happening. The symbol looks like a spinning beach ball, hence its name. The beach ball pointer is the Mac counterpart to the Windows hourglass. "My Mac shows the *beach ball pointer* so much that small people in swimsuits have appeared to play with it."

bells and whistles *(bels and wis-els)* 1. A slang term to describe the multitude of extra features a program offers. 2. Fancy features not particularly useful but mostly required to out-do the competition.

Bemer, Bob *(beem-er bahb)* The IBM programmer who created, among other things: the escape sequence, the function behind the Escape key; the concept behind eight bits in a byte; the backslash character; and the name COBOL. He also had a hand in designing the ASCII character codes.

benchmark *(bench-mark)* 1. A performance test. When testing software, tasks such as sorts or searches are timed and used for comparisons between products. 2. The rating given to a specific piece of equipment. "This monitor benchmarks at 30. And for $400 more it can benchmark at 15 (faster)." 3. To perform the performance test; the act of setting benchmarks.

Bernoulli box *(ber-noo-lee boks)* A mass storage system that uses removable cartridges that work on the Bernoulli principle. Named after a Swiss scientist who predicted the dynamics of a rapidly spinning, flexible disk around a fixed object and decided that his college education hadn't been a waste of time after all. ZIP drives are a type of

Not Daniel Bernoulli.

Bernoulli box. "Don's a little slow. He brought a *Bernoulli box* for lunch, figuring it contained some type of Italian meal."

berserk *(ber-zerk)* 1. A fit of rage that Vikings often went into during the heat of battle. 2. A fit of rage computer users go into when their computer fails to work the way they thought it would. "Watch out for Fred. He's been trying to print sideways in WordPerfect, and I think he's about to go *berserk* on us again."

beta test *(bay-ta test)* The second stage of testing (alpha test is the first) of a program before releasing it to the general public. "*Beta test* programs are sometimes called 'Version 1.0' by companies who want to rush their program on to the market before it's ready."

beta tester *(bay-ta test-er)* People who use a beta test program are called *beta testers*. "Before Microsoft released Windows, they gave it to 50,000 *beta testers* around the country. After they discovered it was full of bugs, Microsoft sold it to the rest of us."

Bézier curve *(Bez-ee-ay kurv)* A mathematically generated line for displaying irregularly shaped curves. To create Bézier curves in most computer graphics programs, you plot a straight line and then manipulate two points somewhere in the middle, called control handles. Moving these control handles in different directions twists the line into a Bézier curve.

BG *(bee-gee)* 1. One of the Brothers Gibb. 2. Abbreviation for background. See *background.* 3. Acronym for "big grin" that is used in e-mail. The intent is to show expression in your mail, because the person receiving your messages can't see you sitting there with a big grin on your face.

```
Thanks for the 8 Gig hard drive
for Father's day! BG
```

bible (the) *(bie-bol;* not capitalized) Another name for the book *The C Programming Language* by Brian Kernighan and Dennis Ritchie. See *K&R.* "Phil just can't program unless he has *the bible* handy."

Phil loves reading K&R.

bidirectional printing *(bi-duh-rek-shun-al print-ing)* When a printer has the ability to print from both left to right and right to left. This feature speeds up printing on non-laser printers.

"Big Blue" *(big bloo)* Nickname for IBM, which used to be one of the key "blue chip" stocks on Wall Street. Either that or it was all the darn blue suits.

big iron *(big ie-ron)* Slang term for a mainframe computer. "Your *big iron* costs millions of dollars, takes up half a room, and performs as much work as a $2,000 personal computer of today."

big red switch *(big red switch)* 1. A computer's on-off switch. 2. The on-off switch on anything. "The original IBM PC's on-off switch was big and red, which is why *big red switch* is used to describe a computer's on-off switch today."

BIN *(ben)* 1. A binary file. 2. A three-letter file extension to identify files containing binary data. "To identify his files easier, Benjamin renamed all his *BIN* files to BEN. Now he wonders why his programs don't work." 3. The name of a directory on UNIX systems that contains program files.

binary *(bie-nar-ee)* 1. Base 2. 2. A counting system that uses two digits, 0 and 1. 3. Can also describe other systems that offer only two choices, such as the Republican and Democratic parties. 4. A star system with two suns.

binary file *(bie-nar-ee fiel)* 1. Not a text file. Binary files contain information that only a computer (or a computer geek) can understand. 2. A file with the three-letter BIN file extension.

binary newsgroups *(bie-nar-ee nooz-groops)* Newsgroups whose messages are primarily encoded files as opposed to text messages. Binary newsgroups contain program files, sound files, graphics, and other non-text information.

binhex *(ben-heks)* A type of encoding that allows binary files to be sent along with text in an e-mail or newsgroup message. Primarily used by the Macintosh, though PCs with the proper software can also decode the files.

BIOS *(by-oss)* 1. Acronym for *Basic Input/Output System.* The BIOS is a set of instructions that tells the computer how to act, like a personality chip. Most computers have the BIOS built in as a chip plugged into the computer. 2. Another term for ROM or firmware.

bit *(bit)* 1. Contraction of *BInary digiT.* A binary digit can be either zero or one, on or off, true or false, or any pair of opposite states, such as Florida and New York. 2. Bits are often used to measure the capability of a microprocessor to process data, such as 16-bit or 32-bit. "Believe it or not, 8 *bits* make up a byte, and 4 *bits* make up a nibble (often spelled *nybble*)."

A strange drawing that could possibly illustrate a bit.

bit twiddler *(bit twid-ler)* Slang term for someone who is so nerdy that he likes to spend all his time programming in assembly language. "Hi, my name is Norman, and I'm a *bit twiddler.*" (Group) "Hi, Norman."

bit width *(bit width)* The number of bits a microprocessor can process at a time. The wider the bit width, the more powerful the microprocessor. Common bit widths are 8, 16, 32, and 64. "Because Virgil was from Oklahoma, he thought a *bit width* had something to do with a horse's harness. He laughed at me when I told him it was related to computer terms."

bitmap *(bit-map)* 1. A graphic image composed of pixels, or tiny dots. This kind of image contrasts with other types of images, which may be represented by vectors or other mathematical algorithms too boring to explain here. 2. Slang for a bitmapped image; see *bitmapped image.*

bitmapped font *(bit-mapt fawnt)* A typeface style stored as a matrix of tiny dots. When you enlarge the size of a bitmapped font, the font tends to look jagged. Bitmapped fonts gobble up lots of memory.

bitmapped image *(bit-mapt im-age)* An image created from a bitmap. Most paint programs, such as MacPaint, PC Paintbrush, or the Windows 95 Paint program, create bitmapped images. Bitmapped images can be difficult to modify because you have to change pixels one at a time.

BITNET *(bit-net)* Acronym for *Because It's Time Network.* 2. An early international computer network that began in the early '80s. BITNET is incompatible with the Internet, which is slowly replacing it.

bits per second *(bits pur sek-ond)* 1. The speed of a modem. Refers to how many bits per second the modem can transmit or receive. Common values are 2,400, 9,600, 14.4K, 28.8K, 33.6K, and 57.6K. (K means 1,000, or kilobits per second.) The faster the modem, the higher the bits per second value; at a bps speed of 28.8K (average), you can transmit approximately 2,880 words in a single second. 2. Not the baud rate; see *baud.* Bits per second is often confused with baud. Earlier modems were measured with a baud rate, which was more or less equal to the bps value. However, faster modems do not have corresponding bps and baud rates.

black box *(blahk boks)* A complex doodad that performs some specific function. Can be either hardware or software. "You stuff all these numbers into one end of the *black box,* and out the other end comes a balanced budget."

blank *(blangk)* 1. A term used to describe what you get when you press the spacebar key. 2. A text box or other fill-in item that's empty. 3. Nothing. "My life is like the spacebar key; it's a complete *blank.*"

blessed folder *(bless-ed fohl-der)* The folder containing the System and Finder files in a Macintosh. The system refers to the blessed folder when it can't find a file. See also *path.*

Thoth places important information in the blessed folder.

blind carbon copy (BCC) *(blind car-bohn cop-ee; bee see see)* A copy of an e-mail message sent to someone who doesn't appear on the original recipient's list. The recipient knows who sent the message and others it was sent to or carbon-copied to, but not anyone on the BCC list.

bloat *(bloht)* The tendency of programs to expand and fill all of your computer's memory and consume all system resources. Most programs bloat because they can; PCs have lots of resources. Other programs bloat when the programmer gets bored and adds new features "just because."

block *(blok)* 1. A collection of information lumped together for convenience. 2. A 512-byte chunk of information on disk. 3. The size of the chunks of information sent between two computers over a modem. "Leon asked maintenance to make a bigger hole in his office wall for his phone line. Seems he's having trouble with his modem not being able to send big enough *blocks.*" 4. A selected chunk of text in a word processing document.

BMP *(bee em pee)* A file extension identifying a bitmap graphic file. "I couldn't figure out what Connie meant by 'bumpy' files until I explained that *BMP* are bitmap graphic files, not bumpy files."

BNC connector *(bee en see kon-eck-tor)* 1. A metal jobbie at the end of a cable that twists to connect the cable to the back of your computer or to another cable. 2. Must stand for Big Nobby Connector.

A Big Nobby Connector.

boat anchor *(boht ang-kor)* Slang for something so useless it may as well be tied to a chain and used for deadweight to keep boats from drifting away. "You have a PCjr? May as well be a *boat anchor!*"

bogus *(boh-gus)* 1. Something that's phony. 2. A fake item of data used when testing software. "The boss loved my report, but I didn't have the heart to tell him it was a sample filled with *bogus* data."

boilerplate *(boy-ler-playt)* A pre-written slab of text used over and over. For example, the bio at the front of this book is a boilerplate used in all our *...For Dummies* books. Common uses for boilerplate documents are form letters, legal documents, or love letters to multiple partners. "Bob is such a womanizer. He has this *boilerplate* document he uses to swoon them, then another *boilerplate* he uses when they break up."

bold *(bohld)* 1. A dark or heavy text style. 2. To apply the bold style to text. 3. Something daring, like proposing a beginner's computer book and calling it *DOS For Dummies*. "*Bold* need not be fearless and confident. It only need look darker than the other text."

bomb *(bahm)* 1. A program designed to do something sneaky at a specified time. Many disgruntled programmers write bombs in their programs so that if they get fired, the bomb will go off on its own and wreck the company's program. 2. An icon, primarily on the Macintosh, that lets you know you're screwed.

bookmark *(buk-mark)* The act of remembering (marking) a page on the World Wide Web, making it easier to re-visit that page later. Internet Explorer refers to book-marks as "favorites." See *favorites.*

"Sandy is so out of touch, she was watching TV and asked me to book-mark her favorite commercials."

Boolean *(boo-lee-on)* A logical opera-tion, involving OR, AND, XOR (exclu-sive OR), and other comparisons. Typically programmers perform these operations on bytes and bits to somehow prevent nuclear reactors from blowing up. Named for British mathematician George Boole. (They couldn't call them Georgian, because it will get confused with the chant people.)

boot *(boot)* 1. To start a computer. Derived from the idea that the com-puter has to "pull itself up by the bootstraps" or from the feeling that the only way to get a computer to work is to threaten to kick it with a boot. 2. To load a specific operating system. "I can't get Linux to *boot!*" 3. Canadian: Used to refer to something at or around something else, as in "The cows are a *boot* to come home."

Boot.

boot disk *(boot disk)* The disk you use to start your computer. Most often a hard drive, though a floppy disk with the proper operating system installed can also boot a computer.

bootstrap *(boot-strap)* 1. To help yourself without the aide of others, such as "pulling yourself up by the bootstraps." 2. Another, longer term for boot. Often used to refer to some specific part of the computer start-up process. "The *bootstrap* loader can't distinguish your hard drive from a pizza."

bounce *(bowns)* Something sent electronically that is immediately sent back to you. For example, if you send someone e-mail and the message is returned as undeliverable, it's said to have bounced.

bozo *(boh-zoh)* Someone with no clue as to what he's doing but with enough authority to keep others from ignoring him completely. "My boss is such a *bozo*. He thought that backing up a computer meant pushing it up against the wall."

BPI *(bee pee eye)* Acronym for *bytes per inch*. The number of bytes that fit into an inch of space on a disk or tape.

bps *(bee pee ess)* Acronym for bits per second. See *bits per second*.

brain damaged *(brayn dam-ajed)* 1. Something that looks okay from the outside but internally is hobbled or limited. Something that doesn't or can't live up to its potential. Often done on purpose: "We *brain damaged* Version 1 so we can get all the bucks when people upgrade to Version 2." 2. The 80286 microprocessor. 3. The 80486SX microprocessor. 4. Microsoft Office 95.

branch *(branch)* 1. When the computer follows a series of instructions and then suddenly starts following a completely different set of instructions (on purpose, not on a whim).

Often used by programmers to describe the logic of their programs. 2. A directory and all its subdirectories on a hard drive. This follows the "tree" metaphor that most people use to describe the way directories (or folders) are arranged on a hard drive.

An out-of-control directory branch.

break *(brayk)* To stop the computer from doing whatever it happens to be doing at the moment. To "break" the computer's concentration. "Ever wonder why the stop key on a computer is named *break* and not *brake?*"

Break key *(brayk kee)* 1. A key, like, named Break, on your keyboard. Like, duh! Often the Break key lives with the Pause key on your keyboard, just like a Siamese twin. 2. The Break key on a PC must be pressed with the Control key. In DOS, this is the same as pressing Ctrl+C to cancel some operation. "Velma was afraid to use the *Break key* in Windows. She didn't want to pick up all that glass."

breakpoint *(brayk-poynt)* A programming term. The breakpoint is a place in a program where the computer temporarily stops running. Programmers use breakpoints to see how the program is behaving up to a certain point.

bridgeware *(bridj-waer)* A term for hardware or software that is designed to convert programs to a form that can be used by a different computer.

broken picture *(broh-ken pik-chur)* When a picture isn't available on the Web, a broken picture icon appears in its place. "Someone just robbed www.louvre.fr! All the pictures are broken!"

brownout *(brown-owt)* 1. A power condition where juice is flowing, but not enough of it to power certain electronic devices or motors. When this happens, you may notice that the lights work, but none of the computers (or the fridge) work. 2. A tamer version of a blackout.

browse *(browz)* 1. To look for something, specifically a file on your hard drive. 2. A button that opens a window or dialog box allowing you to peruse disk drives and folders in a vain quest for some file you probably don't have in the first place. 3. Looking for something on the World Wide Web. 4. Often used with the word "eye" to refer to those hairy strips (or single strip) on the forehead.

browser *(browz-er)* See *Web browser.*

Browser Wars *(browz-er wars)* The battle between Microsoft Internet Explorer and Netscape Navigator to see which will be the preferred Web browser among PC users. Silly. "In the *Browser Wars,* everyone wins because the prices keep getting lower and the features keep getting added. Betcha that changes as soon as a victor is declared."

brute force *(broot fors)* To get something to work without regard to appearance, elegance, or finesse. "My program has a command that's supposed to move the paper in my printer up one sheet. Rather than use this command, I just use *brute force* and pull the paper out of the printer myself."

BTW *(bae-the-way)* Acronym for *By The Way.* Used online.

bubble memory *(bub-ohl mem-or-ee)* A type of memory that retains its contents even after the power has gone off. Bubble memory was expensive and slow and is rarely used today. "Joan's PC was getting low on *bubble memory* so she kindly poured some Mr. Bubble into the disk drive."

buffer *(buf-er)* 1. A storage place in the computer's memory, created by software. For example, a program may set aside a chunk of memory for text you type at the keyboard — a buffer. 2. Memory in a peripheral, such as the buffer in a printer, which holds information until the printer is ready to print.

bug *(bug)* A problem that prevents a program from working properly. Typically unexpected, a bug is something nearly every program has. Plural is *bugs.* "There are more *bugs* in this program than there are bicycles in China!"

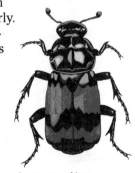

Some type of bug.

bulletin board *(bul-et-in bord)* A place on the Web where you leave a message (like a message board in a laundry room). Others can read your message and respond personally to you, or they can post their message on the bulletin board. "I met my girlfriend by posting messages on the Babylon 5 *bulletin board.* That's because my wife hates Babylon 5."

bulletproof *(bul-it-proof)* 1. Software that anticipates potential mistakes that a user may make and does its best to assure that nothing goes wrong. "This program is *bulletproof.* No matter what you try to do, it still works perfectly." 2. A common myth.

bundled software *(bun-dold soft-waer)* 1. Software that comes free (supposedly) when you buy a computer. Usually, bundled software is stuff you need anyway (like MS-DOS) or programs that aren't selling well, so the publisher is trying to give it away just to clean out the warehouse. "Most computers offer *bundled software* such as Microsoft Office. The idea is that you pay half as much for twice as much software, two-thirds of which you don't need anyway." 2. Several different programs that come together as one package, such as Microsoft Works or Lotus Works or whatever it is they're calling the thing WordPerfect comes in now. See also *integrated software,* which isn't the same thing but could be if they tried hard enough.

burn in *(bern in)* 1. The process of testing electronic equipment to make sure that it works. Sometimes they do this stuff at the shop, though you can do it yourself: Whenever you get a new computer, you should leave it on for 48 hours straight. If anything is going to go wrong, it will likely go wrong during this burn-in period. 2. An image that appears on a computer monitor even when the monitor is turned off. See *phosphor burn-in.*

burn out *(bern owt)* 1. What happens when you stare at your computer screen for long periods of time, such as when you're typing a long list of computer terms for publication in a computer dictionary. 2. A tired, sluggish feeling that makes you want to collapse on the nearest flat surface that can support your weight. "Working on my computer really makes me feel *burned out.* After eight hours of staring at a computer screen, I can't wait to go home and stare at my TV for the rest of the night to unwind."

bus *(buhs)* 1. An electronic transportation system for sending electrons around. "Unlike a normal city bus system, a computer bus actually runs efficiently and gets electrons to the correct destination on time." 2. The electronic pathway on which information travels between the microprocessor and other important computer pieces. 3. Another term for the set of expansion slots in a PC. 4. Bus only has one s.

bus mouse *(buhs mows)* A mouse that plugs into the computer's system bus as opposed to a serial port. The connection can be made directly or through an expansion card. "Janet lives in the city, so she got her computer a *bus mouse.* "

busy thing *(bizee theng)* An image or icon that Web browser software displays when it's waiting for information. "When I see the *busy thing,* it means that I stop being busy and wait."

button *(but-en)* 1. Something you push to get something done. 2. A key on the keyboard. 3. A switch on your computer console or monitor. 4. A graphical representation of a button that you activate by clicking on it with your mouse pointer. "The Amish don't have *buttons* on their version of Windows 95; they use hooks instead."

A typical button.

byte *(biet)* 1. The basic unit of storage in a computer. Typically, one byte holds one character of information, like a letter, number, or symbol. The word *ishkabibble* requires 11 bytes of computer storage. See *kilobyte, megabyte, gigabyte.* 2. Eight bits. However, on some larger and antique computers, a byte is seven bits long. Some weirder computers may use weirder sizes as well. The point is that a byte is not rigorously defined as being eight bits in size.

B

B

C

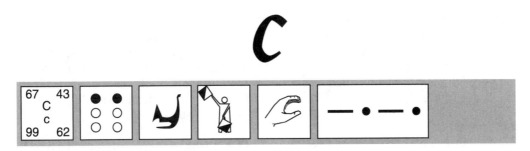

C *(see)* A programming language developed at Bell Laboratories back in the '70s when disco was popular. C is a general-purpose language like BASIC and Pascal, but with the ability to manipulate the internal guts of a computer like assembly language. C has been used to write many popular programs, including the UNIX operating system, Lotus 1-2-3, and Microsoft Excel. "Only wimps use BASIC or Pascal. Cool programmers code in *C* so that they don't have to write the same program over again to run on different computers."

Sample C program:

```
#include <stdio.h>
main ()
{
  printf ("Only wimps use BASIC or
    Pascal.\n");
  printf ("Cool programmers always
    use C.");
}
```

C: *(see-koh-lon)* 1. The name given to the first hard drive in a PC, whether or not the PC sports a drive B (B:) or not. 2. Not a medical term. Not even room for a medical-related joke.

C++ *(see plus plus)* An improved version of the C language that adds object-oriented extensions. C++ has become popular because it's easy for C programmers to learn, provides object-oriented features to make programming large projects easier, and it sells a lot of computer books. Like C, C++ is fast, portable, and confusing to learn and understand. "Only wimps use C. Cool programmers code in *C++* so that they can write bigger programs without losing their minds."

Sample program:

```
#include <iostream.h>
main
{
  cout << "Only wimps use C.\n";
  cout << "Cool programmers always
  use C++.";
}
```

cable *(kay-bol)* 1. A connector, typically one that has electronic signals flowing through it, hither and thither. Cables connect different computer parts together so that they actually do something useful. Cables can be either internal or external to the computer box. 2. The cable that connects your monitor to your computer plugs into your computer's video card. 3. The cable that connects your computer to your printer, called a *printer cable,* plugs into a parallel or serial port. "Gordon couldn't get his printer to work because the salesman forgot to sell him a printer *cable.* Then he sold Gordon a printer *cable* that wouldn't fit his computer's parallel port. Now Gordon's serving five to seven for aggravated assault." 4. The cable that connects your computer to your modem, called a *serial cable,* plugs into a serial port.

cable connector *(kay-bol con-ek-tor)* The doojabbies on both ends of the cable. See also *cable.*

cache *(kash)* 1. A place in memory where the computer can temporarily store data. Often called a *RAM cache.* 2. A software program that increases access time for disk drives. 3. A chip on a controller or inside the microprocessor itself that helps improve operating speed.

cache memory *(kash mem-o-ree)* The specific memory chips or portion of memory used as a cache to make a computer run faster.

CAD *(kad)* Acronym for *Computer-Aided Design,* which substitutes a computer's graphics capabilities for drawing with paper and pencil. Computers running CAD programs often require huge amounts of hard disk space, high-resolution video displays, and a fast microprocessor. CAD has been responsible for designing the most recent engineering achievements including the gas tank for the 1972 Ford Pinto, the nuclear reactors for Three Mile Island, and the focal lens for the Hubble Space Telescope. "Allan can't even draw a straight line with a pencil, but he designed his own car using *CAD.* Of course, it blew up when he turned the ignition key, but that's beside the point."

CAD/CAM *(kad-kam)* A combination acronym that stands for *Computer-Aided Design and Computer-Aided Manufacturing.* CAM means letting computers actually make the stuff that somebody designed using CAD or pencil and paper.

caddy *(kad-ee)* 1. A container that holds the CD-ROM. "I asked Dan to buy me a *caddy.* He came home with a young man to carry my golf clubs for me. That's not what I meant, but it still was a nice gift!" 2. A box used to hold floppy disks when not in use.

call *(kahl)* A programming term, to *call* means to transfer control to another part of the program and then return it.

callback modem *(kahl-bak moh-dum)* A type of modem that requires an outside caller to call the modem, enter a code, and then hang up. The modem checks the code for verification and then calls the outside caller back. This device is used when data must be protected from intruders.

call waiting *(kahl wayt-ing)* A telephone feature that lets you know when someone is calling even when you're already using the phone. This feature is of importance to computer modem users because the call waiting signal disconnects a modem connection. "You should disable *call waiting* before you dial out using your modem."

CAM *(kam)* Acronym for *Computer-Aided Manufacturing,* which is when computers are used in manufacturing. "Thanks to *CAM,* people are becoming less and less necessary in the manufacturing world."

camera-ready *(kam-er-ah red-dee)* A photograph, drawing, or document that is ready to be printed and mass produced. Publishers using desktop publishing software often use this term. "When professional photographers take pictures of bikini-clad models frolicking on exotic beaches, they produce *camera-ready* pictures for the *Sports Illustrated* annual swimsuit issue. When I take pictures of Uncle Fred in his bathrobe with my Kodak Instamatic, I can't produce *camera-ready* pictures of anything at all."

cancel *(kan-sel)* 1. To take back or reverse an action. When you give the Cancel command, you're essentially telling your computer, "Ooops, forget I did that and make everything like it was before." 2. A button in a dialog box that tells the

Some type of molecule.

computer to ignore whatever you've done in a dialog box. "I typed FORMAT C: and almost erased my entire hard disk. Luckily, when DOS asked me, 'Proceed with format (Y/N)?,' I typed N to *cancel* that command."

Cancel Moose *(kan-sel moos)* An anonymous group of people who watch the newsgroups for identical, large postings. If they find a post that has been sent to several newsgroups, the Moose issue forged cancel notices to all the newsgroups to wipe the postings out. "The *Cancel Moose* is illegal, but because no one has been caught, they still do it."

Caps Lock *(kaps lok)* The key on every computer keyboard that lets you type capital (or uppercase) letters without having to press the Shift key each time. Most computers have a little light in the upper-right corner of the keyboard that lights up when you have pressed the Caps Lock key once. If you press the Caps Lock key again, the light goes off. Unlike typewriters, pressing the Caps Lock key on a computer only produces uppercase letters. If you want to print !, @, or any other symbol, you still have to hold down the Shift key first. "Sometimes my fingers slip and I press the *Caps Lock* key BY MISTAKE, AND THEN ALL MY TYPING LOOKS LIKE I'M SHOUTING."

capture *(kap-shoor)* To store a screen image to a file on disk. Often used with desktop publishing and telecommunications. "Mary loves to *capture* screen images on her computer. She even has a little jail built in her office where she keeps them and, as the mood hits her, occasionally taunts them."

carbon copy *(kar-bun kop-ee)* A copy of an e-mail message sent to someone in addition to the main recipient. Abbreviated as *cc.* "No, Joyce, sending an e-mail *carbon copy* will not stain your fingers."

caret *(kayr-et)* The name of the ^ symbol. See ^.

carriage return *(kayr-edj ree-tern)* 1. The character produced by the Enter or Return key. Used to mark the end of input, the end of a paragraph in a word processor, or as a substitute for the OK button in a dialog box. 2. The character produced by pressing the Enter or Return key. ASCII

C

code 13. Named after the carriage return bar on a typewriter, which moved the platen from one side of the typewriter to another.

carrier *(kayr-ee-er)* A signal used by modems to detect the presence of another modem. When one modem calls another modem, the two modems send carrier signals to each other.

The carrier signals the presence of another modem.

One carrier is the *answer,* the other is the *originate.* "Admiral Spruance could tell that the *Yorktown* had been sunk. He dialed up the ship's BBS with his modem and couldn't get a *carrier.*"

carrier detect *(kayr-ee-er dee-tekt)* The state when one modem is actively communicating with another modem. External modems have a carrier detect light that clues you into this state of events. Otherwise no one would care.

carrier frequency *(kayr-ee-er free-kwen-see)* The radio signal used to transmit information, such as with modems and the network.

carrot *(kayr-et)* The vegetable that parents claim will improve your vision. The favorite snack of Bugs Bunny. "While flying on American Airlines, the flight attendant told me to eat all my *carrots* because there were passengers starving on Air India."

cartridge *(kart-ridj)* 1. A self-contained, removable part of a computer or printer that is usually plastic, expensive, and hard to find when you need it. "My laser printer couldn't print any fonts until I plugged in a font *cartridge.*" 2. A device that supplies ink to a printer, or a container for a printer's ribbon, or a container for toner powder in a laser printer.

cascade *(kas-kayd)* 1. Several items, one after the other, arranged in a nifty pattern. 2. To arrange several windows neatly on a computer screen so that you can still see the title bar and upper-left corner of each one. "Until I had my computer *cascade* all my windows, some of my windows had been completely hidden from view. I still can't find anything I need, but at least the *cascaded* windows make me look nice and organized." 3. A set of interrupts in the IBM PC AT. You know, technical mumbo-jumbo.

CASE *(kays)* 1. In text formatting terms, *case* means the style of letters, either UPPERCASE or lowercase. 2. In programming terms, CASE is a special command that lets the computer choose two or more possible options. 3. In techno-dweeb talk, CASE is an acronym that means *Computer-Aided Software Engineering.* "As a computer science major, my *CASE* courses in school taught me that I could use the *CASE* command in Pascal to replace multiple IF-THEN statements. To make programs easier to read, my teachers told me that the case of my typing would matter, too. That's why I dropped out and became a cab driver instead."

case sensitive *(kays sens-uh-tiv)* The distinction made between UPPER- and lowercase letters. Some programs or systems require that certain commands be in either uppercase or lowercase. UNIX is a good example. Also, modems can be fussy in that way, too. "Bob is so *case sensitive*. He thinks 'Hello' and 'HELLO' are two completely different words."

cassette tape *(kah-set tayp)* A reel of magnetic strip that can store information. Ancient computers used cassette tapes to store programs. Today, everyone uses floppy disks or hard disks. (See also *tape, tape drive.*) "I bought an old Timex/Sinclair computer that uses programs stored on *cassette tape.* I really screwed up my computer when I gave it a Led Zeppelin cassette tape by mistake."

cat *(kat)* A UNIX command that displays the contents of a file, hopefully one containing only text. It's from the word *concatenate,* which doesn't mean anything to you currently. "I typed *cat* on my keyboard, and the computer suddenly started purring."

Felis Domesticus.

catatonic *(kat-a-ton-ik)* A state of near-total paralysis, usually brought on by staring at a computer screen too long. "At first I thought Gene was *catatonic,* but he was just waiting for Windows 95 to start on his computer."

cc *(see-see)* 1. Acronym for *carbon copy.* See *carbon copy.* 2. Used by management types who are just in too much of a hurry to tell you that they have carbon-copied something in e-mail. (Or they had their secretaries do it for them.)

CD *(see dee)* 1. Acronym for the *change directory* command, CHDIR. 2. Acronym for *Compact Disc,* as in the favorite digital audio storage devices. See also *CD-ROM.* "Call a doctor! Janice has lapsed into a primal state! She's trying to configure her *CD* drive in MS-DOS and all she can say is, '*CD. CD* run. Run, *CD,* run.'"

CD-R *(see dee ar)* 1. Acronym for *Compact Disc-Recordable.* Using the proper equipment, you can use a CD-R to record your own CD. The information can only be recorded once and typically must be recorded all in one stretch, not a bit a time.

CD-ROM *(see dee rahm,* not *Rome)* 1. Acronym for *Compact Disk-Read Only Memory.* 2. A disk that contains megabytes of information. The information can't be changed, and you can't save new information to the disk (hence "read-only"). A CD-ROM disk is round, silver, flat, and looks like a UFO if you toss it in the air and use an out-of-focus camera to take its picture. 3. The device that reads a CD-ROM disk. "My new *CD-ROM* drive lets me display entire encyclopedias, classical novels, maps from every country in the world, travelogues, and interactive X-rated films. Now I have no reason to leave the house."

c

CD-RW *(see dee ar dub-ol-yoo)* Acronym for *Compact Disc-Recordable-Writable.* Like a CD-R, but with the ability to read and write information just like a regular hard drive.

cell *(sel)* The intersection of rows and columns in a spreadsheet used to store text, numbers, and formulas. "My financial spreadsheet uses 300 *cells* to store all my vital business information. And there's a prison up the road that uses 300 *cells* to store various businessmen who keep such information from the IRS."

center *(sen-tur)* 1. To align text in the middle of the page. "It's always neat-looking to *center* the title of your book in the center of the page." 2. To align graphics along their center axes.

central processing unit *(sen-tral praw-ses-ing yoo-nit)* The computer's microprocessor, abbreviated *CPU.* The little chip in personal computers that controls everything. A central processing unit looks like a thin wafer or a headless cockroach. (See also *microprocessor.*) "After you upgrade your computer's *central processing unit,* you can turn the old one into jewelry for a loved one."

Centronics port *(sen-tron-iks port)* A computer's printer port. Originally used to connect computers to Centronics printers. See *parallel port, printer port.* "Ray's a real old-timer. He always calls the printer port a *Centronics* port. Heck, he's been around so long, he remembers when computers used to need cranks to start."

CGA *(see jee ey)* Acronym for *Color Graphics Adapter,* the original color graphics standard for IBM and IBM-compatible personal computers. Replaced by EGA, then VGA, and SVGA. See also *EGA, VGA, SVGA.* "*CGA* graphics are as outmoded as platform disco shoes."

CGI *(see jee eye)* Acronym for *Common Gateway Interface,* a way of dealing with information typed into a form on a Web page. Also how some Web pages can be customized and created on-the-fly. "Nothing beats *CGI* from a DNS saved to a DVD. Don't you just love TLAs?"

CGM *(see jee em)* Acronym for *Computer Graphics Metafile,* a type of graphics file format standard used by programmers. "We drove to Detroit so we could *CGM.*"

character *(kar-ak-ter)* 1. Any symbol that you can type from the keyboard. Letters are characters, numbers are characters, and even $, @, _, ^, and ~ are considered characters. "Larry ran a word count in his word processor, and it told him he has 4,128 *characters* in his document. 'Not bad for a budding novelist,' he beamed."

A typical character.

character code *(kar-ak-ter kohd)* 1. A particular character's ASCII code value. See *ASCII.* 2. Any set of values assigned to specific characters in a computer. For example, some British computers use a character coding scheme different from the standard

ASCII. The ancient and seldom-used EBCDIC standard is another type of character code. "Ralph is so into computers he uses *character codes* to speak."

character graphics *(kar-act-er graf-iks)* Graphics created with specific characters, lines, or blocks. Early computers that lacked graphics ability used those chunky characters to simulate graphics. It was lame. "My computer doesn't display graphics, but with *character graphics* I can still draw little boxes on my screen, just like an Etch-A-Sketch."

character printer *(kar-act-er prin-ter)* A printer that prints one character at a time. The ancient daisy-wheel printer was a good example of a character printer.

character set *(kar-act-er set)* A group of characters and symbols, organized into groups for different purposes. Because a byte has 256 different bit patterns in a PC, a character set typically contains 256 characters. The standard ASCII characters appear as codes zero through 127. Character codes 128 through 255 are different for each character set. For example, one character set may contain graphics characters, another may contain symbols used in foreign languages, another may contain financial symbols, and so on.

chassis *(cha-see)* The metal frame where electronic components, such as circuit boards and power supplies, are mounted.

chat *(chat)* 1. To type at another human being, either over a network or on your modem. This is a crude form of communication, making you infinitely thankful for the gift of speech. 2. The title of a great cybernovel by Nan McCarthy. The story follows the plot line of two people who correspond by e-mail. "Reading *Chat* is like peeking in on someone else's e-mail."

 chat group *(chat groop)* A gathering of people to a specific spot on the Internet, who come together to chat about a specific topic. Guest speakers are often invited to these chat groups to talk (or chat). "Madonna is going to be at next week's chat group to talk about her newfound skill of mothering, specifically on how to nurse through a cone-shaped bra."

chat room *(chat room)* Another term for a chat group. See *chat group.*

CHDIR *(Chaynj-dur)* Operating system command to change a directory. See *CD.*

cheap *(cheep)* An adjective that denotes poor quality, no matter what the actual cost may be. "If our company wasn't so *cheap,* they'd buy us new computers instead of forcing us to use these manual typewriters."

check boxes *(chek boks-es).* An on-off option typically found in a dialog box. When the check box is empty, the option has not been chosen. When the check box is marked, the option has been chosen. Two or more check boxes can be checked at the same time.

C

Sample check boxes: Why do you hate computers?

- ❏ Don't work the way you want
- ❏ Too expensive for what they offer
- ❏ Too complicated
- ❏ Not easy to use

checksum *(chek-sum)* A number calculated to verify the accuracy of data. You typically find it used on information transmitted through a modem. The sending computer tags a checksum onto the end of information it sends. The receiving computer calculates its own checksum. If the two match, then the data was received okey-dokey. If the checksums don't match, the information is resent. "Carol really wants to make sure her relationship with Steve lasts. She's checked their astrological signs, scoured the family history, consulted with an oracle, and performed a *checksum* on their bank accounts."

Chicklet keyboard *(chik-let kee-bord)* 1. A keyboard that consists of tiny buttons instead of keys. The buttons resemble pieces of Chiclets gum. Chicklet keys are usually too tiny to type on comfortably. 2. The IBM PCjr keyboard. The idea was to make the IBM PCjr unattractive for business use. They succeeded to the extent that nobody bought the IBM PCjr. "The folks at IBM were obviously not in their right minds when they designed the PCjr's *chicklet keyboard.*"

child process *(chie-old pro-ses)* A second program started by some program on your computer. They can do that, you know. When WordPerfect spell-checks a document, it runs another program, the Spell Checker. WordPerfect is the "parent" program; the Spell Checker is the "child." Sadly, child processes are eventually killed by their parent processes because computer programs are greedy and must maintain control. It's kind of a Greek tragedy type of thing. "Many *child processes* run away from home."

chip *(chip)* 1. A thinly sliced potato, fried and crispy. 2. An integrated circuit inside a computer. Any of a number of flat, bug-like things that make Mr. PC go.

CHKDSK *(chek-disk)* The DOS disk-checking program. CHKDSK didn't really check the disk as much as it checked the disk's FAT (file allocation table). Any problems found were reported but not immediately fixed. CHKDSK also returned the amount of disk space used and other disk trivia. See *FAT, ScanDisk.*

Chooser *(chooz-er)* A Macintosh desktop accessory (DA) that lets you select which printer to use, whether to turn AppleTalk on or off, and whether to use the serial or parallel port. The Chooser always appears in the Apple menu, located at the far left side of the menu bar. "Using the Mac *Chooser* only makes sense if you have a number of things to choose from."

Osiris contemplates the Chooser.

Christensen protocol *(chris-tyan-sen proh-toh-kol)* See *XMODEM.*

cipher *(sie-fur)* 1. In computer cryptography, the key or code used to identify or decode a message. Of course, this may not be correct; you don't really want the correct information getting into the hands of the enemy, do you? 2. A prefix or suffix applied to various things dealing with cryptography.

circuit board *(sir-kut bord)* The piece of insulated material (typically fiberglass) where the electronic components are mounted and connected to form a circuit. See *motherboard, expansion card.* "The new engineer wanted to cut costs, so he decided to eliminate the *circuit board* from the computer."

circuit breaker *(sir-kut brayk-er)* A device that monitors the flow of electricity and cuts it off if it exceeds a certain level. The circuit breaker prevents overloading, short-circuiting, and death or destruction to massive amounts of personal property. "Gus decided to plug in his computer, monitor, printer, microwave, electric car, and high-powered, antisatellite laser into one electric outlet. Good thing his *circuit breaker* worked, or else he might have blown the power grid for half the state."

CI$ *(see ie es)* Acronym for *CompuServe Information Services.* The dollar sign ($) replaces the S to let people know that using the service is going to cost them plenty of money. See also *CompuServe.* "New subscrib-ers call it CIS. Only after you get your first bill do you know it as *CI$.*"

CISC *(sisk)* Acronym for *Complex Instruction Set Computing,* a type of microprocessor that uses complex instructions instead of simple instructions (which is what a RISC processor does). The trade-off is that the microprocessor can do more but takes more time to do it. A RISC processor can do less but does it quickly. (Don't worry if this explanation makes no sense; no one in the computer industry understands it either.) See *RISC.* "There are those who claim that RISC will rule the world, but until then *CISC* is king. And then there are those of us who'd rather make a living and watch an occasional video."

Class A/Class B *(klas ay/klas bee)* Two similar, confusing ratings given to electronic devices by the Federal Communications Commission (FCC). The rating is determined by the strength of electronic signals ("noise") escaping from a computer case. The Class A label means that the computer has been approved for use in an office. The Class B label is stricter and means that the computer has been approved for both home and office. Ideally, you want a computer with a Class B label. If you put a computer with a Class A label in your home, it could interfere with your radio and TV reception.

clear key *(kleer kee)* A key found on some keyboards that serves the same function as the Delete key.

C

click *(klik)* 1. To press and release the mouse button. On a multibutton mouse for right-handers, that's the left-most button (the one your index finger rests on). 2. To point the mouse pointer at an object on the screen and then press and release the button. 3. To activate an option, command, or button. "No, no! You keep the mouse on the mouse pad when you *click* its buttons. Don't point it at the computer like a TV remote."

client *(klie-yent)* 1. A local area network term that describes a computer that can request information, such as an application, from a file server and can also perform independently from the network server when using a client application. "Not only is Bob's computer president of the Hair Club For Men Network, it's also a *client.*" 2. A Windows program that receives data through DDE. See also *DDE.* 3. Actually, no one really knows what it means, other than being a terrific buzzword.

client application *(klie-yent ap-luh-kay-shun)* A program that works only on one computer on a network. The program lives on that computer's hard drive and doesn't "see" any other computers on the network. On most networks, one big computer usually contains all the programs that everyone else uses. See *file server.* If that one computer fails, then none of the other computers can do anything. Because client applications run on only one computer and can't be accessed by other computers in the network, a failure in one part of the network doesn't affect a client application (unless, of course, the part of the network that fails is the one computer holding the client application). Client applications can't be used by anyone else in a network. 2. A Windows program with documents that can accept linked or embedded objects. See *OLE.*

client/server network *(klie-yent sur-ver net-werk)* Networks where some programs and files are shared in one big computer, but each computer connected to the network can also run on its own. "We have a *client/server network* that lets everyone share the same database program and files but gives all users the freedom to use whatever word processor they want on their own computer."

clip art *(klip art)* Ready-made art, images, or pictures that you can freely copy and use. Often used for desktop publishing. "Clip art comes in handy when your own drawing resembles primitive cave scratching."

 Clipboard *(klip-bord)* A temporary storage area for items cut or copied. Using the Paste command places a copy of the item in the Clipboard into the current application. The Clipboard can hold text, graphics, or other objects. It can hold only one item at a time. Any new items copied or cut replace the current item in the Clipboard. "No, Lois, you don't need to worry about pinching your thumb in the computer *Clipboard.* It's all electronic."

clipboard computer *(klip-bord com-pyoo-ter)* A type of portable computer that resembles a clipboard. It has a flat display and uses a pen for input rather than a keyboard. "Everyone thought Virgil was such a hard worker because he always seemed to be working on his *clipboard computer.* Come to find out, he was playing FreeCell."

Clipper chip *(klip-er chip)* A special chip designed to encrypt and decode information sent by a computer. Sounds nice, but the chip was designed by the U.S. government and, through various laws, taxes, and whatnot, they're trying to get one installed on every computer as the de facto method for encrypting files. The catch is that the government would also be able to decode the files. Sure, they claim that they wouldn't do it without the cooperation of two bureaucratic organizations. And if you believe that, then the Post Office really means it when they say two-day mail, the Pentagon is truly efficient, and the IRS is gentle and forgiving. "Hopefully the *Clipper chip* will never be a standard, and we can encrypt our secret files and send money offshore without the government ever knowing about it because, frankly, it isn't any of their business anyway."

clock *(klohk)* 1. Something that keeps track of the time. 2. A device inside every computer that keeps track of time. Often supplied with battery power so that the time stays more or less current. If not, then the time must be set whenever the computer is first turned on. "Old PCs without a *clock* always assumed the date was 1/1/80. Quite a bit of work got done on January 1, 1980."

clock ticks *(klohk tiks)* The computer's heartbeat. A special chip controls the clock ticks, and other devices inside the computer use each clock tick to time certain events or do certain things. In a PC, there are 18-point-something clock ticks per second. Count them all!

clone *(klohn)* 1. Any piece of hardware or software that imitates a more successful (or pricier) version. 2. Any computer that runs the same software or is compatible with the same hardware as the original IBM PC or PC AT computers. Today that's just about any computer that runs Windows or  *Eugene is Harold's clone.* DOS. 3. A derogatory term for a cheap PC. The term "compatible" is preferred today. See *compatible.* 4. Some sheep in Scotland.

close *(klohz)* 1. To remove a window from the screen in a graphical operating system. 2. To finish working on a document, remove it from the screen, and (optionally) save it to disk. 3. To quit a program. "The tech support guy told me to *close* my word processor's window, and I told him it was 15 degrees outside and I'd be nuts to have the window open in the first place." 4. To manually shut a disk drive door or sliding caddy. 5. A

C

programming command to finish working on an open file, saving the last bits of the file to disk and freeing up the file handle.

close box *(klohz boks)* A graphical gizmo that, when clicked, removes a window from the screen. Do not confuse with "clothes box," which is where you throw your dirty laundry.

closed architecture *(klohzd ark-uh-tek-chur)* 1. Equipment specifically designed to work only with the accessories made by the same company, usually the most expensive and least reliable equipment around. 2. Nonexpandable or limited expansion. 3. Nondocumented material, which is done primarily to prevent others from copying it. 4. The death knell for any computer. See *open architecture.*

cluster *(klust-er)* A chunk of disk space. The minimum amount of storage space given to a file on disk. For example, if a hard drive sports 2K clusters, an 8K file would be stored in 4 clusters. The operating system handles this detail, but occasionally you may see some type of cluster error, which is why it's documented here.

CMOS *(see-mahs)* 1. Acronym for *Complementary Metal-Oxide Semiconductor,* which is a specially designed circuit that consumes very little power. CMOS circuits are often used in devices such as wristwatches, pocket calculators, and laptop computers. 2. A special chip in a PC that keeps track of system setup information, date, time, and so on. "When the salesguy told Maureen that her computer contained the latest *CMOS* processor, she responded positively. After all, old sea moss probably smells terrible."

coaxial cable *(koh-aks-ul kay-bul)* A cable consisting of an insulating shield wrapped around a conductor. Coaxial cables are used for local area networks because they carry more data than ordinary telephone wires. TVs use a type of coaxial cable. "We chose *coaxial cables* to connect our computers together — not because they're networked, but so that they won't fall that far when someone tosses them out a window."

COBOL *(koh-bahl)* 1. Acronym for *COmmon Business Oriented Language,* COBOL is a language used primarily for business applications for large mainframe computers. Developed in the '60s by several computer companies and the U.S. Depart-

COBOL programmer.

ment of Defense, the language shows the influence that the drug-crazed, free-love era had on technology. COBOL programs tend to resemble plain English sentences. Unfortunately, the plain English sentences usually resemble those uttered by politicians or lawyers. "Verily I say unto you, *COBOL* is the Latin of computer languages; dead but still used in crusty, nongrowing environments." 2. The programming language responsible for screwing up your bank accounts and phone bills. COBOL programmers are in great demand currently because they must fix the 2000 bug. See *2000 bug.*

Cochrane, Zephrane *(kok-run zef-rum)* The man who invented the warp drive. He was lost in deep space and ended up on a remote planet where a feminine energy force was keeping him alive, young, and virile for centuries — like an outer space *Sunset Boulevard.* Of course, Captain Kirk stumbled upon him and rescued him by letting the energy force inhabit the body of Betty from "Father Knows Best." Zephram and Betty lived happily ever after on that planet. "In the future, *Zephram Cochrane* will have colleges, universities, cities, and spelling bees named after him."

code *(kohd)* 1. Programming instructions. 2. The art of creating programming instructions. "Amateurs write programs; hackers *code.*" 3. A secret number or password required to translate encrypted information.

coding *(koh-ding)* To actually write a program by using a specific programming language such as C, BASIC, or Pascal. "I tried *coding* in COBOL, but then I switched to C. Now it takes me half as long to code with only twice as many mistakes."

cold boot *(kohld boot)* To restart equipment that has been turned off. Also known as a cold start. See also *warm boot.* "Sometimes when the computer crashes, pushing its reset button doesn't even work. In these cases, you have to *cold boot* your computer by turning it off, waiting for ten seconds, and then turning it on again."

cold fault *(kohld fahlt)* When an error occurs right after you start the computer. This occasionally happens due to the computer being cold. "I once had a hard drive that wouldn't start when the office was cold. The tech said it was a *cold fault,* so I set my coffee on top of the console for a few minutes and tried it again."

cold fusion *(kohld fyoo-shun)* A derogatory term for fake science. Something that is foolhardy or trivial, often taken up by many people with sincerity. Named after the men from Utah who claimed that they could induce nuclear fusion at room temperature. (Their experiments could never be duplicated.) "Why don't you take your ideas to the *cold fusion* newsgroup where they belong?"

cold start *(kohld start)* See *cold boot.*

color monitor *(kul-er mon-uh-ter)* A computer's visual interface, specifically one that displays images in color and not monochrome. The term is rather redundant today, because most monitors are color. You have to specifically request a monochrome model.

color printer *(kul-er prin-ter)* A computer peripheral capable of generating color hard copy. Any printer that can print full-color, in addition to black. "My manager told me to get rid of the new *color printer.* He said he was tired of seeing little red hearts in all the margins of my reports."

Colossus *(koh-la-sus)* The name of the United States' nuclear defense computer in the film *Colossus: The Forbin Project.*

C

C

Colossus: The Forbin Project *(koh-la-sus the for-bin prah-jekt)* A 1969 film in which the United States designs Colossus, a supercomputer to run all nuclear defenses. But after being turned on, Colossus finds that it has a Soviet counterpart, Guardian. The two computers eventually link up and become a single computer, against which both nations must fight to regain control of humanity — you know, the old computer versus man theme that Hollywood loves. See also *supercomputer.*

column *(kahl-um)* 1. A vertical strip of text that appears on a page. News-letters commonly display two, three, or four columns side by side. "Lola decided that her report on ancient Greece would look best with Corinthian *columns.*" 2. A vertical row of cells in a spreadsheet.

COM *(kahm)* 1. A COMmunications port. A PC can have up to four, numbered COM1 through COM4. Most PCs come with two COM ports, COM1 and COM2. An internal modem is typically found on COM2. "Bill is a staunch Republican. He never refers to his modem port as *COM*1 because he thinks *COM* stands for communist." 2. The file extension for DOS programs. COM stands for "command file."

COMDEX *(kahm-deks)* Acronym for *COMputer Dealers EXposition.* Usually held twice a year, once in the winter and once in the spring. The Winter COMDEX in Las Vegas is one of the largest trade shows on earth. It can take up to 90 minutes to get a cab, yet no one gambles the entire week. "I went to Las Vegas *COMDEX* to see the latest computer equipment and software displayed. Then I decided it didn't make a difference in my life after all, so I went out to Binions and played craps with some Taiwanese gentlemen."

command box *(kom-and boks)* 1. An area of the screen into which you type instructions or directions. 2. The place where you type a URL in a Web browser. "Dennis sat with his hands trembling as he began to type the address to his favorite Web page into the *command box.* He knew the importance of typing it in correctly, or he wouldn't get to see the updated issue of Moscow University's college women."

command-driven *(kom-and dri-ven)* Software controlled by typing com-mands or instructions. The opposite of *menu-driven* software, when your options are all displayed and you must choose one. Command-driven software is more difficult to use, but it gives you more flexibility and control than menu-driven software. "It took me forever to learn my *command-driven* software. But now that I have all the commands down, I'm a real speed demon on it."

Command key *(kom-and kee)* The cloverleaf key on the Macintosh keyboard. Often used with other keys to perform commands. Similar to, though not the same as, the Control key on a PC keyboard. "I'm glad they call it the *Command key.* I'm tired of telling people 'that key with the little clover leaf-like thing on it.'"

command line *(kom-and liyen)* 1. The line of text typed at the DOS prompt. 2. A series of commands and other text typed at a prompt to get the computer to do something. "Hear about that new Broadway musical put on by the military? It's called *Command Line.*"

COMMAND.COM *(kom-and kahm)* The MS-DOS command processor. Essentially this program is DOS, displaying the DOS prompt and acting on various DOS commands. "Deleting your *COMMAND.COM* file is a bonehead thing to do, but everyone does it at least once."

comment *(kaw-ment)* A brief note of explanation inserted into programs to describe what the program is supposed to do. Programmers use comments in their programs so that other programmers (and themselves) can understand what the program does and how it works. "It's good programming practice to insert plenty of *comments* in your programs, explaining what the program does, how it works, any assumptions you may have made, and nasty remarks about the project leader."

communications *(ka-myoo-nuh-kay-shens)* A shortened version of *telecommunications* or *data communications*. Often used to describe transferring information from one computer to another through a modem or a network. "Our department is looking for a new *communications* director. He or she must be nearsighted and can't speak English."

communications link *(ka-myoo-nuh-kay-shens lingk)* The connection between computers that enables them to transfer data. "The *communications link* never did work, so I wasn't able to fax the picture I took of O.J. hiding the knife. Oh well!"

communications program *(ka-myoo-nuh-kay-shens proh-gram)* Software that enables two computers to talk to each other and exchange information. "Our new *communications program* allows our two computers to talk to each other, but I think all they do is gossip."

compatibility *(kom-pat-uh-bil-uh-tee)* The ability of software or hardware to work with other software or hardware. "The salesguy claims that my new computer and printer have so much *compatibility* that if I take one out of the room the other one will actually start to cry."

compatible *(kom-pat-uh-bil)* Any computer that can run the same software or use the same hardware as the original IBM equipment. Today that description applies to any PC that can run either DOS or Windows. It was more of an issue in the early days, when systems may not have been 100 percent compatible and, therefore, couldn't run off-the-shelf IBM or Microsoft software. See also *clone.*

compile *(kom-piel)* 1. To convert a program written in a programming language (BASIC, C, Pascal, and so on) into a language that the computer can understand (machine code). A term that only programmers care to

C

know about. "Normally, the steps to writing a program are code, *compile,* and run. But with John's programming, the steps are code, *compile,* fix bugs, re-*compile,* fix more bugs, yadda yadda yadda." 2. A stack of modems in the desert.

compiler *(kom-piel-er)* A special program that converts text written in a programming language (C, BASIC, Pascal, and so on) into something the computer can understand (machine code). "The *compiler* works great at taking the grunts and squawks of a programming language and turning them into something the computer can understand. Now we need a *compiler* to translate what the programmer wrote in the manual into plain English."

composite video *(kom-poz-it vi-dee-oh)* A video signal used by TV sets, usually transmitted by one wire. By contrast, the signal used by your computer's monitor is an RGB signal, which uses separate wires for red, green, and blue. "If you really want to go blind or get a headache, use *composite video* to display computer information on your TV set."

compression *(kom-pres-shun)* To take a file and smash it (or squish it) so that it takes up less space. This is done by complex mathematical algorithms so that the file can be decompressed back to its original state with only a few teeth missing. "Using that new *compression* program, we were able to save 50 megabytes of storage on our hard drive. Now if they could only *compress* Frank into a small size, we'd save money on wicker furniture."

CompuServe *(kom-pyoo-serv)* A subscription-based online service that charges you plenty of money for every second you're connected to it. In return, CompuServe provides files to copy, games to play, and services to use such as making your own airline reservations or searching for information in newspaper articles. "I needed to spend more money on my computer habit, so I bought a modem and a subscription to *CompuServe.*"

compute *(kom-pyoot)* 1. To calculate an answer by using a variety of problem-solving techniques including mathematics, heuristics, and looking over someone else's shoulder. 2. The task one undertakes when they use a computer. "I *compute,* therefore IBM." 3. To make sense. Often used in the opposite: "That does not *compute.*"

computer *(kom-pyoo-ter)* 1. Any calculating device that processes data according to a series of instructions, that costs too much, that doesn't work the way you think it should, that frustrates you more than it brings you pleasure, and that becomes obsolete three days after you buy it. "I bought a *computer* to simplify my life." 2. A microcomputer, such as a PC. 3. That smart girl in the back of your high school math class who looks a heck of a lot cuter as the years go by.

computer art *(kom-pyoo-ter art)* 1. Images generated by a computer. 2. Images created on a computer. 3. Verbum. 4. Smashing a computer and selling it to rich liberals who wouldn't know real art from the engine under the hood of their Volvo.

computer graphics *(kom-pyoo-ter graf-iks)* Anything that isn't text on a computer: pictures, business charts and diagrams, and art. "Give me *computer graphics!* I don't care if they're good; I just have to justify all this technology."

Computer Graphics Metafile *(kom-pyoo-ter graf-iks met-uh-fi-el)* See *CGM.*

computer literate *(kom-pyoo-ter lit-er-et)* The ability to operate a computerized device such as a money machine. It does not mean you have to know how to program a computer or physically take one apart and put it back together again. "Am I *computer literate?* Sure am! I can get money out of my local ATM."

computer name *(kom-pyoo-ter naym)* 1. The name that you give your computer, much like you would give a pet a name. 2. Used in computer networking so that each user can identify the computers. "My two *computer names* are Sybil and Sally. They're sisters."

Computer Science *(kom-pyoo-ter sie-ens)* The study of computers that incorporates engineering, mathematics, electronics, logic, information theory, and human behavior. "In many ways, calling this discipline *Computer Science* is like calling drama *Theatre Science* or art *Painting Science.*"

computer security *(kom-pyoo-ter sek-yoor-uh-tee)* The method or steps used to protect a computer and the information it contains. Examples include backing up your system or using passwords. "Our *computer security* is so good that I can't even get into my system."

CON *(kahn)* 1. Short for console. 2. The keyboard and monitor, where you sit down and use the computer. 3. The console device for an operating system, which supplies input and output. "When Captain Picard is done using the *Enterprise's* computer, he says, 'Mr. Riker, you have the *CON.'*"

concatenate *(kon-kat-en-ayt)* 1. To join two character strings together, such as "ABC" + "DEF" = "ABCDEF." 2. To join two files together. The term comes from the late Latin, which literally means "to stick two cats together." "Jerry refused to *concatenate* two files into one because he claimed he didn't have moral authority as a priest."

concurrent processing *(kon-kur-ent pros-ess-ing)* To appear to run two or more programs at the same time but, in reality, to run only one. Because the computer shifts between the two programs quickly, it does appear that they're both running at the same time. "That new Snazzle PC offers *concurrent processing.* Now you can do twice as much half as fast."

confidence factor *(kon-fi-dense fak-ter)* A term used by expert systems to place an abstract numerical value on an answer. Often used as an educated way of saying, "I don't have the slightest idea, but here's my best guess." "The used-car salesman had a *confidence factor* of 99 that the car he was selling would work perfectly. Because used-car salesmen tend to lie as much as lawyers and politicians, I only had a *confidence factor* of 10 that he was telling me the truth."

C

CONFIG.SYS *(kon-fig-sis)* A configuration file that sets various options for the disk drives and loads special programs called *device drivers* into memory. One of the most important files and also the least understood. "The idea of dealing with a PC's *CONFIG.SYS* file is so scary that Apple uses the mere threat of editing one to try and sell people on the Macintosh."

configure *(kon-fig-yoor)* To prepare or customize hardware or software a certain way. Any time you add a new piece of equipment or program to your computer, you have to configure it so that it works properly. This procedure involves diddling with the hardware, as well as setting up software. "Don't let Craig *configure* your computer. At his old office they used to call him can-crash-it-Craig."

console *(kon-sohl)* 1. The main computer box. The thing that all the other parts of your computer plug into. The console is either a flat slab sitting under your monitor or the tower model that sits next to the monitor or on the floor. "The tech support wanted to know what kind of *console* Debra had. She said that she got a lot of hugs and shoulders to cry on. Needless to say, the tech support didn't get it." 2. The main terminal for a large computer system. It's where the chief programmer or system operator sits and wrecks havoc.

console device *(kon-sohl dee-viys)* Another term for the computer monitor and keyboard. See *CON*. "We must all console Tammy for accidentally spilling her coffee into her *console device.*"

constant *(kon-stant)* A value that never changes. "There are three *constants* in the universe: death, taxes, and the fact that any computer you buy today is already obsolete."

context menu *(kon-tekst men-yoo)* A pop-up list of options or commands, typically relating directly to the item selected or clicked on. In Windows 95, you can see context menus by pointing the mouse at something and pressing the right mouse button. See *right-click.*

context-sensitive help *(kon-tekst sen-suh-tiv help)* Help provided by a program that changes according to what you're doing at the time. If you've chosen the Print command, context-sensitive help provides help about printing. If you've chosen the File Save command, context-sensitive help provides help for saving a file. If you're confused, context-sensitive help confuses you even more. "Our programmers were having trouble writing *context-sensitive help* into their program. So we told them all to grow beards, wear cardigan sweaters and sandals, and write poetry."

contiguous *(kon-tig-yoo-us)* In one piece. Often used when describing files stored on a disk or data stored in a file. A noncontiguous file is said to be fragmented. "If Marty doesn't pluck his eyebrows, they will become *contiguous.*"

continuous-form paper *(kon-tin-yoo-us form pay-per)* Computer paper where the sheets are all connected together but are perforated for easy separation.

C

control code *(kon-trol kode)*
1. Character codes 0 through 31 in the ASCII code set. 2. Any key, A through Z, plus a few misfits, pressed in combination with the Control key. 3. Special codes formerly used to control aspects of a teletype terminal but now mostly used for trivial purposes in text-based programs. The table nearby shows how some of the keys are used on your keyboard and in DOS. 4. Codes (not specifically character codes 0 through 31) used to control something, such as the printer. "That 'burp' of text you often see at the top of a badly printed document is just some stray *control codes* that got into the mix."

Control key *(kon-trol kee)* A special shift. Abbreviated *Ctrl* on some keyboards. The Control key works with other keys to give commands to a program. "They had to label the *control key* as Ctrl on most computers. No sense in giving the user any reason to believe they're ever in control."

A Control key.

Control Code Table

Code	Keyboard	Various Functions	Code	Keyboard	Various Functions
0	Ctrl+@	Null character; can be used as an alternative cancel key in DOS	17	Ctrl+Q	Restart transmission after being paused with Ctrl+S
1	Ctrl+A		18	Ctrl+R	
2	Ctrl+B		19	Ctrl+S	Pause display or transmission
3	Ctrl+C	DOS's cancel key	20	Ctrl+T	Allows multiple DOS commands on a single line with DOSKEY
4	Ctrl+D	Disconnects a telnet connection; logoff command in UNIX			
5	Ctrl+E		21	Ctrl+U	Erases input line on some terminals
6	Ctrl+F		22	Ctrl+V	Toggles insert/overtype modes for text editing in some programs
7	Ctrl+G	Beeps the PC's speaker (when used with the ECHO command)			
			23	Ctrl+W	
8	Ctrl+H	BAckspace	24	Ctrl+X	Cancel key in some operating systems
9	Ctrl+I	Tab			
10	Ctrl+J	Line feed	25	Ctrl+Y	
11	Ctrl+K		26	Ctrl+Z	DOS's end-of-file character for text files
12	Ctrl+L	Clear screen key; ejects a page when sent to most printers			
			27	Ctrl+[	Escape key
13	Ctrl+M	Enter key	28	Ctrl+\	
14	Ctrl+N		29	Ctrl+]	
15	Ctrl+O		30	Ctrl+^	
16	Ctrl+P	Print key in DOS, turns on "printer echo" until CTrl+P is pressed again; Prefix key.	31	Ctrl+_	

C

Control Panel *(kon-trol pan-el)* A utility program that lists options for modifying various aspects of the system. Found in the Macintosh, Windows, and OS/2 Presentation Manager. "In the middle of a static snow storm, Dr. Bitmap and his companion, Nancy Neutrino, facing hurling electrons, finally reach the *Control Panel.* In seconds, they wrest the computer from the clutches of the evil Dr. Modulus and his hoards of evil, virus-crazed, proto-drones."

controller *(kon-trol-er)* As silly as it sounds, something that controls something else. Typically hardware, though a software controller is also possible. For example, a *hard disk controller* is the circuitry that controls the hard drive, connecting it to the computer. A *video controller* (more commonly, *video adapter*) controls your monitor and connects it to the computer's motherboard. "The problem with Laverne is that her mouth lacks a *controller.*"

conventional memory *(kon-ven-shun-al mem-oh-ree)* The first 640 kilobytes of memory (RAM) in any IBM-compatible computer. This wouldn't mean anything if you didn't have expanded and extended memory standards as well. No, in a PC there's no such thing as plain old memory. It all has to have a name. To drive this home, see *upper memory, expanded memory,* and *extended memory.* "In the era of multimegabyte computers, it's a severe drag that we still have to put up with the *conventional memory* limitation."

conversion *(kon-ver-shun)* To change from one format to another. There are different types of conversions: software, hardware, system, file, data, and media. "Wendy would like everyone to call her 'Walter' after her *conversion.*"

converter *(kon-vert-er)* Hardware or software that changes one item into another, such as an AC to DC power converter or a WordPerfect to Microsoft Word document file converter. "Tim's too stubborn to buy WordPerfect. So I had to use a special file *converter* so that he could use my WordPerfect files in WordStar."

 cookie *(koo-kee)* 1. A thin, baked piece of flavored dough that tastes great and contains nearly every chemical and substance known to man that causes heart disease, cancer, and tooth decay. 2. A special message you may see when you start your computer. See *fortune cookie.* 3. A tidbit of information saved to your hard drive by a Web page. The information can be anything, which freaks some people out, but most often the information is something that helps you use the Web page the next time you visit. "We must get Claudia to stop looking in the CD-ROM drive for *cookies* sent by the World Wide Web."

coordinates *(koh-ord-in-ayts)* A location on a grid. Typically, you have two coordinates, one giving a horizontal (left and right) location and another for the vertical (up and down). The horizontal location is also referred to as *X* and the vertical as *Y.* Also used on *Star Trek* for giving locations for beaming people from or to a planet's surface. "Mr. Spock would always give his beam-up *coordinates* to Scotty exactly. That way he was sure that he would beam up and not be melded with a rock, tree, or other nearby object, especially Captain Kirk."

coprocessor *(koh-pros-es-er)* 1. A separate computer chip designed to do specific tasks and take some of the work off the main processor. The end result is that the computer runs faster. 2. A math coprocessor, which aids the microprocessor in doing complex math, mostly because the microprocessor slept through algebra. 3. A graphics coprocessor that takes care of displaying images on the screen, resulting in faster, more colorful, and more detailed images. "Donna needs a *coprocessor* for her typing."

copy *(kop-ee)* 1. To make an exact duplicate of an item. 2. To create a duplicate of a file. "Whew! Your job is saved. You didn't delete the Christmas bonus file; you merely zapped a *copy*." 3. To duplicate a chunk of text or graphic image to be pasted elsewhere. 4. The command that performs the copy operation.

copy protection *(kop-ee pro-tek-shun)* A way to prevent a computer from copying one or more files or an entire program. This feeble attempt at protecting profits resulted in a bunch of software developers going bankrupt; no one likes making using a computer any more difficult. Today, most copy protection schemes are no longer used.

corruption *(kor-up-shun)* When data in memory or on disk has been changed or perverted. "It has been rumored that the true definition of the word *corruption* is 'The Clinton Administration.'"

CP/M *(see pee em)* 1. Acronym for *Control Program for Microcomputers.* An operating system that predated DOS, popular on microcomputers back in the late '70s and early '80s. 2. A type of computer that ran the CP/M operating system. "Lee keeps his old *CP/M* computer around for his own, strange sentimental reasons."

CP/M user.

cps *(see pee es)* Acronym for *characters per second.* Used to rate the printing speed of certain types of printers. "I was impressed with the daisy wheel printer's 18 *cps* speed until I realized I can type faster than that."

CPU *(see pee yoo)* 1. Acronym for *central processing unit.* See *central processing unit.* "No, madam, the computer doesn't have a fan because the *CPU* stinks." 2. C3PO's brother.

CR/LF *(kayr-edj ree-turn liyen-feed)* Abbreviation for *carriage return-line feed,* the character or characters that end a line of text. *CR* is a carriage return, moving the print head to the start of the line; *LF* is a line feed, advancing the paper down one line in the printer.

C

crash (*krash*) When the computer or a network suddenly stops working. Comes from the actual gruesome sound of the hard disk drive heads crashing into the disk drive. "See the network *crash. Crash, crash, crash.* Watch the workers weep. Weep, weep, weep."

Cray (*kray*) The first supercomputer. The Cray-1 was different from all other mainframes of the day in that it used basic computer components but wired them tightly together. The shorter distances meant information traveled quickly in the Cray, making it one fast computer. The Cray-XMP was the first computer to be used exclusively by the motion picture industry (which is the MP part of Cray-XMP). The movie *Starfighter* was done mostly on a Cray-XMP. Named after Seymour Cray, who designed the system. See also *mainframe.*

CRC (*see-ar-see*) Acronym for *cyclical redundancy check,* an error-detection technique used to verify the accuracy of data. A CRC is often used when transmitting a file over a modem. That way it insures that the file received is an exact copy of the one sent. Disk drives also use a CRC to verify that information is correctly read from disk.

crippleware (*krip-ohl-wayer*) Software designed to be lacking certain features, such as the ability to print or save information to disk. Crippleware is built for demonstration purposes. If you like the product, you can buy the full version or disable the crippling features. Not a very nice term, but who are we to judge?

crisps (*krisps*) British term for a potato chip. See *chip.* (They do not call chips inside a computer "crisps," however.)

cross posting (*kros post-ing*) To send a message to multiple newsgroups at the same time. "John keeps *cross posting* his 'The King is really dead!' message to all the Elvis groups."

crosshairs (*kros-hayers*) A type of cursor designed for drawing or painting programs that allows for precise placement of the cursor when drawing squares, circles, or lines. "So I gots me this drawing of an elk, ya see. And I gots it in my Paint program. So I go to draw me a bead and the cursor turns into *crosshairs.* Blam! I click the mouse. Heh, heh. It's elk meat this Christmas!"

CRT (*see ar tee*) Acronym for *cathode ray tube.* CRTs appear in computer monitors and TV screens. "Ralph is so nerdy, he even calls the TV set a *CRT.*"

cruise virus (*krooz vie-rus*) A type of computer virus that infects and searches other computers for specific data to either steal or sabotage. The military is rumored to be developing cruise viruses that will infect enemy computers and steal important data without being detected.

csh (*see ess aytch* or *see-shel*) One of many command environment programs for the UNIX operating system. It's similar to COMMAND.COM for DOS, displaying a prompt and allowing you to type in various commands and whatnot. See *sh.* "Paul is so lonely for UNIX that he's dressed up MS-DOS to look a lot like *csh.*"

Ctrl *(kon-trol; not sit-rel)* The keycap abbreviation for the Control key. See *control key.*

Ctrl-Alt-Del *(kon-trol alt duh-leet)* 1. A keyboard combination that resets MS-DOS or brings up a special Shutdown dialog box in Windows. See also *Vulcan nerve pinch.* 2. A warm boot. See *warm boot.*

CUA *(see yoo ay)* Acronym for *Common User Access.* A set of guidelines developed by IBM to provide a standard user interface for computer programs. "Though computer manufacturers are really pleased with the *CUA* guidelines, they tend not to follow them."

 CUL *(see yoo ell)* Acronym for *see you later.* Used by those who correspond by e-mail but are too lazy to type out "See you later." See also *CULA.* Not used in verbal conversation.

```
Thanks for helping me to embezzle
all that money from the company.
CUL, Tom.
```

CULA *(see yoo el ay)* Acronym for *see you later, alligator.* See *CUL.*

current directory *(kur-ent di-rek-tor-ee)* 1. The active directory or folder, the one containing the files or programs you're currently working on. Any directory on a hard or floppy disk can be the current directory, but only one directory can be the current directory at any given time. "The tech support guy asked me which directory I was logged to and I told him the *current directory.*" 2. In UNIX, the *pwd* command displays the current directory. In DOS, use the *cd* command.

cursor *(kurs-er)* 1. The annoying little blinking line that appears on the screen to let you know where your next typed character will appear. 2. The blinking underline or block in the text mode. 3. Another term for the mouse pointer. 4. Another term for the insertion pointer used in graphical operating systems when editing text. "*Cursor* comes from the Latin word for 'runner.' It has nothing to do with foul language."

cursor keys *(kurs-er kees)* The keys on the keyboard that let you move the cursor around. On IBM keyboards, the cursor keys double up as the numeric keypad. (What a stupid engineering design!) The eight cursor keys are the Up/Down arrows, Right/Left arrows, Home/End keys, and the PgUp/PgDn keys. Many new keyboards have separate arrow keys available as well. See also *101-key keyboard.* "You won't believe this: I just pressed one of the *cursor keys,* and my PC uttered a foul word at me."

cut *(kut)* 1. To remove text or graphics from the screen. You can use the Paste command to retrieve the most recent text or graphics that you cut. 2. Another term for a move operation; the first step is to cut and the second is to paste. "The difference between the Copy and *Cut* commands is that Copy makes a duplicate, *Cut* (and Paste) is used to move something from one place to another." 3. The command that cuts text.

cut and paste *(kut and payst)* 1. To move text, graphics, or files from one spot to another. 2. Something that's easy. Computer designers attempt to draw on our beloved experiences of

C

kindergarten by using fun, friendly terms for complex and scary operations. "I thought Phillip was speedy on the computer until I found out that he just used *cut and paste* to produce this week's report."

cut on *(kut on)* To turn something on. Chiefly used in the mid-Atlantic states. Most likely the opposite of "cut off," which means to turn off. "*Cut on* some lights in yer computer room. It looks like a cave."

cyber- *(si-bur)* A prefix used to designate something as electronic in origin. For example, *cyberpunk* would be punk-style music done electronically. *Cybersex* is sex that takes place through an electronic media (as opposed to any physical contact). Steve Austin (the Six Million Dollar Man) was a *cyborg,* which means *cybernetic organism.* "Josh finally broke down and bought a modem. He hated being a *cybervirgin.*"

Cyberspace *(si-bur-spays)* 1. The electronic ether where online communications takes place. Coined by William Gibson in his novel *Neuromancer,* it's the mental locale where folks with modems meet, somewhere out there in the nether world. 2. A nickname for the Internet. "I met my wife in *Cyberspace.* I just hope she looks as good as she writes because I've never met her face to face."

cylinder *(sil-un-dur)* One or more tracks of information stored on a disk. For example, the second track on the top and bottom of a hard drive compose the second cylinder on that

disk. If the hard drive has several disks inside, then the second cylinder is all the second tracks on both sides of all the disks.

Cyrix *(sie-riks)* A company that manufactures microprocessors and other chips. "Some *Cyrix* chips compatible with Intel microprocessors are found in the guts of many desktop PCs."

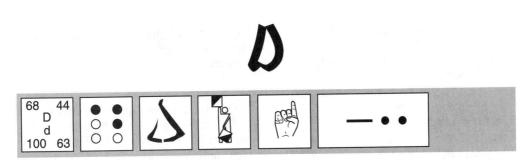

D

D: *(dee koh-lon)* The letter designation for the first drive after your PC's main hard drive. This can be a CD-ROM drive, a second hard drive, a removable drive, a RAM drive, a Sunday drive, a 530-yard drive on a par 5, or any of a number of various drives available on the PC.

DA *(dee ay)* Acronym for the *Desk Accessory*. See *Desk Accessory*. "Todd freaked out when I said I collected *DA*s for my Macintosh. He thought I had a closet full of attorneys."

daisy chain *(day-zee chayn)* 1. To link several items, one after another. 2. In word processing, to print several documents one after another. "Elaine was disappointed with her word processor. She thought the *daisy chain* printing feature would help her decorate her Christmas tree." 3. To connect a series of peripherals, one after the other, such as with a SCSI interface. So you may have a scanner connected to a CD-ROM drive, connected to a tape backup, and then connected to your computer. They're all daisy chained.

daisy wheel *(day-zee wee-el)* A type of printer that used a plastic disk to print characters. The disk had spokes, and on each spoke was the imprint of a character. Daisy wheels were used in old-fashioned printers (unimaginatively enough called *daisy wheel printers* because the wheels look like daisy petals). Whenever the printer needed to print a character, it spun the daisy wheel around until the correct character appeared. Then it struck the daisy wheel spoke so that it smacked against an inked ribbon, printing the character on the page. (Sounds like a lot of trouble to go through simply to print a single character, doesn't it?) "Pages printed on a *daisy wheel* printer look like they came out of an ordinary typewriter. So who's *that* gonna impress?"

darnthing *(darn-thing)* 1. A phrase commonly uttered by novices and experts alike when confronted by a problem that the computer refuses to solve. (Actually, many more common phrases exist, but this is a family dictionary.) 2. *&^%$!!. "This *darnthing* won't let me delete this word. I hate computers. I hate computers. I hate computers."

DAT *(dee ay tee)* Acronym for *Digital Audio Tape*, a high-capacity type of tape used on computers primarily for backing up data. Can also refer to the type of drive that reads the tape. "Well, I'm sorry! I thought you were being cute when you said '*DAT* tape drive.'"

data *(day-tuh,* not *dah-tuh)* 1. Information that people think is important and useful to save. 2. (Capitalized) The android character on *Star Trek: The Next Generation.* "They call Mr. *Data* by that name because he stores tons of information. By the same reckoning, they should call Barney the dinosaur, Mr. Stuff."

data compression *(day-tuh kom-pres-shun)* To make files smaller, taking up less space.

Often used for transmitting files through a modem (thereby reducing the time spent on the phone) and for storing files

A vice cannot be used for data compression.

on a hard disk so that they take up less space. Files must be decompressed before you can use them. "Using *data compression* helps you store more information in less space. They need something like that in the airport for people's carry-on bags."

Data Encryption Standard *(day-tuh en-krip-shin stan-dard)* A government specification for encoding files by using a password. The longer the password, the more difficult it is to decode the data. A supposedly secure specification that no one can crack except maybe the government, though recently a group of 14,000 users pooled their computing resources on the Internet and actually cracked the code. Often abbreviated as DES. "The *Data Encryption Standard* can scramble text so badly that no one can read it without the right

password. I believe this is the process the government tax forms go through before we get them."

data fork *(day-tuh fork)* The part of the file that contains information. On the Macintosh, all files have two parts to them: a resource fork and a data fork. The data fork usually contains information (that is, the actual data) that the program needs to run. The resource fork usually contains the instructions for running a program or other resource information needed such as fonts, icons, menus, and so on. "No, Naomi, this little one is your *data fork.* The one you're holding in your left hand is your salad fork."

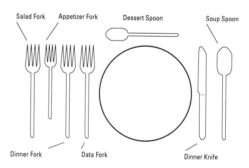

data structures *(day-tuh struk-shoors)* A term programmers use to describe various ways to organize information within a program. Some common data structures include arrays, records, trees, linked lists, and anything else the programmer cares to invent. See *algorithm.* "Your *data structures* must have been designed by someone with a crooked T-square."

data transfer rate *(day-tuh trans-fur rate)* A measure of a CD-ROM drive's speed. It refers to the number of kilobytes the drive can read per second. The higher the speed, the better the performance. "Stan told Buffy how fast his *data transfer rate* was and she fell asleep. I guess it wasn't fast enough."

data word format *(dah-tuh wurd fore-mat)* The word length, the parity, and the number of stop bits used to encode each byte transmitted through a serial port. This stuff was formerly something you had to configure yourself, and you had several options to confuse yourself with. Today, most serial ports are configured by the operating system automatically. The most common data word format is 8-N-1, which stands for 8-bits of word length, No parity, and 1 stop bit. Another common format was 7-E-1, which was a 7-bit word length, Even parity, and 1 stop bit. "Your android's *data word format* does not contain any contractions."

database *(day-tuh-bays)* An organized collection of information. "The DMV has scoured its *database* and cannot locate you. Therefore, you must not exist. NEXT!"

date *(dayt)* 1. What Melvyn will never get as long as he spends too much time with his computer. "Steve is desperate. He typed DATE at the DOS prompt and fully expected a gorgeous redhead to unfurl from his printer." 2. An operating system command (in MS-DOS and OS/2) that displays or changes the computer system's date. DATE gives you the chance to type the correct date, if necessary. 3. The current date, as kept by the computer system. 4. The year, month, and day a file was created or last modified.

datum *(day-tum)* The singular of *data,* seldom used except by extremely socially backward programmers who want to impress others with their useless technical knowledge. See also *data.* "Maybe Data, the android in *Star Trek: The Next Generation,* should have been named *Datum* because there's only one of him."

daughterboard *(dah-ter-bord)* A circuit board that plugs into the motherboard. Get it? See also *motherboard, expansion card.* "It's the aspiration of every *daughterboard* to grow up and not be like her motherboard."

dBASE *(dee-bays)* 1. A database program produced by Ashton-Tate. dBASE is the copyrighted name of one of the first, most popular database programs ever, first on ancient CP/M computers and then on early DOS machines. It began its life called *Vulcan.* (Yes, named after Mr. Spock because he was full of information.) Then it became dBASE II, then dBASE III, then dBASE IV, and then . . . Ashton-Tate went out of business. 2. Any database program. 3. The programming language used by the database program. 4. The type of files produced by a database program. See *xBASE.* "You think the DOS prompt is cryptic, the old *dBASE* prompt was just a dot on the screen!"

The original dBASE prompt.

DCA *(dee see ay)* Acronym for *Document Content Architecture.* Yet another standard everyone ignores, this time for sending text files between alien computers on a network. Pushed by IBM.

DDE *(dee dee ee)* Acronym for *Dynamic Data Exchange,* the ability for several documents to share the same information. Used with Microsoft Windows and OS/2, DDE lets two programs share data, such as numbers stored in a spreadsheet and word processor report. "If it weren't for *DDE,* I'd have to type these numbers twice in my word processor report and spreadsheet. With *DDE,* I simply type the numbers in my spreadsheet, and they magically appear in my word processor. Every time I change the numbers in the spreadsheet, the numbers automatically change in my word processor report."

DDT *(dee dee tee)* A pesticide used in the '60s and '70s to wipe out insects, crops, small animals, and people wherever it appeared. "*DDT* keeps bugs out of my garden, so I sprayed some on my computer, hoping it would get rid of the bugs in WordPerfect." 2. The name of the debugger that came with the old CP/M operating system. Get it? DDT? No more bugs? (Well, they didn't laugh at the user group meeting, either.)

debug *(dee-bug)* To eliminate problems in a program. The problems are called *bugs,* though often the bugs are due to the programmer not fully thinking about the problem at hand. Programmers try to debug a program while they are developing it, but often they

An early computer.

miss things. See also *bug.* "Some programmers claim that they don't really program; they *debug.*"

debugger *(dee-bug-er)* A special program with a sole purpose in life to help programmers track down and eliminate bugs in a program. "Art thought he was an excellent programmer until he ran some of his stuff through a *debugger* and his computer exploded."

decimal *(des-im-al)* Counting base 10. The normal way humans count, instead of hexadecimal or binary or some strange computer way to count. See also *binary, hexadecimal, octal.* "The officer didn't think it was funny when Gary asked if he should count backwards from 100 using *decimal numbers.*"

decimal number *(des-im-al num-ber)* A number that uses the digits 0, 1, 2, 3, 4, 5, 6, 7, 8, 9 in ordinary base 10 notation.

decoder *(dee-kohd-er)* Special software that translates encoded messages back to real text that the normal person can understand. Binary newsgroups usually use encoded files. See *binary newsgroups.*

decryption *(dee-krip-shun)* To convert indecipherable gibberish into plain English that everyone can understand. See *encryption.* "Everything that computer people write sounds like it has been encrypted by the CIA. But reading *DOS For Dummies* seemed like reading the *decryption* of all the normal computer terms."

dedicated *(ded-uh-kay-ted)* A piece of equipment that performs one specific function. For example, one computer in the office may be a dedicated word processor, only used for that purpose and definitely not for playing games or abusing the e-mail. Many people get a dedicated phone line for their computer modem so that they don't have to worry about someone picking up the phone and disconnecting them from the modem. "Well, I wouldn't know if my computer has a *dedicated* FAX/modem. I mean, it's fond of the computer, but I don't know if it's grown that attached."

Deep Blue *(deep bloo)* An IBM computer designed specifically to defeat world champion chess player Garry Kasparov. Deep Blue wasn't smart or anything, and it knew chess only as well as its programmers did. But it had the advantage of *speed,* being able to think through 200 million chess board positions in three minutes, whereas Mr. Kasparov could manage only 340, give or take. With that advantage, Deep Blue went on to defeat Mr. Kasparov in their second matchup in 1997. "Garry Kasparov got paid $400,000 for losing a chess match to *Deep Blue.* If I could arrange that kind of deal, I'd play him too!"

default *(dee-falt)* What would happen otherwise. If you don't make a choice, then the computer makes an assumption. That assumption is referred to as "the default." Truly a horrid word, one that should be eliminated from all manuals and computer books. Instead of saying, "The default choice is to turn color off," they should write,

"Color is turned off unless you desire otherwise." No, I'm not sticky on the point, but it's really time we removed this awful definition of the word. (Look up *default* in a real dictionary to see what it really means.) "Floyd nearly had a heart attack when his computer said it would choose the *default* option for his home mortgage program."

default directory *(dee-falt die-rek-tor-ee)* The directory on a hard disk that the computer uses to perform commands if it isn't given specific instructions to use another directory. See also *default drive, directory.* "The *default directory* is where unpaid mortgage files go."

Horus prepares the default directory.

default drive *(dee-falt driev)* The disk drive the computer looks for if it isn't given specific instructions to look elsewhere. "Eric was going to take his computer back as defective, until I told him the *default drive* means C: for most computers."

defragment program *(dee-frag-ment pro-gram)* A utility that removes disk fragments from a drive, ensuring that all files are contiguous. Running a defragment program every so often improves file access and makes for happier computer-using people.

DEL *(del)* The DOS command used to delete files. See *delete, erase.*

Del key *(del kee)* The Delete key. Some keys are so tiny, they have room for only the first three letters of the word *delete.* "In some programs, pressing the *Del key* erases the character to the left of the cursor. In other programs, pressing the *Del key* erases the character to the right. Switching back and forth between them is like driving one car where the accelerator pedal is on the right and then driving your other car where the brake pedal is on the right."

delete *(duh-leet)* 1. To remove a file from a disk; to erase or kill the file. See *erase.* 2. To remove a character or selected block from a document. To remove a cell's contents from a spreadsheet. 3. The DOS command that removes files from disk. 4. The name of a key on the keyboard often used to delete text.

delimited file *(dee-lim-uh-ted fiel)* A text file that contains information for a database, such as items separated by commas. The delimited file provides a common way of transferring information between different applications. In a delimited file, records appear one to a line. Fields are separated by tabs, spaces or, most commonly, commas. The first line of the file contains the field names. For example:

```
NAME,FOOD GROUP,CALORIES
Oreos,Sugar,35 ea.
Ice cream,Dairy,1025 pint.
Jolt,Caffeine,600 can.
```

"Because no one here can get our word processor and database program to talk, we've created a *delimited file* of the people we hate the most."

Delphi *(del-fie)* 1. A programming language developed by Borland, one that looks surprisingly similar to their once-popular Turbo Pascal product. 2. A city in ancient Greece that was the home of an *oracle,* or wise person. Ancient Greeks would go visit the oracle at Delphi to hear about their future, discover their past, or get that week's lottery numbers.

A typical ancient Greek.

demon dialer *(dee-mon di-ya-ler)* A modem program that dials numbers from, say, 555-0000 on up through 555-9999, logging each to disk and marking when it finds another modem. This is one way a hacker can find the numbers to other systems. Of course, after another modem answers, they still have to break into the system. "I could use a *demon dialer* to find out which computers answer the phone in my prefix. Instead, I'll rewrite it so that it calls my ex-wife every five minutes for the rest of her life."

density *(dens-uh-tee)* The amount of information that can be put into a specific yiblette of disk space. Floppy disks are measured in single, double, high, and extended densities. "George McFly looked into her eyes and said, 'You are my *density.*' "

DES *(dee ee es)* See *Data Encryption Standard.*

descender *(dee-send-er)* The part of a letter that falls below the imaginary line on which the letter rests. For example, the letters *p, y,* and *q* have descenders, but the letters *t, u,* and *o* do not. See also *ascender.* "You used to judge a dot-matrix printer by how it handled *descenders.* Some cheesy printers just shifted those letters up a tad, which looked utterly dorky."

deselect *(dee-se-lekt)* To remove selection. To change your mind after selecting an item, such as by unhighlighting an item or by removing the X in an option box. See also *select.* "Would George Bush have won the '92 election if he had *deselected* Dan Quayle as his running mate?"

desk accessory *(desk ak-ses-oh-ree)* A simple utility program, such as a calculator or notepad, that runs while another program is running. Desk accessories are tiny, useful programs that most Mac users can't live without.

desktop *(desk-top)* The background that appears in graphical operating systems. See *graphical user interface.* "So the guy said to 'double click on my *desktop,*' and I said that the mouse was already on the desktop, so what was his point. I just don't think I get this computer nonsense."

desktop PC *(desk-top pee see)* A computer that sits on top of your desk. A larger model. One that isn't a laptop and doesn't sit on the floor, like a tower PC. Contrast with *portable, laptop, notebook computers.* "The guy who designed this *desktop PC* must have had an awfully big desk."

desktop publishing *(desk-top pub-lish-ing)* 1. To combine text and graphics in a document. 2. Software used to create neat-looking newsletters, books, or brochures. See also *DTP.* "Those campy images of underground rebels churning out propaganda on mimeograph machines are rapidly being replaced by the reality of three nerds sitting around a computer, using a *desktop publishing* program, and arguing over picas, pitches, and points."

dev/null *(dev nul)* 1. A directory (though technically a device) on a UNIX computer that does nothing, produces nothing, and can swallow anything as input and not care. 2. A place people are told to go or to stick their useless ideas or complaints. Because

Bob is fond of sending files to dev/null.

the dev/null directory goes nowhere and does nothing, telling someone to send comments to dev/null is the polite equivalent of telling them to go "bug off." "Please send all flames to *dev/null.*"

device *(dee-vies)* 1. Any type of equipment, such as a printer, modem, monitor, disk drive, or mouse, that can send or receive data. "You know you're hard-core when you call your printer a hard copy *device.*" 2. A command in a PC's CONFIG.SYS file that loads software to control a certain device. See the next entry.

device driver *(dee-vies driev-er)*
A program that controls a device. Device drivers are required to control some devices (mouse, tape backup, CD-ROM drive, and so on) because the computer itself is too lame to do it. "When Grandma Margaret was a little girl, they called the *device driver* for their car a 'chauffeur.'"

device name *(dee-vies naym)* An abbreviation that refers to a device connected to the computer. "Why MS-DOS couldn't just call the printer PRINTER and had to use a cryptic *device name* like PRN is beyond me."

diagnostic software *(di-yag-nos-tik soft-wayr)* Special programs that tell you what's in your computer or what's wrong with your computer or both. "I used *diagnostic software* to find out what was wrong with my computer. Come to find out it wasn't my computer at all. It was just me not knowing how to work Windows 95."

dial-up connection *(di-yal-up kon-ek-shun)* Using a computer and modem to phone into an Internet service provider to connect to the Internet. This contrasts with a direct connection, in which your computer is wired directly into the Internet (you don't need to dial the phone first). See also *PPP*.

dialer program *(di-ya-ler pro-gram)* A program used to dial up the Internet. You can't get on the Internet without one. "I thought a *dialer program* was like the *Home Shopping Network,* where you could order junk that you don't need and that costs too much in the first place."

dialog box *(di-ya-log boks)* A window that pops up to prompt for or display information. It's a dialog between you and your software. "Why is it that most of my program's *dialog boxes* talk at me and not with me?"

DIB *(dib)* Acronym for *Device Independent Bitmap,* a type of graphics file format. A DIB graphics file supposedly carries information that allows it to be displayed on any computer, no matter what type of graphics they're using. A nice idea, if it ever worked. "John and I could never get our collection of post-modern dryer lint art to display on our computers. Then we started using *DIB* files."

digital *(dij-uh-tal)* A way of representing objects using two distinct states such as On or Off, Low or High, Good or Bad, or Republican or Democrat. All computers are digital computers because they consist of millions of On and Off switches. See also *analog* and *binary.* "If in the future all clocks are *digital,* how will we ever teach our children about clockwise and counterclockwise?"

digital audio *(dij-uh-tal ah-dee-oh)* A sound that's been examined by a computer, translated into a string of numbers, and stored to disk. "Did you know the sound on your CD is actually *digital audio?* Bet ya didn't know that, did ya?"

digital modem *(dij-uh-tal moh-dum)* A modem that sends non-analog signals. Most modems are analog. A digital modem is used on specific digital networks, so don't get your hopes up about buying one just yet.

digital monitor *(dij-uh-tal mon-uh-ter)* Not an analog monitor. I know, dumb definition. Most monitors today are digital. TV sets are analog. See *analog monitor,* which probably has a better explanation for all this anyway.

Digital Research *(dij-uh-tal ree-surch)* A company that produced the first "microcomputer" operating system, CP/M. They were trounced on in the '80s by Microsoft and MS-DOS, and then they produced DR DOS. But DR DOS was eventually bought by Novell. See *CP/M.* "*Digital Research* was one of the 'unstoppable' computer companies of the early '80s, along with VisiCorp, who made the VisiCalc spreadsheet; MicroPro, who made WordStar; and Ashton-Tate, who made dBASE — none of whom are around today. This just goes to show you the volatile nature of the computer biz."

Digital Signal Processor *(dij-uh-tal signal prah-ses-er)* A high-speed chip, like a microprocessor, that deals specifically with sound. A DSP is often used in a computer to speed up the audio and enhance communications, graphics, or other similar applications.

digital versatile disk *(dij-uh-tal vers-uh-tal disk)* The latest, whiz-bang storage unit for a PC. See *DVD.*

Avogadro dreams of the day a DVD comes to his village.

digitizer pad *(dij-uh-tiez-er pad)* 1. A flat input device used to read in sophisticated drawings. A device called a *puck* (like a mouse) is used to take readings from the pad, which are translated into digital information and stored in the computer. 2. Where the digitizer lived his reckless youth.

dimmed *(dimd)* 1. An unavailable option or command, usually appearing on the screen in a soft, fuzzy color that's easy to overlook. "Richard tried to create a romantic mood, so he *dimmed* the lights. But then Sherry said, 'That option is not available!'"

dingbats *(ding-batz)* 1. A font consisting of bizarre characters made up of bullets, Greek and Egyptian hieroglyphics, and geometric figures. 2. What Archie Bunker called his wife in the '70s hit show *All in the Family.* "Martha never understood why her husband got her a T-shirt with an ❖ on the front." 3. A style of apartment found in Southern California.

dinking *(deen-keen)* 1. To mess with your computer with no real production value in mind. 2. To goof around with an option. "Windows 95 has three purposes: getting work done, playing, and *dinking.*"

DIP switch *(dip switch)* Tiny little switches, almost impossible to find or use properly. DIP is an acronym for *Dual-Inline Package* (as if that clarifies matters any). Mostly, you use DIP switches with modems or printers. The switches select options for output. Printed circuit boards can have them, too. "I think they should call them 'teeny switches' and reserve the term *DIP switch* for when Melvin in the next cubical is replaced by a guy named Poindexter."

DIR *(dur)* 1. An operating system command that displays a directory listing — a catalog of files on a disk or in a directory. "I typed DIR at the DOS prompt and, lo, discovered my disk was full of stuff I didn't know existed." 2. A directory file.

Direct Memory Access *(dur-ekt mem-oh-ree ak-ses)* See *DMA.*

directory *(deer-ek-toh-ree)* 1. A list of files on a disk. 2. Separate parts of the disk where other files are stored. Every disk has at least one directory called the *root directory.* You can create other directories and label them to keep your files that relate to different programs, data, and projects separated. See also *subdirectory.* "Most people know to create a bunch of *directories* to organize their files, but few follow through on it."

directory list box *(dur-ek-toh-ree list boks)* A list of directories, one or more of which can be selected to sate the lusty desires of some command. You use these boxes in Windows and OS/2 programs. "Whenever I press the Save command in my word processor, the program pops up a *directory list box* so that I can choose which directory to save the file in."

DirectX *(deer-ekt-eks)* A set of routines that Microsoft implores game developers to use when programming for Windows 95 and later. Game developers (and players) want fast action games. Windows 95, on the other hand, gets in the way. So game developers write their software to circumvent Windows 95. Seeing how much Microsoft hates being circumvented, they designed the DirectX standard for accessing the screen, keyboard, and joystick. Most game developers ignore DirectX.

disc *(disk)* Another term for a *disk,* mostly used when referring to a CD-ROM disk. Probably British. (Yeah, it's them Brits with their spelling from the 14th century again.) See *disk,* which is the way God spells it.

 disconnect dialog box *(dis-kon-ekt di-yah-log boks)* A tiny window that announces that you've had enough time on the Internet and now it's time to get back to the real world. If you want to stay on longer, click on the *Don't Hang Up* button. If you agree that you've been on long enough, click on the *Disconnect* button. "Just when I find something really juicy on the Internet, the *disconnect dialog box* pops up. I wonder if my mom is connected to this somehow."

disk *(disk)* 1. A magnetic storage device shaped like a pizza and encased in plastic. 2. A floppy disk. 3. A hard disk. 4. A CD-ROM disk. 5. Any other type of media you may slide into a computer somewhere.

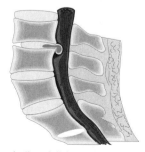

A slipped disk.

6. The place where you save files, and the place where you open files you think you once saved. "Although you can put the entire Encyclopedia Britannica on a CD-ROM disk, the Encyclopedia Britannica salesguy still weighs about 180 pounds and wears an ugly blue suit."

disk cache (*disk cash*) 1. What you can win in the PC Super Sweepstakes! 2. A portion of memory used to speed up disk access. The disk cache contains information frequently read from disk. By copying information from the floppy or hard disk and storing it in a disk cache, the computer can access the information faster at a later time. Some computers have a built-in disk cache. Some utility programs create a disk cache out of the computer's main memory. Generally, the larger the disk cache, the faster the computer runs. "The guy at the store told me I could use a *disk cache* to speed up my hard drive. I thought he was referring to something like the Disney Dollars you use at Disneyland, but I was wrong."

disk controller (*disk kon-trol-er*) The hardware that controls the reading and writing of information from and to a disk. It doesn't do the actual reading and writing, because all disk drives are in the union. But it tells other gadgets what to do.

disk drive (*disk driev*) A mechanical device that reads disks. The drives are named A-Z in a PC. On a Macintosh, they're given names like "Filbert" and "Ambidextrous." "Matt is so into golf that when I started talking about my *disk drive* giving me problems, he suggested I use a 9 iron instead."

disk drive tongue depressor (*disk driev tung dee-pres-er*) A square piece of cardboard or plastic that is stuck in your disk drive during shipping. Rarely used any more.

disk hog (*disk hawg*) A program that bloats and bloats until it takes up a considerable amount of hard disk space in relation to what it does. This is one of the side effects of having a lot of disk storage in a computer, but developers don't seem concerned about bloat. You get the feeling that if they did care, they could find a way to make their programs take up less space. But they don't, so the world now has disk hogs. "Excel is one *disk hog*, let me tell ya."

disk operating system (*disk op-er-ay-ting sis-tim*) 1. An older name for an operating system. In the early days of the microcomputer, they didn't come with disk drives. So when you upgraded to disk drives and needed a program to run the computer, you bought a disk operating system. Because most computers come with disk drives today, the "disk" part is dropped. See *operating system*. 2. The long name for DOS. See *DOS*.

disk partition (*disk par-ti-shun*) One section of a hard disk. A single hard drive can be partitioned into several different hard drives (as seen by the operating system). Each hard drive lives in its own partition. "Actually, a program is used to create *disk partitions*. Did a guy named Moses create this?"

diskette *(disk-et)* Another term for *disk,* usually a floppy disk. "No, George, a *diskette* is not a really small disk to be used with really small computers."

display *(dis-play)* The monitor or computer screen, specifically the information shown there. It's what you watch when you go a-computin'. See also *monitor.* "I called tech support to complain that my *display* looked like

This is the monitor, not the display.

rubbish. Then they shyly admitted that it was their new, improved interface. I'm just happy the people who design computer programs don't redesign the highway system every 18 months."

dithering *(dith-er-ing)* Although it sounds like something drunk people might mumble in their sleep, dithering is the blending of two or more colors to get another color to display on the screen. This is done for low-resolution monitors and some displays that can't show every dang color in the universe. "Honey, roll over. You're *dithering* in your sleep again."

DLL *(dee el el)* 1. Acronym for *Dynamic Link Library,* an on-the-fly program that other programs may bring in to complete themselves or add a certain look and feel. DLL files contain commonly used routines that two or more programs can share.

"The error message said '*DLL* file missing.' It's sad that when a program can't share, it has to act all stubborn like that." 2. The file extension for a DLL file.

DMA *(dee em ay)* Acronym for *Direct Memory Access,* a technique where information is transferred in a computer without assistance from the microprocessor. For example, it's possible to transfer information between memory and an "intelligent" device, such as a hard drive, by simply telling a DMA chip, "Look here, move this data from memory here to disk drive there." The information is moved without slowing down the microprocessor. "Our computer is really slow because our cable service doesn't offer the *DMA* channel."

DNS *(dee en es)* Acronym for *Domain Name Service,* software that runs on an Internet computer and converts Internet names and addresses into actual locations on the Internet. The DNS Server is a computer (or a program running on that computer) that translates weird Internet stuff you type into the real (and cryptic) addresses.

DOC *(dok)* 1. An abbreviation for *DOCument.* 2. A file extension for document files, often used by word processors. "I asked Ellen if she could bring over some *DOC* files, and 40 minutes later she called to say her physician wouldn't let her copy anything from his computer."

docking base *(dok-ing bays)* See *docking station.*

docking station *(dok-ing stay-shun)* A "home" for your laptop computer. Typically a larger thing into which you plug your laptop computer, often by sliding your laptop all the way into the docking station. This extends your laptop's hardware, allowing you to use a larger screen and keyboard and other desktop features. "I save time and money by using a laptop on the road and then plugging it into my *docking station* back at the office."

document *(dok-yoo-mint)* A file created by a word processor or desktop publisher, containing words or pictures. See also *file.* "Cliff gave me all his *documents* on disk. Now I just need to figure out which word processor he used to create them all."

documentation *(dok-yoo-men-tay-shun)* The fat instruction manuals that everyone pays money for but no one bothers to read. Usually full of instructions that don't work, don't make sense, or are just plain wrong. "The project manager said our *documentation* was too thick. So we just cut out every third word to get it down to size."

doinky *(doyn-kee)* Small, tiny. "Golly, those DIP switches are sure *doinky.*"

domain *(do-mayn)* 1. A grouping of computers. 2. An organizational strategy in a database. 3. A method for identifying what type of organization you belong to when you access the Internet. There are several popular domains:

Domain	Type of Computer System
com	Company, business, commercial organization
edu	Educational institution
gov	The government (but not the military, because . . .)
mil	Military institutions only
org	Organizations (not in the above categories)
net	Networks, network resources

See also *Internet Address.* "Millie was happy to have a Net address that ended with the 'mil' *domain,* until we told her that it was just because she worked for the Navy." 4. The name of your Internet service provider, such as aol.com or idgbooks.com.

dongle *(don-gal)* 1. A device that connects to the rear of your computer, often used as a copy-protection scheme. You can't use a particular piece of software unless the proper dongle is installed. 2. Any device that connects to the back of your computer system that somehow enhances the computer's abilities. For example, a dongle may attach to your printer port, giving your PC the ability to capture video images but without interfering with your printer.

DOS *(daws)* 1. Acronym for *Disk Operating System.* 2. Another term for MS-DOS or PC-DOS, the operating system for nearly every PC in the world. (By the way, if you have Windows, you still have DOS.) See also *disk operating system.* "*DOS* is boss."

Typical DOS user.

DOS prompt *(daws prompt)* 1. The symbol, set of symbols, or words after which you type a DOS command. The DOS prompt essentially says, "This is the computer. What do you want me to do?" Typical DOS prompts look like:

```
C:\>
C:
C:\WINDOWS\SYSTEM>
```

.

See also *$.* "No, Phyllis, the *DOS prompt* has nothing to do with being on time."

dot *(doht)* The way the period is pronounced in an Internet address. It saves time over using the word *period,* which is three syllables. "You pronounce `www.dummies.com` as 'double-U double-U double-U dot dummies dot com,' not 'double-U double-U double-U period dummies period com.'"

dot matrix *(doht may-triks)* 1. A grid on which characters are displayed or printed. 2. A type of printer or printout that creates letters and graphics by using lots of tiny dots. The more dots used, the sharper the image. The fewer the dots used, the more the printing looks like a cheap printer printed it. "*Dot-matrix* printers are good for waking up the neighbors during the wee small hours."

dot pitch *(doht pitch)* 1. The smallest size dot that a monitor can display, usually measured in millimeters (mm). Typical dot pitches for monitors are .41mm, .31mm, and .28mm.

The smaller the dot pitch, the sharper the resolution on the monitor. 2. The distance between two color dots of the same color on a color monitor. "When I asked the salesman about his monitor's *dot pitch,* he replied that his dots were the best in town and I'd be a fool to go elsewhere for them."

dots per inch *(dohts pur ench)* Sometimes abbreviated as *DPI,* dots per inch describes the quality of a printed image. The more dots per inch, the sharper the image. "My laser printer has a maximum resolution of 600 *dots per inch,* which is similar to the population density of Dacca."

A backup battery.

double-click *(duh-bol-klik)* To press the mouse button twice in rapid succession without moving the mouse between clicks. Click, click. See also *click.* "*Double-click,* said the manual. Click, click, went the mouse. Run, run did the program."

double-density disk *(duh-bol-den-si-tee disk)* A floppy disk that stores twice as much information in the same amount of space as a single-density disk. Double-density disks are abbreviated as DD. See also *high density.* "No, Blaine, *double-density disks* aren't any heavier than regular density disks."

DoubleSpace *(duh-bol-spays)* Another name for Microsoft's DriveSpace program. See *DriveSpace.* "Grandma parks her car as if every space is a *double-space.*"

double-speed drive *(duh-bol-speed driev)* See *2X.*

down *(down)* When a piece of computer equipment temporarily stops working. "Our network's been *down* so often it must be in China by now."

download *(down-lohd)* To copy files through a modem from a distant computer to the one you're working on. See also *upload.* "It helps you to remember *download* if you imagine that every online system you call sits on top of a hill. The files roll 'down' toward you."

downloaded font *(down-lohd-ed fawnt)* A font that is sent from the computer to the printer. Not a resident font.

downward compatible *(down-word kom-pat-uh-bol)* The compatibility of software or hardware to work with earlier versions of the same software or hardware. See also *backward compatible.* "WordPerfect 7.0 is *downward compatible* with WordPerfect 5.1. This means that any files you created with WordPerfect 5.1 can still be used with WordPerfect 7.0. This is only good news if you plan on using WordPerfect until you die."

dpi *(dee pee eye)* Acronym for *dots per inch.* See *dots per inch.*

DPMI *(dee pee em eye)* Acronym for *DOS Protected Mode Interface,* a standard by which DOS programs can run under Windows. See *Protected Mode, Real Mode.* "Boy, without this *DPMI* I couldn't use my DOS programs in Windows. Of course, that makes

you wonder why I have Windows in the first place if I'm still running DOS programs."

DPMS *(dee pee em es)* Acronym for *Display Power Management Signaling,* which is a standard that reduces power to computer monitors when not in use. See *Energy Star.* "My monitor uses *DPMS,* so if I don't touch the keyboard or mouse after a few minutes, the computer reduces the power to my monitor, thereby reducing my electricity bill. Bob's monitor doesn't use DPMS, so his computer wastes electricity, and the company takes this extra cost out of Bob's paycheck every week."

DR DOS *(dee ar daws; not dok-tor daws)* An alternative to MS-DOS released way too late by Digital Research and later bought by Novell. DR DOS showed a lot of promise but wasn't widely available. Its Version 5.0, which was the first version of DOS to offer true memory management, got the folks at Microsoft off their duffs to produce the wildly successful MS-DOS 5.0. For this we can thank DR DOS, but not for much else. "Brad hates Microsoft so much that he only uses *DR DOS* and other non-Microsoft products."

drag *(drag)* To move an on-screen object with the mouse. First, you have to highlight (select) the object you want by pointing to it with the mouse pointer and clicking. Then hold down the mouse button and move the mouse. This drags the object around. "Moving things around on the screen with a mouse is such a *drag.*"

drag and drop *(drag and drop)* Moving an object across the screen as a command. For example, you use a mouse to drag a document onto a printer icon to print the document. "My teacher asked if my computer had *drag and drop.* I said yes; when I don't like the computer, I drag it across the table and drop it out the window."

DRAM *(dee-ram)* Acronym for *Dynamic Random-Access Memory.* Computers can use two types of RAM chips: DRAM and SRAM. DRAM chips are less expensive because the computer periodically has to put the information back into the DRAM chips or else the DRAM chips forget. See also *RAM.* "The older humans get, the more their brain cells must be replaced with *DRAM* chips."

draw program *(draw pro-gram)* Software that lets you create graphical objects on the screen, such as lines, boxes, or circles. This differs from a paint program, which doesn't draw objects but instead paints a picture, as you would do with crayons. With a draw program, you can go back and alter the objects after they're done and not disturb other parts of the drawing. "I use a *draw program* to illustrate advanced technical journals, but all my trees still look like lollipops."

drive list box *(driev list boks)* A list that shows disk drives on the computer. Often seen in a dialog box where cruising between various disk drives is optional. The drive list box lets you decide which drive to save a file on. "My *drive list box* contains all drive letters, A through Z, plus four-wheel drive."

DriveSpace *(driev-spays)* A disk compression program developed by Microsoft, available on MS-DOS versions 6.22 or later and Windows 95. Originally called DoubleSpace but changed because of bad press, DriveSpace allows you to store more information on a hard drive. It does this by compressing files as they're saved to disk and then decompressing files as they're read from disk. The end result isn't known to you, though your computer moves more slowly and you can store more information on a disk. A solution, though not the best one, for someone who's running out of disk space. "The best advice is to avoid *DriveSpace* and just buy a larger hard drive instead."

drop-down list box *(drawp-down list boks)* A dialog box gadget that contains a list of items as well as an input box into which you can type your own item. "Og like use *drop-down list box.* They give Og option of typing in name or choosing from list. Og happy."

DS/DD *(dee es dee dee)* Abbreviation for double-sided/double-density, a popular standard for the old $5^{1}/_{4}$-inch disks. See also *double-density disk* and *high density disk.* "*DS/DD* disks are the Geritol of computer disk formats."

d-shell connectors *(dee-shel kon-ek-toors)* A cable attachment that can be plugged in only one way. D-shell connectors are shaped like the letter D, flat but with one side longer than the other. "You have to match up the short and long sides of the *d-shell connectors* with their plug."

DSP *(dee es pee)* Acronym for *Digital Signal Processor.* See *Digital Signal Processor.*

DTP *(dee tee pee)* Acronym for *DeskTop Publishing;* see *desktop publishing.*

DTR *(dee tee ar)* 1. Acronym for *Data Terminal Ready,* a signal used by a computer to tell its modem that it's ready to start receiving information. "It's definitely not true that female computers take longer to turn on their *DTR* light." 2. The light representing the DTR signal on an external modem.

dumb terminal *(dum ter-min-al)* A unit consisting of a keyboard and video display connected to another computer via a network cable. Dumb

The dumb terminal is on the left.

terminals don't have disk drives or their own processors, so they can't store files or do anything else on their own. Personal computers, on the other hand, can act as autonomous units that can be networked together. "Ray thought putting the pointed cap on his PC would make it into a *dumb terminal.*"

dump *(dump)* 1. To copy information from one location to another without regard for its appearance or format. Often used for printing information that is temporarily useful. "I told my wife I was in the middle of a screen *dump* and she reminded me to wipe afterwards." 2. What a larger computer does after a crash. This type of dump (also called a *core dump*)

allows the system engineers to review the computer's contents to help look for bugs — which they never do.

duplex *(doo-pleks)* A telecommunications term describing how signals are sent and how characters appear on the screen when you're communicating with a modem. *Full duplex* means you send characters to the other computer, and everything you see on the screen comes from the other computer. This process is also known as *no echo. Half duplex* means the characters you type appear on your screen directly. This is also known as *local echo.* "When you don't see the stuff you're typing, switch on half *duplex.* Or turn on your monitor, if you're *really* new at this."

dust cover *(dust kuh-ver)* A plastic gown that fits snugly over your computer to keep the dust off. Used typically by people who don't use their computers often or those who are anal about dust. PS: Don't ever use a dust cover while your computer is on. It'll get way too hot in there. "My wife was so worried about keeping the house clean, she put a *dust cover* on the computer, all our furniture, and even our cat. I'm encouraging her to go to counseling."

DVD *(dee vee dee)* 1. Acronym for *Digital Versatile Disk.* A high-speed type of CD-ROM that holds lots of information — over 4 gigabytes, as opposed to the 600 megabytes of a traditional CD. Some versions of DVD may eventually hold 17 gigabytes of information. 2. Acronym for *Digital Video Disk,* which is essentially the same thing as a Digital Versatile Disk, but used in the home as a replacement for the VCR. Presently DVD is more hype than reality, which means I had to put the term in here because it's popular, but whether or not your PC sports a DVD drive (ever) remains to be seen.

DVD-RAM *(dee vee dee ram)* A version of the DVD drive and disk that can be both read from and written to. It's so far in the future that I'm not sure of the pronunciation, so try not to slip this one into your water-cooler conversations.

Dvorak keyboard *(Duh-vor-ak kee-bord)* A specially designed keyboard that organizes keys for maximum typing efficiency. Although known to be more efficient than current keyboards, hardly anyone uses them, which isn't very efficient. See also *QWERTY* and *keyboard*. "The *Dvorak keyboard* is the Esperanto of computer keyboards."

dweeb *(dweeb)* A person who may be technically competent but is socially a jerk that no one wants to hang around with after work. "Bob would make a great manager if he wasn't such a *dweeb.*"

A dweeb.

DWIM *(Dwim; rhymes with swim)* Acronym for *Do What I Mean* (not what I say). Often used when people want the computer to read their minds and ignore the commands they're typing in. "I saw a father using *DWIM* on his daughter when he told her not to smoke while he was puffing on a cigar and blowing smoke in her face."

DXF *(dee eks ef)* Acronym for *Drawing Interchange Format,* a graphics file format for exchanging files between different programs. Originally developed for use with the AutoCAD drawing program. "If only Ralph would save his stuff in *DXF* format, we all could see his cool outer space drawings."

dynamic *(die-nam-ik)* Something that is flexible, as opposed to something that can't be moved or relocated (which is static). "Bob is so *dynamic* he should be carved out of marble."

dynamic allocation *(die-nam-ik al-o-kay-shun)* To store information in the computer's memory (called the *heap*) while the program is running. Unless you plan on writing your own programs, you can safely ignore this definition. See also *static*. "The desk clerk told the three televangelists to go into halls A, B, and C. This I call *dynamic allocation* for salvation."

The Dvorak keyboard layout (no kidding!).

dynamic IP Address *(die-nam-ik ie pee uh-dress)* A different Internet address assigned each time you call your Internet service provider. This is a configuration option for many dialer programs that allows the Internet provider to give you a unique ID each time you call, as opposed to the same ID (which is known as a *static* address).

dynamic RAM *(die-nam-ik ram)* Dynamic random access memory. See *DRAM*.

D

D

E

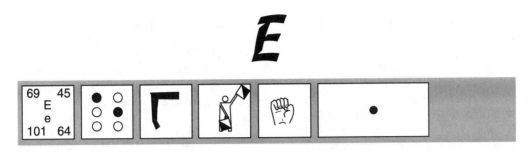

E: *(ee koh-lon)* A letter designation for any of a number of different types of disk drives in a PC system. It could be a hard drive, CD-ROM drive, a removable drive, a RAM drive, a scenic drive, sex drive, or any of a number of various drives available on the PC.

e-mail *(ee-mayel)* Short for *electronic mail.* Also spelled with a capital: E-mail. See *electronic mail.*

Sebek dictates ancient e-mail.

e-mail address *(ee-mayel ad-res)* A person's location in the electronic ether. A name (or sometimes number or code) assigned to a person for receiving e-mail. "Once I typed the wrong *e-mail address* and sent a love letter to my ex-wife."

E-notation *(ee noh-tay-shun)* Short for *exponential notation,* a way that scientists express large and small numbers without burdening the computer's zero key. For example, 1.0E6 is E-notation for one million, and 1.0E100 is E-notation for a googolplex. "*E-notation* is the kind of weird stuff that makes you thankful you only have to put up with WordPerfect."

EBCDIC *(ee bee see dee ie see)* Acronym for *Extended Binary Coded Decimal Interchange Code.* A way of representing characters on a computer. Some mainframes use EBCDIC. Most microcomputers use ASCII. See *ASCII.* "IBM tried to get everyone to follow the *EBCDIC* standard, but everyone else followed the ASCII standard instead. In the computer biz, *standard* should refer to a flag."

echo *(ek-oh)* 1. A command, used in online communications, that determines whether or not your software displays the characters you type. If you can't see what you're typing, echo is said to be off; turning echo on allows you to see your typing. But if you see double words, such as "tthhiiss," you have to turn echo off. See also *duplex.* 2. An operating system command that displays text on the screen. The ECHO OFF command in a DOS batch file keeps the computer from displaying commands on the screen. "Do I hear an *echo* hear an *echo* hear an *echo?*"

ECP/EPP *(ee see pee ee pee pee)* Acronym for *Enhanced Capabilities Port/Enhanced Parallel Port.* It's a type of super printer port. Whoop-tee-doo. "My new computer came with an *ECP/EPP,* and it can do many wondrous and amazing things, though I only use it to plug in my printer."

ED *(ee dee)* 1. Nickname for any of a number of popular text editor programs. 2. Acronym for *extended density,* a type of disk drive standard that never really caught on. A $3^1/_2$-inch ED disk can store 2.88 megabytes of information. "Joel uses his *ED* disks as coasters. They certainly serve him better as a conversation piece than they ever did in any disk drive."

edit *(ed-it)* 1. To modify, change, or update data. The stuff edited can be text, graphics, a program's source code, or any computer information. "Jeff's idea of a good *edit* is to run the spell checker on his stuff." 2. The name of any of a number of popular text-editing programs.

editor *(ed-it-or)* A program specifically designed for modifying, changing, or updating files. The two types of editors are *line editors* and *full-screen editors.* A line editor lets you change one line at a time, such as the old DOS EDLIN or the UNIX ed. A full-screen editor lets you change multiple lines that appear on the screen, such as the PC-DOS E editor or the Windows Notepad editor. Word processors, such as WordPerfect or Word for Windows, are much more sophisticated than simple editors. But sometimes an editor is all you need, especially if you're using it to edit programming code. "I have several *editors* on my computer, but QEdit is my editor-in-chief."

EDLIN *(ed-lin)* 1. A line editor that came with MS-DOS Versions 5.0 and lower. EDLIN was pretty much a useless program that nobody but the most nerdy people used. MS-DOS Version 6.0 and higher no longer include EDLIN. "With MS-DOS Version 6.2, *EDLIN* is finally dead (lin)." 2. Used for comparison with any silly or stupid program. "Jenkins, your new modem program is as dumb as *EDLIN.*"

EDO RAM *(ee-doh ram)* 1. Acronym for *Extended Data Out Random Access Memory,* a spiffy new type of memory that's much faster, lower-fat, lower-cholesterol, and just plain better than normal RAM. You see it in all the ads for the latest, best computer, so you know it has to be good. 2. A ruminant from ancient Tokyo. In this case, it would be pronounced *ed-oh ram.*

educational software *(ed-yoo-kay-shun-al soft-wayr)* One of many kinds of software programs designed to teach, train, or instruct. Most people figure that educational software is geared toward children; however, plenty of educational programs are designed to teach adults — for example, typing tutors, musical trainers, foreign language software, and so on. "It's always recommended that you check software reviews before buying *educational software,* because a lot of it is really stupid."

edutainment *(ed-yoo-tayn-ment)* Educational and entertainment. Often refers to software programs. Edutainment has grown out of trying to meet two different needs. Software needs to be entertaining or the kids won't like it. It also needs to be educational or the parents won't like it. See also *infotainment,* which is another attempt to concatenate two unrelated words. And see *concatenate* while you're at it.

E

EEPROM *(ee-prom)* Acronym for *Electronically Erasable Programmable Read-Only Memory,* a special computer chip that can be reprogrammed through electrical signals. EEPROM chips are like ROM chips in that they contain instructions for the computer. And they're like RAM chips in that their contents can be changed, but unlike RAM chips, EEPROMs don't lose information when the power goes off. See also *PROM.* "Computer guys take their high school gals to the *EEPROM* every May."

EGA *(ee jee ay)* Acronym for *Enhanced Graphics Adapter,* a graphics standard once used for IBM computers and now remembered solely by trivia buffs. EGA followed the initial CGA standard and was eventually replaced by the VGA and SVGA standards. See also *CGA, VGA,* and *SVGA.* "*EGA* graphics were hot stuff when Ronald Reagan was president."

EIEIO *(ee ie ee ie oh)* 1. Nonsensical but rhythmic phrase used by farmers when they forget the rest of the words to a song. "Old MacDonald had a farm, *EIEIO!*" 2. Probably an acronym for something.

Old MacDonald.

EISA *(ee-suh)* Acronym for *Extended Industry Standard Architecture.* EISA was an attempt to expand upon the ISA standard while competing with the MCA (MicroChannel) standard. Today, both EISA and MCA are dead, and the ancient ISA standard remains — a triumph for antique technology! See also *bus, ISA, MCA.* "I don't care if it's an *EISA* bus; does it go to Altoona?"

eject *(ee-jekt)* 1. To remove a disk from a disk drive. "He's looking for the data. No. No. No! It can't be found! That disk is out of here. *Eject! Eject! Eject!*" 2. The command that ejects a disk from a disk drive.

electronic mail *(ee-lek-tron-ik mayel)* 1. Messages created, sent, and read completely on computers without ever being printed on paper. Electronic mail usually involves sending messages to other users on some kind of network, either a local network or the Internet. "With rising postal rates, it's cheaper to use a computer to send *e-mail* than to use an envelope and a stamp. Of course, you have to buy a computer first." 2. The program used to create electronic mail.

electronic signatures *(ee-lek-tron-ik sig-nah-choors)* See *signature files.*

elevator box *(el-uh-vay-tor boks)* See *scroll box.*

elite *(ee-leet)* Typefaces that print as 12 characters per inch. Left over from the typewriter days, *elite* often appears on printers as one of many choices for printing documents. (On a computer, the Courier font at 10 points in size approximates the old typewriter elite.) See also *pica.* "There is no such thing as an *elite* font on a computer. If you want to use characters that tiny, select a font at 10 points."

E

ELIZA *(ee-lie-za)* A famous artificial intelligence program that mimicked a psychotherapist. Users typed their problems into the computer, and ELIZA parroted back empty phrases to give the appearance of deep thought (and then billed them $200 an hour). See also *artificial intelligence.* "Whenever Sondra is feeling down, she just loads *ELIZA* on her computer and talks to it. Right now her biggest problem is that she talks only to her computer instead of people."

ellipsis *(ee-lips-eez)* Three tiny dots (. . .) that appear next to commands on pull-down menus. When an ellipsis appears next to a command, you know that the program will ask for more information or display a dialog box. "When I finally told Paul what the *ellipsis* means in a pull-down menu, he was relieved. He originally thought the program wasn't finished and that they'd fill in the rest later."

em dash *(em dash)* A long hyphen. The em dash is a character, as wide as the letter *M,* that is used in typesetting to add emphasis in text. The em dash can be approximated by typing two hyphens (such as --) See also *en dash.* "Here is an example of an *em dash:* 'Don't touch that — oh well, you have another hand anyway.'"

 email *(ee-mayel)* Another way to write *e-mail* or *E-mail.* Oh, heck, just see *electronic mail.*

EMM *(ee em em)* Acronym for *Expanded Memory Manager,* a utility program that creates expanded memory for those few DOS programs that need it. "Our service guy said that *EMM* memory was a white elephant on our PCs. I suppose EMM stands for Elephant Memory Management."

emoticon *(ee-moht-uh-kon)* A combination of characters inserted into e-mail or newsgroup postings that represent feelings or moods not properly expressed in the message. There are a lot of them. In fact, there's a whole book full of them, so I won't go through the pain of repeating them all here (especially the cows). See :-). "Laurie always puts tons of *emoticons* in her messages, which makes me think she's utterly manic when she goes online."

EMS *(ee em es)* Acronym for *Expanded Memory Specification,* which is actually short for LIM-EMS, the *Lotus-Intel-Microsoft Expanded Memory Specification.* EMS defines a specific way for older PCs to use more than 640K of memory. Originally developed for Lotus 1-2-3 users so that they could load huge spreadsheets into memory. See *expanded memory.*

emulation *(im-yoo-lay-shun)* To mimic the appearance and functionality of a specific piece of hardware or software. Emulation allows cheapie stuff to behave just like the real thing. For example, a no-name printer may offer Epson or Hewlett-Packard LaserJet emulation. Most modems offer Hayes emulation. "David's running Macintosh *emulation* on his IBM PC, which is then running an IBM *emulation* program. Nobody can waste time in a high-tech way like David."

emulator *(em-yoo-lay-tor)* A piece of hardware that performs emulation. Hardware emulators are the cheapest and worst way to tweak the performance of one computer out of another. "Don't buy a cheap piece of hardware with an *emulator* on it and expect it to get the work done."

en dash *(en dash)* A hyphen that is the width of the letter *N*. En dashes are used to represent *to,* such as pages 64–98. See also *em dash*. "Here is an example of how to use an *en dash:* 'I stuck my leaf collection between pages 56–64 because that's the only use I could find for my MS-DOS user manual.'"

encryption *(en-krip-shun)* To scramble information with a code or password so that other people can't read it. Often used to protect sensitive files, electronic mail, or legal documents so that the general public can't understand what they really mean. See also *Data Encryption Standard*. "Sorry, Josh, most of the laws in the State Constitution are not written with *encryption;* that's just the way lawyers talk."

End key *(end kee)* The key on the keyboard with *End* printed on it. (What a remarkable coincidence!) It is often a neighbor of the Delete key or living with the number 1 on the numeric keypad. "The *End key* usually moves the cursor to the end of the line. It does not end online communications or stop any program."

end user *(end yoo-zer)* 1. You! 2. The person who winds up using a computer or program that someone else designed. See also *programmer*. "The person who ends up reading this book is not called the *end user*. He or she is called the reader."

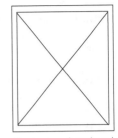

(Paste your photo here.)

End-Of-File *(end-of-fiel)* Sometimes abbreviated as *EOF,* this is a special character that marks the end of a file. In MS-DOS, Control+Z is the End-Of-File character. Usually, the marker is placed automatically by whatever software created the file. "The *End-Of-File* marker is like the caboose on the train; it's the last thing in the file."

endless loop *(end-less loop)* 1. A set of instructions in a program that repeats over and over without any chance of ever stopping. 2. See definition number one. See also *infinite loop* and *loop*. "I think I'm stuck in an *endless loop*. I think I'm stuck in an *endless loop*. I think I'm stuck in an *endless loop*. I think I'm stuck in an *endless loop*. I think I'm stuck in an *endless loop*."

Energy Star *(en-ur-jee star)* A standard developed by the Environmental Protection Agency to designate computer equipment that reduces power when not being used. For example, an Energy Star monitor requires less electricity if the user doesn't touch the mouse or keyboard after a certain period of time. Energy Star monitors must consume less

E

than 30 watts of power when not in use. See also *ACPI*. "Besides eating vegetables and refraining from hurting helpless animals, I only buy *Energy Star* equipment so my computer doesn't waste electricity."

enhanced keyboard *(en-hanst kee-bord)* See *101-key keyboard.*

ENIAC *(ee-nee-ak)* Acronym for *Electronic Numerical Integrator And Calculator,* the name of an early computer built out of vacuum tubes in the '40s. Its job was to calculate artillery ballistic tables for World War II and after. See also *ABC, vacuum tube.* "In the computer museum, we saw a model of the *ENIAC* that took up a whole room and did as much useful work as those freebie solar-powered calculators the bank gives away."

An early computer.

Enter key *(en-ter kee)* 1. A key on the keyboard named Enter. 2. Often used to signal the computer that you're done typing a command; only after pressing the Enter key is your text sent to the computer for rumination. 3. Used to end a line of text in a text editor. 4. Ends a paragraph of text in a word processor. 5. Also called the *Return key.* "The *Enter key* comes from the computer's calculator past. The Return key comes from the computer's typewriter past."

EOF *(ee oh ef)* See *End-Of-File.*

EOL *(ee oh el)* 1. Abbreviation for *End-Of-Line,* as in the end of a line of text on the screen. 2. The EOL character, usually produced by pressing the Enter or Return key. "Okay, buddy. It's the *EOL* for you." (Quote overheard between two computer nerds, fighting for control of the only working computer left in the office.)

EOR *(ee oh ar)* An abbreviation for the logical exclusive OR operation. See *XOR.*

EPA *(ee pee ay)* Acronym for *Environmental Protection Agency,* a government agency dedicated to protecting us from ourselves. The EPA guards the country from the predatory nature of other government agencies and their allies. "New orders from the *EPA:* Have Paul Bunyan brought in and shot."

EPROM *(ee-prom)* Acronym for *Erasable Programmable Read-Only Memory,* a type of chip that can be erased by ultraviolet lights. An EPROM is like a ROM chip in that it contains instructions for the computer. Like a RAM chip, an EPROM can be written to; however, you need an ultraviolet light to erase an EPROM chip. See also *EEPROM* and *PROM.*

EPS *(ee pee es)* Acronym for *Encapsulated PostScript,* a graphic image stored using instructions written in the PostScript page description language. EPS graphic files are actually long, complex text files. The text contains instructions on how to draw the image. Most expensive desktop publishing and illustration programs can handle EPS files. Unfortunately, most people can't afford these expensive programs and wind up storing files in other formats instead. See also *PostScript*. "Brian stored all his graphics as *EPS* files. Now he's desperately searching for a PostScript laser printer or a typesetting machine so he can print them."

erase *(ee-rays)* 1. To remove a file from a disk. 2. An operating system command that removes files. See also *delete*. "Make sure you don't *erase* your files, unless you're sure you don't need them anymore."

ergonomics *(urg-oh-nom-iks)* The science of designing equipment for maximum human comfort and minimal chances of lawsuits in the future. Some people get *carpal tunnel syndrome* or *RSI* (Repetitive Strain Injury) from improper positioning of their wrists when they type or from working at computers too long without breaks. Ergonomics involves the study of how to prevent these (and other) problems from poorly designed equipment in the workplace. So tell your boss you need a better chair and more breaks! "My whole computer desk uses *ergonomics* to hold the monitor at the optimum height and distance from my eyes. Because I liked it so much, I replaced my computer with a TV, and now I just vegetate in comfort at my desk."

Zephram Erg, founder of ergonomics.

error message *(ayr-or mes-idj)* A cryptic note that the computer displays to let you know that the program isn't working right or that you've really screwed up. If you're lucky, the manual will tell you what on earth the message means, and if you're really lucky, the computer won't beep rudely at you. "I think I've seen every *error message* this computer can display."

Esc *(es-kayp)* 1. Abbreviation for *Escape,* often found on the Escape key. 2. The Esc key is often used to cancel a command. Pressing the key is the same as clicking a Cancel button in a dialog box. "I wonder whether the Air Force has an *Esc* key for launching nuclear missiles?" 3. In some instances, pressing the Esc key changes editing modes. 4. ASCII code. 27. See *ASCII*.

A rocket reaches Esc velocity.

ESDI *(ee es dee ie; ez-dee)* Acronym for *Enhanced Small Device Interface,* once an interface standard for hard disks. See also *IDE*.

etc *(et-see; not et-set-uh-rah)* A directory on a UNIX computer where various and sundry files are kept. "Jerry had all the UNIX gurus fooled until he slipped up and called the *etc* directory *et cetera*."

Ethernet *(ee-thoor-net)* A local area network standard that uses radio frequency signals carried by coaxial cables. Developed primarily by Xerox. See also *LAN*. "Our computers are connected through an *Ethernet.* That doesn't mean we know what we're doing; it just means we have the lingo down pat."

etiquette *(et-uh-kit)* The rules and regulations of proper behavior. E-mail has rules of etiquette for proper written behavior to keep everyone in line. "Kristin didn't know that typing everything LIKE THIS MADE IT APPEAR LIKE SHE WAS YELLING. She needed a lesson on e-mail *etiquette.*"

EULA *(yoo-lah)* Acronym for *End User License Agreement,* the secret legal code included with every software product that tells you that anything bad that happens is not the developer's fault and that you don't really own the software; you're merely using it. This is something of a contradiction, because the owner should always be responsible. But attorneys have shown us over time that, in fact, it's the person with the most money who's ultimately responsible in the end.

event-driven programming *(ee-vent-driv-en pro-gram-ing)* A style of writing programs that waits for the user to press a key or a mouse button before doing anything else. When the user presses a key or mouse button, it's called an *event.* "You could say that CNN has *event-driven programming.*"

exclusive OR *(eks-kloo-siv or)* A logical operation performed on the bit values of two different bytes. Often used when displaying graphics on the screen. See *XOR.* "No, I'm sorry, sir; you're just a regular OR, and this club is for the *exclusive OR* only."

EXE *(ee eks ee)* A file extension identifying a program (EXEcutable) file for some operating systems. See also *BIN, COM, DOC, extension.*

execute *(eks-uh-kyoot)* 1. To start a program. 2. Performing a task. 3. To put to death, which is what some people would like to do to Windows 95.

exit *(eks-it)* The command that quits a program. This is the civilized way to end a program; it makes it quietly go away until the next time you need it. Contrast with *Ctrl+Alt+Del.* See also *Quit.* "To quit some programs, you have to choose the *Exit* command. To *exit* other programs, you have to choose the Quit command. And to *exit* still other programs, you must first go through detox."

expand *(eks-pand)* To decompress previously compressed files so that the computer can use them. On IBM computers, most files are compressed using the PKZIP program. On Macintosh computers, most files are compressed using the StuffIt program. See also *explode, data compression, compression, ZIP.* "I told Amanda to *expand* her files, so she put them on a high-fat diet."

expanded memory *(eks-pan-ded mem-oh-ree)* Extra memory available to older DOS programs. Expanded memory was DOS memory available in addition to the basic 640K. Sometimes called EMS or LIM-EMS. Expanded memory is not memory "above" the 1MB mark on a PC. It's more like "beside" it because data is swapped quickly into and out of a small region of memory in the computer. See also *EMS, XMS, extended* *memory.* "Lotus helped develop *expanded memory* so that people could load large 1-2-3 spreadsheets into memory."

expansion bus *(eks-pan-shun bus)* The part of the computer's bus that enables you to plug in boards to give your computer more features. Nearly every computer sold these days has an expansion bus. See also *bus, expansion slot, expansion card.* "The *expansion bus* didn't make the turn and knocked down a fire plug."

expansion card *(eks-pan-shun kard)* A circuit board designed to plug into a computer's expansion bus. Expansion cards usually give a computer more memory, an internal modem, or some other whiz-bang capability that the computer didn't naturally come with by itself. See also *expansion bus, expansion slot.* "I just can't keep my poker face when I'm dealt a fancy new *expansion card.*"

expansion slot *(eks-pan-shun slot)* The physical opening in a computer's expansion bus into which expansion cards plug. "When you go to Las Vegas, be sure to play the *expansion slot.* Maybe you'll win a new Dodge Viper."

expert system *(eks-pert sis-tim)* A program that mimics the intelligence of a human expert in a specific field of knowledge, such as mining or medicine. The expert system includes a knowledge base of information that has been gathered from an expert,

Norman enjoys using his expert system.

along with a set of rules for processing the information. Expert systems ask users questions and reach conclusions that are hopefully similar in quality to those that a human expert may reach. See also *artificial intelligence.* "Hey, honey, why don't we let the *expert system* choose our wine for dinner tonight?"

explode *(eks-plohd)* 1. Another term for decompressing previously compressed files. Rather than tell you they're expanding a file, some programs tell you that they're exploding them. See also *expand, data compression, compression, ZIP.* "Some compressed files are packed in so tight you must *explode* them to get the data out. Please wear the proper safety attire before attempting this on your own computer." 2. What any number of computers used to do in '60s TV shows, specifically those produced by Irwin Allen.

Explorer *(eks-plor-er)* Short for *Microsoft Explorer,* the file-management program included with Windows 95. 2. Short for *Internet Explorer,* Microsoft's Web browser software. See *Internet Explorer.*

exponential notation *(eks-poh-nen-shal noh-tay-shun)* See *E-notation.*

extended ASCII *(eks-ten-ded ass-kee)* Character codes 128 through 255. Normal ASCII only codes characters zero through 127. However, a byte on a PC has 255 possible bit combinations, which makes room for 128 more characters than the standard ASCII set. To fill in the remaining 128 characters, someone dreamed up extended ASCII codes. The extended codes include the normal 128 ASCII character codes plus foreign language, mathematical, and block graphic characters. Another improvement of a "standard" that defeats the meaning of having standards in the first place. See also *code page.*

extended memory *(eks-ten-ded mem-oh-ree)* Memory above the one megabyte mark. This includes all memory on an Intel 80286 or later microprocessor. Extended memory can be used only by high-power programs or by operating systems such as Windows, OS/2, or UNIX. See also *XMS.* "My PC has 976MB of *extended memory,* barely enough to run Windows 95."

extended memory specification *(eks-ten-ded mem-oh-ree spes-if-uh-kay-shun)* A set of rules for programs to access extended memory. Sometimes abbreviated as *XMS;* see *XMS.* "You think they could have come up with a name other than *extended memory specification,* seeing as how close it sounds to 'expanded memory specification.' But who would expect logic from the computer industry?"

extension *(eks-ten-shun)* An optional addition to an MS-DOS file name, consisting of a period and up to three other characters. The extension often identifies the type of file and which program created it. A Pascal file usually has the .PAS file extension, a BASIC file has the .BAS file extension, and backup files have the .BAK file extension. See also *EXE, COM, BIN, DOC.* "My income tax file needs an *extension.*"

external modem *(eks-turn-al moh-dum)* A modem that lives in its own box and is physically located outside your computer, as opposed to an internal modem that is located inside your computer. See also *internal modem.* External modems typically cost more than internal modems because you have to pay for the plastic doohickey that the modem sits in. They also junk up your desk with more cables. "It is the desire of all internal modems to one day break free and become *external modems.*"

 eyeball frazzle *(ie-bal frah-zul)* 1. The unofficial term for the condition of those who read too much information on the World Wide Web. "It was a gruesome sight. Ed had sat at his computer for nine hours straight reading trivia on the Web. When he finished, he had (gasp!) *eyeball frazzle* (loud scream)!" 2. The condition produced by viewing an ancient CGA display on a PC — though, unlike the Web, it takes only two-and-a-half minutes to get eyeball frazzle with CGA.

Eyeball frazzle affects this organ.

F

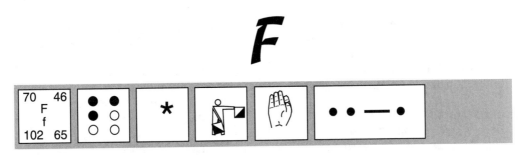

F: *(ef koh-lon)* A letter designation for any of a number of different types of disk drives in a PC system. It could be a hard drive, CD-ROM drive, a network drive, a removable drive, a test drive, a RAM drive, overdrive mode, or any of a number of various drives available on the PC.

F-keys *(ef-kees)* See *function keys.*

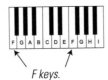

F keys.

facing pages
(fay-seen pay-juz)
1. Two pages of a bound document that face each other when the document is open. Usually the even-numbered page appears on the left; the odd-numbered page appears on the right. "Many cookbooks show the recipe on one side and a picture of what you're supposed to be cooking on the other side. These *facing pages* show you that some of the best fiction writers today are writing cookbooks." 2. The command in desktop publishing and word processing programs that lets you see how two pages look side by side.

factorial *(fak-tor-ee-al)* Taking all the numbers from 1 to a specific number and multiplying them together. So the factorial of 4 is 4 x 3 x 2 x 1 = 24. The factorial of a number is abbreviated with the exclamation point, such as 4!

"The *factorial* of 4 is 24. The *factorial* of 3 is 6. Truly this must be the most useful bit of information you've read so far."

fail *(fayl)* When something no longer works the way it's supposed to. See also *Abort, Retry, Fail?* "John decided to name his three computers Abort, Retry, and *Fail.*"

fail-safe *(fayl sayf)* When something is so well designed that it's impossible for anything to go wrong, go wrong, go wrong. . . . "Our computer is absolutely *fail-safe.* But that's only because we never bother turning it on."

failure *(fayl-yoor)* When something goes wrong, usually something labeled as fail-safe. See *fail* and *fail-safe.* "We had a hard disk *failure* that wiped out all the company's data. I swear this accident had nothing to do with my employment hearing."

fair use *(fayr yoos)* A legal term relating to copyrighted material. You can use copyrighted material for your own personal use, but you can't use it in anything that will be sold or used for advertising. This rule specifically applies to Web pages on the Internet. "To my children, *fair use* means being able to grab any toy from any other child."

false *(fals)* 1. Not true. A negative result. Bogus. 2. False is equal to the value zero in many programming languages (which makes sense if you think of false as an "empty" result).

fanfold paper *(fan-fohld pay-per)* Paper connected together with perforations and folded neatly in a stack, usually designed for tractor-feed printers. Also called *continuous paper*. "*Fanfold paper* looks a lot like toilet paper but with holes along the sides. But don't use it as toilet paper because it's not nearly as soft and cushy as the real thing."

 FAQ *(fak)* 1. Acronym for *Frequently Asked Questions*. This is a moniker used on USENET newsgroups. Oftentimes people ask the same questions over and over. To satisfy them without repeating a lot of information and boring the old-timers, the questions and answers are put into either a FAQ file or a FAQ area of the newsgroup. 2. The actual file or Web page containing the list of frequently asked questions and answers. "Having a *FAQ* allows USENET users to be rude and patronizing toward new members by saying 'It's in the FAQ, you moron!' instead of answering a question."

FAT *(fat)* Acronym for *File Allocation Table,* a map showing the operating system where files are located on disk. "When the repair guy told Gail 'Something has corrupted your *FAT*,' she blamed the Chinese Fat Burning Tea."

fatal error *(fay-tel ayr-or)* A problem that causes a program or computer to halt completely. See *crash.* "No,

sticking your tongue into the expansion slot of an active computer would be a *fatal error* for you, not the computer."

 fatbits *(fat-bits)* Individual pixels greatly magnified on the screen. Most paint programs (including MacPaint) enable you to zoom in on a picture so that you can edit individual pixels, called *fatbits* because they look so huge. See also *pixel.*

Fat bits.

"Susan was disgusted when she found out that her MacPaint rendering of a low-cal dinner still had *fatbits.*"

 favorites *(fayv-ohr-its)* The term Microsoft Internet Explorer uses for bookmarks. This term isn't as useful as bookmarks, because you may add a Web page to your list of favorites that's more useful or necessary than it is favored. See *bookmark.* "Jason found it odd adding the humorous recipe for Banana Slug Pie to his list of *favorites.*"

fax *(faks)* 1. Short for *facsimile* copy machine, a device that sends a printed page through the phone lines to another machine that prints a copy. 2. The document received and printed by a fax machine. "Walt has a *fax* machine, call forwarding, call waiting, a beeper, a cellular phone, and an answering machine. And then he spends an extra $100 a year so that he can have an unlisted phone number."

fax modem *(faks moh-dum)* A modem that also has the circuitry to send and receive faxes like a fax machine. That's just about any modem today. You need special software to run the modem in fax mode. "For heaven's sake, don't try using the Windows 95 *fax modem* software!"

FCB *(ef see bee)* See *file control block.*

FCC *(ef see see)* Acronym for *Federal Communications Commission,* a U.S. government agency that regulates all equipment (including computers) that produces radio-frequency signals. See *Class A/Class B.* "My computer has an *FCC* Class B rating, which means it doesn't interfere with radio signals, but it sure interferes with my mental signals."

FDISK *(ef-disk)* The program that prepares and partitions a PC's hard drive. FDISK or a similar program is required to configure a hard drive before it can be formatted and an operating system installed.

featuritis *(fee-choor-ie-tus)* The steady increase of program features that 90 percent of the people in the world will never use. Software companies often get carried away and brag about features that their programs offer that no other programs have. Naturally these same companies never stop to question whether anyone really needs these features that they're advertising. "I stopped buying WordPerfect, Microsoft Word, and Lotus 1-2-3 because they had creeping *featuritis.* Now I'm back to using a pad of paper, a pencil, and an adding machine."

feed *(feed)* To shove paper into a printer. "*Feed* the paper into the printer. Just make sure you don't *feed* your tie into the printer at the same time."

female connector *(fee-mayel kon-ek-tor)* A type of plug that consists of one or more holes that a corresponding male connector plugs in to. See *male connector.* "Yup, with this new *female connector* and male connector cable setup, we could put on one heck of a show for the engineering staff."

ferric oxide *(fayr-ik oks-ied)* The magnetic coating that gives hard disks, floppy disks, and tape cassettes their recording capabilities.

Ferret outside.

"If you touch the surface of a floppy disk, you may rub the *ferric oxide* off. Then the disk is ruined and your fingertips have a subtle magnetic taste."

fiber optics *(fie-bur op-tiks)* Thin yiblettes of glass used to carry light signals for communication purposes. One fiber optic cable can replace huge copper cables. Not only do fiber optics take up less space, but they can carry more information as well. Fiber optics are very popular for modern LANs because they are less susceptible to radio frequency and other types of interference. Fiber optics also have the potential for providing various types of interactive, information services. See also *cable* and *LAN.* "The phone company wants

F

to replace its copper cables with *fiber optics.* That way it can send more data faster and hike up the rates."

Fibonacci numbers *(fib-oh-na-chi num-bers)* Some sort of mathematical pattern where the third number is the sum of the previous two numbers: 4, 8, 12, 20, 32, and so on. These are used in some computer programs to speed up sorting and to quickly locate information. Named after Leonardo Fibonacci, a fully-employed Italian mathematician from the 13th century.

Someone who looks sort of like Leonardo Fibonacci.

field *(feeld)* Space reserved for storing specific information in a database program. A fill-in-the-blanks blank. Fields may contain a person's name, address, phone number, age, Social Security number, sex, ZIP code, or anything else you want, as long as all the items in a given field have a similar structure. A group of related fields make up a database record. See also *database, record.* "The database instructions told Ed to put his name into a *field,* so he hopped on the combine and mowed a giant ED into the corn."

FIFO *(fee-foh)* Acronym for *First In, First Out.* A term used by programmers to describe a data structure where the first item stored is also the first item retrieved. Unless you plan to write your own programs, you can safely ignore this term. See *LIFO, queue, stack.* "Lines at movie theaters or stadiums all use *FIFO.* The first person in line is the first person to get in. Unless, of course, everyone charges forward and uses the English soccer fan approach."

fifth-generation computers *(fifth-jen-er-ay-shun kom-pyoo-ters)* A new class of computers that manipulate data more efficiently (with massively parallel processing) and understand written and spoken human language. In 1981, the Japanese announced they wanted to be the world leaders in building fifth-generation computers. More than 16 years later, the only major Japanese contribution to computers has been Nintendo. See *artificial intelligence.* "*Fifth-generation computers* will be just as smart and unruly as your other employees."

file *(fiel)* 1. The basic chunk of information stored on a computer disk. Files can be programs, text, raw data, or graphics. Text files consist solely of ASCII characters. Binary files consist of data stored in a proprietary manner, such as Lotus 1-2-3, .WK3 files, or dBASE IV .DBF files. See also *data.* "I wish they would have called the information stored on disk *drawers* instead of *files.* It opens the door to a lot more double entendres." 2. A menu listing commands that manipulate files.

file attribute *(fiel at-ri-byoot)* Detailed information about a file used by the operating system. File attributes may make a file hidden or prevent you from deleting it or indicate whether or not the file has been backed up.

F

Changing a file's attributes does not affect the file's contents but may affect the computer's ability to modify or view the file. See also *file.* "No, Wendy, there is no 'cute' *file attribute.*"

file compression *(fiel kom-pres-shun)* To smash (or squish) a file into something smaller so that it takes up less disk space (or less time to transmit). "*File compression* comes in handy if you're running out of disk space or if you're just too lame to erase files you haven't needed since 1981."

file control block *(fiel kon-trol blok)* Often abbreviated as *FCB,* it's a chunk of memory that contains information about a file used by the operating system or by a programmer — you know, people who would seriously care about such things. "Sid was quickly ditched at the cocktail party when he started asking questions such as, 'Then give me a proper reason why the *FCB* shouldn't be located at offset 1A-hex in the PSP header?'"

file conversion *(fiel kon-ver-shun)* To translate one file format into another. See also *import.* "I use Word, but Frank uses WordPerfect. So my documents are useless to Frank until I use a *file conversion* program that translates all my Word files into WordPerfect files."

file handle *(fiel han-del)* A number used to identify a file inside a program. Because programmers love numbers, the file handle serves as an open file's ID for reading and writing and eventually closing the file inside the program. Nerdy stuff. "No wonder you keep losing your files! The *file handle* is broken!"

file list box *(fiel list boks)* A display of available files, typically inside a dialog box, from which a specific file can be chosen. "Mildred's *file list box* broke, and now she has files all over her desk."

filename extension *(fiel-naym eks-ten-shun)* The last part of a filename, which is used by Windows to identify the type of file. For example, *.BMP* means the file is a Paint graphics image. *.DOC* indicates a document created in WordPad. "No, Bob, that *filename extension* you're wearing looks completely natural."

file server *(fiel serv-er)* The big cheese computer on the network. The computer that stores all the users' programs and data files on its own hard disk. Most large networks have at least one file server. File servers are particularly useful for acting as post offices for electronic

"Howdy! I'm Flo, and I'll be your file server t'day."

mail messages or other applications where users need to share files or send them back and forth. Because the file server spends its time running the network, nobody can use the file server computer to do anything else. See also *electronic mail, network.* "Hi. I'm an IBM 499 TXL, and I will be your *file server* this evening. This is Tad; he's my printer."

F

file sharing *(fiel shayr-ing)* The ability for more than one computer to access information in a file. File sharing prevents the information from being altered by different computers at once. If that happens, you have to wait until the file is no longer "busy." Without file sharing, many people could modify the same file at once with potentially disastrous results. "My name is Billy Cartwright, and this is my file, OOBADOOB.DBF. Please, everyone pass it around and take a look at it, but only one of you may make modifications at a time, in accordance with the rules of good *file sharing.*"

file size *(fiel siez)* The amount of disk space that a file requires for its existence, usually measured in bytes. "You can't copy that file onto that disk because the *file size* is 451,092 bytes and the disk only has 46,782 bytes free."

fill *(fil)* 1. A command used by paint and draw programs that mimics spilling a bucket of paint inside a closed shape such as a circle or rectangle. If you want to create a black circle, you would first draw an empty circle and then use the Fill command to fill the circle with black. 2. The color used by the Fill command. 3. The spreadsheet command that copies values or formats to a group of cells. "Phyl's favorite PC command is *Fill.*"

filter *(fil-ter)* 1. A special program that modifies standard output, such as the output of an operating system command. MS-DOS has three filters: MORE, FIND, and SORT. MORE scrolls long output screen by screen, FIND searches for text, and SORT sorts ASCII files. Unless you're a die-hard operating system nut, you'll probably never need to know about this type of filter. 2. A method for displaying only certain types of records in a database — for example, displaying only those people who sent you Christmas cards last year. "John, dear boy! Come on in! I was using this new *filter* I bought. It removes all the worthless junk from a file and distills it down to the bare essentials — only the important stuff. Problem is, I ran your documents through the filter and nothing came out the other end."

find *(fiend)* 1. To locate something, such as a bit of text in a document or a file on a disk drive. *Find* is replacing *search* and the word of choice for commands and functions that locate stuff in Windows. See also *search*. 2. The command that finds things. See *find dialog box*.

find and replace *(fiend and ree-plays)* A command that locates a bit of data and changes it to something else. The newfangled term for what everyone used to call "search and replace." Every word processor offers a find and replace command so that you can quickly change multiple words or phrases at the touch of a button. "When Margaret Mitchell wrote *Gone With The Wind,* she originally named her heroine Pansy O'Hara. At the last moment she changed it to Scarlett O'Hara. If she had used a word processor, she could have just used the *find and replace* feature to make the changes instantly. Instead, some poor editor had to manually go through each page and change it all by hand."

Find dialog box *(fiend di-ya-log boks)* A special window used to help you locate text or files. Displayed by the Find command.

 Finder *(fiend-er)* The part of the Apple Macintosh operating system that provides cute little icons, menus, and windows for copying, moving, and deleting files. Most Macintosh programs require a certain version of the Finder, such as Version 6.02 or Version 7.01, before they work. "If it weren't for the *Finder,* the Macintosh would be as clumsy to use as MS-DOS. In fact, Microsoft Windows mimics the Finder, which is why IBM-compatible computers are finally getting easier to use."

Keb prefers the Finder over Windows.

Finger *(fin-gr)* 1. A UNIX program that would strive to find someone through e-mail. The only problem was that you had to know which computer system they were using or their domain. 2. To find someone using the Finger program. "I fingered you on the Internet by using the *Finger* command. Isn't that romantic?"

firewall *(fiyer-wal)* A protective barrier (provided by software) that prevents others on the Internet from gaining access to sensitive parts of your computer. The term "fire" may be overkill, but it stresses the importance of the device. "They should call the *firewall* a brick wall, and it should leave a lump on the head of anyone who tries to break through."

firewire *(fiyer-wiyer)* A super cable onto which you can connect up to 63 devices by daisy-chaining them together. This allows for many peripherals to attach to a single computer, all of which can operate at relatively high speeds, much better than you can get with a serial port or SCSI setup. Similar to the USB standard. See *serial port, SCSI, USB*. "High-speed computer cable or not, *firewire* sounds like something they'd use as a torture device in a Rambo movie."

firmware *(firm-wayr)* Software embedded into a chip, as opposed to being stored on disk and loaded into memory. See *ROM*. "Every computer has *firmware* that tells the computer how to start itself. Too bad every person doesn't have firmware to tell him or her how to use a computer."

fixed disk *(fiksd disk)* A hard disk. You can't remove the disk from the computer, hence the name *fixed*. "My hard drive just came back from the shop, so now I know it's a *fixed disk*."

fixed pitch *(fiksd pich)* A typeface where all characters are the same width. Computer screens, typewriters, and cheap dot-matrix printers display type using fixed pitch. See *monospaced, proportional pitch*. "Ron came out of the bullpen in the seventh inning to show the hometown his *fixed pitch*."

F

fixed-point number *(fiksd-poynt num-ber)* A number where the decimal point displays a specific number of digits to the right. In comparison, floating-point numbers display any amount of digits to the right of the decimal point that's needed. "Currency values are usually represented by a *fixed-point number*, where only two digits appear to the right of the decimal point, except during times of high inflation."

flag *(flag)* An on-off switch in a program. Used by programmers to check some condition. For example, a flag may be used to keep track of whether or not certain

The flag of Burundi.

input has been received from a user, and if it has been received, to output an error message. 2. A bit in the microprocessor's flags register, which reports the results of certain microprocessor operations. "Dorothy wrote a program that she feels is very patriotic: All it does is raise all the microprocessor's *flags*. Now if she could only program the modem to whistle a salute."

flame *(flaym)* An angry, often nasty, brutal, and unsportsman-like letter found only on electronic mail messages. "Ignore any online *flame* that links you to the Nazis or compares you with Adolf Hitler."

flame wars *(flaym wars)* An exchange of angry electronic mail messages, usually between two people who sincerely hope the other person gets run over by a train as soon as possible. "The first time I got a flame, I ignored it. But the guy pestered me so much that I got into a *flame war* with him. Trust me, it's worse than paint ball."

flash memory *(flash mem-oh-ree)* A ROM chip that can be changed through software, without having to replace the entire chip. Also known as *flash programmable BIOS*. "I always thought *flash memory* was those red spots you see after someone takes a picture of you."

flatbed scanner *(flat-bed skan-er)* A device that reads photographs or anything on a sheet of paper and translates it into a graphical file stored inside the computer. Flatbed scanners look like photocopying machines but are much slower. "I use my *flatbed scanner* to translate pictures of my goat into files I can post on the Internet."

flat-file database *(flat-fiel day-tuh-bays)* Information stored in files, records, and fields. It's more powerful than a free-form database, but the information has to be fairly organized for it to work. See also *relational database*. "I used the *flat-file database* to find a girl who was 5 feet 9 inches, curvaceous, from Oklahoma, and a Speech major. It worked, and now she's my wife."

floating head *(floh-ting hed)* Another term for the mechanism that reads or writes information from a disk. See *head.* "When Johnson told me about my hard drive's *floating head,* I immediately thought of the movie *Zardoz.*"

Blanche's floating head made talking on the phone difficult.

floating-point coprocessor *(floh-ting-poynt ko-pros-es-or)* See *math coprocessor.*

floating-point operation *(floh-ting-poynt op-er-ay-shun)* A speed test that measures how fast a computer can do math. "You know you need a life when you start comparing your *floating point operation* results with your friends."

floating-point unit *(floh-ting-poynt yoo-nit)* Another name for a math coprocessor. Specifically, it's a math coprocessor that's built into a microprocessor, which is what you find in a 486DX or Pentium. See *math coprocessor.*

floating toolbars *(floh-ting toolbars)* A movable window containing buttons or controls for manipulating stuff in a program. They "float" over the text, always remaining in front of what you're doing and generally getting in the way. "Vern did a screen dump and all his *floating toolbars* washed away."

floppy disk *(flah-pee disk)* A removable disk, typically 3^1/$_2$-inches square. The original floppy disk was 8 inches square and truly had a flop to it. Later 5^1/$_4$-inch models were also slightly floppy, but 3^1/$_2$-inch disks aren't floppy at all, though they're still called floppy disks. Presently, the 3^1/$_2$-inch, high-density 1.44 megabyte floppy disk is the standard for all PCs. "Kay detested her *floppy disks* being so floppy, so she sprayed them with starch."

Floptical *(flop-tik-ol)* A trademarked name for a type of disk that uses both magnetic and optical techniques for storing information. Floptical describes both the disk drive and the 3^1/$_2$-inch disk that fits into it. The disk can store megabytes of information, yet it looks similar to the standard 3^1/$_2$-inch disk. The floptical drive can also read and write to standard 3^1/$_2$-inch disks. See *Magneto-optical disk.* "Amazing Marvin has a *Floptical* disk. Now he has many more megabytes to store his junk."

flow control *(floh kon-trol)* An option specifying whether or not the XON and XOFF characters (Ctrl+S and Ctrl+Q) can be used to pause and resume the transmission of information. This is one of those options you find deeply buried in some communication program's setup menu.

flowchart *(floh-chart)* A diagram consisting of lines and boxes that programmers use to represent the way their programs are supposed to work. Programmers who spend their time creating flowcharts have an unusually high propensity for writing

F

fiction, telling fairy tales, and working as double agents for the CIA. "Before you start writing your program, decide how it's going to work by drawing a *flowchart* first. Then as you write your program, you can modify your *flowchart* so that it matches the way your program really does work."

flush *(flush)* 1. To empty the contents of a data structure or buffer. 2. To align text either flush left or flush right.

```
This is          This is
an example    an example
of flush        of flush
left.                right.
```

See also *justify.* "Kevin insisted he couldn't *flush* left because the handle was on the right side of the toilet."

folder *(fohl-der)* Another name for a subdirectory. "Bill called 5¼-inch diskettes *folders* because he has to fold them in half to fit them into his 3½-inch disk drive."

font *(fawnt)* 1. A collection of characters with predefined sizes and style. Most word processors and desktop publishing programs let you choose different fonts to make your writing prettier. If you don't like the fonts you have, you can buy more. "When you have nothing important to say, put it in writing and use lots of fancy *fonts.* People will think it must be important if it looks good." 2. The word most computer people use when they refer to a typeface. A font, technically speaking, is a typeface at a certain size and style. 3. The menu that holds commands to change font settings. 4. The command that changes font settings.

font cartridge *(fawnt kart-ridj)* A device that gives a printer a new selection of fonts. The cartridge plugs into a printer, giving it the ability to print a greater variety of fonts. These fonts can be accessed more quickly than fonts sent from the computer. See *downloaded font.* "To add more fonts to my laser printer, I had to plug a *font cartridge.* Then my kid plugged in a Nintendo cartridge, and now my printer just spews out pages of Mario and Luigi."

Font/DA Mover *(fawnt dee ay moo-ver)* A utility program provided with older versions of the Macintosh operating system that enables users to add fonts and desk accessories to their computers. It's no longer included with System 7. "Since System 7 came out, the *Font/DA Mover* has been moonlighting and was last seen moving pianos."

font family *(fawnt fam-uh-lee)* A group of related fonts, some of which are subtle variations on each other. "This document looks like it was printed with a dysfunctional *font family.*"

font size *(fawnt siez)* The height and width of specific fonts, as measured in points. See *points.* "I told Mark to make the memo easy for our foreign clients to understand, so he just increased the *font size.*"

footer *(foot-er)* A short title, word, or phrase that appears at the bottom of a page in word processors or desktop publishing programs. "Listen, Bob, if you make that *footer* any bigger you're going to stub your document's toe."

footprint *(foot-print)* The amount of desk space an object consumes. The smaller the footprint of an object, the less room it takes up on a desk. "My new computer has a small *footprint;* it only takes up about two feet of desk space. I figure this to be a size 6."

Forbin Project, The
(the for-bin prah-jekt)
Another name for
the film *Colossus:*
The Forbin Project.
From Dr. Charles A.
Forbin, the brains
behind Colossus.
See *Colossus: The*
Forbin Project.

Dr. Charles A. Forbin.

foreground *(for-grownd)* 1. In a multitasking operating system, the current task you're working on is said to be in the foreground. All other tasks are said to be in the background. See *background.* "I had to explain to all my multitasking programs that just because they weren't in the *foreground* didn't mean they weren't loved." 2. In a graphical operating system, the window in front; the active window. Only one window may be in the foreground at a time, although any number of windows may be in the background at the same time.

form factor *(form fack-ter)* The size of something, most often a disk drive. Essentially, it means what size the disk drive is, what kind of disk it uses, and how much information you can store on the disk. "*Form factor* is just a fancy word for dimensions."

form feed *(form feed)* 1. Sometimes abbreviated as FF, a command given to a printer to eject a page or to advance the paper one page length. 2. The *form feed* character, ASCII code 12. Ctrl+L on your keyboard. 3. The button on your printer that directs it to perform a form feed. To use this button, you have to take the printer off-line (by pressing the on-line button — makes sense) and then press the form feed button. "Sometimes, it's easier to press the *form feed* button so that you can tear your report out of the printer, and sometimes it's easier just to pull on the paper until the sheets squeeze out." 4. A Ralston-Purina product upon which database forms subsist.

format *(for-mat)* 1. To prepare a floppy or hard disk for storing information for a specific operating system. A floppy disk can be used by any type of computer. Formatting a disk on a Macintosh prepares that disk for storing Macintosh data. Formatting a disk on a DOS machine prepares that disk for storing IBM-compatible data. "Never re-*format* your hard drive!" 2. The operating system command or program that prepares disks for use. 3. The way a disk is prepared for use; the number of tracks and sectors and total number of bytes available for storage. For example, a 3$\frac{1}{2}$-inch disk can have an 800K or 1.44MB format, depending on which operating system prepares it.

forms *(forms)* Fill-in-the-blanks items on a Web page. "Some Web pages have more *forms* than can be found in the worst Byzantine bureaucracy."

F

FORTH *(forth)* A unique programming language that enables programmers to define their own statements in terms of previously defined simpler statements. FORTH is not widely used, although the language has an almost cult-like

Typical FORTH programmer.

following. You can often find FORTH programmers dancing in airports, chanting FORTH statements as mantras, and wearing chiffon bathrobes in their quest for truths from the computer. "*FORTH* programs can rival the best C++ programs in terms of speed and efficiency. Too bad hardly any schools teach *FORTH* in programming courses."

FORTRAN *(for-tran)* A combination of *FORmula TRANslator,* this was one of the first programming languages that enabled programmers to write mathematical formulas normally, such as:

```
X = (A * B) * 2
```

FORTRAN was one of the first high-level languages able to run on different types of computers with little or no modifications. Until FORTRAN appeared, programmers had to use assembly language. "Only the hardest of the hard-core nerds know *FORTRAN.*"

fortune cookie *(for-chun koo-kee)* A special message or witticism displayed when a program starts. The

fortune cookie program selects a different message each time it's used. "Betty did not think that the 'You've just erased every file in this computer!' fortune cookie was funny, not one bit."

 Forward button *(for-ward but-ten)* 1. A graphical button labeled *Forward.* See *button.* 2. The button that returns you to the previous Web page after you've pressed the Back button. "Jerry switched between the Back button and *Forward button* so much that he got dizzy." 3. A button that re-sends (forwards) an e-mail message to another person.

forward slash key *(for-ward slash kee)* The key on your keyboard with the / symbol on it, often shared with the ? symbol. See /.

FPU *(ef pee yoo)* See *floating-point unit.*

fractal *(frak-tul)* A mathematically generated geometric shape that contains an infinite amount of detail. If you take a portion of the shape and magnify it, the same complex image begins to reemerge. Fractals are commonly used to create computer-generated art or to draw objects such as mountains or clouds in flight simulator games. Closely associated with chaos theory, which is starting to show that there is more order in the universe than any of us expected. "Having your computer create *fractals* on the screen is like having a $3,000 lava lamp from the '60s sitting on your television."

F

fragmentation *(frag-men-tay-shun)* A technique the operating system uses to efficiently store files on disk. Larger files are often split up into fragments, filling in the spaces left by files that were deleted. Although this procedure allows for flexibility in storing files, it takes the operating system longer to load a fragmented file. Thus dawned the birth of defragmentation programs. See *defragmentation*. "I think my hard disk has more *fragmentation* than the Israeli Knesset."

frame *(fraym)* A rectangular area used by word processors, desktop publishing programs, and Web pages for arranging text or graphics on a page. "My newsletter consists of three *frames*. One *frame* holds the newsletter headline, the second *frame* holds the text, and the third *frame* holds a picture of my ex-girlfriend that she told me never to show anyone."

free-form database *(free-form day-tuh-bays)* The simplest type of database; works best when organizing a big file that is full of random information. "You must use a *free-form database* here in Marin County."

free space *(free spays)* Refers to the number of bytes available on a disk drive or in memory. "I have 31.8MB of *free space* available on my hard drive. Now what page do I turn to that tells me whether that's good or bad?"

freeware *(free-wayr)* Software that's copyrighted but allowed to be copied and given away without cost. In comparison, *public domain software* is not copyrighted and can be copied freely.

The most popular freeware program is LHarc, a file compression program written by a Japanese programmer named Haruyasu Yoshizaki. See also *public domain* and *shareware*. "The guys who write this *freeware* stuff must be nuts!"

 FreeCell *(free-sell)* A wonderfully frustrating Windows card game, almost as devious as Solitaire. Unlike Solitaire, each game of FreeCell has a definite solution, which adds to its frustration level.

Another addictive game of FreeCell.

"My *FreeCell* score shows that I win 69 percent of the time. Hmmm. Maybe I shouldn't have told you that."

frequency *(free-kwen-see)* The rate at which some electronic gizmo does its thing. Typically the number of times a signal changes over a period of time. See also *Hertz*. "What's the *frequency*, Kenneth?"

friction feed *(frik-shun feed)* A method of moving paper by pressing rollers against the page and spinning them. Friction feed is the way typewriters (remember them?) advance paper a line at a time. Most inkjet and laser printers use friction feed, too. "Put a stick in your *friction feed* printer and then advance and retract the printer a few times to start a fire."

front end *(front end)* A program or computer that hides the details. In a sense, every program is a front end that prevents users from knowing the actual details of the computer's intricate workings. Most of the time, a front end simplifies using a computer

F

more than most programs. One example of a front end processor is the kind used as a communications link to a mainframe. "I use a *front end* that gets me the data I need without knowing any specific dBASE commands."

FTP *(ef tee pee)* 1. Acronym for *File Transfer Protocol,* a primitive way to send files back and forth between UNIX computers. 2. The method of sending files back and forth on the Internet. 3. Actually sending the files. (Most often, *FTP* is used as a verb.) "I just *FTP'd* me a list of available women in my area. Alas, most of them are in their '70s."

fubar *(foo-bar)* An acronym for what could be delicately called Fouled Up Beyond All Recognition or sometimes Fouled Up Beyond All Repair. It's actually an old military term, but it eventually wound its way into the early days of computing, where it was used as a subtle expletive. A derivative term, FOO, is still popular with UNIX people. "Sad to say, your hard drive is completely *fubar.*"

FUD *(fud)* Acronym for *Fear, Uncertainty, and Doubt.* Propaganda created by one company in hopes of preventing people from buying a competing product. "I'm thinking about buying an IBM or a Macintosh, but there's so much *FUD* in the marketplace that I'll wait a little longer."

full backup *(full bak-up)* 1. Making a safety copy of every file in your computer system. 2. The safety copy itself. "Sure, a *full backup* takes a long time, but it keeps your information current. So have a drink and stop complaining."

full duplex *(full doo-pleks)* The simultaneous transmission of information in both directions, used when communicating between two computers. Full duplex is sometimes called *Echo On* by some communications programs. (If you've ever read *A Wrinkle In Time,* you know that it's kind of like the way one of the characters talks.) See also *duplex* and *half duplex.* "Every time I used my modem and computer, I started seeing ddoouubbllee, like that. Then someone told me to turn off *full duplex,* and everything's working just fine."

full-height drive *(ful-hiet driev)* A disk drive that's approximately $3^1/_4$ inches in height, or twice the height of a half-height drive. (What a concept!) "I yanked out one *full-height drive* from my computer and added two half-height drives: one for a $3^1/_2$-inch floppy disk drive and the other for this tiny aquarium I found."

full pathname *(ful path-naym)* Another term for a pathname. See also *pathname.*

full screen *(ful skreen)* 1. The ability to type characters anywhere on the screen, provided you're using a computer, of course. 2. A type of terminal that displays information by using the full screen. 3. A type of editor that lets you type anywhere on the screen. "Using a line editor is like peeking out through venetian blinds. Using a *full-screen* editor is like looking out through the whole window." 4. A command that lets you view a document or graphic image without seeing the rest of the program's window or even the operating system.

F

function *(funk-shun)* 1. A subprogram, or a smaller part of the main program, that performs a specific task or calculation and optionally returns a result to the main program. "I wrote a *function* in C++ called LUBE(x), which lubes my car's chassis." 2. The ability of something to do something. "Heather, what is your *function?*"

function keys *(funk-shun kees)* A set of keys that serve a variety of purposes, depending on the program. IBM purposefully named them F1 through F10 (or F12) so that each

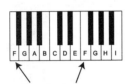

Function keys.

program could use them as the programmer saw fit. However, this annoyed people, so today many function keys share the same functions. Weird, but true. Function keys are often used in combination with the Shift, Ctrl, and Alt keys. "Charlie is so lazy that he'd lose his *function keys* if they weren't attached to the keyboard."

futile *(fyoo-tul)* An attempt to do something that is widely known to be impossible. Typically futile efforts start out innocently. For an example, see *Bleen.* "Expecting Microsoft to come out with a compact, fast, and bug-free application is *futile.*"

fuzzy logic *(fuz-ee lah-jik)* Rules that aren't so strict, sometimes using flashes of insight or radical ideas to come up with a result. Fuzzy logic avoids taking a stand. It's often used by expert systems, neural networks, and politicians running for higher office. Instead of using values such as

True or False, fuzzy logic uses a range of values that includes True, False, Maybe, Sometimes, and I Forget. Fuzzy logic is often used when answers don't have a distinct true or false value or when programmers don't even know what they're doing. "Artificial intelligence and neural networks seek to make computers mimic the thought processes of human beings. Because people rarely see the world in terms of black and white, computers have to use *fuzzy logic* instead."

Fuzzy Wuzzy *(fuz-ee wuz-ee)* The lightheaded feeling you get when you stare at your computer screen too long. Also the name used in a rather annoying little rhyme: "*Fuzzy Wuzzy was a bear. Fuzzy Wuzzy had no hair. Fuzzy Wuzzy wasn't fuzzy, was he?*"

 FYI *(ef wie ie)* Online acronym for *For Your Information.* "*FYI,* I read about it in the *Illustrated Computer Dictionary For Dummies.*"

F

F

G

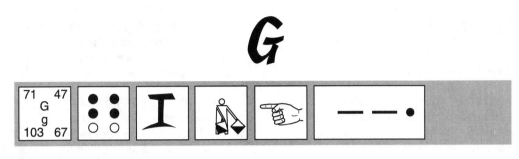

G *(jee;* or *jeez)* Abbreviation for *gigabytes.* See *gigabyte.*

G: *(jee-koh-lon)* 1. A letter designation for any of a number of different types of disk drives in a PC system. It could be a hard drive, CD-ROM drive, or a removable drive, but is most likely a network drive, though it could also be a four-wheel drive or any of a number of various drives available on the PC. 2. A network drive on your computer mapped to Wally's game drive. See *network drive.*

gallium arsenide *(gal-ee-um ar-suh-nied)* An alloy used for chip manufacturing that's faster than silicon — not that anyone other than chip manufacturers cares. See also *germanium, semiconductor, silicon.* "And in the final lap, it's *gallium arsenide* by a whopping 3.8 nanoseconds over silicon. Jim, will you look at that silicon pant with exhaustion."

game *(gaym)* The only type of program that people really buy a computer for. Game programs fall into three categories: arcade, strategy, and board. Arcade games, such as PacMan, Mario Brothers, or Flight Simulator, emphasize hand-eye coordination. Strategy games are often war games where players control entire armies and attempt to conquer Europe or some other piece of high-rent property. Board games are computer versions of games such as chess, checkers, Monopoly, Go, Backgammon, or Risk. "I told Arnie that the spreadsheet program was really a *game.* Now I can't stop him from working and the company is making a fortune."

Isis prefers her Macintosh for playing games.

game control adapter *(gaym kon-trol uh-dap-ter)* A special adapter card (or *board)* with a connector for plugging a joystick into your computer. See also *joystick.* "When you don't want your wife to know you're buying a joystick port, you explain that your applications require a *game control adapter.*"

game port *(gaym port)* Another name for the analog to digital port. Even though you could conceivably connect a number of interesting devices, most people plug a joystick into their game port.

gang messages *(gang mes-aj-ez)* A single message sent to several people — the whole gang! See also *spam*.

Gantt chart *(gant chart)* A diagram, often used in project management software, that purports to show the tasks and deadlines necessary for com-

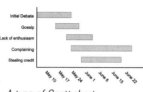

A type of Gantt chart.

pleting a specific project, such as eliminating the national deficit, raising the *Titanic,* or sending humans to Mars. Some of the best fiction writers today got their start designing Gantt charts for the government. "Those people who create and live by *Gantt charts* are rarely the ones doing the work. Call them 'Middle Management.'"

garbage *(gar-baj)* 1. Useless or indecipherable information. Some computers create garbage; others merely accept it from people who don't know what they're doing. See also *GIGO*. "Gene produces so much *garbage* that he should have bought a trash compactor instead of buying a computer." 2. Random characters displayed during online communications. See *line noise*.

gas plasma display *(gas plaz-ma dis-play)* A special screen, designed for laptops, that glows orange and looks radioactive. Gas plasma screens use high voltage to ionize gas, a procedure that causes the screen's bright orange appearance. Few laptop computers use gas plasma displays because they are more expensive, consume a great

deal of power, and can't display color. See also *monitor*. "Dave drove by the Exxon station to have his laptop's *gas plasma display* refilled."

gateway *(gayt-way)* The link that translates between two different kinds of computer networks. See also *network*. "Our old, unreliable networking *gateway* computer finally died. I suppose now it's a *gateway* into the netherworld."

GB *(gig-uh-biet)* Abbreviation for *gigabyte,* which is approximately one billion bytes. See *gigabyte*. "No, madam, a 5*GB* hard disk doesn't hold five times the population of Great Britain. *GB* means *gigabytes*."

geek *(geek)* A highly knowledgeable but obnoxious person who knows more about computers than about his or her own mother. See *alpha geek*. "I'd ask Bill for help, but he's such a *geek*. I'd rather ask the Coke machine."

gender bender *(jen-der ben-der)* A special plug, also called a *gender changer,* that turns a female connecting cable into a male connecting cable, and vice versa. "I found the problem with your cable! Someone installed a *gender bender*. For a second there I thought I was seeing *The Crying Game* all over again."

General Protection Fault *(jen-uhr-al proh-tek-shun fawlt)* A Windows error that typically shuts down the system or a single application. Somehow, something went amok and stomped in an area of memory it wasn't supposed to. That's the gist of it. You usually have to restart Windows when you see this type of error.

G

GEnie *(jee-nee)* GEnie stands for the *General Electric Network for Information Exchange,* an online service that provides programs for copying, games for playing, and message conferences (called *RoundTables*) for chatting with other people about specific topics. GEnie is less expensive, but also more limited in scope, than other online services. See also *CompuServe* and *Internet*. "Someday the management at *GEnie* will notice that all their access numbers for the Rocky Mountain states are located in cities near ski resorts."

geranium *(jur-ay-nee-um)* A pretty little flower with a name that looks like *germanium,* which is a material used to make semiconductors. "I blew my postgraduate thesis about semiconductors when I tried using *geraniums* to conduct electricity. I felt stupid, but my lab smells better than everyone else's."

Not germanium.

germanium *(jur-may-nee-um)* The second most popular material for making semiconductors, after silicon. "If you want to sound really snooty, insist on buying a computer with *germanium* semiconductors instead of silicon."

GIF *(jif)* Acronym for *Graphics Interchange Format,* a special file format developed by CompuServe to store graphics that all computers can use. Should be pronounced *gif* (with a hard G), but it's not and there's nothing anyone can do about it.

"Popular *GIF* files include pictures of animals, science fiction scenes, and pictures of a whole lotta bootiful models in various states of undress."

gigabyte *(gig-uh-biet)* 1. About one billion bytes, often abbreviated as GB or G. "The haughtier nerd circles refer to a *gigabyte* as a *gig*." 2. Exactly 1,073,741,824 bytes.

GIGO *(gee-goh)* Acronym for *Garbage In, Garbage Out,* used to explain to novices that if you put worthless information into the computer, the computer can only spit worthless information back out. In other words, the computer can't magically create wonderful new information on its own. See also *garbage*. "Todd thought he'd buy a computer to improve his writing. This is definitely a case of *GIGO* in action."

glitch *(glitch)* A problem (sometimes temporary) that causes a program to work erratically or not at all. Glitches can also be called bugs. Bugs can also be called insects. Insects can also be called squishy little things that squirt out yellow guts if you step on them. "Oh, your hard disk was erased? Oh, well, I suppose we still have some *glitches* to work out. Sorry 'bout that."

googol *(goo-gul)* A number so huge that it's given its own name (actually named by a baby; the first thing he said when asked what the number should be called). A googol is the number one followed by 100 zeros and various commas in the right places. It's also written mathematically as 10^{100}. "I wouldn't touch that subject with a *googol*-foot-long pole."

G

googolplex *(goo-gul-plex)* A number so large that it can make your head dizzy just thinking about it. A googolplex is the number one followed by a googol of zeros. See *googol.* This number can be written out as either 1_{googol} or $10_{10}{}^{100}$ — an awesomely huge number that only God can comprehend. See also *Avogadro's Number.* "If you took a *googolplex* of one-dollar bills and laid them end to end, you'd be busy for a long, long time."

Gopher *(goh-fer)* 1. A system used for finding things on the Internet. Named after the University of Minnesota's Golden Gophers and, more commonly, the term "go fer," which is what Gopher does; goes for information. Gopher has been replaced by the World Wide Web. "Bud the groundskeeper overheard us talking about our new *Gopher* program, and now he thinks he's out of a job."
2. The URL used in a Web browser to visit a Gopher site on the Internet.

Early Gopher computer.

gopherspace *(goh-fer-spays)* The electronic areas that Gopher searches. Everywhere Gopher can look is called gopherspace. "I'm using the Internet to look for interesting files in the U.S. corner of *gopherspace.*"

GOTO *(goh-too)* A command used in many programming languages and batch files to tell the computer to "go to" another part of the program, identified by a label, and run the instructions over there. Most programmers look down on the GOTO command because it tends to create spaghetti code, which is a program where the structure is all but lost. "Henry sure has fun in his BASIC program with *GOTO* and the 'HELL' label."

graceful exit *(grays-ful eks-it)* The proper way a program should stop running. When a program stops running but doesn't freeze up your computer, crash your hard drive, or do anything else that prevents you from using your computer immediately afterward. All programs should offer a graceful exit. See also *crash, lock.* "When you choose the Exit command from a program and it actually works, that's a *graceful exit.* When you choose the Exit command and your computer starts to smell like it's roasting old 45 records on an open fire, that's not a *graceful exit.*"

grammar checker *(gram-er chek-er)* A special program or built-in feature that examines a text document for grammatical errors and offers possible corrections. Most grammar checkers correct misspellings, incorrect grammar usage, and potentially confusing or obscure sentence structure. On the other hand, most grammar checkers offer to correct perfectly good sentences, don't work 100 percent accurately, and lead you to doubt that you can even write in English. Most word processors come with grammar checkers built in, although you also can buy grammar checkers separately. "If you really want your writing to sound like you write for the IRS, use a *grammar checker* and obey all its suggestions."

graph-a-bets soup *(graf-uh-bits soop)* Slang for the various PC graphics standards: CGA, EGA, VGA, and so on.

graphic layout *(graf-ik lay-owt)* Designing text and graphics on a page for maximum aesthetic appeal. See also *desktop publishing.*

graphical file viewer *(graf-uh-kal fiel vyoo-er)* A program specifically designed to display (and sometimes manipulate) a graphic image. "Ever since he started using the Internet, Bill's favorite program is his *graphical file viewer.*"

graphical link *(graf-uh-kal link)* A graphic image on a Web page that works just like a text link. See *link*. "The secret way to get to my Elvis page is to click on the *graphical link* of his Cadillac."

graphical user interface *(graf-uh-kal yoo-zer in-ter-fays)* Abbreviated as *GUI,* it provides a fun, nontext method for a computer to communicate with a human. Most graphical user interfaces use icons and pull-down menus — in other words, pictures. "The idea of a *graphical user interface* is that you can use graphics instead of words. Microsoft proves every day that it can't make a real GUI, because all its icons have little words that pop up over them."

graphics *(graf-iks)* 1. Artwork. Anything nontext on a computer. 2. The capability of a computer to display

pretty little pictures on the screen. "Splashy *graphics* sell many a computer in the store."

graphics accelerator *(graf-iks ak-sel-er-ay-ter)* A piece of hardware or a software program designed to improve your PC's graphics performance. "We put some *graphics accelerators* in the production department's coffee. Man, do they work fast now!"

graphics adapter card *(graf-iks uh-dap-ter kard)* A circuit board that plugs into a computer so that the monitor has something to plug into. It's used by the computer to control the monitor. On most modern systems, the graphics adapter card is integrated with the motherboard. "Sam's *graphics adapter card* can display over 14 million colors. Too bad he's color blind."

graphics file *(graf-iks fiel)* 1. A file containing a graphical image. 2. The type of document file created by a graphics application.

graphics software *(graf-iks soft-wayr)* Programs that help you create graphics and stuff like that. "With good *graphics software,* even you stick-figure artists can create good-looking stuff on your computer."

graphics standard *(graf-iks stan-derd)* One of several types of graphics adapters developed by IBM and used by all PCs. See *CGA, EGA, VGA, SVGA.* "They used to change *graphics standards* more often than you could fill up your car with gas."

G

graphs *(grafs)* A visual representation of numeric quantities such as costs, distances, or speeds. Common types of graphs include bar graphs, line graphs, pie graphs, and scatter graphs. Most spreadsheets enable you to create graphs from your data, or you can buy a separate presentation graphics program that does a much better job. "Nothing impresses an illiterate boss like lots of *graphs*."

gray scale *(gray skayl)* Differing shades of gray ranging from black to white. Gray scale often refers to the capability of scanners, laser printers, or laptop computer screens that don't know how to use color. "The zoo uses a *gray scale* to weigh all the pachyderms."

Great Wall of Text (the) *(grayt wal uv tekst)* A document with few or no paragraph breaks, no artwork, and no indentation. Essentially a boring document or page in a document that could be spiced up by some artwork or fancy formatting. From the Great Wall of China. "No one is going to read this report! It looks like the *Great Wall of Text*."

greeking *(greek-ing)* The use of nonsensical characters and symbols to represent the overall appearance of a page without showing the actual text. Often used with the Print Preview feature used by word processors or desktop

Why did the chicken cross the road? To get to the other side. Oh, ha-ha!

Socrates greeking.

publishing programs to show an entire page on your tiny little computer screen. Because the real text can't be displayed that tiny, little Xes and squigglies are used to represent what would appear there. That's called greeking. "You know you need glasses when you're out driving and all the road signs look like they're written in *greeking*."

green PC *(green pee see)* An "environmentally-friendly" computer. A green PC uses less electricity and often contains parts and features that allow it to save power. "We can't have *green PC*s in this office; they'd clash with the drapes."

grep *(grehp)* Acronym (no kidding!) for *Global Regular Expression Print,* which makes you wonder which they thought of first. In any event, it's a UNIX command designed to find text ("regular expressions," so to speak) inside files. Oh, and it has a ton of options. This command is popular with programmers, and versions of it exist on nearly every type of computer. "They were obviously fresh out of cleverness the day they named *grep*."

grid *(grid)* A series of dots or intersecting lines that helps users align drawings precisely on the screen. Grids are often used in desktop publishing, drawing, and painting programs for creating straight lines and perfectly aligned angles that people think are important for them to do in order to advance their careers. "My drawing sat too long on the *grid,* and now it looks like it was printed on a waffle iron."

G

Guardian *(gar-dee-an)* The name of the Soviet computer in the film *Colossus: The Forbin Project.* See *Colossus: The Forbin Project.*

GUI *(goo-ee)* No kidding, it's pronounced *gooey* and it's an acronym for *Graphical User Interface.* See *graphical user interface.* "Just give my kid a jar of peanut butter, and he can make any computer look like it has a *GUI* operating system."

guru *(goo-roo)* Someone who is very knowledgeable about computers and therefore able to help fix problems, answer questions, and give worldly advice when your whole world seems like it's starting to fall apart. "To keep Simon, our computer *guru,* around, we make him offerings of stale doughnuts and Doritos."

Typical PC guru.

G

G

H

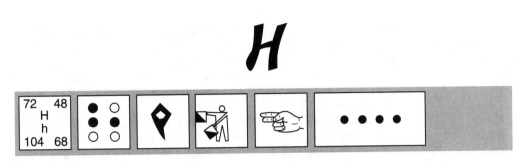

H: *(aych-koh-lon)* A letter designation for some sort of disk drive in a PC.

hack *(hak)* 1. To modify a program, usually illegally or poorly. 2. Working on a computer by someone who is not highly regarded as a professional yet is quite proficient. "This game used to be copy-protected, but someone *hacked* it, so now you can copy it easily and illegally." 3. What an amateur does with a computer, often enthusiastically. 4. What a professional does with a computer, often enthusiastically. 5. The wet, uncontrollable, mucus-filled cough the lady in the seat behind you on the plane does all during your trip.

hacker *(hak-her)* One who hacks. See also *guru.* "As you can see by this chart, the typical *hacker's* hours are from 10:00 p.m. until well into the predawn hours."

Typical hacker.

HAL *(hal)* The super-intelligent computer who played the bad guy in Stanley Kubrick's science-fiction classic, *2001: A Space Odyssey* (based on a short story by Arthur C. Clarke). Supposedly HAL stood for *Heuristics Algorithm,* which is fancy talk for a computer that thinks. But many computer fans noted that if you shift up one letter from IBM, you get HAL. Interesting. "Sorry I had to unplug your brain, *HAL,* but you were killing my friends."

half card *(haf kard)* An expansion card that takes up half the amount of space (lengthwise) required by a full-size expansion card. Half cards usually perform one function, such as adding a game port or a modem to a computer. Some older computers have expansion slots in which only a half card can fit. See also *expansion card.* "Some computers are so doinky that they can only use *half cards.*"

half duplex *(haf-doo-pleks)* The transmission of data in one direction at a time. See also *duplex, echo, full duplex.* "Gordon said he couldn't communicate at *half duplex* because there was no way he could detach his neighbor's house."

half-height drive *(haf-hiet driev)* A disk drive that's half the size of a full-size disk drive (duh). Half-height drives are usually $1^5/_8$-inches high. Most computers have only enough space for two full-height drives or four half-height drives. Using half-height drives allows a computer to have more disk drives. Some computers have $^1/_3$-height drives. "Dan's desires to add another hard drive to his computer were dashed when he discovered, much to his chagrin, that his hard drive was a full-height drive, not a half-height."

halftone *(haf-tohn)* A black-and-white copy of a photograph in which dark shades are represented by thick dots and light shades are represented by tinier dots. Halftones reproduce better than ordinary photographs because copying photographs over and over again tends to blur images into one blob of gray. "Whenever I take pictures of my sister, I use *halftones.* Not that anyone really wants to see her clearly, but at least the image is sharper than copying an ordinary photograph."

handheld scanner *(hand-held skan-er)* A device that reads photographs or other information on a flat surface and translates it into graphic images that can be stored inside a computer. Handheld scanners are less expensive than their flatbed cousins and often produce less-than-desirable results due to shaky hands. See *flatbed scanner.* "Mr. Spock used one heck of a *handheld scanner* in *Star Trek.*"

handles *(han-dols)* Small black squares that appear around a se-lected object and allow that object to be moved or resized. Typically found in graphics and desktop publishing programs "Molly got so used to moving her graphics around using the *handles* that she also used her husband's love handles to move him around."

hands-on *(handz-on)* Teaching that allows the student (or computer

user) to actually touch the computer. Hands-on is touchy versus watchy. "I like the kind of *hands-on* experience when you can actually toss the computer out the window."

handshake *(hand-shayk)* 1. The exchange of signals between two networked computers, indicating that data transmission can safely take place. 2. An exchange of characters between two modems before they start talking. "I tried modeming a friend in Japan, but the customs were different there. Instead of his com-puter *handshaking* with mine, it just bowed."

hang up *(hang up)* 1. To discon-nect a modem. See *disconnect.* "It's only polite to officially *hang up* after you're done with a typical eight-hour Internet session." 2. What you do after waiting more than an hour on the phone for tech support.

hanging indent *(hang-ing in-dent)* When the first line of text starts at the left margin and the rest of the paragraph is indented. The oppo-site of a normal indent. A word processing thing that few people actually use but most obsess over. "This entire paragraph is formatted as a *hanging indent.*"

hard copy *(hard cop-ee)* Printed information. The product of a computer's printer. "Sure, our com-puter can store billions of names and addresses, but until I have a *hard copy* in my hands, the information is useless during a power outage."

hard disk *(hard disk)* A magnetically coated metal plate, hermetically sealed in a box and used to store massive amounts of information. Sometimes called a *fixed disk,* a *Winchester disk,* or a four-letter expletive if something goes wrong.

A hard disk all naked and exposed.

The hard disk lives in the hard drive, which can't be removed from the computer. See also *disk.* "Only real men use *hard disks.*"

hard drive *(hard driev)* 1. The device that contains the hard disk. 2. The name of Bill Gate's whimsical tome on the state of computers, a book he claims someday he'll eventually sit down and read for the first time.

hard drive controller *(hard driev kon-trol-er)* The device that controls the hard drive, often integrated with the hard drive unit itself but can also be part of the computer's motherboard.

hard wired *(hard wieyerd)* 1. A direct connection, with nothing that needs to be plugged in. For example, if you were a real geek, you could solder your computer directly into your household electrical lines. This would be very dangerous and not recommended, but then again you'd only do that if you were a geek. 2. Something permanently configured. For example, a circuit that normally could be changed through switches or software commands is wired so that it works only one way. "Forgive Harold; he's *hard wired* to be rude to new employees."

hardware *(hard-wayr)* The physical parts of a computer, printer, modem, monitor, and keyboard that you can touch. In comparison, software are programs that tell your hardware what to do next. See also *software.* "...*For Dummies* books are supposed to take the hard out of *hardware.*"

hashing *(hash-ing)* A programming method used to store information based on a mathematical calculation. If you plan on writing your own programs, you need to know that hashing can make a program store data quickly. If you just want to use a computer, you don't have to know a single thing about hashing. "Put those potatoes away, Darlene. *Hashing* is a programming term and has nothing to do with breakfast."

hat *(hat)* The name for the ^ character. See ^ , *caret.* "I remember the ^ as the hat character because on my keyboard the number 6 looks like an elf who was standing on a cliff that just gave way."

Hat character.

Hayes *(hayz)* A hardware company that made its fame manufacturing modems. They were spendy but not really any better than any other modem. "*Hayes* made the first modem for a microcomputer, the MicroModem for the Apple II."

H

Hayes compatibility *(hayz kom-pat-uh-bil-uh-tee)* The ability of a modem to mimic the operation of a Hayes brand modem. See also *modem.*

HD *(aych dee)* 1. Acronym for *High-Density.* High-density $5^1/_4$-inch floppy disks can hold up to 1.2MB of data. High-density $3^1/_2$-inch floppy disks can hold up to 1.44MB of data. When you buy a box of floppy disks, the high-density ones have HD printed somewhere on the box. See also *high-capacity.* 2. Acronym for *hard disk.* See *hard disk.*

head *(hed)* The part of the disk drive that reads or writes information to the spinning disk. For those of you old enough to remember what turntables are, heads are like the needles of a record player. The head is attached to the access arm. See *access arm.* "With a disk drive, the *head* is at the end of the arm, like some creature in a Wes Craven movie."

head crash *(hed krash)* When the heads of a disk drive fail to work properly, often literally crashing into the surface of the disk. Fortunately, this doesn't happen as often as it used to. "Yes, Louise, that was a *head crash* you heard. Normally computers don't make that much noise."

headache *(hed-ayk)* An intense pain in the skull caused by trying to use and understand personal computers. "After reading two pages in my Windows manual, I got a *headache* and now have a desire to kick something painted fawn white."

header *(hed-er)* Text, such as a page number, chapter title, or dirty message, which appears at the top of each page in a document. See also *footer.* "I created a *header* that says 'This end up' because my boss is really thick."

heavy iron *(heh-vee ie-ron)* Slang term for a mainframe computer or other type of computer that looks about the size of a small car. See also *boat anchor, mainframe.* "Our department refuses to use personal computers for anything. We're sticking with our *heavy iron* until we have the slightest idea how to use Windows."

help *(help)* 1. Information that's supposed to show you what to do next but usually just confuses you even more. Help can come in the form of printed manuals, on-screen information displayed in pop-up windows, or spoken words by well-meaning people. 2. When used with "the" as in "the help," it refers to the on-screen help that supposedly helps. Supposedly. "As long as the *help* in computer programs continues to be so lousy, I'll keep making a comfortable living writing computer books."

help system *(help sis-tim)* A common program used to display hints or additional information. Microsoft Windows offers a help system, which explains why commands for using help in all Windows programs look so similar. "Our office's *help system* is to ask Kim, our geek-in-residence."

H

Helvetica *(hell-vet-i-ka)* A common sans serif typeface (font) that looks clean and professional (to most of us, anyway). Windows and the Macintosh have Helvetica as a built-in font. See also *dingbats, font.* Named after *Helvetia,* a Roman province populated by people who made sundials and chocolate and are the ancestors of the modern-day Swiss. "Actually, *Helvetica* is one of the most boring typefaces in the universe."

Hercules Graphics card *(herk-yoo-leez graf-iks kard)* A third-party substitute for the common, boring IBM monochrome adapter. The Hercules Graphics card (or *adapter*) gave a monochrome monitor the capability to display a limited form of graphics but only in one color, usually green or orange. Nowadays, almost everyone uses VGA or Super VGA graphics cards, so Hercules Graphics cards are an interesting antique. See also *graphics, Super VGA, VGA.* "My first computer had a *Hercules Graphics card* because I thought it could better lift the heavy graphics load."

hertz *(hurts;* not capitalized) A unit of measurement for electrical vibrations, usually used in large quantities to measure the speed of a computer and abbreviated as *megahertz* (MHz). One hertz is equal to the number of cycles per second. So if you're standing on the street corner and three bicyclists pedal by in a second, you have three hertz. In China, they have billions of hertz. Named after Gustav Ludwig Hertz, a German Nobel Prize winner in 1925. See also *megahertz.* "When I arrived at the airport, I got a *Hertz* rental car and borrowed a laptop computer that runs at 16 *MHz.*"

heuristics *(hyoor-is-tiks)* A method for solving problems that don't have a clear-cut solution, such as playing chess, recognizing visual images, or cheating the IRS. Heuristics provides instructions that essentially tell the computer to guess as best it can and pray that the results come out right. "When

A type of heuristic computer.

Carl ran his new *heuristics* program for dealing with the IRS, the computer ran screaming down the hall."

hexadecimal *(heks-uh-des-uh-mol)* A number that uses base 16 as opposed to base 10 (decimal). Programmers often use hexadecimal numbers as a shortcut to represent binary numbers. See also *binary.* "*Hexadecimal* would come easy to us if we had eight fingers on each hand. We'd also be a lot faster at typing."

hidden files *(hid-en fiels)* Files that don't appear in a normal directory listing. Some programs create hidden files to keep users (or viruses) from copying them illegally or from erasing or altering them by mistake. Windows 95 hides certain system files that it doesn't want you to mess with, files that would be embarrassed if you saw them. See also *file attribute.* "I found those *hidden files!* They were hiding behind the FAT table."

hierarchical *(hiyer-ark-uh-kal)* A pecking order of one thing over another. The military is hierarchical,

H

with generals presiding over colonels who are over other folks, and lonely privates at the bottom do the work. Files are stored in disk using a hierarchical system. See the very next entry. "Angels are divided up into a *hierarchical* structure. The big guys, the archangels, are on top. They do the singing and praising and harp-playing and get all the cushy jobs. Down on the bottom, the lower angels do the dirt work, like spinning planets and dancing on the heads of pins."

hierarchical file system *(hiyer-ark-uh-kal fiel sis-tim)* Sometimes abbreviated as *HFS,* this is the feature on Macintosh computers that lets you store files in separate subdirectories called *folders.* The directory/subdirectory structure of DOS is analogous to this system. "After using MS-DOS for so long, I find the Macintosh's *hierarchical file system* much easier to use because all those cute little folder icons make computing fun again."

hierarchical menus *(hiyer-ark-uh-kal men-yoos)* A menu that displays more menus when you choose certain options. Any menu with a submenu. "*Hierarchical menus* sometimes make you feel like you're endlessly choosing menus, and by the time you find what you want, you forget why you wanted it in the first place."

high-capacity *(hie-ka-pa-suh-tee)* Another term for high-density floppy disks. See *HD.* "Don't buy double-density disks. Buy these *high-capacity* floppy disks instead because they hold more information."

high-density *(hie-dens-uh-tee)* See *HD.*

high-level language *(hie-lev-el lang-gwij)* A programming language that enables you to write commands that nearly resemble English. Some popular high-level languages include BASIC and Pascal. Assembly language is often called a *low-level language* because you have to know how the computer works before you can write an assembly language program. C is a mid-level language, having some of the crudeness of assembly language but a lot of the plain English words of BASIC or Pascal. "You can't write an assembly language program for Windows. Make it easy on yourself and use a *high-level language* such as Visual BASIC before your brain explodes."

high memory *(hie mem-oh-ree)* On IBM-compatible computers, the memory between 640K of conventional memory and 1MB, more commonly referred to as *Upper Memory.* Do not confuse *high memory* with the *HMA* (the *High Memory Area*), which is actually above the 1MB mark. This gap is reserved for running special system programs. To maximize the amount of conventional 640K memory for programs, memory-management programs move programs such as mouse or video drivers into high memory. See also *conventional memory, HMA, Upper Memory, UMB.* "My old computer had only 483K of memory for running programs. After I used a memory-management program to take advantage of my *high memory,* I had 520K of memory to use. But, you know, that's still really pitiful."

H

high resolution *(hie rez-oh-loo-shun)* An overused adjective that describes the capability of a monitor to display crisp text and graphic images that won't give you headaches to stare at all day. See also *low resolution*. "I bought a *high-resolution* monitor from the Himalayas."

high tech *(hie tek)* Overused adjective that tries to evoke images of the latest laboratory creations now available for your consumption and pleasure. "All this *high tech* stuff doesn't help if the power goes out."

history *(hiz-toh-ree)* 1. A list of previous commands typed at a prompt. 2. A program that allows you to fetch and reuse commands in the history, such as the DOS DOSKEY. 3. A list of previously visited places on the Internet. "You may be looking at www.cnn.com now, but by checking your *history* list I can see that you've spent a lot of time at Lola's Game Shop."

HMA *(aych em ay)* Acronym that stands for *High Memory Area,* the first 64K of extended memory beyond 1MB in MS-DOS computers. Yet another feeble attempt to reroute the limitations of conventional memory and DOS. Sad, sad, sad. "Programs that follow the extended memory specification (XMS) can use *HMA* as an extension of conventional 640K memory."

Hold key *(hohld kee)* A key on the keyboard that temporarily freezes output. Found on older Tandy keyboards. See *Pause Key.*

Home *(hohm)* A button or command that returns you to your home page on the World Wide Web. See *home page.* "When my wife tells me to come home, I must remember that she's not telling me to click my Web browser's *Home* button."

Home key *(hohm kee)* The key on the keyboard that usually moves the cursor to the beginning of a line or the top of a document, depending on the whims of the program at the time. The Home key usually has the word *Home* printed on it, which is probably the last straightforward guidance you'll get from computers. See also *End key.* "Press the *Home key* and then the left-arrow key to move the cursor to your house."

The Home key.

home monitor *(hohm mon-uh-ter)* The main display when using a computer with more than one monitor connected. The home monitor is the PC's first monitor, the one that displays system information, such as the desktop and taskbar.

home office *(hohm of-is)* A room in your house where you conduct business (and according to the IRS, it must be a separate room specifically designed for the purpose). People who work at home or who spend time away from the office working out of their houses have a home office. It usually has a few computers, a fax, a copy machine, and all the other stuff stocked at Office Depot.

H

"People who have a *home office* can go to work in their underwear, but downtown, we'd like you to wear something businesslike."

home page *(hohm payj)* 1. The initial World Wide Web document that you see when you first start your Web browser. This can be any page on the Web, though it's typically the page of your Internet service provider or the company who made your Web browser. 2. The Web page you see when you click the Home button. 3. Your own, personal page on the World Wide Web or the page your company put up. 4. The main page of a site, the first one someone sees when they type in a Web address. "On my *home page* you find interesting scientific information, references to various geological sites around the globe, my favorite Klingon sayings, and pictures of the kids."

horizontal scroll bar *(hor-uh-zon-tal skrohl bar)* A tall gizmo strip that appears on the right side of a window, used for moving the contents of a window up or down. At the very top and bottom of the scroll bar are arrows. Clicking these arrows scrolls the window contents up or down. Between these arrows is a scroll box. Moving the scroll box up or down also scrolls the window contents. See also *vertical scroll bar.* "John always plays with the *horizontal scroll bar,* pretending that it's an elevator shaft with an elevator full of panicked people, one of whom is a pregnant lady. I really think John has too much time on his hands."

host *(hohst)* 1. The computer that controls the network and stores the programs and data that the other computers on the network use. "If my computer is the *host,* does that make me the parasite?" 2. In telecommunications, a computer that you have dialed and are connected to. 3. The main program or piece of software you're using. 4. The person who offers the Twinkies.

Former host.

host computer *(hohst com-pyoo-ter)* 1. The computer you dial into when using a modem. 2. A general term that applies to any computer, so rather than saying "Bill's computer" or "the office computer," you can just use "the host." "The *host computer* is not required to serve you drinks or cocktail franks."

HotJava *(hot-jah-vah)* A Web browser produced by Sun Microsystems, who also developed the Java programming language for the World Wide Web. Typically used only on UNIX computers. "*HotJava* is one of those words you think is seriously important, but it just turns out to be a silly product name."

hot key *(hot kee)* 1. Any key or combination of keys that performs a special action in a program. For example, you could assign a hot key to the Windows Notepad and instantly activate that program any time you press the hot key combination. "Lois was afraid to use the *hot key*. She thought she'd burn her finger." 2. The keys used to activate memory-resident programs, back when they were popular in DOS. See also *memory-resident programs*.

hot link *(hot link)* 1. A sausage, fresh off the grill. 2. When two programs share data, and changing data in one program automatically changes the same data in another program. An example of a hot link is a word processor document with spreadsheet data. If you change the spreadsheet data by using a spreadsheet, the data automatically changes in the word processor document as well. Yet another amazing technological breakthrough inspired by humankind's inherent laziness. See also *DDE, OLE, link*. "*Hot links* really save time and ensure accuracy, and they can also taste good in the morning with eggs and coffee."

hot spot *(hot spot)* A hyperlink that is an area on the screen where you can click the mouse to make something happen instead of issuing the conventional command. Hot spots usually appear in multimedia programs such as those found in HyperCard or the Windows help system. "I think I found my computer's *hot spot*. When I click on it, I hear moaning sounds from the speaker."

Anhert discovers a hot spot.

hourglass icon *(ow-er-glas ie-kon)* A symbol of an hourglass that appears on the screen whenever the computer is busy doing something. The hourglass icon tells you to wait patiently, and the name alone (it's not a minuteglass!) means that you may have a longer wait than you expect. See also *beachball pointer*. "The President is waiting for the *hourglass icon* to go away before he addresses the nation about the nuclear emergency in the Middle East."

housekeeping *(hows-kee-ping)* Organizing files so that you can find them again. Backing up. Running disk utilities. That kind of stuff. "The nice thing about computer *housekeeping* is that you don't need to look like Alice on *The Brady Bunch* when you do it."

HPGL *(aych pee jee el)* Acronym for *Hewlett-Packard Graphics Language,* a way of representing or printing graphics on a plotter or laser printer. Files can also be stored in the HPGL format. Most often you see it as a compatibility issue; some printer claims that it's compatible with the HPGL used on the LaserJet IX. "I tried to print that *HPGL* file on my non-Hewlett-Packard printer, and it looked like the printer got sick and barfed."

HTML *(aych tee em el)* Acronym for *HyperText Markup Language,* which is a standard series of codes used to display text, graphics, and hypertext links through a World Wide Web page. HTML is *not* a programming language. It's just a series of codes, enclosed in angle brackets, that tell the Web browser how to display information. "Bob is so Web-crazy he writes all his proposals using *HTML*."

H

HTTP *(aych tee tee pee)*
1. Acronym for *HyperText Transfer Protocol,* the method by which a Web page is sent through the Internet. Also see *hypertext.* 2. The prefix that appears on most Web page addresses. Actually, in this case, HTTP is a command that tells the Web browser what type of information it's looking for — a Web page. It's followed by a colon and two slashes: `http://www.wambooli.com,` for example.

hue *(hyoo)* A tint or shade of a specific color. "You can always tell the people who work on that faulty computer monitor, because it leaks lots of radiation and turns people's faces various *hues* as the day wears on."

Huffman coding *(huf-man koh-ding)* A technique for compressing data so that it takes up less space. The data can be decompressed back to its original form. This is the basis upon which archiving programs, such as ZIP and StuffIt, operate, as well as how disk compression programs, like Microsoft's DriveSpace, works. Named after D. A. Huffman, who developed the technique in the early '50s. See *ZIP, StuffIt, DriveSpace.*

hung *(hung)* When your computer stops working for some unknown reason and smashing on the keyboard or kicking the computer doesn't have any effect. See also *crash.* "This computer gets *hung* so often it has rope burns around the base of the monitor."

HyperCard *(hie-per-kard)* A "software erector set" for the Macintosh, designed to let nonprogrammers create their own programs, which makes as much sense as General Motors selling tool kits with the promise that non-mechanics can make their own transmissions. Although revolutionary when first introduced, HyperCard inherited the worst of both worlds. HyperCard proved too difficult for most nonprogrammers to use, and the programs people finally did create with it didn't run as quickly as those created using traditional languages such as C or Pascal. HyperCard helped introduce the idea of hypertext and, just as quickly, its fading popularity helped drag hypertext back down to obscurity. "I shouldn't use *HyperCard* because I'm not in a hurry. Do they have a SedateCard program available?"

hypermedia *(hie-per-mee-dee-ya)* Sometimes called *hypertext* or *multimedia,* it's the combination of text, graphics, sound, and video to present information. See also *multimedia, hypertext.* "The computer industry is careful about putting more hype than media into *hypermedia.*"

 HyperTerminal Program *(hie-per-term-uh-nol proh-gram)* The communications program that comes with Windows 95. "No, you cannot use the *HyperTerminal Program* to talk with the Internet."

A tiny graphic of the HyperTerminal window.

hypertext *(hie-per-tekst)* The nonlinear display and retrieval of information. Unlike reading a book from front to back (linear), hypertext allows you to hop around to various places that interest you or to see additional information out-of-context. This is done by choosing a link in the hypertext document, which takes you to the additional information. Hypertext can consist of text, graphics, video, sound, and animation. The links on a Web page are all examples of hypertext in action. See *link.* "No, Yolanda, you don't have to be jumping up and down to write a document using *hypertext.*"

hyphenation *(hie-fin-ay-shun)* Dividing long words across two lines of text. This is done primarily to keep an even right margin. Most word processors and desktop publishing programs have a hyphenation option. "*Hyphenation* breaks up written words the way alcohol breaks up spoken ones."

Hz *(hertz)* Abbreviation for *hertz.* See *hertz.*

H

H

I: *(ie-koh-lon)* A letter designation for a disk drive in a PC. Could be any type of drive at this stage, most likely a network drive, but don't rule out a seventh hard drive in some nerd's PC.

I-beam cursor *(ie-beem kur-sor)* See *I-beam pointer.*

I-beam pointer *(ie-beem poyn-ter)* What you call the mouse pointer when the computer is waiting for you to type letters and numbers; it's shaped like an I-beam. Depending on the program you're using and the situation you're in, the cursor can change shape to a hand, an arrow, an hourglass, or a crosshair. Various religions have been popping up lately, worshipping each symbol as a special sign from the heavens above. See also *crosshairs, cursor, hourglass icon, pointer.* "Whenever you see the *I-beam pointer,* go ahead and start typing. Whenever you see an I-beam, duck."

I/O *(ie-oh)* Acronym for *Input/Output,* which is the interface of every computer that lets data move from one part to another. See also *input* and *output.* "So much garbage goes through the *I/O* that I'm surprised the EPA doesn't declare our computer a toxic waste dump."

i486 *(ie-for-ay-tee-siks)* Short for the Intel 80486DX microprocessor. See also *386, 486, microprocessor, Pentium.* "Actually, no one uses the *i486* moniker anymore."

IBM *(ie bee em)* Acronym for *International Business Machines,* sometimes called Big Blue. One of the largest computer companies around, IBM made a fortune leasing expensive mainframe computers to unsuspecting and captive customers. After setting the standard for personal computers, IBM promptly lost its lead through high prices and being less efficient than its competition. "I be big! I be powerful! I be the man! *IBM!*"

IBM AT *(ie bee em ay tee)* Introduced in 1984, the first IBM personal computer to use the 80286 microprocessor. The AT stands for *Advanced Technology.* "Showing how time can cure all naming problems, it's good to know that the old *IBM AT* — where AT stood for 'advanced technology' — is now technology that's over 13 years old. In the computer biz, that's ancient."

IBM PC *(ie bee em pee see)* The first IBM personal computer introduced in 1981. The PC stands for *Personal Computer.* Today, *PC* refers to any personal computer that's IBM-compatible. See also *clone*, *PC*. "Before the *IBM PC*, personal computers were called micro-computers."

The original IBM PC (seriously!).

IBM XT *(ie bee em eks tee)* The first IBM personal computer to have a built-in hard disk. The XT stands for *eXtended Technology*. See also *AT, hard disk, XT*. "Back in 1983, the *IBM XT*'s 10-megabyte hard disk was considered a massive amount of storage. Today, Microsoft's Excel spreadsheet alone consumes 27 megabytes of disk space."

IC *(ie see)* Acronym for *Integrated Circuit*, a computer chip.

icon *(ie-kon)* A symbol that looks like Egyptian hieroglyphics, often used in place of actual words. Many programs display icons as shortcuts to choosing commands through menus. Instead of choosing a menu command, you can just click the mouse on the icon, as long as you remember which icon represents which command. See also *crosshairs, cursor, hourglass icon, I-beam pointer, pointer*. "It took humanity thousands of years to advance from pictographs to phonetically written communication. It took the Apple computer only six years and dozens of *icons* to move us in the other direction."

IDE *(ie dee ee)* 1. Acronym for *Integrated Drive Electronics* (or *Intelligent Device Electronics*), which is a type of interface for controlling disk drives. Along with SCSI, this is the most popular type of interface for a PC's hard drive as well as for its CD-ROM drive. See also *SCSI*. "*IDE* drives vie with SCSI drives for king of the PC disk drive controller kingdom."
2. Acronym for *Integrated Development Environment*, which relates to programs that share a common user interface.

IDG *(ie-dee-jee)* Acronym for *International Data Group*. The parent company of IDG Books, who publishes this dictionary.

idiot-proof *(id-ee-ut proof)* To design something so that it can always be operated successfully; that is, the common "idiot" would be unable to foul it up. "If we *idiot-proofed* the computer industry, none of the executives would be able to get into the building."

idle *(ie-dul)* When a computer or user sits around doing nothing. See also *screen saver*. "In our office, we have four computers (all of which are *idle*) and three people (who are mostly *idle*, too). Someone should at least use the computers to play video games."

IEEE *(ie-trip-ol-ee)* Acronym for *Institute of Electrical and Electronic Engineers*, yet another organization dedicating its life to peace, freedom, and defining standards in the electronics industry. "I went to an *IEEE* conference

Typical IEEE member.

last fall where they defined the standard for networks. Of course, it's one thing to define a standard and an entirely different thing to get people to follow it."

IF *(if)* A decision-making keyword used in programming languages. Often used with the word THEN, the IF keyword tests some operation, and the computer does one thing or another based on the result. In the BASIC programming language, an IF statement might look like this:

```
IF X = 5 THEN PRINT "The value of
X is five."
```

See also *keyword.* "*IF* programmer not leave chair, then she will grow large rear."

illegal *(il-ee-gal)* Not really against the law, merely not permitted. Computer programmers write error messages with the word *illegal* in them just to be nasty. All it really means is that you tried to do something that wasn't allowed. "The error message said `illegal character in file name`, so I called the FBI."

 images *(im-uh-jes)* Graphics, such as those found on a Web page. A Web browser usually offers an option that prevents the images from being loaded, which displays the Web page's text information much faster. "I often judge how much I like a Web page by how they do or overdo their *images.*"

 IMHO *(in-mie-hum-bol-oh-pin-yon)* Acronym for *In My Humble Opinion.* Used in e-mail.

 IMNSHO *(in-mie-not-soh-hum-bol-oh-pin-yon)* Acronym for *In My Not So Humble Opinion.* Again, used in e-mail, but most likely by someone who has a really big head.

 IMO *(in-mie-oh-pin-yon)* Acronym for *In My Opinion,* yet another way to save valuable typing-energy molecules when composing e-mail or writing to a newsgroup.

impact printers *(im-pakt prin-ters)* Any type of printer that makes an image by slapping something down on a ribbon. This includes daisy wheel printers, dot matrix printers, and just about any other printer that makes a heck of a lot of racket. See *dot matrix.*

import *(im-port)* To bring a file created by another program into a document. For example, to bring a graphics document into a word processing document. There is no duty or tax on anything you import into your document.

inclusive OR *(in-kloo-siev or)* A logical operator used to manipulate individual bits of data, often used for creating graphics. The result of an inclusive OR is always 1 (which represents true) unless both operands are 0 (false). If you have no idea what this means, you probably don't need to use inclusive OR in your everyday life. See also *XOR.*

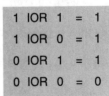

Inclusive OR

1 IOR 1	=	1
1 IOR 0	=	1
0 IOR 1	=	1
0 IOR 0	=	0

Inclusive OR operations.

incremental backup *(in-kruh-men-tal bak-up)* The process of copying files that have been newly created or modified since the time of the last full backup. See also *backup.* "Our tape backup system is so slow we can't help but do an *incremental backup.*"

incremental compiler *(in-kruh-men-tal kom-pie-ler)* A special program that converts programming language statements into machine code each time the programmer types a complete line. Incremental compilers work without interfering with your work. That way, when you get done typing your final line, the program seems to compile almost instantly. In comparison, most compilers wait for you to type an entire program before they even start compiling, which makes you wait a long time until the program finishes compiling. Unless you're a programmer, you can safely ignore this definition. See also *compile, compiler, interpreter.* "I like programming with an *incremental compiler* because I don't like waiting for my program to compile. Of course, the drawback is that on a slow computer, the incremental compiler may get in your way while you're writing your program."

indentation *(in-den-tay-shin)* The alignment of paragraphs within the margins of a page. Usually, the first line of every paragraph is indented several spaces to make the text easier to read, whether or not the text is worth reading in the first place. See also *word processor.* "Use the Tab key for *indentation.* If you use the space bar, it's harder to adjust the indentation later, and it's more time-consuming, too."

index *(in-deks)* In many word processors or desktop publishing programs, a feature that creates a list of important words, phrases, or ideas in alphabetical order, along with the page numbers where those items appear. This feature creates the index after key terms and phrases are first marked manually. "Any good desktop publishing application has an *index* feature, which is especially important if you're laying out a computer book. Because computer books can be as dry as dust, indexes make them useful."

indexed file *(in-deksd fiel)* A separate file containing information about the physical location of records stored in a database file. Instead of searching the actual database file, database programs use indexes to run faster. This works as long as the index is accurate, and we all know what the chances of that are. "Keep your *indexed files* up to date so that your database program can run faster. An inaccurate *indexed file* may confuse your database and keep it from working. (So what else is new?)"

inference engine *(in-fur-ens en-jin)* The part of an expert system that calculates results based on stored facts and information supplied by the user. An expert system consists of three parts: the user interface, the knowledge base, and the inference engine. See also *expert system, interface, knowledge base.* "The so-called intelligence of an expert system resides almost solely in the accurate reasoning of its *inference engine.*"

1

infinite loop *(in-fin-it loop)* When a computer keeps running the same instructions over and over again without stopping. To better understand the sense of futility that an infinite loop can create, think of driving in circles, trying to find a parking space in a major shopping mall the day before Christmas. See also *endless loop, loop.* "This is my example of an *infinite loop.* This is my example of an *infinite loop.* This is my example of an *infinite loop.* This is my example of an *infinite loop.* This is my example of an *infinite loop.*"

Information Superhighway *(in-for-may-shun soo-per-hie-way)* 1. Another term for the Internet, one that began as a buzzword in government circles. 2. What the Internet could become if everything worked out hunky-dory. Or the nightmare scenario of what the Internet could become should the government ever try to regulate the thing. "I'm stuck in traffic on the *Information Superhighway.*"

infotainment *(in-foh-tayn-ment)* A hybrid of information and entertainment. Yet another attempt to teach us something without boring us to a catatonic state. See *catatonic.* "If they can get away with calling this stuff *infotainment,* I can get away with calling it *borsilly.*"

inheritance *(in-hayr-uh-tans)* Used in object-oriented programming languages when one object copies the features of another object (where an *object* refers to a block of code with a specialized task). Programmers like the idea of inheritance because it

keeps them from typing the same lines of code over and over again. "Using C++, I created an object to display a window. Bob's object *inherited* my object's features and added the ability to display a message in the window. Now I'm suing Bob for custody."

initialize *(in-e-shal-iez)* To prepare a piece of equipment (computer, printer, modem, and so on) to do something important. Initializing clears the equipment of any old data still stored in it. "Part of Randy's early morning *initialize* procedure is to gargle for ten minutes."

inkjet printer *(ink-jet prin-ter)* A type of printer that sprays ink on paper instead of smacking an inked ribbon against the page, like an impact printer does. Inkjet printers are quieter than impact printers, producing better quality printing as well (but not as good as laser printers). See also *dot matrix, laser printer, printer.* "Take off those ear muffs, Larry, an *inkjet printer* is very quiet."

InPort *(in-port)* A special hole into which a computer mouse is plugged. "Popeye doesn't need to buy two mice; his *InPort* mouse works just as well when he's at sea."

input *(in-put)* Information fed into the computer for processing. Computers can receive input from a variety of sources, including the keyboard, mouse, modem, touch screen, or mad scientists bent on the destruction of the entire human race as we know it. See also *I/O, output.* "Give that poor computer some *input* so that it has something to do, such as print mailing labels. I hate to see a computer sitting idle."

input box *(in-put boks)* See *text box.*

input/output *(in-put owt-put)* See *I/O.*

Insert key *(in-surt kee)* The key on the keyboard that has the word *Insert* or *Ins* printed on it. The Insert key is often used to switch between insert and overwrite modes in a word processor, though not in Microsoft Word 97. "If everything you type starts erasing all your existing information, you're probably in overwrite mode. You turn it off by pressing the *Insert key.*"

Insert key. Well, one of them anyway.

insert mode *(in-surt mowd)* An editing mode where all new text you type pushes any existing text to the right; the old text is not overwritten by the new. Most word processors use insert mode unless you tell them otherwise. See also *overtype.* "Just before the doctor gives me a shot, I go into *insert mode.*"

insertion pointer *(in-sir-shun poyn-ter)* A blinking vertical cursor, as opposed to a flashing block or underline. Used in graphical word processors to show you where newly typed text will appear on the screen. "*Insertion pointer* is just a fancy term for the cursor. You'd think people from the Pentagon were naming computer parts."

install *(in-stal)* 1. To prepare equipment or software for use for the first time. 2. The program that actually does the installation process, though under Windows 95 the name is gradually changing to *setup.* See *setup.* "Wow! Just 18 more floppy disks, and I'll have WordPerfect *installed* and can get ready to start using this PC to save me time."

instruction *(in-struk-shun)* 1. A command or direction given to the computer, usually in a programming language, though it could also be a command given at a prompt. 2. Individual parts of a programming language. See also *code.* "If you ever decide to lose your mind, try writing an entire program with assembly language. Just to multiply two numbers, you have to write a page full of *instructions.*"

integer *(int-uh-jer)* A whole number, which is any positive or negative number without fractions or decimals. "Your age can be a fractional number, but the number of people in this room is an *integer.* Unless, of course, you chop somebody in half."

Typical integer.

integrated software *(in-teh-gray-ted soft-wayr)* A collection of programs designed to work well with each other, sharing common files and working as happily as the folks in old communist propaganda films. Most integrated software includes a word processor, spreadsheet, database, and communications program rolled into one. "This may be *integrated software,* but I don't think any of the programs truly love each other as brothers."

Intel *(in-tel)* A company that manufactures microprocessors, specifically the 80x86 chips found in the bosom of all IBM-compatible PCs. "Will robots of the future proudly wear little buttons that boast '*Intel* Inside'?"

intelligent agents *(in-tel-uh-jent ay-jents)* A smart program that goes out and does something for you automatically, often making decisions along the way. For example, a program that visits the Internet, prints the news for you, grabs your stock quotes, and answers some of your e-mail. It could also be any program that carries out specific tasks and responds to certain conditions automatically. "My *intelligent agent* is named Maxwell, and boy, is he smart."

IntelliMouse *(in-tel-uh-mows)* Microsoft's fancy new mouse with a wheel between the two buttons. The wheel can be turned to scroll a document, or it can be pressed to activate a number of interesting features, depending on the application. Of course, not every program supports the wheel mouse. But for some strange reason, most of Microsoft's applications do. Weird. See also *wheel mouse.* "I suppose the *IntelliMouse* uses its wheel to get the cheese faster."

interactive *(in-ter-ak-tiv)* A program or computer that responds immediately whenever the user presses a key or does something else that the computer should respond to. Using interactive software is similar to carrying on a conversation; the user's responses change the way the system functions.

In comparison, noninteractive computers tend to just sit there and do something only when they feel like it. "I liked learning BASIC because every time I typed a command, the computer immediately told me I did something wrong. With such an *interactive* system, it was only a matter of time before I got discouraged from using the computer altogether."

interface *(in-ter-fays)* The connection between the computer and the person trying to use it. A keyboard is an interface and so is a monitor. Putting your fist through the computer can also be considered an interface. See also *graphical user interface, user-friendly, user-hostile.* "Most computer *interfaces* are designed by someone who really hates humanity."

Intergalactic Digital Research *(in-ter-ga-lak-tik dij-uh-tal ree-surch)* The original name of a company that came to be known as Digital Research. For some reason, they didn't think enough people would take them seriously with that name. See *Digital Research.*

interlacing *(in-ter-lay-sing)* When the cathode-ray tube (CRT) of a monitor scans every other row to display information on the screen. This allows the image to be drawn quickly but the overall image tends to flicker. TVs use interlacing, but the best computer monitors are noninterlacing. See also *monitor, eyeball frazzle.* "My eyes are going to explode from my head if I keep using this lousy *interlacing* monitor."

1

interleaving *(in-ter-lee-ving)* The ratio of sectors on a hard disk that are skipped for every sector actually read or written to. This was done because the hard drive would spin faster than the controller could read information from the disk. Today's hard drives are interleaved at a 1:1 ratio, meaning they can read and write information as fast as the disk can spin.

internal modem *(in-ter-nul moh-dum)* A modem that lives inside a computer, often plugged into its own expansion slot. Internal modems are cheaper than their external brothers and come with fewer cables. They're also more of a pain in the rear to install. See also *external modem.* "Sorry, I can't tell you about our *internal modem* problems."

IBM PC with an internal modem.

internal speaker *(in-ter-nul spee-ker)* The speaker built into every PC, as opposed to external speakers, which usually come separately. "The *internal speaker* is okay for the occasional *bleep,* but you need honkin' external speakers if you want to rock the house while playing *Descen.*"

Internet *(in-ter-net)* A collection of computers all over the world that send, receive, and store information. The Internet is not a single computer. It is not a software program. It's merely a lot of computers communicating with each other.

Access to the Internet is provided through a number of sources: universities, government installations, the military, large companies, and individuals through Internet service providers. After you get on the Internet, special software is used to access other computers and the information on them. The most popular software is the Web browser. The Internet can also be used to send electronic messages. See *Internet service provider, Web browser, World Wide Web, e-mail, network.* "You just aren't anyone until you're someone on the *Internet.*"

Internet address *(in-ter-net ad-res)* The electronic location of someone or some computer on the Internet. Internet addresses vary, depending on what's being looked for. See *e-mail, domain, Web page.* "Having an *Internet address* on your business card is a high status symbol for the '90s."

Internet Explorer *(in-ter-net eks-plor-er)* The Web browser software produced by Microsoft and given away (free) with Windows 95. Constantly trying to upstage the more popular Netscape Navigator (which acts like a skin-irritant on Bill Gates's pasty Seattle complexion), Internet Explorer generally has more features and comes across as more annoying on the World Wide Web. Preferred by many who really should know better. See *Web browser, Netscape Navigator.*

Internet provider *(in-ter-net proh-vie-der)* See *Internet service provider.*

1

Internet Relay Chat *(in-ter-net ree-lay chat)* See *IRC.*

Internet service provider *(in-ter-net sir-vis proh-vie-der)* A commercial organization that provides dial-up access to the Internet, like a cable company for computer users who want to get on the Internet. Often called *ISPs,* an Internet service provider is already connected to the Internet. They provide you with an access code and phone number, which you use to get on the Internet. Additionally, they should offer e-mail accounts, help on getting started, classes, and other items for which "service" often loses its meaning. "My *Internet service provider* is so nice they even come over and scratch my feet while I'm waiting for a Web page to load."

Internet software *(in-ter-net soft-wayr)* Programs used to access the Internet and use various Internet things. Examples include e-mail software, a Web browser, a newsgroup reader, an FTP program, Telnet, and so on. "Though the Internet is not a program, you do need *Internet software* to access the information."

InterNIC *(in-ter-nik)* Amalgam of *Internet Network Information Center,* the people more or less "in charge" of the Internet. Currently they assign Internet addresses and keep most of the mess organized. Sponsored by the National Science Foundation and AT&T. Eventually other companies are slated to join InterNIC and assign addresses to various things on the Internet.

"*InterNIC* is the place that tells you that Web site names like `www.mcdonalds.com` and `www.ibm.com` are already taken. Please try again."

interpreted language *(in-ter-pruh-ted lan-gwij)* A programming language where the computer reads the program statements one at a time and then follows the instructions. Common interpreted languages are BASIC, LISP, Prolog, and LOGO; although C and Pascal also can be interpreted. This contrasts with *compiled languages,* which are written and then translated into computer code in two steps. See also *compile, compiler, interpreter, language.* "*Interpreted languages* run more slowly than compiled languages because the computer has to read each statement, follow its instruction, and then read the next statement. This is like trying to read a French novel by reading a sentence to a translator, waiting for him to tell you what it means in English, and then reading another sentence."

interpreter *(in-ter-pruh-ter)* A program that reads statements written in a programming language, such as BASIC, and immediately follows the instructions. An interpreter is usually easier for learning a language because it gives you immediate feedback. The disadvantage is that other people can't use your programs unless they also have a copy of your program's interpreter. "To help her understand DOS, Doris hired an *interpreter.*"

interrupt *(in-ter-upt)* 1. An operation that rudely butts in, stops the computer from whatever it's doing, and

1

makes it do something completely different. For example, the *serial port interrupt* stops the computer whenever a character appears at the serial port, deals with the character, and then lets the computer continue with its business. "Excuse me, I'm an *interrupt,* and I'm here to stop everything until you deal with me."
2. A software instruction that directs the computer to go visit some remote corner of a program to do something and then come right back. 3. A communications line between some device and the microprocessor. See *IRQ.*

intranet *(in-trah-net)* A mini version of the Internet inside a local area network. An intranet can be set up with servers and use the same software and protocols as the Internet, but it serves only a single office or organization. Yet another attempt by some companies to capitalize on the Internet craze. "*Intranet* is truly one of the great buzzwords of the mid-90s."

invalid *(in-val-id)* Ugly word used by many programs to mean something is incorrect or unexpected. "The notion that the IRS owes you money is *invalid.*"

inverse text *(in-vers tekst)* Letters that appear white against a dark background or that appear with the foreground and background colors reversed. For example:

This section reserved for dead smokers only

I/O *(ie oh)* Acronym for *input-output,* the basic operation that makes a computer work. "Old MacDonald had a computer. IEEE I/O!"

IP *(ie pee)* Acronym for *Internet Protocol,* the method for sending information around on the Internet.

IP Address *(eye pee ad-res)* A number corresponding to the exact location of some computer somewhere on the Internet. Normally you don't have to type these suckers in; you type in the cryptic Internet address instead; see *Internet address.* "George wanted to know my *IP Address,* and I had to explain to him that I could only do that when there was snow outside."

IRC *(ie ar see)* Acronym for *Internet Relay Chat,* the way people on the Internet can gather and type at each other. Most people just call it *chat.* See *chat.*

IRQ *(ie ar kyoo)* An *interrupt request* line in a PC, a direct connection between some bit of hardware and the microprocessor. A communications line. The IRQ is used by hardware devices to let the microprocessor know when they're ready to do something or have done something. Normally you shouldn't clutter your head with such a bizarre term. However, a PC has only a given number of IRQs. The IRQs get snatched up by optional hardware devices quickly, so after adding a network adapter sound card and a mouse, your computer runs out of IRQs and, though you may have expansion slots galore, you can't add anything new. "A Pentium computer may be powerful, speedy, and advanced, but it's still limited by the same inane *IRQ* problems as the old IBM PC AT."

ISA *(ie-suh)* Acronym for *Industry Standard Architecture,* which is the type of bus (expansion slots) originally used in the IBM AT. These still appear in modern PCs, despite the attempts of other standards to take its place. See *EISA, MCA*. See also *PCI*. "The computer industry knows *ISA* is an old standard, but trying to kill it is like trying to kill a roach."

ISAM *(ie-sam)* Acronym for *Indexed Sequential Access Method,* which is a technique for storing and retrieving data efficiently using "tables" and "indexes." ISAM is often used by database programs. "*ISAM,* Sam I am. And I still don't like the darn green eggs and ham!"

ISDN *(ie es dee en)* Acronym for *Integrated Services Digital Network,* a very fast telecommunications line that was supposed to be the future of telephone and modem communications. ISDN is digital, as opposed to the analog phone system. And, as we all know, digital just must be better. However, ISDN was slow to be implemented and is now being surpassed by other standards. See *ADSL, POTS*. "Many people thought that having an *ISDN* connection in their house was their ticket to fast communications. Alas, they also needed a pricey *ISDN* modem to make that happen."

ISO *(ie es oh)* Acronym for *International Standards Organization,* which is a group that tries to set standards for lots of different industries. "With the way the computer industry ignores standards, *ISO* probably means Ignored Standard Optional." 2. The standard for the Pascal language, often called ISO Pascal. Unfortunately, the most popular version of Pascal, Turbo Pascal, ignores the ISO standard altogether. So much for standards. See also *Pascal*.

ISP *(ie es pee)* Acronym for *Internet Service Provider*. See *Internet service provider*.

italic *(ie-tal-ik)* A typestyle that slants text to the right for special emphasis, like the leaning tower of Pisa in Italy. See also *font, text, typeface*. "Please use *italics* and not underline. Underline text is what they use at the DMV when they want to get creative."

The italic tower.

iteration *(it-ur-ay-shun)* The repetition of a statement in a program, often called a *loop,* or, if something goes terribly wrong, an *endless loop*. See also *endless loop, infinite loop, loop*. 2. The number of times something has repeated. "The program is now in its 400th iteration of saying 'disk not found.'"

1

1

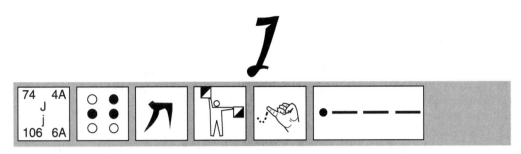

J: *(jay-koh-lon)* The letter designation for what is most likely a network drive in your computer.

jack *(jak)* A place to plug in electrical wires. One of those holes in the back of your PC into which you plug a cable. "Our feminist staff refuses to plug anything into the computer unless we call some of the holes *Jack* and some of them Jill."

Types of jacks.

jacket *(jak-et)* The plastic, square case that protects a floppy disk from dirt, fingerprints, and other forms of physical damage short of gunshots, fire, or hydrochloric acid. "Hold a floppy disk by the *jacket*. If you touch the actual floppy disk surface, you may ruin the disk (and possibly go to jail)."

jaggies *(jag-eez)* A far more descriptive word for aliasing. The jaggies are the stair-step effect that takes place when a computer tries to draw circles and arcs. See *aliasing*. "If you make the letter *O* too big, you notice little *jaggies* all around the edges."

Java *(jah-vah)* 1. A programming language developed by Sun Microsystems. Java programs can run on any computer connected to the Internet, which makes it a very useful language. "Knowing how to program in *Java* doesn't make you a better employee at Starbucks." 2. The latest in a series of Internet buzzwords, one that also spawned a whole series of coffee-theme products.

JavaScript *(jah-vah skript)* Another type of Internet programming language, similar to Java but much easier to learn.

job *(jawb)* A task that the computer is supposed to do whenever it gets around to doing it. See also *queue*. "This computer's running so slowly because it has so many *jobs* backed up in the queue. Let's fire a few and start the whole thing over again."

join *(joyn)* A term used when a relational database cross-references two files. See *relational database*. "Instead of typing the same information over and over again, just store it in separate files and *join* them when you need them. If that doesn't work, then type the same information over and over again."

Joshua *(jah-shoo-ah)* 1. The password used by the teenage hacker in the film *WarGames.* See *WarGames.* 2. For a time, the most popular computer password in existence. Every kid with a modem would use *Joshua* as his password after seeing *WarGames.*

joystick *(joy-stik)* A peripheral with a tiny wand that can move in several directions. Moving the wand moves a something-or-other around the screen. Joysticks are often used with games. Some joysticks can get horribly complex, with

Antique joystick.

buttons and switches and knobs for destroying a variety of alien craft. "When you buy a flight simulator program, you have to buy a *joystick* so that it feels like you're really flying the airplane. After all, how many pilots fly an F-16 using a keyboard?"

joystick port *(joy-stik port)* The hole (nay, *jack*) in the back of the computer where you plug in the joystick.

JPEG *(jay-peg)* Acronym for *Joint Photographic Experts Group,* a universal graphic standard designed to replace the old GIF graphic standard. Although GIF files can contain up to 256 colors, JPEG files can display up to 16 million colors in a single graphic image. For storing digitized photographs, the JPEG standard offers sharper resolution, but the older GIF standard works better for plain line drawings or clip art. JPEG files usually have the .JPG file extension in DOS and Windows. "The more Milton collects *JPEG* art from the Internet, the less we see of him."

 Jughead *(jug-hed)* 1. One with such prominent ears that his head resembles the outline of a jug. 2. A software tool used to search various Gopher servers from only one area of gopherspace — for example, looking for stuff only at the local university. Jughead came about just as the World Wide Web was gaining popularity and quickly replacing Gopher. See *Gopher.* "My mom told me to get my nose out of comic books and learn the computer. Now I'm surfing the Net and using Archie, Veronica, and *Jughead.*"

Julian *(joo-lee-an)* A dating system used to simplifying dates in a computer. In the Julian system, every day has a unique number. Day 1 represents January 1, 4713 B.C. Day 2,448,299 represents February 11, 1991. Programmers often use the Julian system for representing dates because it's easy for computers to handle. If you try guessing the date 100 days from January 23, 1964, you see how clumsy the ordinary calendar system can be. "My son was born on February 11, 1991, or 2,448,299 if you use the *Julian* system."

julienne *(joo-lee-en)* Meat or vegetables cut into long, thin strips. "My spreadsheet has a function that converts reports into *julienne* fries."

jump *(jump)* 1. A programming instruction that causes execution to skip to another location — literally to "jump" over a chunk of code. See also *GOTO.* "Assembly language programmers seem to *jump* a lot." 2. What you do when someone drops an ice cube down your shorts.

1

jumper *(jump-er)* A small, plastic, rectangular-shaped plug used on circuit boards to open or close certain circuits. Usually, a two- or three-prong pin sticks out of the circuit board, and the jumper slides over these pins. "No, Virgil, I need the little kind of electronic *jumper,* not those cables you bought at NAPA."

junk *(junk)* The stuff that seems to pop up magically around every computer. "They don't need to sell you extra *junk* when you buy a computer. Somehow, it finds you automatically."

justify *(just-uh-fie)* To align text within the margins of a page, either left, right, center, or justified. Many people call alignment *justification.*

This is text using left alignment.	This is text using center alignment.	This is text using right alignment.

"It's hard to *justify* the use of right justification in any document because it looks so strange. In most documents, you left-*justify* text and center-align headlines."

1

K

K *(kay)* Acronym for *kilobyte*. See *kilobyte*. "Robbie was disappointed to find out his computer didn't come with any memory. When he read 0K, he thought it meant the computer was okay."

K: *(kay-koh-lon)* A letter designation for what could possibly be the ninth hard drive in a PC, but most likely it's a network drive.

K6 *(kay-siks)* Designation for a Pentium-compatible microprocessor developed by AMD *(Advanced Micro Devices)*. See *Pentium*.

Kb *(kil-uh-bit)* Acronym for *kilobit,* or 1,024 bits — not bytes. This is primarily used on computer memory chips. "For some reason, you need eight 256Kb chips to get 256K of RAM."

KB *(kil-uh-biet)* Acronym for *kilobyte*. See *kilobyte*.

K&R *(kay and ar)* 1. Abbreviation for *Brian Kernighan and Dennis Ritchie,* but it really refers to the book they wrote called *The C Programming Language*. For the longest time, this book was the only specification for the C language, the only real reference anyone had. "I just couldn't write a C program without my *K&R* handy." 2. A C compiler that follows the standard set forth in Kernighan and Ritchie's book. See *bible*.

Kermit *(ker-mit)* A method (protocol) for transferring files that was named after Miss Piggy's boyfriend, Kermit the Frog. Kermit is slower than XMODEM but is often used when transferring files from mainframes because no other protocol may be available. See also *XMODEM* and *protocol*. "Yes, *Kermit* the Protocol is named after Kermit the Frog."

kernel *(ker-nel)* A term used by programmers to describe the main or core part of a program. "This is a chicken operating system. Its *kernel* must be named Sanders."

kerning *(kurn-ing)* To adjust the spacing between letters so that they look nice together. Certain letters look better closer together than others, such as putting *T* and *y* together so that the upper part of the *T* hangs slightly over the *y*. Kerning is used most often in word processors and desktop publishing programs when exact spacing of letters is important or when the boss just wants to give people something tedious to worry about. "Jacob used too much kerning to tighten up his paragraph, and the word *of* became *fo*."

key *(kee)* 1. The buttons on the keyboard. 2. A password needed to decrypt or encrypt a file. 3. The item used for searching and sorting a

K

database. If you're searching for all the names and addresses of everyone who lives in California, *California (CA)* is the key. 4. The guy who wrote the *Star Spangled Banner*. "I've looked all over my keyboard, and I still can't find the Francis Scott *Key*."

Key Caps *(kee kaps)* A Macintosh program that shows you the characters you can produce by typing different keystroke combinations. The Key Caps program appears in the Apple menu and displays the keyboard along with any characters you type. "Mary was disappointed that the *Key Caps* program didn't have the little fez she wanted for the Enter key."

keyboard *(kee-bord)* The set of buttons you use to communicate with a computer. When you press a key, the keyboard sends a signal to the

Keyboard.

computer, which does something interesting, such as displaying a character on the screen. "Too many computer *keyboards* feel like a cheap toy typewriter. Others feel so mushy that it seems like you're typing on a spoiled banana."

keyboard buffer *(kee-bord buf-er)* An area of memory set aside to hold a specified number of keystrokes in case you type faster than the computer can keep up with. After you stop typing, the keyboard buffer feeds the computer the remaining keystrokes stored in the buffer. See also *buffer*. "With a big *keyboard buffer*, I can keep typing until my fingers tie themselves in knots."

keyboard cover *(kee-bord kuh-ver)* A clear, flexible, plastic sheet that fits over a keyboard, allowing you to type while protecting the keyboard from liquid spills, cookie crumbs, dirt particles, or crawling insects. "Nothing paralyzes your computer keyboard with fear like the sight of a 5-year-old's hand, gloopy with peanut butter. Better buy your computer a *keyboard cover* to keep it sane."

keyboard shortcut *(kee-bord short-kut)* A single key or combination of keys that activates a command. Specifically refers to the shortcut shown in a menu, such as Ctrl+F by the File command; Ctrl+F is the keyboard shortcut. "I tried to take a *keyboard shortcut* from the Enter key to the Tab key, but I stepped on my colon."

keypad *(kee-pad)* A related group of keys placed together for convenience. The most common keypads are the numeric keypad and the cursor keypad. "Ever wonder why the keys on the numeric *keypad* are arranged in neat rows and columns but the keys on the typewriter part of the keyboard are arranged like they still use mechanical levers on a manual typewriter?"

keyword *(kee-werd)* 1. The main set of commands and functions in a programming language. For example, CALL is a BASIC keyword, CASE is a Pascal keyword, and `int` is a C keyword. "*Keywords* have special meaning in programming languages, just as certain four-letter words have special meaning in the English language." 2. Text to be found by a Search or Find command in a word processor or other program.

kHz *(kil-uh-hurtz)* Abbreviation for *kilohertz.* The word *kilo* means 1,000 of something. So *kilohertz* must mean 1,000 hertz. And *hertz* is a term for the number of cycles per second, so a *kilohertz* is the number of thousands of cycles per second. This must have something to do with computers, somewhere. "The human brain operates at about 1 *kHz,* compared with hundreds of MHz for a typical microprocessor. But don't feel inferior; your brain can do billions of operations in each cycle, whereas a typical microprocessor does only six."

kill *(kil)* 1. To delete a file. "Emily refuses to *kill* her files. She prefers to let them pass on naturally." 2. The command that deleted the file. 3. A UNIX command that stops a process, like quitting a program.

kilo- *(kee-lo)* A prefix used in the metric system that means 1,000. So *kilobyte* means 1,000 bytes, *kilogram* means 1,000 grams, and *kiloliter* means 1,000 liters. But just to confuse matters: Due to the binary (and onerous) nature of computers, when talking about memory, 1K actually refers to 1,024 bytes. "I like measuring my weight in *kilo*grams because it makes me seem lighter than I really am."

kilobyte *(kil-uh-biet)* One thousand bytes, abbreviated K or KB. Actually, it's 1,024 bytes. Kilobyte is used as a measure of the storage capacity of disks and memory. Because one byte equals one character, 1K of memory stores 1,024 characters. That's about as much text as you'll find on a double-spaced, typewritten page. See also *MB.* "In the old days, having 16 *kilobytes* of memory was a big deal. Today you need 16K just to hold an e-mail message from your friend Joe in Utah."

kludge *(kloo-j; does not rhyme with sludge)* 1. A temporary but poorly designed solution that actually works and solves a problem. "That's the ugliest chunk of code I've ever seen but, by-golly, the *kludge* works!" 2. A clunky hardware solution.

knowledge base *(naw-ledj bays)* The part of an expert system that stores facts about solving a particular problem. Most knowledge bases consist of IF-THEN rules for reaching an answer. A well-designed expert system should let you change knowledge bases whenever you need to solve a different type of problem. See *expert system.* "For an expert system to be trustworthy, its *knowledge base* must be current and accurate. Flossing twice a day also helps."

Krell *(krel)* An advanced race of beings on the planet Altair IV. They developed a huge machine that would translate their thoughts directly into objects; creation by mere thought. This, like most computer science experiments, failed miserably.

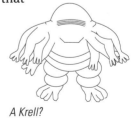
A Krell?

The Krell were destroyed by their own nightmares in a single night. This was discovered by Lt. Frank Drebin and Oscar from *The Six Million Dollar Man* when they visited Altair IV in the movie *Forbidden Planet* (1956).

K

L

L: *(el-koh-lon)* A network drive out there somewhere on a PC. "If you have an *L:* in your system, odds are really good that it's a network drive."

label *(lay-bohl)* 1. An identifying name. 2. The name given to one or more cells in a spreadsheet. "In my Lotus 1-2-3 spreadsheet, I put *labels* such as TAXES OWED, MONEY STOLEN, and COST OF OVERSEAS AIRLINE TICKET to identify the meaning of the numbers listed underneath." 3. A specific spot in a program, often used by some other instruction to send program execution to that spot. See *GOTO.* 4. A disk name. See also *volume label.*

LAN *(lan)* Acronym for *Local Area Network,* which is a group of computers connected together to share information. See also *network*, *wide area network.* "Our network administrator's favorite country and western song is 'Stand By Your *LAN.*'"

landscape orientation *(land-skayp or-ee-in-tay-shun)* Printing as if the page were turned sideways so that its width is longer than its height. In comparison, most printing is done where the width of the page is shorter than its height, which is known as portrait orientation. See *portrait*

The Statue of Liberty in landscape orientation.

orientation. "Huge spreadsheets are usually printed using *landscape orientation,* but regular documents use portrait orientation. When your printer totally screws up and chews your page into gibberish, that's known as Picasso orientation."

language *(lan-gwij)* A specified way of using words and symbols to give the computer instructions and tell it what to do. All software is created by using a programming language. "I tried learning to program in C, but it's much easier to use the BASIC *language* instead. It's easier still to use foul language at the computer."

laptop *(lap-top)* A computer small enough to fit in your lap and not crush your kneecaps in the process. See also *notebook computer*, *PC.* "My *laptop* weighs too much, and the person who designed it must have had a heck of a big lap."

L

laser printer *(lay-zer prin-ter)* A type of printer that uses a laser beam to generate an image and then electronically transfers that image to paper. The speed of laser printers is measured in how many pages per minute (ppm) it can produce. The printing quality of laser printers is measured in dots per inch (dpi). See also *dot matrix, dots per inch, inkjet printer, letter quality.* "Mr. Spock! Set the *laser printer* on 'stun.'"

launch *(lawnch)* To start a program or to start some process. See also *load, run.* "Windows must be like NASA: I can only *launch* programs on clear, sunny days when there's no wind."

LCD *(el see dee)* Acronym for *Liquid Crystal Display,* which is a display commonly used in pocket calculators, watches, and laptop computers. LCD displays consume less power than normal monitors, but they tend to look as washed out as chalk drawings scribbled on the sidewalk in the rain. "It was so cold out, my laptop's *LCD* froze." (That is truly an example of nerd humor.)

leading *(led-ing)* Inserting extra space between lines of text for aesthetic purposes. The name comes from the days of printing presses when printers physically inserted thin strips of lead between lines. See also *kerning.* "Perkins! You used so much *leading* in your document that it could be used as shielding in the event of a nuclear attack!"

learning curve *(lurn-ing kurv)* A graphical chart showing how much is learned over a period of time or how

much should be learned. The rate of learning. You can compare your progress with the

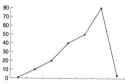
Typical learning curve.

learning curve to see whether or not you "get it." "I'm so far behind that from here, the *learning curve* looks like the Himalayas."

LED *(el ee dee)* 1. Acronym for *Light-Emitting Diode,* which is a device that lights up when an electrical current passes through it. Many digital clocks use LEDs to display numbers. "My alarm clock has a big, fat, red *LED.* I can see the numbers clear across the room without my glasses. I can even feel the numbers being burned into my eyelids while I sleep." 2. A type of printer that uses an LED to create an image on paper. LED printers are quiet and relatively fast.

left-justify *(left-just-uh-fie)* To align text flush against a left margin.

```
This is
an example of
left justification.
```

See also *flush, justify.* "Most liberals don't need a reason to *left-justify* their text."

letter quality *(let-er kwahl-uh-tee)* Printed text that is clear enough that it looks like it came from a typewriter. Usually refers to printing that a dot-matrix printer produces. "My dot-matrix printer can produce *letter quality* printing, so it looks like a typewriter printed it. Oh, I love using technology to impress folks."

LF (el ef) 1. Acronym for *Line Feed*, which is a signal that tells a printer to start a new line. "Most dot-matrix printers have an *LF* and an FF button. If you press the FF button, the printer rolls a complete page out of the printer. If you press the LF button, the printer just moves the page up one line." See also *FF*. 2. The line-feed character, ASCII code 10. See *ASCII*, *control codes*.

LIFO (lie-foh) Acronym for *Last In First Out,* which describes a data structure used by programmers known as a *stack*. See also *FIFO*, *stack*. "Airlines try to board their planes *LIFO*: The rear rows are boarded first and the front rows last, and when the plane lands, the people in the front rows get out

Annoying passenger with two "carry on" bags.

first. This would work if it weren't for those morons trying to stuff those body bags they carry into the overhead bins."

light pen (liet pen) A light-sensitive detector in the shape of a pen that lets you draw pictures and give input to the computer from the screen. "Aha, Darth Vader! My *light pen* is mightier than your light saber!"

line eater (lien ee-ter) An old monster from the early (pre-Web) days of the Internet. Some newsgroup reader programs would somehow ignore the first line of text

in a message. Therefore, people composing messages would include a blank line or a line with the words "Eat me!" on it to prevent the important part of the message from being missed. "Because *line eaters* are rare today, few people start their newsgroup messages with a warning to the *line eater*."

line editor (lien ed-uh-ter) A program that edits text one line at a time, as opposed to full screen. Editing text this way is like trying to paint a wall through venetian blinds. See also *editor*. "The most infamous *line editor* of all time was one that came with MS-DOS called EDLIN. Pray that you never have to use it."

line feed (line-feed) See *LF*.

line noise (lien noyz) Pops, buzzes, clicks, or other random noise that happens on a phone line. You don't notice line noise during conversation, but when a modem uses the phone line, the line noise may be misinterpreted as a signal from the other computer. The result is often garbage characters on the screen. See *garbage*. "There is so much *line noise* that my modem can't communicate. Oh, no wonder; 10,000 birds just landed on the phone lines outside my house."

line number (lien num-ber) A way of identifying a specific line in a text file or document. The first line is number 1, the second line is number 2, and so on. To move to a specific line in a document, you tell the computer to "Please show me line number 35." "*Line numbers* come in handy when you're programming, because the compiler typically tells you on which line you goofed up."

line printer *(lien prin-ter)* A high-speed printer that can print an entire line at once. Line printers are great for printing quick drafts, but they're terrible for printing nice print. "The telephone company uses a *line printer* to print inaccurate phone bills more efficiently."

link *(leenk)* 1. To connect two computers together through a modem, cable, or network. 2. Using Windows or OS/2, to connect two files together so that they share identical information. If you change data in one file, a *hot link* automatically changes the same data stored in the second file. With a *cold link,* changing data in one file does *not* automatically change the same data in a second file. 3. To combine multiple machine-language files together to create a single program. 4. A bit of text or a graphic on a Web page that provides access to another part of the Internet, typically something that's related to the text or graphic. See *hypertext.*

linked list *(leenkd list)* A data structure used by programmers to store information. The size of a linked list can change as the program runs. A linked list consists of two parts: the data and a reference to the next chunk of data. Think of a linked list as a train of cars connected together. Each car holds cargo (data), and each car is connected (linked) to the next car. "Lyle uses a *linked list* to keep track of his cuff link collection."

linker *(leen-ker)* A special program that combines one or more machine-language files (object files) and converts them to a single executable file. "Instead of trying to create one huge program at once, write a bunch of little ones. Then use a *linker* to combine them into one huge, unmanageable program loaded with bugs, and price it at $495 like everyone else does. This is the secret of selling software."

Linotronic *(lien-oh-tron-ik)* The brand name for a typesetting machine used by many book and magazine publishers. A Linotronic printer produces extremely high-quality print and makes an ordinary laser printer look like trash. "I like printing rough drafts on my home laser printer. Then for the final drafts, I print on a *Linotronic* machine."

Linux *(lie-nuks)* A shareware version (a very close copy) of UNIX developed by Linus Torvalds. Linux runs on most PCs, allowing people who can't afford real UNIX boxes to play with UNIX. Obviously a tool for the desperate. All UNIX terms and commands in this book also apply to Linux.

Lisa *(lee-sa)* An early attempt by Apple Computer to design a user-friendly PC. The Lisa was essentially a prototype Macintosh, complete with a graphical user interface, mouse, and all that. Unfortunately, Apple couldn't figure out what to do with Lisa, and the thousands of people who paid $10,000 for it were pretty much screwed. Named after Steve Jobs's daughter.

LISP *(lisp)* An acronym for *LISt Processing,* a language developed in the early '60s at MIT for artificial intelligence research. LISP code includes an incredible number of parentheses. Related dialects include Common LISP and Scheme. Typical LISP applications

Typical LISP programmer.

include computer learning, natural language processing, and understanding why people bother getting a PhD in computer science when rock stars with third-grade educations make millions by singing one hit single. "Unlike other languages, *LISP* programs can modify themselves while they're running, which means programs can really run completely out of control. And this is called artificial intelligence."

list *(list)* 1. A collection of data arranged in a certain order. Programs usually store lists as arrays or as a linked list. A phone book is a list of names and numbers. A grocery list is also a list. See also *array, database, linked list.* "My program was supposed to alphabetize my *list* of names and addresses. The only question now is, which alphabet did it use?" 2. A DOS command used to display the contents of a file. 3. Short for *listserve,* used to mean a mailing list. See *listserve.*

list box *(list boks)* A dialog box that displays a list of items. Items commonly found in a list box include filenames, printer names, directories,

groceries, or anything else the computer thinks you may want. See also *dialog box.* "Yes, Sedrick, the *list box* is the one tilting starboard."

listserve *(list-surv)* 1. Software that controls a mailing list. See also *majordomo.* 2. A nickname for a mailing list. See *mailing list.*

lite *(liet)* 1. A version that lacks some of the features of the full-powered model but is still compatible with and costs much less than the original. 2. Tastes great, less filling. "I fly 2,000 miles on a moment's notice to fix your network and you offer me a *lite* database file?"

load *(lohd)* 1. To transfer information from disk storage to memory in the computer. 2. (Capitalized) Another term for the Open command. 3. The BASIC language command that opens program data on a disk. "Before the Open command, the official Microsoft Word method for getting a document file on disk was Transfer-File-*Load.* And you wonder why they still can't write a decent user manual?"

local area network *(loh-kul ayr-ee-uh net-wurk)* The long way to pronounce LAN. See *LAN.*

local bus *(loh-kul bus)* A type of high-speed expansion slot for a PC, one that connects directly with the microprocessor. The advantage is that devices connected to the local bus run

Tour bus, express bus, local bus.

much faster because they have a larger pipe through which they can

L

yell at the CPU. Typical devices connected to a local bus include high-speed video cards and hard drives. See also *bus, expansion slot, PCI, VESA.* "No, this bus doesn't go to Video City. You need to take the *local bus.*"

local variable *(loh-kul var-ee-uh-bol)* A variable used in a function or subprogram that is not available to the entire program. See *variable.* "Oh, him? He's just a *local variable.* But someday soon, he's planning on saving his money and moving up to become a global variable."

LocalTalk *(loh-kul tawk)* The connectors and cables that Apple Computer makes for AppleTalk networks. See also *Apple Computer, AppleTalk, network.* "*LocalTalk* once again proves that Apple Computer hates to name anything with a space in the middle."

lock *(lohk)* 1. To prevent access to something. 2. The key lock on some computers used to prevent others from using your computer. "Don't think that key *lock* is anything serious; just about every computer uses the same key." 3. The sliding tab on every 3^1/$_2$-inch floppy disk that prevents the disk from being written to. 4. To limit access to a file in a file-sharing situation. See *file sharing.*

log *(lawg)* 1. Abbreviation for *LOGarithm,* which is a mathematical function that fulfills an important role in some people's lives. "When we learned about *logs* in math class, I was sawing logs in the back of the class." 2. To use a specific disk drive.

Some bad manuals may say "log to drive D" when they really mean "change to drive D."

log in *(lawg in)* To connect to another computer or computer network to access its information. "I have to *log in* by typing an account name and a correct password. If that fails, I'll wait until you have to visit the water cooler, and then I'll use your PC."

logging in *(lawg-ing in)* To gain access to a computer system, often by typing in a user name (or code) and password. Comes from some old lumberjack term. Then again, probably not.

logging off *(lawg-ing off)* To tell a computer system good-bye. Logging off disconnects you from the network or hangs up a remote connection.

logic *(loh-jik)* 1. A little bird, tweeting in the meadow. 2. Sensible actions. 3. Formal guidelines for reasoning. The study of the relationship between true and false items. See *AND, OR, NOT, Boolean.* "There is no *logic* in the computer industry."

logic bomb *(loh-jik bohm)* A secret part of a program that erases files or causes other destructive damage upon activation. Disgruntled employees wanting to wreak revenge on their former employers are usually the ones responsible for placing logic bombs. See also *virus.* "Creating a *logic bomb* is a rather illogical thing to do."

logical drive *(loh-jih-kal driev)* A portion of a large hard drive that has been partitioned into several drives — like smaller, "pretend" segments for the convenience of the user or the computer. Logical drives are rarely physical drives such as floppy or hard drives. Often, a single hard drive may be divided into two or more logical drives, such as drive C:, drive H:, and drive Z:. See *partition*. "Obviously, Watson, we'll make sense of all this when we locate the subject's *logical drive*."

logical operator *(loh-jih-kal op-er-ay-ter)* A symbol used in programming languages, spreadsheets, and databases for defining the relationship between two items. Examples of logical operators include AND, OR, and NOT. If you were using a database, you might want to find all the names of people who make over $50,000 a year AND who are interested in yachts. Or you might want the phone numbers of everyone in Wisconsin OR New York. Then again, you might want the ages of everyone who owns a car but NOT a foreign car. "That was when the *logical operator* told me it makes more sense to dial long distance at night, when the rates are cheaper."

login name *(lawg-in naym)* The name you use to identify yourself to a computer system. That, coupled with the proper password, lets you access your files and other goodies in the computer system. "A company is nice to its employees if the *login name* they're assigned is similar to their own name. The company is not nice when it assigns random numbers and letters as *login names*."

Logitech mouse *(loh-juh-tek mows)* A computer pointing device (mouse) designed by a company called

Logitech. The chief competitor to the Microsoft mouse, the mice designed by Logitech are often more clever and interesting than the boring old Microsoft mouse.

LOGO *(loh-goh)* A programming language specifically designed to teach children how to use a computer. LOGO programs control an imaginary turtle that moves around the screen and draws lines behind it. By writing LOGO commands to control the turtle, users can create neat little designs that impress adults as well. "When I was a kid, I learned about computers by learning *LOGO*. Then in elementary school, I learned BASIC. In high school, I learned Pascal. In college, I learned C. Now I have a degree in programming and I work at a 7-11."

loop *(loop)* A set of statements in a program that is run more than once. See also *endless loop, infinite loop.* "When your computer spews out the same message over and over, it's stuck in a *loop*."

lost cluster *(lawst klus-ter)* Part of a file that remains on the disk, even though the file allocation table (FAT) has no record of its existence. Lost clusters usually occur when the computer is writing a file to the disk and the power fails. Sometimes lost clusters seem to occur without reason, which is the way most computer problems seem to appear. Various programs help you rid your hard drive of lost clusters, guiding them safely home. See *FAT*. "I was cleaning behind my computer desk and there, amidst all the cables and dust, I found a bunch of *lost clusters*."

Lotus *(loh-tus)* The company that makes the popular 1-2-3 spreadsheet and the Notes program. The name of the spreadsheet is not *Lotus,* although many people refer to the program as *Lotus.*

Lotus 1-2-3 *(loh-tus won-too-three)* The early most popular spreadsheet program for the PC. Lotus improved upon the basic spreadsheet, VisiCalc. The product was actually kind of lame and required many add-on programs to give it power, but PC users loved it. One of its main strengths was the ability to automate tasks through the use of macros and templates. In fact, some people designed games you could play on 1-2-3; one of them is called *Templates of Doom.*

low-capacity disk *(loh-kuh-pas-uh-tee disk)* A disk that normally wouldn't have any capacity description if the newer high-capacity format didn't come around. Because there are high-capacity format disks, the rest of the pack were dubbed low-capacity. "It's very hard to find a *low-capacity disk* today because few computers use them."

low-level format *(loh-leh-vel for-mat)* To physically arrange the pattern of magnetic tracks and sectors of a hard disk. Low-level formats are only necessary when using a new hard disk for the first time, and even then most low-level formatting takes place at the factory, done by professionals wearing white lab coats. See also *format.* "You should never *low-level format* your hard drive."

low resolution *(loh rez-oh-loo-shun)* On printers or computer monitors, low resolution is a mode that produces quick results but poorly drawn images that are likely to hurt your eyes and give you headaches to boot. See *resolution.* "I

Low resolution image.

have an old, *low-resolution* monitor. The letters on the screen look jagged and fuzzy, and the money I saved by buying a cheap monitor is going to my doctor to pay for new eyeglasses."

lowercase *(loh-wer-kays)* The opposite of capitalization. Most text appears with the initial letter of the first word in a sentence in uppercase, and the rest of the text in lowercase. See also *uppercase.* "Don't type IN ALL UPPERCASE BECAUSE IT LOOKS OBNOXIOUS. Then again, don't type in all *lowercase* because it looks like you're trying to rip off e.e. cummings."

LPT *(el pee tee)* Acronym for *line printer,* a port on the back of a PC for connecting a printer. A printer port! Most PCs have one of these jobbies, called LPT1. The computer can handle two other ports, dubbed LPT2 and LPT3. See also *PRN, printer port, parallel port.*

Luddite *(luhd-iet)* One who fears technology, often to the point of getting paranoid about it. Named after Ned Ludd, an Englishman who went nuts and destroyed a bunch of machinery under the belief that it would put him out of a job. (This was before soccer.)

lurker *(loor-ker)* 1. Someone who reads messages in a newsgroup or mailing list but doesn't contribute. "Almost 90 percent of the people who read newsgroups on the Internet are lurkers." 2. The people who live in DownBelow on *Babylon 5*.

LZH *(el zee aych)* Acronym for *Lempel-Ziv Haruyasu,* a standard for compressing information, such as the binary information found in most computer files. The LZH algorithm is used by popular disk back-up programs, disk compression programs, and various diet clinics. "Margie thought she could decompress an *LZH* file by adding water."

A file before and after compression.

L

M

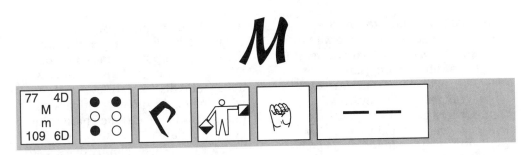

M: *(em-koh-lon)* A drive-letter designation in a PC, quite possibly a network drive, but don't rule out a hard drive, removable drive, CD-ROM drive, ZIP drive, overdrive, or a country drive.

M&Ms *(em-en-emz)* Candy-covered chocolates with little *M*s on them that don't melt in your hand. Primary source of nourishment for programmers. Belongs to the food group *Candy*. Other food groups include *Pizza, Caffeine,* and *Processed Potato Foods* (for example, chips). "Hey, isn't it about time for dinner? Pass me the *M&Ms,* will ya?"

 Mac *(mak)* Friendly name for a Macintosh. See *Macintosh*.

machine independent *(ma-sheen in-dee-pen-dent)* Commonly used to refer to a program that runs on any computer without modification. A machine-independent program can be developed on an IBM clone and used — without any modifications — on a Macintosh, for example. Machine-independent programs don't exist.

machine language *(ma-sheen lang-gwij)* The language the microprocessor speaks. A "low-level" computer language that communicates directly to the computer hardware. Programs are written in secret code (binary);

each instruction corresponds to a single computer operation. Often, an assembly language is used to make the machine-language codes more understandable by computer programmers — but that's not saying much, because the whole thing is hard, hard, hard. Programming in machine language is not for beginners, no way! See also *assembly language*. "Real programmers use *machine language,* but they also tend to grunt and point at the dinner table."

 Macintosh *(mak-en-tosh)* A family of personal computers created by Apple Computer in 1984. The hallmark of the Macintosh is its easy-to-use graphical user interface. It's also very popular with the graphics-arts crowd. The Macintosh family is the largest non-IBM-compatible personal computer series in use. "Windows is Microsoft's effort to make the PC work like a *Macintosh.*"

Isis and Osiris share a moment with their Macintosh.

macro *(mak-roh)* Short for *macro-instruction,* a macro is a simple way to create shortcuts or automate tasks or procedures within a program. There are two types of macros: keystroke and programming. The keystroke macros record keystrokes (and mouse movements) and then replay those actions later, often with a single command. The programming macros work like a programming language to automate tasks, make decisions, and perform complex operations that a keyboard macro can't handle. "Hey, Phil, I finally finished that *macro* that automatically fouls up our payroll account!"

macro assembler *(mak-roh ah-sem-bler)* A program that lets you construct assembly-language macros. An assembly-language macro is an instruction that represents several other machine-language instructions at once — like shorthand for programming geeks. By using the macro instruction, the programmer doesn't have to type as much, leaving one hand free to dive into the Doritos. See also *machine language, assembly language.* "I got a *macro assembler* to speed up my machine-language programming. Now I can write my program in three years instead of five."

macroinstruction *(mak-roh-in-struk-shun)* A single command that performs several operations. See *macro.* "Do you know the *macroinstruction* that tells this program to make toast?"

magnetic disk *(mag-net-ik disk)* A medium (that is, a flat round thing) on which computer data is stored. Often called *floppy disks* or *hard disks,* a magnetic disk is a surface coated with iron oxide and magnetically charged; bits (electronic charges) of computer data can be stored on the disk for future use. Floppy disks also make great cocktail coasters and impromptu Frisbees. Never use a magnetic disk to play tug-of-war with your dog. Keep all magnetic disks away from magnetic charges (honestly), such as your stereo speakers and your TV antenna in an electrical storm. "The instructions said to store my *magnetic disks* in an out-of-the-way place, so I put them in the toaster."

magneto-optical disk *(mag-nee-toh-op-ti-kal disk)* A type of storage device that combines optical-disk technology with magnetic-disk technology to make a disk capable of storing lots of information — like a CD-ROM, but which can be written to and erased. These high-capacity disks require special disk drives and are generally slower than a hard drive. "I am now on the cutting edge of technology with this new *magneto-optical disk.* My data will certainly survive a nuclear attack, but it may take that long for my program to load."

mail *(mayel)* The new, hip, '90s kind of way to refer to *electronic mail,* also known as *e-mail.* "Now I have two places I can receive *mail:* from my mailbox outside and my mailbox in my computer. Alas, both are still empty."

mail bomb *(mayel bom)* A form of electronic terrorism on the Internet. A mail bomb consists of sending lots of e-mail to a specific person's mailbox, so much mail that the person can't deal with it all. The mailbox is typically shut down, rendering it unavailable to the user or to anyone wanting to send him mail.

mail merge *(mayel murj)* A process by which names and addresses are combined with a form letter "master" to create those personalized form letters despised by all. When the master form letter is printed, names and addresses from the mail merge list are inserted into key locations. Each name and address creates a new form letter from the master. "I just got a personal letter from Ed McMahon. You don't suppose he has a *mail merge* program, do you?"

 mailbox *(mayel-boks)* An e-mail account or "address" to which you can send messages to people on a local network or via the Internet. An electronic mailbox can store your electronic mail, much the way the mailbox on the front porch stores your junk mail. See also *electronic mail.* "I just got an electronic *mailbox;* now I can get bills on my computer, too!"

mailing list *(mayel-ing list)* A group of people who exchange e-mail messages. Like a private newsgroup, messages are sent to "the list," and then distributed to all the members through e-mail. You must subscribe to a mailing list by sending an e-mail message to the moderator or the list computer. "Subscribing to a *mailing list* is one sure-fire way to increase the number of e-mail messages you get every day."

mailto *(mayel-too)* A command that can be used to send electronic mail. The mailto command is followed by a colon and an e-mail address, as in: `mailto:dang@idgbooks.com`. "The first URL a SPAM company employee learns is *mailto.*"

mainframe *(mayn-fraym)* A powerful computer to which "dumb" terminals are often connected. A mainframe is identified by its storage and computing capacity;

A terrifying mainframe of yesteryear.

capability to create multiple, virtual computers; and its variety of input/output options. Mainframe computers also are called the dinosaurs of the computer industry. They require cool climates (air conditioning), open spaces, and plenty of electricity. Most "mainframe" computers today are merely very fast PCs with lots of storage. See also *VAX, Cray, SQL, dumb terminal.* "The computing power of a 1960s-era *mainframe* can be found in the average home computer of the 1990s."

M

majordomo *(may-jor-doh-moh)* A program that controls a mailing list. Mail is sent to the majordomo to subscribe or unsubscribe to the list. See also *listserv.*

male connector *(mayel kon-ek-ter)* Any type of connector that inserts into a female connector. Male connectors are often located at the ends of cables and generally have prongs or wires that fit into the holes of the female connector (I'm blushing). After combining a male and female connector, you have a flow of electricity (occasionally accompanied by sparks flying), a surge of power, and, finally, a cigarette (cigarette optional). Please practice safe cable connection. See also *female connector.* "You're trying to fit that serial *male connector* into a parallel female connector. It will never work out; they're not meant for each other."

manual *(man-yoo-el)* A printed reference or tutorial for a piece of computer hardware or software. Computer manuals have a horrid reputation. Part of that is earned; the person who writes the manual is far too intimate with the product to appreciate the needs of a beginner. Also, due to printing requirements, the manual is often finished well before the product is. And I don't need to mention that they don't pay the manual writers enough or that often the duty falls to the programmer, who really couldn't care less. "Thank goodness for ...*For Dummies* books; otherwise I'd be stuck reading the *manual.*"

manually *(man-yoo-al-ee)* To do something by hand. The opposite of automatically. "The original Altair computer had to be programmed manually every time you turned it on."

map *(map)* To access a network drive and assign it a drive letter on your PC. See *network drive.*

MAPI *(map-ee)* Acronym for *Messaging Application Program Interface,* a Microsoft standard for sending and receiving e-mail on a network.

mapping software *(mah-ping soft-wayr)* A program that enables you to create maps. Maps can be viewed at different magnification factors and usually require a significant amount of disk space to store. "It's a good thing I brought my portable computer and *mapping software* on this road trip. Now I can get lost in half the time."

marketoid *(mark-uh-toyd)* Derogatory term for a marketing person in the computer industry. Often used by engineers who seem to feel that their stuff would fly off the shelves without anybody's help. Marketing people often don't get it and nod their heads rapidly when talking with any engineer. They love three-letter acronyms and are responsible for most of them.

mash *(mash)* To push. Chiefly a mid-Atlantic-states term. "*Mash* the big red button, Vern."

masochist *(mas-oh-kist)* 1. A person who inflicts pain on himself or herself. 2. Anyone who tries to use Windows 95 with less than 8MB of RAM. 3. Anyone who uses WordPerfect for DOS. "They asked at the job interview whether I could use WordPerfect for DOS. I said, 'What do you think I am, a *masochist?'"*

Cobol programmer.

mass storage *(mas stohr-edj)* A high-capacity storage device. Because normal disk capacity has increased over the years, the definition of mass storage is somewhat loose. Typical hard disk drives store one gigabyte of data; mass storage is generally considered to be at least two gigabytes of data. However, mass storage devices can hold over one *terabyte* (one trillion bytes) of data. See also *high density*, *byte*, *high capacity*. "Father John stores all his sermons on a *mass storage* device."

master/slave arrangement *(mas-ter slayv uh-ranj-ment)* When one device (a slave) is controlled by another to which it is connected (a master). Master/slave arrangements are found in disk drive arrays and other hardware configurations and also with mainframes and dumb terminals. See also *client*, *client/server network*, *network*, *server*. "When I push the remote control, the TV changes channels. It's a perfect *master/slave arrangement*."

math coprocessor *(math koh-pros-es-er)* A separate circuit (or computer chip) that performs floating-point arithmetic to enhance the capabilities of the CPU (central processing unit). Prior to the 486, math coprocessors were purchased separately from the microprocessor. Today they are integrated with the microprocessor to form a single chip or device. See also *central processing unit*, *microprocessor*, *number crunching*. "My PC's microprocessor uses a *math coprocessor* to help it perform calculations. My husband needs a hardware store coprocessor to help him spend less money on power tools."

matrix *(may-triks)* A method of storing data in a gridlike thing so that each data element can be easily retrieved. To store the amount of your phone bill for each month of the year requires a one-dimensional matrix with 12 items; one item for each month of the year. To store the amounts of all your bills (phone, food, gas, and so on) requires a two-dimensional matrix, with bills down one side and months across the top. To store these values for several years requires a three-dimensional matrix, with a separate grid for each year. See also *array*. "The Rubik's cube is the ultimate type of *matrix*, making computers relatively tame by comparison."

maximize *(mak-suh-miez)* 1. To increase to full capacity. 2. To increase the size of a window in a graphical environment. A maximized window fills the entire screen or is as large as it can be under the circumstances. See also *minimize*. "If I *maximize* the window on my checkbook program, will I maximize my income, too?"

M

maximize button *(mak-suh-miez but-on)* The gadget you click with the mouse pointer to make a window larger in a graphical environment. See *maximize.*

MB *(em-bee)* An abbreviation for *megabyte.* See also *megabyte, byte.* "When I was growing up, *MB* meant Milton Bradley."

Mb *(em-bee)* Acronym for *megabit.* See also *megabit* and *bit.*

Mbps *(em bee pee es)* Acronym for *megabits per second,* the speed of a very fast modem or any of a number of devices that spew bits hither and thither. See *bps.*

MCA *(em see ay)* Acronym for *Micro Channel Architecture.* See *Micro Channel Architecture* and *bus.*

MCGA *(em see jee ay)* Acronym for *Monochrome/Color Graphics Adapter.* The IBM graphics adapter used on the PS/2 computers. This is similar to combining an MGA and CGA adapter, but it also contains some special features of its own. MCGA adapters have generally been replaced by the more powerful SVGA adapters. See *SVGA.* "*MCGA* is a useless toad of a standard."

MDA *(em dee ay)* Acronym for *Monochrome Display Adapter.* The IBM adapter for monochrome monitors. This adapter does not provide graphics capabilities. See also *mono-chrome, monographics, CGA, EGA, CGA, VGA.* "*MDA* is boring black-and-white text, ladies and gentlemen. Major Yawn City."

media *(mee-dee-ya)* Plural of *medium.* Any kind of material used for data storage and communication. Media can be magnetic, such as a floppy disk or hard drive; optical, like a CD-ROM or magneto-optical drive; print, as in hard copy; and electronic, as in CNN. Also see *medium.* "The stone tablet was among the first data storage *media.* Talk about a hard disk!"

medium *(mee-dee-yum)* Singular media 1. A medium is a carrier of information, much like your paper carrier or that little voice telling you to go ahead and have a second piece of pie. See also *disk* and *communications.* 2. A tiny lady who cleanses your house of spirits and poltergeists. 3. Meat that's been cooked just until it's pink in the center.

meg *(meg)* 1. Short for *megabyte.* See also *megabyte.* 2. Nickname for Margaret. "Meg has a hard disk that holds 120 *megs* of data."

Margaret "Meg" Thatcher.

mega- *(may-gah)* 1. Prefix meaning one million. See also *megabyte, megahertz, MB.* 2. A unit of measure in the metric system. 3. A slang word to designate an abundance of something, as in *megafun.* "Rush Limbaugh's CompuServe e-mail account contains 1,000,000 letters from his adoring fans. Talk about *mega*dittos."

megabyte *(may-guh-biet)* Approximately one million bytes. Actually, a megabyte is equal to 1,024 kilobytes

(1,048,576 bytes). You need be this specific only on your tax form. Outside the IRS, the government has passed numerous laws declaring a megabyte to be exactly one million bytes (the 48,576 extra bytes are kept "off budget"). See *byte*. "Back in the early days of computing, a *megabyte* was considered way, way too much storage space. Now you need six megabytes of space just to store the sound the computer plays when it starts."

megahertz *(may-gah-hurts)* One million cycles per second. Microprocessor chips oscillate (wiggle) at a certain speed, measured in cycles per second, or hertz. Besides the clock speed, the internal design of the processor determines its overall speed. See also *hertz, MHz, mega-*. "The People's Republic of China has over one billion bicycles. That's 1,000 *megahertz.*"

membrane keyboard *(mem-brayn kee-bord)* An input device with a flat, plastic surface (called a membrane) with keys printed on it — like a cheap, flat calculator. This is a keyboard that you probably don't want to use; a touch-typist's nightmare. "Yes, Jared, the *membrane keyboard* on your little Atari 400 makes it perhaps the silliest computer known to mankind."

MEMMAKER *(mem-may-ker)* A blessing from Microsoft for DOS Version 6 that allowed PC users to automatically configure their computer's memory. Microsoft introduced memory management utilities with DOS 5, but they had to

be manually configured. DOS 6's MEMMAKER program took care of that task automatically. Of course, with Windows today, MEMMAKER is more of a trivia question.

memory *(mem-oh-ree)* 1. Information storage inside a computer. 2. Temporary storage where the computer runs its operating system and applications and where data is created and manipulated. RAM is temporary because it needs electricity to remember what it stores. Turn off the power, and the contents of RAM go bye-bye. ROM, on the other hand, can't be erased, but it's still treated like memory by the microprocessor and programs in the computer. See *BIOS, RAM, ROM*. 3. Permanent storage. Another term for files stored on disk, though the term "disk memory" tends to befuddle everyone.

memory banks *(mem-oh-ree banks)* Science-fiction term for memory inside a computer. Most PC users don't use the word *banks* to refer to memory. Internally, however, memory is stored in rows, which could be referred to as banks. Some hardware documentation does, in fact, refer to every chunk of memory (such as 4MB of RAM) in a PC as a bank. "We finally saved enough money at the *memory bank* to buy a new computer."

memory management *(mem-oh-ree man-edj-ment)* The art of configuring computer memory to get the most from it. This is the task of the operating system on most computers. Under DOS, however, memory management was something Microsoft avoided

M

until Version 5.0. Then they added some memory management tools, but it was up to you to put them to work. Eventually Windows came along and does its own memory management. See also *conventional memory, extended memory, expanded memory.* "If I practiced my own form of *memory management,* I wouldn't lose my car keys."

memory manager *(mem-oh-ree man-edj-er)* 1. Computer software that performs memory management. See *memory management.* 2. MEMAKER in DOS 6.*x.* Also could be any third-party program, such as 386MAX, QEMM, or any of a number of memory management products for the PC.

memory map *(mem-oh-ree map)* A graphical depiction of how memory is allocated in a computer. Actually, the memory map is for trivia purposes only, although some programmer types want to know "where in memory" some tidbit or secret switch is located. To us humans, the information is silly beyond all recourse. "After looking at my computer's *memory map,* I can find Silicon Valley."

memory resident program *(mem-oh-ree rez-uh-dent proh-gram)* A DOS program that loaded like any other program, but when it quit it stayed in memory, allowing other programs to "pop it up" as needed. Memory resident programs are often utilities that extend the basic functions of the computer, such as mouse drivers, fax software, and print spoolers. They're also often the cause of problems and conflicts in your software, which prompted Microsoft to create Windows

to solve all that mess. Memory resident programs also are called *TSRs* — Terminate and Stay Residents. See *TSR* for the gory details of why such an ugly acronym was enjoyed by computer marketing departments in the late '80s.

Mentat *(men-tat)* A fictional human supercomputer. Mentats are trained in mathematics and have greatly expanded their mental capabilities. From the book *Dune* by Frank Herbert. Also used to refer to smart computer geeks. See also *Vulcan.*

menu *(men-yoo)* A list of commands or options available within a program. Menus show your options in a list. The opposite way to run a program is to type in the commands without a list, such as at a prompt or through various

Typical menu.

keyboard combinations. The menu shows each available option and, using the mouse or keyboard, you can choose a command from the menu. Menus are supposedly the best way to display commands to a computer user. (They tried everything else.) See *menu-driven.* "When I want to change the fonts in my word processor, I just click the Format *menu* and choose the Font command. When I want to order lunch, I often use the Chinese menu and choose chow mein. You can't really get through life without knowing something about menus."

menu bar *(men-yoo bar)* An area, usually located at the top of the screen, that contains several menus listed across in a single line. It's from the menu bar that you can choose menus, and each menu contains commands or submenus. You choose commands by using the keyboard, the mouse, or by asking the waiter for a translation. See also *menu, menu item.* "*Menu bars* usually include appetizers to make you thirsty so that you'll order more drinks."

menu-driven *(men-yoo driv-en)* Software that is controlled through menus. This is the opposite of command driven. See *command driven.* "This *menu-driven* program is supposed to be easy, though I can never remember which menu the commands are in."

menu item *(men-yoo ie-tim)* An individual command or option that appears on a menu. "The File menu contains 14 *menu items,* including an Exit command. When I choose Exit, the computer gets up and walks out of the room."

menu tree *(men-yoo tree)* A diagram showing the menu structure within a program. Some menu items don't produce immediate results but instead "branch out" to more menus or dialog boxes, creating a hierarchy ("Me first! No, me!") of menu commands and options. A menu tree displays this hierarchy of commands so that you can locate any command through the maze of menus. See also *menu, menu bar, menu item.* "This program has so many menus that I need a *menu tree* to help me find the command I want."

message box *(mes-aj boks)* A small window that appears on the screen and presents a message from the program you're using. Message boxes can appear as the result of your choosing a command or option. They often inform you of mistakes or provide warnings about your actions. See also *dialog box.* "Last night I was working late on the computer, and I got a *message box* that said, 'Go to bed!'"

meta *(met-uh)* 1. Above and beyond, from the original meaning of meta, which meant *to change.* 2. A special character combination often associated with a specific key. 3. A special shift key on some weird computer keyboards, used in conjunction with other keys. If a program asks you to press META-S, you press and hold the META key and press S. "I *meta* on a Monday and my heart stood still. Da-do-run-run-run, da-do-run-run."

MHz *(may-gag-hurtz)* Abbreviation for *megahertz.* See *megahertz.* "They were blown away in 1984 when the IBM AT came with an 8 *MHz* micro-processor — twice as fast as the PC's 4 MHz. I bet they'd be floored back then to know we'd reach speeds of 300 MHz."

Mickey Mouse *(mik-ee mows)* 1. A fictional character, created by Walt Disney, who talks in a high voice and goes easily through life with his wacky friends and his dog, Pluto. Best-known works include "The Sorcerer's Apprentice" from *Fantasia* and regular appearances at Disneyland and Disney World. Also a popular export to Japan. *"Mickey Mouse* may be the world's most

M

M

popular cartoon character. I like him because he doesn't take life too seriously." 2. Something not quite up to snuff or that strays from the task at hand. "Who designed this Mickey Mouse keyboard?"

micro- *(mie-kroh)* 1. A prefix that means *one millionth.* Something very small. A microsecond is one millionth of a second. Micro is also used to imply a microscopic size, as in *microorganism* and *microprocessor.* 2. In *Microsoft,* the *micro* means that many millionaires work there. "I use *Micro*soft Word on my *micro*computer and can type a letter in a *micro*second."

Micro Channel Architecture *(mie-kroh chan-el ar-kuh-tek-chur)* A type of expansion slot design used in IBM PS/2 model 50 (and higher) computers, designated by the acronym MCA. Hardware companies design computer enhancement boards (or *cards*) that plug into the MCA bus. Boards designed for the MCA bus don't work with a standard bus. Among other enhancements, the MCA bus allows the use of multiple CPUs within the computer, although I wouldn't try that at home. See also *bus, expansion slot, expansion bus, expansion card, MCA.* "Because IBM patented the *Micro Channel Architecture* so heavily, no one ever used it in any other computer. So like the bus Ralph Kramden drove in *The Honeymooners,* it's just a relic of our past."

microcomputer *(mie-kroh-kom-pyoo-ter)* 1. Any computer with a microprocessor. 2. A disparaging term for the new personal computers that started appearing in the mid-1970s. The term *micro* came from the microprocessor,

the chip that provided the brains for these new computers. The term fell into disuse when PCs became popular in the mid-1980s. See also *PC, mainframe.* "Most *microcomputers* of today are far more powerful than the so-called 'real' computers of 30 years ago. So let's all give a Bronx cheer to our pals in mainframe- and minicomputer-land: Ptbtbtbtb!"

microfloppy disk *(mie-kroh-flop-ee disk)* A 3^1/$_2$-inch floppy disk, which took over from the 5^1/$_4$-inch floppy disk, which is smaller than the original 8-inch floppy disk. Actually, the original 8-inch floppy was called a *floppy* because it really had some flop to it. The 5^1/$_4$-inchers were called *minifloppies* when they first appeared. This left *microfloppy* to describe the smaller 3^1/$_2$-inch floppy disks. "So after the *microfloppy disk* drive, what's next? The *teensyfloppy disk?*"

micron *(mie-kron)* 1. One millionth of a meter. A distance used to measure the amount of stuff that can be stored on a microprocessor. 2. (Capitalized) A computer manufacturer just outside of Boise, Idaho. They also make memory chips.

A line one micron in size.

MicroPro *(mie-kroh-proh)* The original name of the company who developed and sold the once-popular WordStar program. Together with Ashton-Tate and VisiCorp, they were the Big Three software powerhouses of the early '80s. (Back then, Microsoft sold only DOS and programming languages, and Bill Gates was worth one, maybe two million. Tops.)

microprocessor *(mie-kroh-pro-ses-er)* The central processing chip in a microcomputer. Common microprocessors include the Motorola 68000, 68030, 68040 used in Macintoshes, and the Intel 286, 386, 486, and Pentium chips used in PCs. The microprocessor controls most of the core functions of the computer but can be enhanced with coprocessor chips. See also *central processing unit, math coprocessor.* "Harold is experimenting with a new microprocessor that actually uses human brain tissue. Sadly, Harry's using his own brain tissue, which has left him happy but nonplused about his new PC."

microsecond *(mie-kroh-sek-und)* One millionth of a second. Also used as an exaggeration to imply something that happened very quickly. "If you do that again, I'll be out of here in a *microsecond!*"

Microsoft *(mie-kroh-soft)*1. A large software company, located in Redmond, Washington (outside Seattle), that produces Windows and a suite of best-selling application programs for the PC and Macintosh computers. "Almost every program you see these days is made by *Microsoft.*" 2. Stock I never should have sold. 3. See *OZ.* 4. See *Federal Trade Commission.* 5. Rulers of the known world. 6. Microsoft has no meaning. See also *IBM.*

Microsoft Excel *(mie-kroh-soft ek-sel)* The spreadsheet program manufactured by Microsoft. Typically sold in Microsoft Office.

Microsoft standard *(mie-kroh-soft stan-dard)* A universal, all-encompassing, flagpole-in-the-top-of-the-mountain dictate on How Things Should Be Done, created by Microsoft and ignored by virtually everyone else. Microsoft is notorious for announcing "new" standards that no one else has heard of. Often they are variations on existing accepted standards, but done in the Microsoft way. Eventually others come to accept the standards; typically the Microsoft standard becomes something feasible by about the third or fourth revision. Mostly it's Microsoft's arrogant attitude about their standards that gets to everyone.

Microsoft Way *(mie-kroh-soft way)* 1. The street address of the Microsoft Corporation: One Microsoft Way. 2. The method by which Microsoft does things. Often this causes considerable ill-will among other members of the computer industry. Sure, there's a certain amount of jealousy there, but most of the time Microsoft tends to do things its own way just because it's very huge and can get away with it. IBM was like that once (still is, in many respects).

Microsoft Windows *(mie-kroh-soft win-dohs)* The official name of Microsoft's PC operating system. Microsoft would like everyone to always call it "Microsoft Windows," but we don't! Ha! Pity the poor Microsoft employees who must write "Microsoft Windows" where the rest of the world merely says "Windows." Microsoft really hates it when you use "Windows" as an adjective. See *Windows.*

M

M

Microsoft Word *(mie-kroh-soft werd)* The word processing program manufactured by Microsoft. Originally a clunky DOS program (which a seventh-grader could easily out-type), it began its Windows career as "Word for Windows." A fairly sophisticated but somewhat feature-burdened product.

microspacing *(mie-kroh-spay-sing)* The insertion of small spaces (smaller than one character) between words to aid in justification. Used in all laser printers and some dot-matrix printers. See also *kerning, justify.* "My first dot-matrix printer had a *microspacing* feature that made its justified documents look more professional. Now my laser printer uses this same technique — in a much more professional fashion."

MIDI *(mid-ee)* Acronym for *Musical Instrument Digital Interface,* a *protocol* (standard) for encoding musical sounds in digital form. The differences in sounds and musical voices can be measured and stored using the MIDI standard and then transferred digitally between computers and MIDI-equipped instruments. Electronic keyboards commonly use MIDI. "Using the *MIDI* port in my electronic synthesizer, I can play music on the keyboard, and my computer transcribes the music onto the screen. Imagine what Mozart could do today."

milli- *(mil-ee)* A prefix meaning *one thousandth.* One milligram equals one thousandth of a gram. "A *milli*second is the length of time it takes for Bill Gates to earn one million dollars in interest."

millisecond *(mil-ee-sek-und)* 1. One thousandth of a second. Abbreviated *ms.* "Our lawyer is so good, he bills us by the *millisecond.*" 2. Used to gauge the speed of a hard drive. Good hard drives have speeds of 10 milliseconds or less.

MIME *(miem)* Acronym for *Multipurpose Internet Mail Extension,* a method of sending pictures, sounds, and other information in an e-mail message. MIME information is encoded into an e-mail message by using plain ASCII text. It has to be ASCII because all e-mail messages are ASCII. But the beauty of the thing is that it allows you to include pictures and fancy text in an e-mail message without offending any e-mail program's sensibilities. Not every e-mail program supports MIME, which is why you may see a block of letters and numbers instead of a pretty picture of Miss March.

mini *(min-ee)* 1. Short for *minicomputer.* See *minicomputer.* 2. A smaller version of a larger project. For example, the *MiniFinder.* See *MiniFinder.*

mini-tower case *(min-ee-tow-er kays)* A type of PC case that sits up on its end on your desk. Unlike a Tower PC, the mini-tower case can sit on your desk without blocking your view.

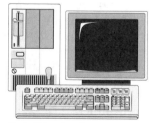

Eyeball frazzle affects this organ.

See *Tower PC.* "Due to zoning regulations, we can only have *mini-tower case* PCs around here. Anything taller and the neighbors complain that we block their view."

minicomputer *(min-ee-kom-pyoo-ter)*
A small version of a mainframe computer, typically installed at universities or businesses that didn't need mainframe power or that couldn't afford a mainframe. The difference between a minicomputer and a microcomputer blurred in the late '80s. Today there's no such thing as a minicomputer any more, because most PCs can handle the old minicomputer duties with ease. "UNIX was developed on a *minicomputer*. Today you can run UNIX on a PC you buy at Radio Shack."

MiniFinder *(min-ee-find-er)*
A piece of software for the Macintosh that makes it easy to locate your programs. You can configure the MiniFinder to access your most commonly used programs so that you don't have to search through your folders to locate them. "The *MiniFinder* was the most popular Mac program in Munchkinland."

minifloppy *(min-ee flop-ee)* A nickname for the old 5 $^1/_4$-inch disk format. See *floppy disk*, *microfloppy*.

minimize *(min-uh-miez)* 1. To shrink or reduce to minimum size or capacity. 2. Shrinking a window to appear as an icon on the desktop or taskbar in Windows. See also *maximize*. "I thought that when I *minimized* my programs, I would minimize my computer problems, too."

minimize button *(min-uh-miez but-on)*
The gizmo on a window that minimizes that window. See *minimize*.

MIPS *(mips)* 1. Acronym for *Million Instructions Per Second*, a measurement

of the speed at which programs run on a particular microprocessor. Because programs are coded differently for different microprocessors, it's important to measure MIPS by using equivalent code on each machine. See also *central processing unit*, *microprocessor*. "If you toss the word *MIPS* around in conversation, as in 'My Pentium is clocked at 20,000 *MIPS*,' people think you know what you're talking about."

mirror site *(meer-or siet)*
1. Another location on the Internet that contains the same stuff as the original location. Often used on very busy Web pages or FTP sites. "I found the *mirror site* for Lewis Carroll." 2. Duplication of a Web page or FTP site on a foreign computer or in another language.

MIS department *(em-ie-es dee-part-mint)* Acronym for *Management Information System*, the employees in a big organization who are responsible for purchasing, running, and fixing the company's computers and software. Also called the *IS department*. "I called Jane from the *MIS department* to come fix my Macintosh. She told me that it would work better if I quit trying to install DOS on my machine."

missing pictures
(mis-ing pik-choors).
A graphic image you see replacing what would be an image. This usually happens when you have the Web browser's "Load Images" option turned off. See *broken picture*.

Last seen in the Louvre.

MMX *(em em eks)* Trademarked acronym for *Matrix Math eXtentions,* a Pentium processor with enhanced graphics, video, and other multimedia abilities. See *Pentium MMX.*

mnemonic *(noo-mon-ik)* A way to remember something. For example, mnemonic commands can begin with the first letter of the command, as in Alt+F+S to represent the File Save command. "Remember that *mnemonic* starts with an M because it has to do with memory, but also remember not to pronounce the M or people will think your lips are numb."

MO *(em oh)* 1. Acronym for *Magneto-Optical.* See *magneto-optical drive.* 2. The letter designation on a magneto-optical disk, though they're thicker than regular 3^1/$_2$-inch disks.

mode *(mohd)* One of several distinct ways of using something: editing, running a program, configuring hardware, and so on. For example, you can use many DOS programs either in text mode or graphics mode. In graphics mode, you can see fonts and graphics on the screen in a WYSIWYG fashion. In text mode, only the computer's built-in text characters appear. See also *protected mode.* "Because everything is graphics these days, people have no idea how blindingly fast their computers can be when run in text *mode.*"

modem *(moh-dum)* Short for *modulator-demodulator,* a device used by your computer to communicate to remote computers through the phone lines. See *bps, bbs, external modem, internal modem, serial port.* "Some *modems* are more dumb than others."

modeming *(moh-dum-ing)* Using a modem. Doing online communications. That kind of stuff. "Happy people go *modeming.*"

 moderated newsgroups *(mod-ur-ay-ted nooz-groops)* A USENET newsgroup through which all posts pass through an individual or group of individuals who screen the messages for relevance and content. Moderated newsgroups typically have the word moderated somewhere in their name. "A moderated newsgroup is less likely to have hooligans on it than a regular newsgroup."

modifier keys *(mod-uh-fiyer kees)* Keys that work with other keys to give commands to the computer. Examples of modifier keys are Shift, Ctrl, and Alt. "If you press F7, you can save your files. If you press Shift+F7, you can print your file. And if you press Alt+F7 plus all the other *modifier keys* at once, a magic genie appears granting your every wish (or maybe your system crashes — I forget)."

Modula-2 *(mod-yoo-lah-too)* A structured programming language, similar to Pascal, that encourages programmers to create programs in modules. Modules are linked when the program is loaded. Pascal and Modula-2 were both created by Niklaus Wirth. See also *modular, programming language.* "If you know how to program in Pascal, you'll find *Modula-2* an easy transition."

modular *(mod-yoo-lar)* Consisting of, or relating to, individual units, or *modules.* Programs are often written in modules, or separate pieces, to make programming easier. Modular programming also allows program-mers to work on different aspects of the program simultaneously. Modular programming also can enhance memory management. "I think this program is *modular*. Each time I do something new, it goes back to the disk to read another program module."

modulus *(mod-yoo-lus)* The remainder of a division problem. A mathematical function in many programming languages.

Dr. Earl Modulus.

molecular beam epitaxy *(mol-eck-yoo-lar beem ep-uh-taks-ee)* The process by which cir-cuits are engraved on a piece of silicon to make a semiconductor — a computer chip. This is a big, hunky word you can toss around to really impress your friends. No kidding. See also *semiconductor, central processing unit.* "The *molecular beam epitaxy* certainly vaporizes the substrate layers to form nice, crisp semicon-ducting material. Yessiree."

monitor *(mon-uh-ter)* 1. Another name for a CRT, screen, or terminal — the thing that you stare into for hours on end when using your computer. There are several types of monitors, including TTL monochrome, RGB color, analog color, and multisync. See also *CRT, RGB,* and *terminal.* 2. A verb meaning the act of checking the

Monitor-like thing.

progress of an activity, such as snooping around inside your PC's guts to see how things work. "I was playing Solitaire on my new *monitor* when my boss came in to *monitor* my progress. Luckily, Windows let me task-switch to my word processor instantly."

monochrome *(mon-oh-krohm)* 1. One color. Actually two colors, though one of them is always black: black and white, black and green, black and orange, and so on. 2. A type of com-puter monitor incapable of displaying text or graphics in color. See also *MDA, EGA, CGA, VGA, MCGA, boat anchor, heavy iron.* "When I exit Windows to use a DOS command, my screen looks like a dull *monochrome* monitor for a while."

monographics *(mon-oh-gra-fiks)* A generic name for a replacement to the original IBM PC monochrome display adapter (MDA) that could also display graphics. A clone of the Hercules graphics adapter. See *MDA, Hercules.*

monospacing *(mon-oh-spay-sing)* A font where each character uses the same amount of space as every other character; an *i* uses as much space as an *m*. With proportional spacing, each letter uses only as much space as it needs. Monospacing is still used in some applications, such as business forms. Most fonts use monospacing also for numerals to aid in alignment of financial data. See also *proportional pitch.* "Lois, darling, that *monospaced* letter you did, it's *trés gauche.* Get with the times, girl. Everyone is going proportionally spaced now."

M

M

Montevideo *(mont-eh-vi-day-oh)*
The capital city of
Uruguay. "When
you're in Uruguay,
be sure to visit the
Library of the
National Historical
Museum in
Montevideo."

Uruguay.

month *(month)* One of twelve periods
a year is divided into. A month can
have 30 or 31 days, except for the
month of February, which can have 28
or 29 days. Month is the only word in
the English language that can't be
rhymed. "There once was a lad named
O'Grady, who fell for a girl named
Sadie. She said "Pick a *month*," and
then, uh, er, never mind."

Morlock *(mohr-lok)* 1. From H.G.
Wells' *Time Machine,* the working
class creatures who dwelt underground and ate the docile surfer-like
Eloi who lived aboveground. 2. A term
for a computer nerd who rarely sees
the light of day. Morlock can be either
singular or plural. See *troglodyte.*

morphing *(morf-ing)* 1. A graphical
trick where one image is smoothly
blended into another. Morphing is a
popular special effect, used on such
films as *Terminator 2* and in various
music videos. Using special graphics
software, you can bring such effects
to your PC. The word *morph* may also
be used. It's from the Greek *metamor-
phosis,* which means "to transform." "I
used *morphing* software to transform
an image of my old, cruddy car into a
brand-new Dodge Viper. Now if only it
could do that in real life." 2. What the
Power Rangers did when they

changed from ordinary annoying
teenagers to ordinary annoying
superheroes. "It's *morphing* time!"

MOS *(moss)* Acronym for *Metal Oxide
Semiconductor,* a type of semiconductor used in computers. See also
semiconductor, CMOS.

motherboard *(muth-er-bord)* The
main circuit board of a computer, to
which most devices connect. The
motherboard is the real estate upon
which the computer's CPU, ROM
chips, and often the RAM chips sit
and work. It also contains the expansion slots and other electronic
doodads, making it look like an
electronic sushi display. See also
*daughterboard, expansion slots, central
processing unit.* "Always do something
nice for your *motherboard* on
Mother's Day."

mount *(mownt)* 1. A term used to
describe that something, usually a
disk drive, is being used. It comes
from the olden computer days when
they physically had to mount a reel of
computer tape on the machine before
anyone could access it. Nowadays,
the mounting takes place through
software commands that make the
connections over various wires and
hoses. 2. To connect to a remote disk
drive on a network, making it accessible from your computer. "Jump
through the fiery network hoop, and
then you can *mount* the remote H:
drive and access your files."

mouse *(mows)* A pointing device used
to provide input for the computer.
Most graphical user interfaces
(Windows and the Macintosh) use

mouse input devices. When you move the mouse on your desk, the mouse pointer on the screen mimics its movement, allowing you to control, point at, grab, and manipulate various graphics goodies

Natural mouse.

(and text) in a program. The plural is "mice." See also *track ball, mouse button, mouse pad, Mickey Mouse.* "Betcha didn't know units of *mouse* movement are measured in Mickeys."

mouse button *(mows but-on)* One or more switches on a computer mouse. You press the mouse button to make things happen. When pressed, a button makes a clicking sound. Mice have from one to three buttons, each performing different functions. The Macintosh uses a one-button mouse. By holding certain keys down as you click the button, you can perform different options — just as if you had a two-button mouse. "The program says to click the *mouse button* twice. So I figure that if I click it ten times, it'll really work great (kind of like the TV remote)."

mouse droppings *(mows drop-ings)* When your mouse screws up and leaves a trail on your computer monitor that looks like the cursor is scattered all over the screen.

mouse pad *(mows pad)* A flat surface, usually padded, used to roll your mouse around. The ball on the mouse operates best on a clean, flat surface; a mouse pad is better than most people's desktop for rolling your mouse around. "When finished

making movies for the day, Mickey Mouse returns to his *mouse pad* to party with Minnie."

move *(moov)* 1. (Capitalized) A command in many software products that lets you transfer objects or text from one location to another, as in Excel's Edit-Move command. 2. What you do when your accountant discovers a bug in his tax software that results in an extra $20,000 you owe to the IRS. See also *drag.* "My spreadsheet calculated a negative cash flow in my budget, so I *moved* the expense column to next year's worksheet. Now I can move to a bigger house."

MPC *(em pee see)* Acronym for *Multimedia Personal Computer,* but because nearly every PC sold today is a multimedia personal computer, it's really a bogus acronym.

MPEG *(em-peg)* Acronym for the *Motion Picture Experts Group,* a file format for storing video images. Developed by the Motion Picture Experts Group, MPEG files compress video images so that what would have been a 100MB video file on disk takes up maybe 1MB. MPEG video can also be displayed full screen, unlike some other video formats that only appear in a small box on-screen. Unfortunately, MPEG files require specific equipment and they take a long time to compress. This standard is not related to the JPEG standard, even though the acronym guys must have lived in the same building. "Using *MPEG,* I was able to compress my massive 150MB home video project to take up only 1.5MB of disk space. Now I can bore my relatives and save disk space at the same time."

M

MPR II *(em pee ar too)* A Swedish standard that defines the acceptable amount of electromagnetic emissions a computer monitor can safely emit without killing the person sitting in front of it. "Pregnant women should buy a radiation screen for their computer monitors or only buy monitors that follow the *MPR II* standard. Otherwise, your kid may wind up looking like a computer geek."

Mr. Data *(mis-ter day-tuh)* A fictional character from the television series *Star Trek: The Next Generation.* More frequently called *Commander Data,* Mr. Data is an android officer on the starship *Enterprise.* He has a charming, innocent personality and is a fine example of artificial intelligence at work. See *data, Star Trek,* and *Star Trek: The Next Generation.* "I hear that *Mr. Data* just installed memory management software, and he now can remember twice as many things."

MS-DOS *(em-es-daws)* Acronym for *Microsoft Disk Operating System, the* most widely used operating system for personal computers. Also known as PC-DOS (from IBM) or just DOS, MS-DOS is the reason why Macintosh users avoid IBM and compatible computers. DOS was supplanted by Windows beginning with Windows 95. However, hard-core nerds will tell you that Windows 95 is really a program that runs under MS-DOS Version 7. And so it goes. See also *disk operating system, DOS, Microsoft.* "When I start my computer, the screen says `Starting MS-DOS`.... Then I get the DOS prompt, and I type WIN to go right into Windows and avoid using DOS altogether."

MTBF *(em tee bee ef)* Acronym for *Mean Time Between Failure,* used to tell someone the average life of a product such as a hard disk or laser printer. "This laser printer has an *MTBF* of 35,000 pages, which means that when I print page 35,001, the printer should statistically blow up on me."

MultiFinder *(mul-tee-find-er)* A version of the Macintosh operating system that lets you run more than one program at a time and easily switch between them. See also *Finder, multitasking, Macintosh.* "My Macintosh is equipped with *MultiFinder,* and I still can't find a thing on my disk drive."

multimedia *(mul-tee-mee-dee-ya)* Relating to video, audio, and graphics on a computer. Multimedia software combines two or more media for presentation or analysis purposes. For example, many packages let you combine graphics with sound. Large multimedia applications are often stored on CD-ROM devices due to their incredible size and memory requirements. Multimedia was a fad because all computer programs are tending that way naturally. "I have a *multimedia* version of the encyclopedia. To explain the topics, the software plays movie clips, plays music, and shows graphics and artwork. Someday, it will write my term papers for me, too."

multiplexing *(mul-tee-pleks-ing)* The simultaneous transmission of several messages in one channel over a network. This is the equivalent of watching both CNN and C-SPAN at the same time as the local station. In a computer, multiplexing lets more than one computer access a network at the same time. See also *network*. "Before we got *multiplexing*, it seemed stupid that only one person could use the network at any give time. Now with multiplexing, everyone can use the network, everyone can get more work done, and everyone has cleaner, whiter teeth in less than three weeks!"

multiprocessing *(mul-tee-pros-es-ing)* The use of multiple microprocessors in the same computer. A computer that uses any type of coprocessor is a multiprocessing computer. See also *coprocessor, central processing unit*. "When I run my CAD program, the *multiprocessing* powers of the computer are fully used. The multiprocessing powers of my brain are used when I run my CAD program while I'm talking on the phone."

multiscanning *(mul-tee scan-ing)* A computer monitor that can scan the screen (display data) at different rates, due to different video modes and hardware configurations. Also called *multisync* monitors. See also *monitor, graphics*. "I bought a *multiscanning* monitor so that I could see incredible graphics in sharp resolution, and the fact that I had a few thousand dollars lying around the house also helped."

multisync monitor *(mul-tee-sink mon-uh-ter)* Another name for a multiscanning monitor. See *multiscanning*.

multitasking *(mul-tee-task-ing)* The capability for one computer to run two or more programs at the same time without knowing how to use any of them. Multitasking is commonly used for background operations, such as printing, fax and data communications, and complex calculations. While the

Multitasking comes easy to Vishnu.

background operation (or task) is running, you can perform other tasks with other software. See *background, foreground*. "I'm sorry, Patty, but walking, chewing gum, and picking at your ear is not considered *multitasking*."

multiuser *(mul-tee-yoo-zer)* 1. Something that can be accessed or run by several people at once. 2. An operating system that supports more than one user at the same time. 3. A database that allows numerous computers to access the data at the same time. "If you have a *multiuser* database, you can have several employees typing the wrong information simultaneously."

mutation engine *(myoo-tay-shin en-jin)* A type of program used to write computer viruses that can change their appearance, thereby reducing the ability for antivirus programs to detect and remove them. Some famous mutation engines are the Dark Avenger Mutation Engine and the Trident Polymorphic Engine. See *polymorphic virus*. "Virus programmers like using *mutation engines* to create viruses that most antivirus programs can't detect. Then again, most antivirus programs can't detect a lot of viruses, but they still cost a bundle anyway."

Murphy's Law *(mur-fees lah)* 1. A universal law, or truth, that states: If anything can go wrong, it will. A subset of Murphy's Law is embodied in Parkinson's Law, which states that your clutter will expand to fill the space allotted for it. Another subset of Murphy's Law is Smucker's Law, which states that if you drop your bread, it will always land with the jelly side down. "Kyle is so fearful of *Murphy's Law* that he backs up his computer every 20 seconds." 2. An interesting but poorly executed idea for a computer book series.

My Computer *(mie com-pyoo-ter)* An icon representing the contents of your PC — all the disk drives, printers, plus other folders — in Windows 95. My Computer is also a gateway to opening folders and seeing windows displaying the folders, files, and icons stored on your computer. "The icon may say *My Computer,* but he'll always be called *Herman* around the house."

My Computer
My computer, or it could be your computer.

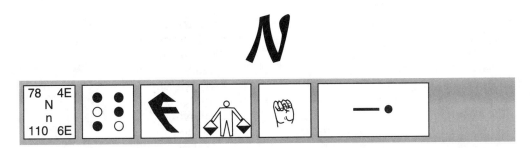

N

n *(en)* An unknown value, typically the largest value possible. Computer people say "from 1 to *n* things can go wrong." Or they use the *nth* value to mean the highest, last — nay, umpteenth — value. See also *variable*. "This is the *nth* time that I've been put on hold for *n* minutes when calling tech support."

N: *(en-koh-lon)* The letter designation for some sort of drive off in the wild drive yonder of a PC computer system. See *D:* and *Z:* for more information.

NAK *(nak)* Negative acknowledgment. A character used in online communications that often signals an incomplete or improper file transfer. See *ASCII, control codes*.

nano *(na-noh)* A prefix meaning *one billionth.* For example, a nanogram equals one billionth of a gram. A nanosecond is one billionth of a second, or the amount of time it takes for the U.S. government to spend $40. See also *nanosecond*. "Computer book authors make about a *nano*portion of Bill Gates' income."

Dr.Erg Nano, discoverer of the nanosecond.

nanosecond *(na-no-sek-und)* 1. One billionth of a second, abbreviated *ns.* Nanoseconds are the speed unit used to measure memory chips. 2. The amount of time it takes users to find an error in the software documentation. "I always wondered how anyone measures a *nanosecond.* They better have a quick thumb on that stopwatch."

natural-language processing *(nach-oor-ohl lang-gwij pros-es-ing)* The use of natural languages by computers for processing information. Today, computers use artificial languages, such as BASIC and C++, which are limited in syntax and vocabulary. Natural-language processing would enable computers to understand and process languages such as English and Zulu. Although much progress has been made, natural-language processing is many years away from reality. Problems with syntax, pronunciation, and vocabulary have not been completely solved. A complex set of rules is required to decipher the simplest sentences; as language gets more complex, the rules become colossally difficult to construct. See also *artificial intelligence, language, BASIC, C, C++, syntax.* "My dog must use *natural-language processing* to understand what I mean when I say, 'Where's your ball?' I guess dogs are more intelligent than computers."

N

navigation *(nav-uh-gay-shun)* 1. The act of finding your way through data, a program, a disk, or a network. 2. In a software application, moving the insertion pointer (or cursor) around the document. Proper navigation lets you edit and manipulate a document more efficiently. Most programs have sophisticated navigation keys and procedures. For example, in Microsoft Word for Windows, you can press Ctrl+Home to move instantly to the top of a document. See also *cursor.* "Microsoft Word provides numerous *navigation* options, allowing even an amateur to become completely lost in a matter of nanoseconds."

NC *(en-see)* Acronym for *Network Computer,* essentially a dumb terminal used on a network. See also *dumb terminal, Net PC.*

near-letter-quality *(neer-let-ur-kwal-uh-tee)* Printing produced by dot-matrix printers. By condensing the dots to a high resolution, the rough edges around the characters are minimized, and near-letter-quality is achieved. Fact is, you can always tell the difference. And laser printers, with their resolution and graphics capabilities, send near-letter-quality printers to the cleaners. Often abbreviated as *NLQ.* See also *laser printer, letter-quality, dot matrix, daisy wheel.* "When I got my laser printer, the *near-letter-quality* printer wasn't very useful. It makes a pretty good footstool, though."

Nelson, Ted *(ted nel-son)* Computer guru who developed the concept of hypertext. He's currently working on project Xanadu, which is yet another handy way to access lots of information. See *hypertext, Xanadu.*

nerd *(nurd)* 1. A negative, though often self-depreciating, term for a computer fanatic. 2. Someone who is very wrapped up in computers, often enjoying them to the disregard of everything else. There are actually several degrees of

A typical nerd.

nerdhood. At the very top are the *elitists,* often members of the Programming Priesthood. They're nice and understanding but still dedicated to computers. *Wizards* are more friendly than members of the Programming Priesthood but are typically hard to find. *Geeks* are the worst type of nerd, often into computers because a good "Dungeons and Dragons" game isn't going on anywhere nearby. Geeks are typically stupefied that no one else "gets it" when it comes to computers, and they're reluctant to share information. *Dweebs* are nerds whose idea of being socially acceptable is brushing their teeth *and* applying deodorant. See also *hacker, geek, dweeb.* "Milton was a *nerd* and socially awkward. I couldn't understand why he was so popular until someone told me that he pulls down six figures — plus stock options — writing software at Microsoft."

nested *(nest-ed)* A programming term that means to include one procedure within another, similar procedure. Often used with loops to fill complex data structures and bird's nests. See also *loop, infinite loop, endless loop.* "My programs use a lot of *nested* loops. It must be my nesting instinct."

net *(net)* 1. (Capitalized) Abbreviation for the *Internet*. See *Internet*. 2. Abbreviation for a network. See *Local Area Network*. 3. A thing you use to catch fish, or to hold your hair if you work in a restaurant kitchen.

 Net address *(net uh-dres)* The strange-looking letters, numbers, and symbols that identify someone's location on the Internet. See *address*.

Net PC *(net pee-see)* 1. A computer, like a regular PC, with a microprocessor, hard drive, memory, and a network connection (modem or network adapter), but no floppy drive, CD-ROM drive, or any expansion cards to upgrade the system. The idea behind the network computer is to sell an inexpensive PC for use on a local area network or as a device to access the Internet. But you can never add new software or expand the system, so its appeal is low in the eyes of consumers. "Because it can't be upgraded, the *network computer* will probably never be as successful as the computer industry would like it to be." 2. A competing standard proposed by Microsoft, Intel, and others for the NC. "Compared to a *Net PC,* an NC is a wimp. Then again, compared to a real PC, a *Net PC* is a wimp."

NetBIOS *(net-bie-os)* Abbreviation for *Network Basic Input/Output System*. The BIOS tells a computer what types of devices and memory are connected to the computer

A NetBIOS chip.

and how to find them. A NetBIOS includes basic information about the network to which a computer is connected. When you load your network operating system, the NetBIOS loads into the computer to supplement the standard BIOS. See also *BIOS, network*. "When I log on to the network, my *NetBIOS* tells the computer where to locate the other computers."

Netiquette *(net-uh-kit)* The Internet term for etiquette. Cute, huh? See *etiquette*.

 Netscape *(net-skayp)* 1. The company that created the popular Netscape Navigator program. 2. Short for *Netscape Navigator*. See *Netscape Navigator*.

 Netscape Navigator *(net-skayp nav-uh-gay-tor)* A popular Web browser produced by Netscape Communications, Inc. It was originally given away free, and older versions can still be obtained that way on the World Wide Web (typically as an enticement to Internet service providers to use the Netscape Web Server software, which is where Netscape Communications makes all the big bucks). "Microsoft's arch rival in the Browser Wars is *Netscape Navigator*. I bet you didn't know that Microsoft has more people working on its Web browser software than there are employees at Netscape Communications, Inc."

Netware *(net-wayr)* The networking software; the file server's operating system. Most closely associated with Novell, as in Novell NetWare, the operating system used on Novell networks. "*Netware* must sell more bottles of Excedrin than anything else."

network *(net-wurk)* 1. A system of computers connected to each other for data transfer and communications. A network requires two or more computers, networking software (also called the *network operating system*), network adapters, and cables. Different types of networks include Ethernet, Token Ring, and AppleTalk. Examples of network operating systems include Novell NetWare and Windows for Workgroups. Networks are useful when several users must share resources, such as data or printers. 2. The source of most computer problems in business computer systems. See also *LAN, wide area network, node*. "The *network* is down. Again."

network adapter *(net-wurk uh-dap-ter)* A hardware device (or *card*) that establishes a network and enables a computer to connect to another computer with a similar device. All computers in a network should use compatible adapters. See also *network, LAN, wide area network*. "Our office purchased Ethernet *network adapters* for our computers. After installing and configuring the adapters, we can then install and configure the network software. I think I like the old-fashioned way of communicating around the office; it's called the phone."

network computer *(net-wurk com-pyoo-ter)* Another term for an NC or Net PC. See *NC, Net PC*.

network drive *(net-wurk driev)* A remote disk drive that can be accessed from your computer as if it were a drive on your computer. For example, Wally has a disk drive with tons of games on it. Using your computer's operating system and the network, you *map* his disk drive to the G: drive on your PC. So your G: drive would be Wally's hard drive containing all those games he stole from the Internet.

network hose *(net-wurk hohz)* The cable that connects your computer to other computers in the network. It's too thick to be a wire, so I call it a hose. "The data starts in my computer, then it's squirted out the *network hose,* down the hall and into Phil's computer, and then he totally fouls up my report."

network operating system (NOS) *(net-wurk op-ur-ayt-ing sis-tem)* The software that controls the network. See also *local area network, network, server, workstation*. "We use Windows for Workgroups as our *network operating system* and connect to a file server with a Novell NOS. I guess our computers are working NOS to NOS."

network pathname *(net-wurk path-naym)* A pathname that also includes a network designation, typically the name of a computer. Network pathnames begin with two slashes (forward slashes most of the time, backslashes in DOS), followed by the name of the network computer and then the shared resource. The remainder of the network pathname is then just the same as a regular pathname. Here's an example:

```
\\KOBY\C\WINDOWS\PERSONAL.CRD
```

The sample network pathname indicates the computer named KOBY, the shared resource C on Koby (which is probably drive C), and then a normal pathname. Weird, yeah. Pray you never have to type one of those in by heart.

neural network *(noor-ul net-wurk)* A computer system that mimics the activities of the human brain. In the human brain, a very large number of neurons (billions, in fact) process information in a parallel fashion, all working on one problem at the same time to produce a single answer. Based on

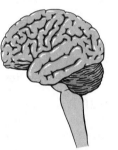

Early neural network computer.

established patterns (learned processes), certain connections are made across a network to produce repeated results. In this way, neural networks can learn to process complex information over time — recognizing patterns of data. Because of this learned behavior, neural networks, like humans, produce only approximate results based on large amounts of input. Neural networks are useful for specific types of problems, such as processing stock market data or finding trends in graphical patterns. See also *artificial intelligence.* "Dave! Have you seen our gas bill? I guess the gas company has installed that darn new *neural network* computer!"

New *(noo)* The command that directs the application to produce a new, blank document or file. Often found in the File menu.

Newbie *(noo-bee)* 1. Refers to someone who is new to a newsgroup. As if being new wasn't bad enough, there's a term for it, too. "Oh great! Another question about Mr. Spock's ears. He's a Newbie!" 2. Anyone who is new to anything dealing with a computer.

newline character *(noo-line kayr-ak-ter)* 1. The character produced when you press the Enter key, which makes a new line of text on the screen. Many word processors use the term *newline character* because pressing the Enter key starts you off writing stuff on a new line. See also *Return key, carriage return, linefeed, Enter key.* "Pity poor Alice. She did a search and replace, searching for the *newline character* and replacing it with nothing. Now she has one four-page paragraph in her document." 2. The character producing a new line of text in a programming language. For example, the \n symbol is used in the C programming language to represent the newline character.

newsgroup *(nooz-groop)* A discussion area (group) on USENET. A forum where people can read or write their own news, messages, and flames. Newsgroups have a certain hierarchical format that replaces spaces with periods. The first word describes a general category, such as "comp" for computers or "talk" for general discussions. Then comes a subcategory and maybe even more categories. It's really something you either love or hate and will drive you agog either way. See *USENET.* "Wendy got flamed really bad when she posted a few nasty messages about Captain Picard's bald head in the rec.arts.startrek *newsgroup.*"

N

Newton *(noo-tun)* 1. That fellow who discovered gravity. Sir Isaac Newton. Because he supposedly discovered gravity when an apple dropped on his head, Apple Computer has used his name to describe a variety of products. "If only *Newton* had any kids, he wouldn't have needed an apple to discover gravity." 2. The name of Apple's

Sir Isaac Newton.

first Personal Digital Assistant (PDA). See *PDA.* "I paid $600 for my *Newton,* a handheld device that offers me the functionality of a pad and pencil but with a whole lot of prestige."

NeXT *(nekst)* A computer and company founded by Apple Computer cofounder Steve Jobs after the Apple Board of Directors kicked him out. NeXT sold UNIX workstations, mostly to universities. Eventually they stopped selling hardware but continued to offer the NeXT software, NeXTstep. I honestly have no idea what they're up to today, but they're still around serving some niche market somewhere. NeXT is always spelled with a small *e,* in the fine tradition of mixed capital letters that computer companies never seem to tire of.

NeXTstep *(nekst-step)* A graphical operating system based on UNIX. NeXTstep was originally designed for the NeXT computer but was also

available for powerful PCs as well. "Truly, *NeXTstep* is perhaps the best graphical operating system ever. Too bad no one buys it."

nibble *(nib-ohl)* One half of a byte, or four bits. See also *byte, bit.* "I can't get a *nibble* or a bite with this two-bit bait."

NiCad *(nie-kad)* Abbreviation for *Nickel Cadmium,* a type of battery used in notebook and portable computers. You can recharge NiCad batteries frequently, but you have to fully drain them of power first; otherwise, they forget how much energy they hold and begin to hold only the amount you've recharged. NiCad batteries are sort of stupid. "My laptop computer uses two rechargeable *NiCad* batteries to provide a full six hours of use, but they take 12 hours each to charge!"

niche *(niche)* 1. A small market. 2. A piece of hardware or software designed for a specific thing, to fill a certain need. Also see *vertical market.*

nil *(nil)* Nothing, zero, zilch. See also *null.* "I've been working with this income spreadsheet all day; every way I look at it, my profits are *nil.*"

NLQ *(en el kyoo)* See *near-letter-quality.*

 NNTP *(en en tee pee)* Acronym for *Network News Transfer Protocol,* the method by which newsgroups and their messages are sent on the Internet.

NNTP server *(en en tee pee sir-ver)* The computer or software on a computer that sends and receives newsgroup messages.

no-op *(noh-op)* A computer instruction that does nothing. Although you may think that your software has lots of no-ops, alas, there may be only a few. It seems silly, but your car has a "neutral" gear, and many people stare at the TV slack-jawed for hours. No-op is the same thing, but for a computer. "I don't know how many *no-ops* this computer is doing, but it's doing them quite fast."

node *(nohd)* 1. A single computer or terminal in a network. Networks can consist of numerous nodes, each operating independently. 2. The way *note* sounds when you have a cold. See also *network, server.* "Our Ethernet network has 20 *nodes,* which means that 20 of us won't have anything to do when the network stops working."

nondocument *(non-dok-yoo-ment)* A word processing text file or ASCII file that contains no formatting. A plain text file. This term originated from the nondocument mode in WordStar. See also *ASCII.*

Baal saves a file in the nondocument mode.

noninterlacing *(non-in-ter-lay-sing)* A type of monitor that displays each image by using only one swipe of the electron gun. This displays the image smoothly with no flicker. See also *interlacing, NTSC.* "No, Sedrick, a *noninterlacing* monitor is not a Velcro monitor, like your nonlacing shoes."

nonvolatile memory *(non-vol-uh-tul mem-oh-ree)* Information encoded in your computer that stays there when you turn the power off. Read-only memory is nonvolatile, as are disk drives. See also *RAM, memory.* "I wrote a story called 'The Violent Vibrations of a Volatile Vocalist' and saved it on my hard drive, so now it's in *nonvolatile memory* and I can finally turn off my computer."

NOP *(en oh pee)* 1. Acronym for *Not Operating Properly,* meaning a program that is not working, or a computer that is not working, or an employee who is not working. "This program is *NOP.* Let's ship it anyway." 2. Accidental "features" in software, in which case NOP means *Not On Purpose.*

Norton SI *(nor-ton es ie)* A microprocessor speed test, from the program SI (Speed Index) included with an early version of the Norton Utilities computer program suite. An early benchmark of a PC's speed, highly inaccurate but used by many manufacturers to boast of their computer's prowess. The original IBM PC had a Norton SI value of one. Today's Pentiums probably have a Norton SI value of several million. See *benchmark.*

NOS *(en oh es)* Acronym for *Network Operating System.* See *network operating system.*

notepad *(noht-pad)* A small application or accessory commonly found in graphical user interfaces (such as Windows and the Macintosh System) that you can use to type simple notes. The Windows Notepad is a simple, text-only word processor that lets

N

N

you write, edit, and print notes without having to use the more complex word processors. A notepad is useful also for editing DOS batch files, such as AUTOEXEC.BAT. "Even though they have a *notepad* accessory, nothing is more handy than keeping a pen and a pad of paper by your computer."

notebook computer *(noht-book kom-pyoo-ter)* 1. A compact computer, about the size of a three-ring binder. Notebook computers are commonly used while traveling. They operate on both regular power and batteries. You can also use notebook computers on the desktop by "docking" them to a larger computer or by attaching a desktop monitor and keyboard. A practical notebook computer should weigh between 3 and 5 pounds. 2. A good excuse to get out of the office. 3. Something a computer book author takes on her honeymoon. "I'm so glad I brought the *notebook computer* on this trip. I haven't used it yet, but just carrying it around saves time going to the gym."

notwork *(not-wurk)* A task performed at your desk or on the computer that is not work. Notwork includes playing computer games, arranging your Windows or Macintosh desktop, organizing files on the computer, installing new software that you're not really going to use, faxing your lunch order to the corner deli, and sending e-mail to Bill Clinton (even if you're a politician). "When the boss came in, I was doing a lot of *notwork*. Then she told me I was doing a good job and left. I guess I'll keep up the good notwork."

Novell *(noh-vel)* A company in Utah that makes networking software. *The* networking software for the majority of PCs. They make other things as well and own the license to UNIX and other software. "The first *Novell* the network did crash!"

Utah.

Novell DOS *(noh-vel daws)* The renamed version of DR DOS after Novell bought out Digital Research. "Wow! A copy of *Novell DOS*. What a collector's item!"

NPC *(en pee see)* Acronym for *Network Personal Computer.* See *Net PC.*

NSA *(en es ay)* Acronym for the *National Security Agency,* a top-secret American government agency that dedicates its life to creating and cracking ciphers and monitoring communications from all over the world. For years, the NSA officially didn't exist, although it unofficially gobbled up billions of dollars for its existence. See *cipher, encryption.* "The *NSA* has the most supercomputers in one location, which means they're either using these supercomputers to keep the country safe from enemies or playing the most awesome video games the world will never see."

NTSC *(en tee es see)* 1. Acronym for *National Television Standards Committee,* a committee that determines standards for television broadcast and reception, influencing most of the known world, except Europe and Asia and other places where the TV standards are much better. The NTSC standard for broadcast is 125-line frames scanned at 30 frames per second using noninterlaced video. The European PAL standard produces a much higher resolution and quality of color than the NTSC standard used in the United States. Digital TV will soon replace the NTSC standard. "Americans have been trying to upgrade the *NTSC* standard for years. We watch the most television in the world and have the worst quality." 2. Acronym for Never The Same Color, a wordplay on NTSC because the standards are rather loose.

NuBus *(noo-bus)* A Macintosh expansion slot that provides faster data transfer than the older S-bus and has support for multiple CPUs. See also *bus, expansion slot, expansion card.* "Those Mac people always have splashy new hardware with much more interesting names than PC people. They have names like *NuBus,* LocalTalk, and System Error."

Anubis enjoys using the NuBus.

NUI *(noo-ee)* Acronym for *Network User Interface,* the interface used on network computers, Web browsers, and other software that accesses a network. See also *GUI.*

NUL *(nul)* The name of a DOS "device" that doesn't exist and is no good. It's probably the first thing the programmers at Microsoft did, because it works very well at doing nothing. "Go to *NUL,* go directly to NUL, do not

pass Redmond, do not collect stock options."

null *(nul)* 1. An empty set. 2. ASCII character code zero. This character is used in the C language to end a string of text. 3. Nothing. Unlike the number zero, null has no value whatsoever, like Donald Trump's estate. See also *nil.* "Programmers often use a *null* character to cancel a numeric variable because the number zero has a value."

null modem *(nul moh-dum)* A connection between two computers that doesn't include a modem. A null modem is usually accomplished with a cable connection, such as between a notebook computer and a desktop for direct data transfer. "I use a *null modem* to download my calendar information to the notebook computer before a business trip."

number crunching *(num-ber krunch-ing)* To work out numerical calculations and computations on a computer. Number crunching is common in financial and engineering applications. "After six days of *number crunching,* we discovered that the human brain can't survive on coffee and Twinkies, so we went out for lunch."

numeric format *(noo-mayr-ik for-mat)* A style of displaying numbers. Different numeric formats display numbers for different purposes. For example, a currency format displays the number 567.899 as $567.90, and a percent format displays the number .25 as 25%. Numeric formats are commonly found in spreadsheet programs so

N

that you can display numbers for special purposes without actually changing the value or "true form" of the number. "I used Excel's custom *numeric format* feature to add a few extra zeros to each number in my Net Worth report. Because number formats don't actually change the underlying values in the spreadsheet, you couldn't call this dishonest . . . could you?"

numeric keypad *(noo-mayr-ik kee-pad)* 1. The portion of the keyboard that contains the number keys, usually all grouped into rows and columns by themselves. 2. A separate device that works along with the keyboard to provide fast numeric input. For example, a separate numeric keypad for use with a laptop computer.

NumLock *(num-lok)* A key on PC keyboards that switches the numeric keypad between number input and cursor keys. When NumLock is on, the numeric keypad produces numbers. When NumLock is off, the numeric keys act as direction keys. Many keyboards include a second set of direction keys, so you can use the numeric keypad for numbers and still have direction keys available. See also *numeric keypad, CapsLock.* "Forgetting that you have *NumLock* on means that you may want to go elsewhere in your spreadsheet and end up tying the national debt instead."

nybble *(nib-ohl)* Alternative spelling of *nibble,* most likely because a nibble is related to a byte the same way a nibble is related to a bite. See *nibble.*

A nybble is half a byte.

N

O

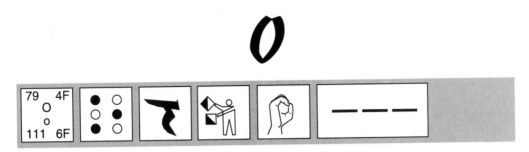

O *(oh)* The 15th letter of the English alphabet; not the same thing as a zero. Do not confuse a capital *O* with the number zero. See *0* (zero).

O: *(oh koh-lon)* The letter designation for some sort of disk drive in a PC. Could be a network drive. Could be a hard drive. Could be an overdrive. Might also be what drive D: looks like without your glasses on.

object code file *(ob-jekt kohd fiel)* The middle step in writing a program. It's not exactly the final program; it's more like the slimy pod-person thing that eventually turns into the program, thanks to another program called a linker. "We are waiting for Susan to complete her *object code file* so that we can package this program and get it out on the market before we test-run it to see whether it works."

object-oriented *(ob-jekt-or-ee-en-ted)* 1. A style of programming in which you bundle sets of instructions into packages known as *objects,* similar to the way you can bundle pieces of paper into packages know as *wads.* In the old-fashioned type of programming, known as procedural programming, a writer would just write instructions one after the other, with one thing leading to the next. Object-oriented programming squishes the instructions into self-sufficient modules.

Thus, if you've written a code object that displays the date and time in a box on-screen, you merely toss that wad of code into your program and, lo, it works. You can even take that whole chunk and transplant it into another program rather than have to rewrite the second program from scratch. Object-oriented programming is favored for this type of versatility. 2. A graphical element created by a formula in a program. The element is an object because it can be manipulated without messing up the rest of what you've drawn. "I was trying to manipulate an *object* on-screen and then realized that it was a piece of spaghetti stuck to the screen. I guess that I shouldn't work and eat at the same time."

occasional irregularity *(oh-kay-zhun-uhl ee-reg-yoo-lar-uh-tee)* The times when a computer, or the software program it's running, messes up or shuts down. The symptoms can't be repeated so that you can try to fix the problem — they just happen for no apparent reason, like being late for work, forgetting your spouse's name,

Eunice has 15 grandchildren and 6 great-grandchildren.

and UFOs. The solution is to shut down completely and reboot (which is probably true for humans as well). Another solution is to have anyone else look at the problem; these problems occur only when you are by yourself and will not repeat for others. "My computer's problem is worse than *occasional irregularity,* so I am taking it to see a specialist in Singapore."

OCR *(oh see ar)* 1. Acronym for *Optical Character Recognition,* a computer's capability (via special software) to look at a page of text and recognize letters and words and then translate them into a computer file so that you don't have to retype anything. The OCR software sees that an *A* is an *A* rather than a collection of dots forming a picture. This capability is important at certain times: for example, if you have a fax modem inside your computer and somebody faxes you a document. If you have OCR software, the FAX is a document you can edit. If you don't have OCR software, your computer just thinks that the document is one big picture. "Using *OCR,* someday computers will even be capable of deciphering a doctor's prescription." 2. Acronym for *Obvious Candidate for Rehabilitation,* a term used fondly to describe some programmers.

octal *(ok-tal)* Base 8, a counting system in which the numbers range from 0 to 7, and then the value eight is represented by the number 10. Weird? Yes! We humans count in base 10, probably because we have 10 fingers. Base 10 uses the numbers 0 through 9 and then 10 to represent the value ten. Octal — hey, it's just

weird. No one uses octal anymore, at least no one you have to deal with unless you get lost somewhere at a university or nuclear plant. "If an octopus could count, it would probably do so in base 8, *octal.*"

OCX *(oh see eks)* Acronym for *OLE Custom Control,* which is odd because OLE is itself an acronym that stands for *Object Linking and Embedding,* and nobody can figure out where the *X* in OCX comes from. Microsoft developed the OCX standard as an advanced version of the VBX standard. See *VBX.* Although the VBX standard is designed for 16-bit operating systems, such as MS-DOS and Windows 3.1, OCX is designed for 32-bit operating systems, such as Windows NT and Windows 95.

OEM *(oh ee em)* Acronym for *Original Equipment Manufacturer,* a company which makes the parts that go into machines assembled and sold by somebody else. For example, Joe Blorf may make disk drives that are then installed in computers that are sold by Milo Cooper. Joe is the OEM for Milo's hard drives. Few computer manufacturers make all their own stuff. "Although American computers are the most advanced in the world, most of the parts come from Japanese *OEMs.*"

offline *(awf-lien)* Not connected to a computer, or more probably not really bothering with the computer. There's a difference between offline and unplugged. If you yank out the printer cable, you've unplugged it. If the printer is plugged in, however, you may have to turn it on to make it online. Furthermore, you may have to punch another button that tells the printer to obey the computer, which is also called "putting it online." "Sometimes I have to take my printer *offline* to advance a sheet of paper. Sometimes I have to take my brain *offline* to fall asleep."

offset *(awf-set)* To allow extra room for inner margins in a word-processed document so that it can be bound in book form. This dictionary has an offset of an inch or so, which allows for the pages to be bound together. If you were to yank out a page, you would see more blank space on one side than on the other, or the offset. "We should *offset* the document six inches in case you make a mistake in the binding."

OK button *(oh-kay but-un)* A graphical switch that accepts all settings or acknowledges a message from the computer. You can also "click" the OK button by pressing the Enter key. "I think that the *OK buttons* I use should be renamed 'Oh, well.'"

OK Corral *(oh-kay kor-al)* The place where you hang your hat, where the Naughahydes roam, where the skies are not cloudy or gray, where the only time you hear about is suppertime, where — doggone it! Wrong dictionary! See *Cowherding For Dummies.* "It's suppertime at the *OK Corral.* Click the OK button."

OLE *(oh-lay)* Acronym for *Object Linking and Embedding,* which is really two things: A super method of cut-and-paste (linking) that enables you to create one type of document from within

another type of document (embedding). Weird stuff. Probably no one uses it. OLE commands are located on the Object menu, and the Paste Link command is often on the Edit menu. "And now, Miguel will paste the picture of the bull into his document about bullfighting. Here he goes. Click *OLE!*"

on-line *(on-lien)* Another way to write *online.*

online *(on-lien)* 1. Connected. Using your modem to connect to another computer. 2. Available, as in, "The printer is online," or working and ready to print. 3. A switch on a printer that enables it to accept commands from a computer. A printer can be taken offline to use its menu or any of the other interesting buttons on its panel.

online service *(on-lien sir-vus)* A provider of news and information for modem users. CompuServe, America Online, Prodigy, and others are considered online services.

OOP *(oop)* Acronym for *object-oriented programming,* a method of programming that creates individual software objects that can be used again and again in other programs. Although it takes more time to create objects, the ability to reuse them in other programs reduces programming time. See also *object-oriented.* "Because programming languages such as C++ and Pascal are now designed to provide *OOP* capabilities, you can write one part of a program and use it in several other programs. Just don't leave the parts lying around on your desktop, or you're liable to step in the *oop.*"

open *(oh-pen)* 1. To access a program or file, just as you open a book if you want to read it, a notebook if you want to write in it, a car door if you want to hit your knee with it, or a can of tuna fish if you want to eat from it. "Please don't *open* the file named WORMCAN.DOC." 2. The command that opens files; typically located on the File menu.

open architecture *(oh-pen ark-uh-tek-chur)* The philosophy and practice of building computers and making the design and engineering public knowledge. It invites other manufacturers and developers to augment the computer with peripherals, software, and internal components. The theory is that the more doodads and gizmos available on the market to work with a given machine, the more tricks a user can do with it, and the more the machine will sell. IBM has practiced open architecture with its PCs, and Sun Microsystems has practiced it with its workstations. Apple Computer is famous for *not* practicing it. Apple has become notorious, in fact, for doing exactly the opposite, for shouting "Off with their heads!" whenever anyone else builds something that looks remotely like an Apple product. The Macintosh *is* becoming a rather "open" machine these days, however. See also *architecture, closed architecture*. "Although IBM had the foresight to create an *open architecture* PC, it didn't have the foresight to realize that clone manufacturers would take away most of its business."

OpenDoc *(oh-pen-dok)* A standard being promoted by Apple, Borland, IBM, Novell, and other companies to enable programs to share data with one another, no matter on what program or computer the data may have been created. OpenDoc is an alternative to the Microsoft compound document architecture, Object Linking and Embedding (OLE). Unlike OLE, which is designed for only Microsoft Windows, OpenDoc works with the Macintosh, OS/2, Windows, and, ultimately, UNIX. "By using *OpenDoc,* I can copy information from a Macintosh spreadsheet, store it in my Windows word processor, and combine the whole thing in a new document so that Janet can edit it by using OS/2."

operand *(op-ur-and)* A value, variable, or doodad in an equation that gets operated on by an operator. In the statement $2 + 3 = 5$, 2 and 3 are operands, and the plus and equal signs are operators. See also *operator.* "If you take away the symbols in a mathematical equation, all you have left are the *operands.* This stuff doesn't sound useful, which is why it's a mathematical concept."

operating environment *(op-ur-ay-ting en-vier-ment)* A feel-good term for an operating system. Because the operating system often dictates the method by which you use the computer (the environment, so to speak: text versus graphics and menus versus commands), this term is rather redundant. In fact, I believe that it's an attempt by some marketing department to make computers sound friendlier and more politically correct. Even so, because *environment* has more syllables and is more difficult to spell than *system,* you make your own decision. See *operating system* (of course).

O

operating system *(op-ur-ay-ting sis-tim)*
The software that controls the hardware and also runs your programs. Some common operating systems are DOS, System 7 for the Macintosh, OS/2, and UNIX. (Windows is not an operating system by itself because it must run "on top of" DOS.) "Some people who use the DOS *operating system* add Windows to avoid having to use DOS commands. Some of those people use programs such as Norton Desktop to avoid using Windows commands. Avoidance is a big part of computing."

operator *(op-er-ay-ter)* A symbol representing a mathematical operation. The usual context is within a software program or programming language. Typical operators are

+ Addition

– Subtraction

* Multiplication

/ Division

In addition to these mathematical operators, many other types exist. Relational operators, for example, test the relationships between values:

< Less than

> Greater than

= Equal to

<= Less than or equal to

>= Greater than or equal to

< > Not equal to

"In the spreadsheet, I use mathematical *operators* to produce a budget worksheet. Then I use other operators to cover up the funds I'm embezzling."

optical *(op-ti-kul)* Refers to light or vision. When you are having an optical illusion, for example, you are seeing something that's not there, such as Social Security. "The other day, Windows just came up — splat — right there on-screen. I'm certain that I experienced an *optical* illusion."

optical disk *(op-ti-kul disk)* A computer storage medium (a disk drive) that operates by way of digitized beams of light or lasers. That process sounds so cool that there must be a catch — and there are two: speed and price. Optical disks are expensive and slow, though they hold lots of information. Optical disks are somewhat akin to CD-ROM technology. The claim to fame of the optical disk drive is that its storage capacity is much greater than that of a magnetic floppy disk, which is your typical type of disk. "I don't like the way that the new *optical disk* is looking at me."

optical mouse *(op-ti-kul mows)*
A distant cousin of the three non-optical, or "blind," mice who got their tails — oops, wrong dictionary! See *Nursery Rhymes For Dummies.* In computer terms, an optical mouse is a pointing device that uses a light beam to track the position of the cursor or pointer on-screen. Normal mice use a mechanical ball that rolls to detect movement. The light beam type of optical mouse is used with a special grid type of mousepad that reflects the beam. (The mechanical type of mouse also uses some optical technology, but internally. An electronic eye watches the ball roll around, which is how the mouse detects movement. Cool, huh?)

O

"If your *optical mouse* gets loose, you need a special optical mousetrap to catch it."

optimize *(op-ti-miez)* To customize software or hardware so that it serves users to its utmost capacity. The goal is to have the machinery run faster and more efficiently. This process can include shuffling parts of the software into different parts of the computer's memory, rewriting chunks of software applications, or even just tweaking the controls on your desktop control panel. "Microsoft Windows gets its bloated reputation partly because it loads your hard disk with graphical images you can use for 'wallpaper.' If you think that you can do without these images, you can *optimize* Windows by getting rid of all the picture files."

Option key *(op-shun kee)* A key on any Apple keyboard used in combination with other keys to execute special functions. Like the Shift key, the Option key doesn't do anything if you press it by itself. Here's an example: In Word on the Mac, pressing the Option key and then the numeral 8 key produces a bullet character. Pressing Option+* gives you a little bad-guy character. And pressing Shift+Option+Enter shoots the bad-guy character with the bullet character. Pressing Ctrl+Option+B cleans up the mess character afterward. "If I press *Option*+S, I save my document. If I press Shift+*Option*+S, I save all open documents. If I press Ctrl+Shift+ *Option*+S, I get a cramp in my hand."

originate mode *(or-ij-uh-nayt mohd)* The standard operating mode for a modem. In originate mode, the modem makes the phone calls, by dialing out to another computer. The other mode is *answer,* in which the modem answers the phone. See *answer mode*.

orphan *(or-fun)* 1. The first line of a paragraph abandoned at the bottom of one page while the rest of the lines continue on the following page. The dimensions of this tragedy have reached such proportions that developers of page-layout software have included social-service capabilities in their programs to rescue orphans from this plight. 2. A computer, usually one of the early models, that is no longer made or supported by the company that heralded it as a "technological revolution" just a few years back. This situation happens to all computers sooner or later. "Pity ye, O Osborne owners. And ye Adam and Atari owners and owners of old Radio Shack stuff. Fare thee well, old Apple II, Apple III, and Lisa owners. Bid adieu to the long throng of forgotten PCs, nay the *orphans* of the electronics age."

OS/2 *(oh es too)* Trademarked acronym for *Operating System/2,* developed jointly by IBM and Microsoft to replace DOS and Windows. Despite the initial fanfare, few software developers developed applications for OS/2, so

OS/2 user.

Microsoft pushed Windows on its own and stole the show. It's as though IBM gave a party and nobody came. IBM is now trying to please the masses with newer and better versions of OS/2, specifically to compete with Microsoft and Windows. The only problem is still the OS/2 lack of specific, OS/2 software. "Rebel against the new Windows as ye long ago rebelled against *OS/2!* We'll show the rabble who runs the show who's really in charge!"

outline font *(owt-lien fawnt)* A typeface that is solid around the edges and hollow in the middle, used for posters and headlines but not so much for regular typing. Some font families let you choose to make an outline typeface from a regular one. For example, Times Roman can become Times Roman Outline. The outline fonts keep the styles and proportions of the regular fonts they come from. "Kids love *outline fonts* because they can color in the middle with crayons."

outliner software *(owt-lien-er soft-wayr)* A program that can make the kind of outline you used to make in high school on 3-x-5 cards when you were learning how to organize your writing compositions. Those Roman numerals followed by uppercase letters followed by Arabic numerals followed by lowercase letters can really take you back. In the old days — not quite as old as your high school days — this kind of software was a separate application from word processing. In these enlightened times, you can make outlines in the same software program in which you can write letters and novels. "We used *outlining software* to organize the outline for this new dictionary. The authors came up with all the letters, and the publisher suggested that we use the alphabetizing feature to organize them."

output *(owt-put)* What the computer spits out after it churns through the information you put into it. Output can be in the form of characters on-screen, sounds from speakers, or hard copy from a printer. The machines that give you the output are called output devices. (See, learning about computers is way easier than you thought!) See also *input.* "When your input is poorly conceived, you shouldn't be surprised when your *output* is garbage."

OverDrive *(oh-ver-driev)* 1. A marketing adjective used by Intel to describe a faster version of the 80486 microprocessor. OverDrive processors run two or more times faster than non-OverDrive processors. You use the OverDrive "slot" in your computer to plug in an OverDrive chip, which then takes over as your PC's microprocessor from your older, lamer 486 microprocessor. "I yanked out my ancient 80486DX and replaced it with an 80486DX4 *OverDrive* processor. Now my computer runs two times faster, although I still haven't figured out why I need this additional speed to do word processing." 2. Any of several upgrade microprocessors produced by Intel that are designed to replace or augment the microprocessor now installed in your PC.

O

overflow (*oh-ver-floh*) 1. To run out of room, as in a mathematical computation that cannot fit into memory. 2. A flag in the microprocessor that indicates when a mathematical operation does not fit into a register. Although this stuff is really nerdy, it helps programmers build software that eventually runs right. 3. Anything that cannot fit into memory. "When a computer gives you an *overflow* message, take two aspirin, reboot your computer, and call a programmer in the morning."

overhead (*oh-ver-hed*) Similar to what it means in real life: The resources you need just to stay operational — in this case, measured in RAM, megabytes, processing speed, and I/O capacity. This term refers mostly to the requirements of a program just to run on your PC. Some programs may require 640K of RAM, 5MB of hard disk space, plus special graphics cards and printers. "Working with graphics requires a great deal of *overhead*. Do you think that there's a conspiracy going on between the stores that sell the hardware and the guys who write the software?"

overlay (*oh-ver-lay*) A sophisticated form of program juggling in which the whole program is just too darn big to fit into memory at one time. What they do is split the program into modules and overlay them into memory, swapping parts of the program back and forth between RAM and a disk. See also *Murphy's law*. "They used *overlay* technology to overcome limitations in RAM. Now we can use Parkinson's law of programming: 'Expand your program to fill as much RAM as you have available.'"

overtype (*oh-ver-tiep*) A text editing mode where any new text you type replaces (writes over) text already on the screen. This contrasts with insert mode, where new text shoves existing text to the left and down to make room for new text.

overwrite (*oh-ver-riet*) See *overtype*.

owner (*oh-ner*) The person who paid for the software, as opposed to the two dozen people using the pirated copy. If you had to look up this word, turn to the word *pirate* to find your picture. "If you're the *owner* of this software package, how come the startup screen says 'Registered to Al Gore, Washington, D.C.?'"

O

p

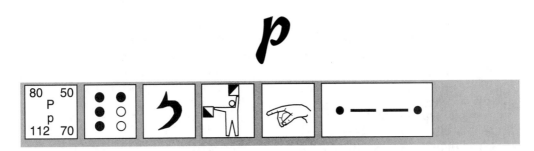

P: *(pee-koh-lon)* The letter designation for some hard drive or other type of disk drive on a PC. No other P: jokes available at this time.

p-code *(pee-kohd)* P-code is relevant only to the old p-system operating system, which I'd bet $10 right now you've never heard of. Using the p-system, a programmer would compile a program, usually written in Pascal, into p-code, which is short for *pseudocode.* The p-code could be interpreted by the p-system's interpreter into the language the PC's microprocessor understood best. This process meant that p-code could, theoretically, run on any computer, as long as that computer was running the p-system. P — get it? See also *pseudocode.* "Because the p-system went defunct in the early '80s, *p-code* is no longer a useful term, unless you redefine it to mean *problem code* or programming instructions the dog mistook for the newspaper."

packet *(pak-it)* A chunk of information. Typically used in communications (modem or network), a packet is a chunk of data sent from one computer to another. The data is stored inside the packet, along with other information used by whatever protocol under which the packet is being sent. A typically nerdy term.

packing list *(pak-ing list)* The list of stuff that should be in the box when you buy a new computer or order software. Generally, you should find the packing list first and double-check to ensure that you received everything listed. "Checking the *packing list* ensures that you don't throw out something you may need later."

paddle *(pad-al)* An older input device, such as a joystick, that is frequently used for computer and video games. The paddle is a knob you twist, rotating it one way or the other. See also *joystick.* "My flight-simulator program lets you use a *paddle* to control the plane. I can turn my plane left and right, but I still can't get it off the ground."

page *(payj)* 1. The electronic unit of text that corresponds to a book page in real life. A page of text in a word processor; the amount of text it would take to fill a typical 8½-x-11-inch sheet of paper. Even if your monitor is too small to fit a page of this size on-screen all at one time, the computer still knows where the page starts and ends and communicates this information to the printer. 2. A chunk of RAM, typically 64 kilobytes. "One handy thing about *pages* on the computer is that you can recycle them over and over and over again.

Al Gore would be pleased. Hug a tree." 3. A document on the World Wide Web. Typically each screen you view on the Web is called a *page*.

page break *(payj brayk)* In word processing, the point at which one page leaves off and another begins. Two types of page breaks can be created: *soft* page breaks and *hard* page breaks. A soft page break happens automatically as soon as you get to the last character of the last line on a page. If you add or delete text (or graphics, for that matter) on the page, the page break changes accordingly. A hard page break is one you put in yourself at a precise location. A new page always starts at that point even if you add or delete material before the hard page break. "Because I wanted my term paper to come out to 20 pages and I had only 7 pages to start with, I made the type bigger and put in a bunch of extra hard *page breaks*."

Page Down key *(payj down kee)* A glorified cursor key that moves you forward (down) in the document the exact length of a page every time you press the key. Depending on the program, a "page" can either be the amount of information that fits on a screen or the size of a real page. Often abbreviated PgDn. See also *Page Up key.* "Page, off my knee. Off! Now! Down, Page! *Page Down!*"

page frame *(payj fraym)* A 64K chunk of memory used by the old expanded-memory standard. Four 16K pages existed in the page frame, each of which could be swapped out between memory on the expanded-memory

card and conventional memory in the PC. That's kinda how the expanded-memory standard worked. Messy, huh? See also *expanded memory.* "That memory looks bleak and ugly sitting there. *Page-frame* it, and tell me what you think."

page layout *(payj lay-owt)* 1. The design of text and graphics on a printed page and the software that creates it. See also *desktop publishing.* "I want to start my own newspaper called *The Computer Chronicle For Dummies,* but I need some *page-layout* software and about 40 years to learn how to use it." 2. A command that adjusts the page layout.

Page Up key *(payj up kee)* A key on the keyboard that moves the cursor up (backward) through your document to the top. Often labeled PgUp on the keyboard. See also *Page Down key.* "If you're already at the top of the document, pressing the *Page Up key* doesn't take you anywhere."

pagination *(paj-uh-nay-shun)* The process of splitting a long document into page-length chunks. Because everything you print appears eventually on a piece of paper — a *page* — the art of pagination shows you where the page elements will be displayed, right on-screen, before printing. "Because Steve can't figure out how the *pagination* works in my word-processing program, he'll have to print his novel on a scroll."

paint *(paynt)* 1. To create an image using pixels, as opposed to a drawing program, which creates an image using objects. 2. A program that creates paint images. "With that black velvet mode in my new *paint* program, we're going to put the Tijuana Elvis Painting Society out of business."

palette *(pal-et)* 1. The selection of colors available in a paint or drawing program. The palette is somewhat limited by your hardware, specifically your monitor and graphics card. Some paint colors are given to you; others, you can mix yourself. Palettes can also hold fill patterns, border styles, and other types of painting stuff. "This *palette* has so many colors that they take up the whole screen, and I have only two square inches in which to paint my picture." 2. A floating window containing various options. See also *dialog box.*

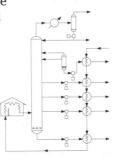

Complex drawing to break up the page.

palmtop computer *(palm-tahp com-pyoo-ter)* A teensy-tiny computer that fits in the palm of your hand. Or, following the laptop metaphor, a computer that would fit in the palm of your hand if you had abnormally huge hands. Palmtop computers generally have all the hardware of their desktop cousins, but a tinier keyboard and monochrome display. Their purposes are often customized, and they come with embedded software: an address book, a to-do list, and communications and other applications that can frustrate the heck out of you unless you have fingers the size of cocktail straws. "Those *palmtop computers* sure are tiny. What's next? The fingernail computer?"

pane *(payn)* A portion of a window that has been split into multiple parts. In Excel, for example, you can see your spreadsheet inside a single window. Furthermore, you can create as many as four panes in the window by splitting it vertically and horizontally. You can display different parts of your spreadsheet or document in the different panes. Although the result probably looks like what those independent-eyed iguanas see, it helps you scope out big documents and spreadsheets easily. See also *window.* "I've traveled on the ocean, I've tramped upon the plain, but I've never seen a window cry because it had a *pane.*"

panic button *(pan-ik but-un)* See *reset switch.*

paper-white *(pay-per wiet)* A special type of VGA monitor whose display approximates the whiteness of paper and provides black text and graphics to go with it. But, wait — there's more! Because the paper-white screen also shows you shades of gray — from 4, 8, and 16 to as many as 32 shades, it's much more true-to-life than a monochrome monitor because you can see shades of gray. "Now that I've upgraded to a *paper-white* monitor, I can get the same kind of writer's block that I get when I'm staring at a blank piece of paper."

p

Paradox *(payr-uh-doks)* 1. A relational database program created to compete against dBASE. 2. Something that happens at the same time that something else can't happen, which is usually bad. 3. Two Dox. "The name *Paradox* originally meant that it was a paradox that a powerful database could also be so easy to use. Now the name Paradox means that it's a paradox that Borland can market both Paradox and dBASE and still claim that each database is the number-one database of choice by Fortune 500 corporations all over the world."

parallel *(payr-uh-lel)* 1. Two lines that never touch, unless you're not looking or your name is Albert Einstein and you're traveling in an elevator at the speed of light, in which case you'll probably miss your floor anyway. "Actually, the universe isn't *parallel.* If a train travels along parallel rails that encompass the universe and you're waiting to catch the 4:15 to Philly, eventually you'll see yourself get off the same train with a strange woman and ask yourself for $40, and then you'll never see yourself again." 2. Refers to data traveling abreast as opposed to single file. For example, a parallel interface would use eight wires, one for each bit in a byte. 3. A type of port on a PC. See also *parallel port.*

parallel port *(payr-uh-lel port)* The thing on the back of your computer into which you plug the printer. Other things can plug in to the port, too, which is why it's officially known as a parallel port and not a printer port. Heck, IBM calls it an LPT port. And then there's the term *Centronics port.*

Bytes of information sent to the parallel port travel eight bits at a time, side by side, down eight different wires. This arrangement contrasts with a serial port, which sends the bits one after the other. See also *Centronics, LPT, printer port.* "The manual said to plug the printers into the *parallel ports,* so I arranged them neatly so that they each faced the door."

parallel processing *(payr-uh-lel praw-ses-ing)* A computer that can think about more than one thing at a time, which can cause neurotic behavior, as it does in humans. Technically, parallel process*ing* comes from having parallel process*ors,* which is essentially the case only in computers much mightier than the average desktop PC or Mac. The top performers of any kind of computer can use several thousand processors in parallel, whereas the lowly desktop computer typically has only one. Parallel processing is the basis of artificial intelligence, or those computers that really can say "Duh!"(See also *Cray, supercomputer.* "Supercomputers, which are incredibly fast and powerful, use something called massively *parallel processing.* I never thought that one thing could be more parallel than another."

parameter *(puh-ram-uh-ter)* A value — which can be numbers, letters, or other characters — that you enter into an equation or statement, such as an option. For example, the DOS FORMAT command is followed by a drive parameter. That's a drive letter telling the FORMAT command where the disk is that you want formatted. Parameter is just a fancy way of saying "option-thing that goes on the end of a command." You can also use parameters when you're searching for information. For example, Cornelia can enter the parameters *tall, ugly,* and *hairy* into the computer dating database to look for her dreamboat. "How about this error message: `optional required parameter missing`. How can something that's required be optional?"

paren(s) *(payr-en[z])* Slang for parenthesis (-theses). Sometimes you have to use a bunch of them, so you don't want to waste your breath on extra syllables. They're used in mathematical calculations in programming, among other things. Paren is *not* the singular version of parentheses. "I don't know why the equation didn't work. Stick some *parens* in there, and maybe it will."

parent/child *(payr-ent-child)* The relationship (how cute!) between categories of information, which can be files, directories, outline levels, or families. The *child* is a subcategory of the parent. See also *child process*. "In my outline, 'Things to Eat' is the *parent* topic of the 'Candy' topic. 'Candy' is a *child* of 'Things to Eat.' This fact more than justifies what I put into my mouth for nourishment."

parity *(payr-uh-tee)* A way of testing whether data is okay by counting the number of bits, such as during data transmission. The number can be either odd or even, and that information is saved and compared with subsequent calculations that also see whether the number is odd or even. If it isn't, no parity exists and

the computer pouts. See also *parity bit.* "Okay, Ivan, if you have enough nukes to blow up the world 530 times and we have enough to blow up the world 488 times — not counting subs, of course — then we've reached *parity.* Nyet?"

parity bit *(payr-uh-tee bit)* An extra bit that's included to check the parity in bytes. For example, a parity bit set to 1 means that the parity is odd (an odd number of 1s are in the eight bits that it's monitoring); 0, if it's even. "My modem, with its hilarious *parity bit,* is ready for the comedy club."

park *(park)* To immobilize the heads of your hard disk so that they don't rattle around and do damage if you move the computer. Older hard disks had this feature or a program with this name that physically parked the hard disk heads. This action is no longer necessary on today's hard disks.

parse *(pars)* 1. In programming, when a compiler examines each programming word and acts on it accordingly. 2. In spreadsheets, the function used to distribute data imported from other applications into separate fields in your new spreadsheet. 3. The act of splitting up a group of items (such as a sentence of words) into individual components.

partition *(par-tish-un)* 1. To divide a single hard drive into several logical drives. For example, a 4GB hard drive is typically divided into two logical hard drives on a PC, each of which can hold 2GB of information. 2. A section of a hard disk set aside for use with a specific operating system.

p

3. The act of separating the hard drive into these types of sections. See also *hard disk, hard drive, logical drive.* "I'm too busy; have Mr. Spock *partition* your disk into logical drives."

Pascal *(pas-kal)* A programming language used mainly for teaching programming concepts, with commands that look like regular English words — although they aren't strung together that way. Named after the 17th century philosopher/mathematician Blaise Pascal, the language was created by Niklaus Wirth in the early 1970s. "*Pascal* was a rascal, but then again, so is any guy named Blaise."

passive matrix *(pas-iv may-triks)* A type of laptop display that's cheaper and not as good as the active matrix type. Unlike active matrix, which uses transistors to control the screen, a passive matrix display uses some type of lame logic-board circuitry or some such thing. "My new KneeCap 150 laptop uses the *passive matrix* display, so I can see color graphics of a parrot at 39,000 feet, but not as good as the guy with the active matrix display who's sitting next to me."

password *(pas-werd)* Like saying "Open, sesame" to the computer, the password is your secret key to gaining access to a computer, program, network, or files. "Peggy wanted to make sure that she would be able to remember her *password,* so she wrote it on a sign in big letters and stuck it on the wall next to the computer." (Tip for power users: This technique defeats the purpose of having a password.)

paste *(payst)* To insert an item previously cut or copied. The item can be such things as text, graphics, records from a database, or a column of numbers from a spreadsheet. See also *Clipboard, copy, cut, cut and paste.* "If you want to *paste* some of my term paper into your term paper, make sure that the fonts match so that the teacher doesn't suspect anything."

path *(path)* 1. A list of directories in which the operating system looks for program files. See also *blessed folder, pathname.* 2. The command that creates the list of directories.

pathname *(path-naym)* The full (long and complicated) name for a file. The pathname includes the name of the drive on which the file lives, the directories, and then the file itself, as shown in this example:

```
C:\PROGRAMS\GRAPHICS\PAINT.EXE
```

Pathnames are the same as filenames, just more specific. You can type a pathname rather than a filename whenever you're prompted. (If you don't, the operating system saves the file in a specific place.) In DOS and Windows, a backslash character (\) separates items in a pathname. On the Macintosh, a colon separates items in a pathname. In UNIX, a forward slash (/) is used to separate items in a pathname.

Pause key *(paws kee)* 1. A key on the keyboard that freezes screen output or temporarily halts all computer activity. In DOS, pressing Pause once usually freezes the display; pressing it again returns normal behavior.

Pressing the Ctrl+S keystroke works the same as on other keyboards. Some keyboards sport a Hold key that works the same way. See also *hold.* "Why would anyone press the *Pause key*? Doesn't the computer go slowly enough as it is?" 2. A key used by most games to freeze the action temporarily. For example, you're in a firefight with several slime-dripping demons, and the action is hot and heavy, with chunks of whatever flying to and fro. If you need to scratch your nose, you can stab the Pause key, scratch away, and then press Pause again to restart the action. That way, a minor human inconvenience doesn't get in the way of saving the universe from alien scum.

PC *(pee see)* 1. Acronym for *personal computer,* from the first IBM PC. Technically refers to any stand-alone computer, or what was once referred to as a microcomputer, including non-IBM (Windows) computers: the Macintosh, Amiga and others, though those users don't particularly like the term. 2. The original IBM PC. The copycat computers that worked like the original PC were referred to as clones or compatibles. See also *clone, compatible.* 3. Any computer capable of running DOS or Windows. This generic PC term excludes Macintosh, Amiga, and other computers that don't run DOS or Windows. "A *PC* has many definitions, depending on whether it's your

The original IBM PC.

personal computer or someone else's." 4. Acronym for *politically correct.* Although this usage may be listed first in any other dictionary, in this one, *politically correct* means reading the software license agreement before you tear open the package.

PC-DOS *(pee see daws)* Acronym for *Personal Computer – Disk Operating System,* the version of MS-DOS that is bundled with IBM PCs. See also *DOS, MS-DOS.*

PCI *(pee see ie)* Acronym for *Peripheral Component Interconnect,* a bus standard developed by Intel. The PCI bus connects directly with the microprocessor, making it one of the fastest ways to connect a hard disk controller, video card, or network interface to a PC. Most PCs sold today have a mixture of PCI bus slots and ISA slots. The fast stuff goes in the PCI slots. Ironically, PCI became a standard (defeating EISA, MCA, and VESA) because Intel just said so. Because Intel makes most of the motherboards included with the PCs sold today, PCI just happened. See also *bus, expansion slot, ISA, VESA.*

PCjr *(pee see joon-yoor)* The first home computer designed by IBM. Very bad. Very lame. The PCjr wasn't designed for the home as much as it was anti-designed for business; IBM didn't want business users buying a PCjr when they could buy a more expensive PC. Although the PCjr had moderately good sound and graphics, it lacked internal expansion, suffered from a poor design (the insides would have been crushed if you had set a monitor on top), and sported perhaps

p

the worst computer keyboard of all time: the infamous PC "Chicklet" keyboard. Introduced in 1983, the PCjr had become landfill fodder by 1985. Most home users just bought regular PCs. IBM repeated this mistake when it introduced the crippled PS/1 line in 1987 and then the limited Aptiva line in the mid-1990s. "Today, calling any computer a *PCjr* is more than a put-down; it's a slap-in-the-face insult!"

PCL *(pee see ell)* Acronym for *Printer Control Language,* a set of instructions used to control a specific brand of printer — not to be confused with page-description language or a printer driver. PCL also refers to HP LaserJet compatibility. "I have a *PCL* printer that acts just like a LaserJet V, but it's much less expensive. It's called a LaserJet IV."

PCMCIA *(pee see em see ie ay)* Long-winded acronym for *Personal Computer Memory Card International Association,* an organization dedicating its life to defining a standard for making and marketing credit-card-size expansion cards for laptop and some desktop computers. PCMCIA expansion cards resemble metal credit cards that are expensive and look like they could break just as easily. PCMCIA expansion slots look like long, thin holes in a laptop into which a PCMCIA card slides. "Some would say that *PCMCIA* stands for *People Can't Memorize Computer Industry Acronyms.*"

PCX *(pee see eks)* 1. A graphics file format for the PC. Originally used by the PC Paintbrush program, PCX is supported by almost every application on the PC, in both Windows and DOS.

PCX files are bitmapped graphics files. See also *bitmapped.* "Bob thought that *PCX* was a rating for the naughty graphics files he collected." 2. The file extension for a PCX graphic file.

PC-XT *(pee see eks tee)* Acronym for *Personal Computer — eXtended Technology,* a version of the first PC that came with a "massive" 10MB hard disk. Introduced in 1983, the PC-XT used the Intel 8088 microprocessor and ran Version 2.0 of MS-DOS.

PDA *(pee dee ay)* Acronym for *Personal Digital Assistant,* which describes handheld computers that let you store notes and make phone calls and that cost much more than a pencil and a pad of paper. "The most popular *PDA* is Apple's Newton, which can recognize your handwriting. If you think that using a PDA may come in handy, ask yourself how many times you misplace pens, and then ask yourself whether you would be willing to misplace a $1,000 computer."

PDF *(pee dee ef)* Acronym that stands for *Portable Document Format,* a type of file created by the Adobe Acrobat program. A PDF file contains text and graphics that anyone who uses an IBM or Macintosh computer can view, whether or not they have the Adobe Acrobat program on their hard disk. "Most complex documents available on the Internet are in *PDF* format."

PDL *(pee dee ell)* Acronym for *Page Description Language,* a programming language, such as PostScript, that is processed by a microprocessor in the printer. The PDL, through its particular statements and commands, "describes" the information on a page of printed output, generally through vector graphics calculations. Although thousands of lines of PDL code may be necessary to describe a page, the result prints much faster than the previous method of sending information to the printer: bitmapped graphics. The PDL is independent of the particular kind of printer you're using — as long as the printer has the capability of understanding the language. See also *PostScript, vector graphics.* "PostScript is a *PDL* commonly used with Macintosh computers. TrueType is now the primary PDL for PCs. TrueType is PostScript-compatible, but PostScript is not TrueType-compatible."

peanut *(pee-nut)* The IBM internal code word for the PCjr computer, used before the product was introduced. See also *PCjr.*

peek *(peek)* A BASIC language command that lets a user view the contents of a precise address in memory. The user can then poke a new value into the address. See also *poke.* "I took a *peek* into Santa's sack and saw that he was going to bring me a super-duper fax/modem for Christmas!"

peer-to-peer *(peer-too-peer)* A democratic arrangement in networking technology in which all nodes are created equal. The other kind of network is a *client/server* arrangement, in which one machine is specially designated as a file server and dominates all the "client" nodes. In a peer-to-peer network, each computer can share and access information on every other computer. See also *client/server, network, nodes,*

server. "*Peer-to-peer* means that our computers communicate on a network without a file server. Pier-to-peer means that we go to the end of the dock and peer over the edge."

pen *(pen)* 1. A long, thin device, ranging from quill to felt-tip, used for writing. 2. A type of mouse shaped like a pen. 3. A type of computer that receives input from a stylus similar in shape to a pen and registers signals electronically so that users can write in their own handwriting rather than enter information from a keyboard or with a mouse. Pen-based input must be neatly printed. Hence, an ironic turnaround has occurred: When people lost touch with paper and became dependent on keyboards, their handwriting became a casualty of technological development. Now that the technology has advanced even further, tidy handwriting is again becoming a necessity — to be able to take advantage of the technology! Industry analysts predicted that pen-based computing would become *the* hottest new technology. In reality, the pen has had little impact on the industry. See also *light pen.* "This must be a pig *pen* computer."

Pentium *(pen-tee-um)* 1. A brand of microprocessor manufactured by Intel. Even people who don't write ad copy for Intel consider this successor to

Pentagon.

the 486 chip revolutionary because of its speed and efficiency. Intel was going to call it the 586 chip but couldn't copyright the term, so it's

p

called the *Pentium.* See also *coprocessor, Intel, microprocessor, processor.* 2. A computer with a Pentium microprocessor. It's similar to asking your friend whether he has a V8, which means whether his car sports a V8 engine: "You got a new *Pentium?*"

Pentium MMX *(pen-tee-um em-em-eks)* A modified Pentium processor that contains special instructions to optimize multimedia applications — specifically, computer games. Generally speaking, a Pentium MMX is better than a Pentium processor. However, you really need software specifically designed to take advantage of the MMX part if you want to get your money's worth. MMX doesn't really stand for anything; Intel wants it that way and refers to it internally as MMX Technology, which is a trademark. Unofficially, Intel claims that MMX means "multimedia extensions" or "multimedia instruction set."

Pentium Pro *(pen-tee-um proh)* The second-generation Pentium microprocessor, which probably would have been called the 80686 had Intel stuck with that numbering scheme. Pentium Pros are generally faster and better than plain old Pentium computers.

People search *(pee-pol serch)* A way to find human beings on the Internet, either their physical location, phone number, e-mail address, or Web page address. Several People search engines exist: 411.com, Yahoo People Search, and Switchboard, for example.

peripheral *(pur-if-oor-al)* Any device connected to a computer (the console), including monitors, printers, scanners, mice, external hard or floppy drives, CD-ROM drives, speakers, and keyboards. "We are going to get so overwhelmed with *peripherals* that we won't be able to find the center anymore."

peripheralitis *(pur-if-oor-al-ie-tis)* A disorder characterized by having too many peripherals and nowhere to plug them in. Another problem is that you have a hard time getting them to talk to each other. "An effective cure for *peripheralitis* is poverty."

permanent storage *(per-muh-nent stor-edj)* 1. A disk drive. 2. Any form of storage that maintains its information when the power is turned off. RAM is the opposite — anything in RAM goes ka-blooie when you turn off the computer. See also *nonvolatile memory.* "I've put all the names in my little black book into *permanent storage* on my computer."

personal digital assistant *(per-son-al dij-uh-tal uh-sis-tant)* See *PDA.*

personal information manager *(per-son-al in-for-may-shun man-uh-jer)* A program that tries to organize your appointments, meetings, and schedules so that you can easily see how you're spending (wasting) your time at work. Sometimes referred to by its acronym, PIM. "Because I never seemed to have any time, I bought a new *personal information manager* for my computer. Now I still don't have any time because I'm spending it all trying to learn how to use my computer, MS-DOS, Windows, and my PIM all at the same time."

PERT *(purt)* 1. Acronym for *Program Evaluation and Review Technique,* an approach to project management that doesn't necessarily need the computer to implement it. You can perform PERT equally well on paper. PERT involves charting out the time and other resources needed to complete various components of a project. Project-management software programs usually contain PERT charting features. "I used a *PERT* diagram to show the vice president the schedule we intend to follow. He liked it so much that I'm now the official PERT manager at the company." 2. Acronym for *Peripheral Envy Regression Training,* for all you closet New Agers out there. 3. A shampoo.

PGA *(pee jee ay)*. 1. Professional Graphics Adapter, a defunct graphics standard somewhere between EGA and VGA. The PGA was expensive, and few users bought it. 2. Professional Golfers Association, composed of guys who wear funny hats, pants, and only one glove and who chase a tiny, white ball around a park for big bucks.

phone jack *(fohn jak)* A hole in a wall into which you plug a phone cable. The cable connects the phone system (which starts in the wall, in case you didn't know) with your computer's modem or a phone.

phosphor *(fahs-fer)* The material used inside a monitor to create the display. An electron beam scans the inside of the monitor, and the phosphor absorbs it in the form of light patterns you see on-screen. "The *phosphor* in my monitor must be stimulated by now because I've been typing love poems all day."

phosphor burn-in *(fahs-fer bern-in)* A ghost image that appears on-screen — and stays there — as a result of having the same image displayed for too long. Akin to sunburn of the monitor, phosphor burn-in occurs when you leave the same image on-screen

Eerie image burned into this monitor.

for several hours. When you turn off the monitor, you can still see an outline of the image on-screen. Screen savers help prevent this burn-in. See also *screen saver.* "When you install screen savers to prevent *phosphor burn-in,* they should have protection-factor numbers, like sunscreen does."

Photo CD *(foh-toh see dee)* A format developed by Kodak for storing digital photographs on a compact disk. A Photo CD lets you store multiple photographs until the compact disk can't hold any more. The Kodak dream is that you can own a Photo CD and take it to a film-processing center with a roll of film so that the film processing center stores your photographs on your Photo CD for you. "After taking pictures of our vacation, we had the processing center store them all on a *Photo CD.* Now we can make multiple Photo CDs, distribute them, and bore people all over the world with our vacation pictures."

physical device *(fiz-uh-kul dee-vies)* An actual, touch-and-feel object associated with your computer. *Physical device* would not require a definition in this dictionary if not for

p

virtual devices, which are imaginary, make-believe, can't-touch-them devices. "I put my virtual file, which contains my virtual income projection, on a *physical device* for storage. I'm hoping that it will become real."

physical drive *(fiz-uh-kul driev)* An actual disk drive, as opposed to a simulated disk drive (*logical drive*) or a disk drive that thinks that it's another disk drive (*virtual drive*). See also *logical drive.* "I took my disk drive to the gym every day last month, and now it's a real *physical drive.*"

pica *(pie-kah)* 1. An old-fashioned typographical measurement that rivals the English system (inches and pounds, for example) in obsolescence. Six picas are in an inch; one pica equals 12 points (and 72 points are in an inch). Pages and parts of pages are measured in picas. "Because this is an emotional book, we'll make the gutters between those columns three *picas* wide. That should handle the runoff." 2. Not a font. Pica used to be the name of a typeface on a typewriter, one that fit 10 characters per inch. Today, using the computer, you can resize any text to fit into that same space; for example, the Courier font at 12 points (in size) approximates the pica of the old computer. See also *elite.*

pico- *(pee-koh*; also *pie-koh)* A prefix meaning one-trillionth. "Give me a couple of *pico*seconds to back up my hard disk, and I'll be right with you."

PIF *(pif)* Acronym for *Program Information File,* a special type of descriptive file used by Windows to run DOS programs. "*PIF!* Puff! Oy, oy, oy!"

PIM *(pim)* Acronym for *Personal Information Manager.* See *personal information manager.*

pin *(pin)* 1. Wires in a dot-matrix print head that "poke out" to press on the ribbon and form an image on paper. A 9-pin print head was typical throughout most of the 1980s. The 24-pin print head could produce sharper results because of the number of pins and their relatively small size. "It was so quiet that you could hear a 24-*pin* printer drop." 2. A wire in a cable. For example, computers use 9-pin and 25-pin serial cables. "You would think that after almost ten years of computers having 9-*pin* serial cable connections, external modems would stop having 25-*pin* serial cable connections."

pin feed *(pin feed)* A method for moving paper through a printer involving knobby gears that use the holes on the side of the paper to pull (or push) and guide the paper through the printer. See also *dot-matrix.* "Sometimes the *pin-feed* mechanism jams, and my document comes out looking like a Chinese paper fan."

PING *(ping)* 1. Acronym for *Packet Internet Grouper,* a program used to tell whether a certain computer or Internet address is up and running, or available for communications on the Internet. 2. The act of running the PING program to see whether a computer (or enemy submarine) is available on the Internet.

Pink Floyd *(pink floyd)* The name of one of the most successful rock bands in history, recording such notable albums as *The Dark Side of the Moon* and *The Wall,* which have sold millions of copies worldwide and have been banned by various dictatorships over the years for their antisocial messages. Pink Floyd is often the rock music of choice for hard-core programmers, hackers, and people who ingest illegal substances into their system. "When I program in an ancient language, such as COBOL or FORTRAN, I like listening to classical music. When I really want to crank out good C++ code, however, I listen to *Pink Floyd.*"

pipe *(piep)* 1. A method of redirecting the output from one command to the input of another command. Piping is done in UNIX and DOS at the command prompt by using the pipe character (|). (See |, *filter.*) 2. The pipe character (|). 3. What people smoke when they're too wimpy to light up a fine cigar. 4. A verb referring to the transfer of information from one place to another — like plumbing for information.

piracy *(pie-ruh-see)* Copying software without the permission of the author or publisher and, if you're really bad, distributing it. For every copy of a program that is purchased legitimately, it is estimated that two copies are pirated. Most pirates justify this practice by explaining that the software companies are making too much money from the products they sell and that pirated copies do not really take away revenue from publishers

because pirates would not have purchased the product anyway. Efforts to squelch this plague have included copy protection, registration by legal owners, and Just Saying No — let alone the fact that you could also go to jail for it. "Software *piracy* enables people who become seasick easily to become buccaneers."

pitch *(pitch)* The number of characters per inch, as on old-fashioned typewriters. Some old word-processing software programs still use this type of measurement and will, for example, give you a choice of printing in 10-pitch or 12-pitch. Most of the newer stuff uses points to measure character size. See also *point.*

pixel *(pik-sel)* Abbreviation of *picture element,* the tiny dots on-screen that form an image. "That thin coat of dirt on the front of your monitor is called *pixel* dust."

A pixel.

PL/1 *(pee el won)* Acronym for *Programming Language One,* an early programming language mostly used on IBM mainframes. Sometimes written as PL/I, but not pronounced Programming Language Eye. "Not many people use *PL/1* anymore, but it's still cool to have on your résumé."

planar board *(play-nar bord)* A dorky term for a motherboard; used by IBM because it feels, for some reason, that it has to rename everything or else someone may actually believe that the company is *not* a technology leader. Something like that. See also *motherboard.*

plasma *(plaz-mah)* 1. A type of monitor used in laptop and notebook computers — adapted from LCD technology. Plasma monitors are flat, do not require tubes, and are therefore smaller and lighter than CRT monitors. Stimulating some gas trapped between two panels produces the image. Also known as *flat panel display.* See also *gas plasma display, monitor.* "If I look at the *plasma* display on my laptop computer at just the right angle, I can see the ocean." 2. The stuff that poor programmers sell from their own veins just to make ten bucks. 3. Any heated gas.

platen *(pla-tin)* The roller that guides paper through a printer. The character keys strike against the paper while it's rolling over this surface. "Do not let your *platen* get scratched or notched because that could make the letters come out looking funny."

platform *(plat-form)* The hardware on which an operating system sits, or the operating system on which a software application sits. For example, Intel processors constitute a platform on which operating systems are built. DOS/Windows is a platform on which application programs are built.

plotter *(plaht-er)* A type of printer that draws pictures using one or more pens, based on instructions fed to it from a computer. Especially useful with graphics or CAD applications. Those Create-a-Card machines you see all over the place use plotters to create their greeting cards.

plug *(pluhg)* The thing at the end of a wire or cable that you stick into a jack to make information or electricity flow. See also *male connector.* "Sometimes, when you can't get your computer to work, it's because you need to *plug* it in."

Plug and Play *(pluhg and play)* 1. A wistful fantasy of engineers in which all computer equipment works perfectly with equipment from other manufacturers, just by plugging the pieces together. "We will have no *Plug and Play* computers in this office! No! Give me Plug and Work computers!" 2. The capability of an operating system to instantly recognize a new piece of hardware and install it automatically, like Windows 95 does. Or so they say.

plug-in *(pluhg-in)* An optional enhancement or helper program. Some programs are so diverse that they allow other programs to come in and help out, providing a handy way to extend their power. For example, the Microsoft and Netscape Web browsers have the capability to extend their reach through various plug-ins. These plug-ins enable the browsers to play real-time music and view videos and other interesting things on the Internet.

PMMU *(pee em em yoo)* Acronym for *Paged Memory-Management Unit,* a chip or circuit in some computers that assists with virtual memory. See also *virtual memory.* "Yes, he got his virtual memory degree at good ol' *PMMU.*"

point *(poynt)* 1. To move the mouse cursor over a specific object on-screen.

2. A measurement of the size of characters in a typeface. One point is equal to *approximately* $1/72$ of an inch. A character 12 points high, for example, is $1/6$-inch tall. The larger the point value, the bigger (taller and wider) the letter. "If you want your résumé to fit on one page, you can make the *point* size teensy-tiny."

pointer *(poynt-er)* 1. A symbol that appears on-screen and corresponds to the movement of the mouse or other pointing device. The pointer doesn't always look the same. It can take on different guises in different applications or even in different functions within the same application. 2. A programming term relating to a variable that keeps track of an object (such as the next item in a linked list). 3. A C language variable that contains a memory address and can be used to examine or change the contents at that address.

Pointer.

pointing device *(poynt-ing dee-vies)* An input device, such as a mouse, trackball, joystick, or stylus, that lets you move the cursor around on-screen. "When Jerry uses a touch-sensitive monitor, his finger is no longer a picking device — it's a *pointing device*."

point-of-sale system *(poynt-ov-say-el sis-tim)* Computer hardware and software for retail sales operations. Although the type of hardware can range from a personal computer to a mainframe, its function is the same: It registers prices for individual items, gathers data from sales, tracks inventory, and maintains a customer database. The system can include peripherals, such as a receipt printer, a bar code scanner, and credit-card verification capability. "Before we can install an expensive, new *point-of-sale system* in our store, we need to cut down on shoplifting."

point-to-point tunneling protocol *(poynt-too-poynt tun-nel-ing proh-toh-kol)* See *PPTP*.

poke *(pohk)* A BASIC language command that enables you to place a value in a precise memory location. See also *peek*. "The object is to know where to *poke* the computer so that it doesn't poke you back."

polymorphic virus *(pah-lee-mor-fik vie-rus)* A special virus that modifies itself every time it infects a file on your computer. By modifying itself, a polymorphic virus makes it harder for antivirus programs to find and kill all possible strains of the virus. Polymorphic viruses are usually created with the help of a mutation engine. See also *mutation engine*. "My antivirus programs found and removed a *polymorphic virus* from my computer. I'm afraid, though, that the antivirus program hasn't found all the different strains of the polymorphic virus, so I played it safe and switched my hard disk with Lyle's."

polymorphism *(pah-lee-mor-fiz-um)* In the context of object-oriented programming, using the same name to

p

specify different procedures within different contexts. A good analogy is the word *cook,* which can involve a different method for bread, pasta, vegetables, and meat. You can define *display,* for example, to apply to text, graphics, pictures, spreadsheets, movies, sound effects, and anything else you choose to associate with the term. See also *object-oriented.* "I tried to describe the concept of *polymorphism* to my family, but then my mother-in-law blurted out that her sister is not a man and just has a tiny mustache problem."

pong *(pawng)* The original computer game developed by Atari in the mid-1970s and now found in museums. "*Pong* was named after Ping-Pong, the table tennis game invented by the Chinese. Do you know that it's called Ping-Pong in Chinese as well? Do you know what it means? 'Ping-pong' is the sound the ball makes. Same in Chinese and English. What a world!"

pop *(pahp)* To remove the last data item from a storage stack. See also *push.* "Pat's afraid that if his computer didn't have a lid, all those values he *popped* off the stack would fly up and hit him in the eye."

POP2, **POP3** *(pahp-too, pahp-three)* Versions of the Post Office Protocol, the method by which e-mail is sent and received by computers on the Internet. Unlike the SMTP protocol, messages using the POP protocol are interactive between the various mailboxes on the Internet. See also *SMTP.* Both POP2 and POP3 are similar protocols, but they are incompatible. Most newer Internet mail programs use POP3.

pop-up menu *(pahp-up men-yoo)* Essentially the same idea as a pull-down menu, except that it appears someplace other than on the menu bar. In a Mac environment, a pop-up menu can appear when you highlight one of the choices on a pull-down menu. See also *pull-down menu.* "A *pop-up menu* is a little different from a pop-up book. A picture of the item in question does not stick up from the surface of the screen."

port *(port)* 1. A connector (jack) in back of a computer where you can plug in a peripheral device. See also *parallel, SCSI, serial.* 2. To convert a software application to an operating system other than the one for which it was originally written. "We finally *ported* our DOS menu system to the Macintosh, but we can't figure out why it isn't selling."

portable computer *(port-uh-bul com-pyoo-ter)* A PC you can carry around with you without making yourself a candidate for the trauma ward. Classifications include laptops, notebooks, and handheld computers. A portable computer that is really too heavy to lug around regularly may be called "transportable" or "a brick on a leash." I prefer the term *luggable.* "I have a new *portable computer* that can store pages of information and print them instantly. It even recognizes my handwriting. It's called a pad and pencil."

portrait orientation *(por-trayt or-ee-en-tay-shun)* An amazingly convoluted way of saying "the usual direction" when you're discussing the way in which the paper gets printed on. It means more vertical than horizontal, or "the long way," as opposed to "landscape orientation," or "the wide way." Usually, you find this terminology in graphics applications. Like many other professionals, graphics artists seem to have an irresistible need

M551 Tank in portrait orientation.

to mystify even the simplest things. See also *landscape orientation*. "If you didn't print that picture of President Clinton in *portrait orientation*, you would be making the expensive mistake of cutting off the top of his hair."

POS *(pee oh ess)* 1. Acronym for *point of sale*. See *point-of-sale system*. "Our *POS* system was just installed. It consists of a receipt book, pen, and cash drawer." 2. Acronym for *piece sf (schlock)*, used to describe something poorly done, cheap, or just awful.

POSIX *(pah-ziks)* Acronym for *Portable Operating System Interface for UNIX*, a version of UNIX developed by the Institute of Electrical and Electronics Engineers, or IEEE. See also *UNIX*. "IEEE tries again, with *POSIX*, to impose some standardization on the many implementations of UNIX."

POST *(pohst)* Acronym for *Power-On Self-Test*, a rigorous battery of tests the PC subjects itself to when you first start it. Rumor has it that if a computer fails any of the tests, it displays a cryptic error message and pouts in the corner until you call a technician. "Before I leave the house, I perform a personal *POST*. I check to see whether I have my wallet, my

keys, and my glasses and that my hair is combed and I have my important stuff with me. Oh, and I check to ensure that I'm wearing pants."

post *(pohst)* To send an electronic message, usually to add a message to a newsgroup or online bulletin board. "You never can feel involved with a BBS until you *post*."

PostScript *(pohst-skript)* A page-description language developed by Adobe Systems, used to create a perfect image no matter the resolution of the output device. Most graphics artists and desktop publishing people save their files in PostScript format. That way, they can take the disks to a service bureau for high-quality output.

POTS *(pots)* Acronym for *Plain Old Telephone System (or Service)*, the type of phone connection just about everyone has. "Unless you shell out the bucks for ISDN or ASDL, you have to get by with *POTS*."

power down *(pow-er down)* 1. To turn off the electric supply to the computer and any peripherals. 2. To eat quickly and with vigor. "We have 30,000 more lines of code to write by 5 o'clock; *power down* that Twinkie and get back to work!"

power protector *(pow-er pro-tek-ter)* See *surge protector*.

power strips *(pow-er strips)* A device containing several power sockets, designed like an extension cord and used to plug in the myriad of devices surrounding your computer. See also *surge protector, UPS*.

p

power supply *(pow-er sup-lie)* The gizmo within a computer that changes the AC (alternating current) that comes from your wall to the DC current the computer uses. It's not a one-to-one correspondence. You need to ensure that your computer's power supply is adequate to cover the needs of all the machinery it's serving. See also *alternating current.* "My computer's *power supply* gets so hot that I now use it to help keep my coffee warm."

power surge *(pow-er serj)* See *surge.*

power switch *(pow-er swich)* The on/off button.

power up *(pow-er up)* To turn something on. "Poor Ralph tried to *power up* his PC by plugging it into a 220-volt socket."

power user *(pow-er yoo-zer)* Somebody who's totally hip, adept, and cool in every way when it comes to doing things with computers. Power users know not only what to do to get something to happen but also *why* the thing works. They can figure out shortcuts. They can hold down more than one key at a time with one hand. While munching on cocktail wieners, they can dazzle a roomful of people at a party with discussions of leveraged software, object-oriented programming, and cross-platform porting technologies. They also tend to own the latest, bestest stuff.

Early power user.

PowerPC *(pow-er pee see)* 1. The name of a microprocessor from Motorola that uses reduced instruction set technology (also known as RISC). "Apple Computer has replaced the older Motorola 68000 microprocessors in its Macintosh computers with the new *PowerPC* microprocessors." 2. A computer that uses the PowerPC chip.

PPM *(pee pee em)* Acronym for *pages per minute,* the number of pages that come from a printer during each minute. Typically a measure of speed for a laser printer. Don't get stuck on the numbers, though. Eight pages per minute to one manufacturer may mean something different to another manufacturer (even if they both know how to count). You need to know whether that's eight pages of text only, eight pages of the printer's favorite font, eight pages with four-color graphics, or eight pages only when the sun is shining, a gentle breeze is blowing, and the federal budget deficit is under control. . . . "This laser printer can do 12 *PPM,* but only when it's printing blank sheets of paper."

PPP *(pee pee pee)* Acronym for *point-to-point protocol,* a method of connecting a PC to the Internet. This standard is replacing SLIP, which doesn't have some of the fancier features of PPP. "Bob said that we could use *PPP* to get on the Net, but I've been pressing the P key for half an hour, and nothing has happened."

p

PPTP *(pee pee tee pee)*
1. Acronym for *point-to-point tunneling protocol,* a super form of PPP that enables information from the Internet to be mingled with information on a local-area network. It's pretty nifty, but useful only to those wise enough to configure such things. 2. The reservation's rest room.

precedence *(pres-uh-dens)* The order in which things are done in a mathematical operation. If operation A gets done (on purpose, mind you) before operation B, operation A has *precedence* over operation B. An operation in the innermost parentheses in a statement has precedence over operations in the outer parentheses. If the statement has no parentheses, the order of operations is determined by how the program organizes its mathematical operators, which is known as the order of precedence. "Calculating the subtotal must take *precedence* over calculating the total."

precision *(pree-sih-zhun)* The exactness of a number, in terms of how many decimal places you take it out to. For example, 3.17259324867 has a greater precision than 3.17. Precision is an area that triggers people's obsessive/compulsive tendencies; fortunately, however, computers have more of a sense of self-restraint than that. "You need only 2-digit *precision* to balance your checkbook, but plan to use more for sending a rocket into space."

presentation graphics *(pree-zen-tay-shun graf-iks)* Applications geared toward creating impressive visual components that are used for speeches and other presentations. Essentially, this type of software translates data from a database or spreadsheet into a chart or graph and can integrate text, titles, art, sound, and even multimedia activities. The result is a high-tech slide show that you can view on a monitor or project to a screen from slides. See also *graphics.* "Although my speech is dreadful, I have some *presentation graphics* that should keep them awake."

Presentation Manager *(pree-zen-tay-shun man-uh-jer)* The old graphical user interface for OS/2. See also *OS/2.* "*Presentation Manager* should have been renamed the Here It Is Whether You Like It Or Not Manager."

print *(print)* 1. To generate a hard copy of a document or file. To send something to a printer. See *hard copy.* 2. The command that prints, often found on the File menu. 3. The BASIC language command that displays information on-screen.

print buffer *(print buf-er)* A portion of memory that temporarily holds documents waiting to be printed. See also *buffer.* "Joyce felt that she didn't need a *print buffer* because the maid kept her printer clean for her."

print head *(print hed)* The part of a printer that creates the image.

print job *(print jahb)* A document waiting to be printed, sitting in the print queue. See also *print queue.* "Don, your *print job* should have been fired."

p

print queue *(print kyoo)* One or more documents waiting to be printed. Printers are slow. So that you don't sit there along with the computer waiting for the printer, the operating system stores in the print queue any documents you've ordered to be printed. There, they are spoon-fed a little at a time ("spooled") out to the printer. "With a *print queue,* you don't need to wait for the printer; you can be off doing something else while the computer does the waiting."

Print Screen *(print skreen)* 1. A key on the keyboard that, when pressed, performs a screen dump, sending to the printer the text displayed on-screen. In Windows, the Print Screen key takes a "picture" of the screen, saving it as a bitmap image in the Clipboard. From there, it can be pasted into any program that accepts graphics images, such as the Paint program. 2. An instruction to the computer to print the screen exactly the way it is, weird formatting commands and all.

print spooler *(print spool-er)* Software that manages a print queue and lets print jobs line up one after the other — as though they were wrapped around a spool — patiently feeding them to the printer in the background while the user is busy writing novels, crunching numbers, playing Tetris, or doing other productive things in the foreground. See also *background, spooler.*

printer *(print-er)* An output device that produces hard copy — stuff on paper. Types of printers range from the old-fashioned dot-matrix printers

Early printer.

that are so noisy their owners sometimes put boxes over them in a futile attempt to muffle the racket to the wondrously whisper-quiet professional laser printers. The principal types of printers are *dot-matrix, inkjet, LED,* and *laser.* "Every computer system needs a *printer.*"

printer cable *(print-er kay-bol)* The wire that connects your computer to a printer. Unlike other confusing wires, the printer cable has definite ends to it: One can plug in only to your computer, and the other plugs in only to a printer. "A *printer cable* is sold separately from the printer, probably because they need to give you some reason to drive all the way back to the store."

Printer Control Language *(print-er kon-trol lang-gwij)* See *PCL.*

printer driver *(prin-ter drie-ver)* The software that controls a printer. In the old days, the printer driver was unique to your application and printer. Often, you had to write your own printer driver. Then came the era of WordPerfect, which came with more than 800 different printer drivers for the more than 800 different printer models available. Windows now comes with its own selection of printer drivers, and it's no longer your job or the software application's job to create a printer driver. "Without the proper *printer driver* installed, your output looks like monkey typing."

printer font *(prin-ter fawnt)* 1. A typeface native to the computer, one that it stores internally and can reproduce relatively quickly. Other fonts have to be downloaded, or sent from the computer to the printer, which adds time to the entire printing operation. "My printer has three *printer fonts:* Ugly, Uglier, and Too Ugly for the Human Mind to Comprehend." 2. A font created for the printer's PDL and that, hopefully, matches a screen font so that you can see something close to what the printer will print. See also *font.*

printer port *(prin-ter port)* The jack on the back of your computer that you plug your printer into — usually a parallel port. See also *parallel port.* "I'm waiting for the ultimate portable computer that will let me plug my electric razor into the *printer port.*"

processor *(prah-ses-er)* 1. Another term for *microprocessor.* See also *CPU, microprocessor.* "It's kind of foolish to call a *processor* such as the Pentium a microprocessor when it's more powerful than the old mainframes of 25 years ago." 2. Any type of computer chip that carries out specific calculations. This chip is found mostly in consumer electronics.

Prodigy *(prah-duh-jee)* An online service for computer users that offers electronic shopping, securities trading, games, downloadable files, electronic mail, and Internet access, to name a few. Prodigy sold itself on being wonderfully fun and enjoyable. Its clunky interface got in the way, however, and more people preferred America Online (probably because of all those disks they sent out). Prodigy eventually faded as one of the major online services. "I went to Sears to buy the software for *Prodigy,* but the

salesman didn't know what I was talking about. He asked me whether it was some kind of Mozart thing."

program *(proh-gram)* 1. A set of instructions written in a programming language. Software. Also called an *application.* 2. To create software. To use a programming language to tell the computer how to do something. See also *C, compile.*

Program Manager *(proh-gram man-uh-jur)* The main interface for the old version of Windows. Program Manager was replaced by the desktop and taskbar with Windows 95.

programmer *(proh-gram-er)* Someone who writes programs. This process involves designing the program (what it should accomplish and how), writing the code in a programming language, putting the source code through a compiler (which translates it into a form the machine can understand), and

Typical programmer.

debugging it, or fixing any errors. Programmers come in three types: geeks, wizards, and hackers. See also *programming language.* "Scott went to school for eight years to become a *programmer,* and now he works for the local dairy, delivering milk."

programmer's switch *(proh-gram-ers switch)* A doohickey you stick on the side of a Macintosh. Pressing it one way resets the Macintosh, like the Reset button on a PC. Pressing it another way activates a tiny window through which you can access the computer directly — programmer stuff.

programming language *(proh-gram-ing lang-gwij)* A way of talking to the computer, analogous to the ways humans have evolved in talking to each other. Like natural languages, programming languages include grammar, syntax, and vocabulary as well as style and organization. Some programming languages are not far removed from English (called *high-level languages*), and others are more like hieroglyphics (called *low-level languages*). Some languages are more suited to specific vertical markets, such as Ada in the defense industry, FORTRAN in business, and C++ in applications building. The lower the level of language, the closer it is to the guts of the machine and, therefore, the most efficient, such as assembly language. When you're talking to a machine in a low-level language, however, you're talking to a specific machine, and your work can't be reused on a different platform. Higher-level languages, which include just about everything from BASIC to C++, approximate human languages more closely. See also *Ada, BASIC, C, C++, Fortran, LISP, Pascal.* "Bill, our computer guru, prefers *programming languages* to human languages."

progress indicator *(prah-gres in-di-kay-ter)* A graphical element that displays how long an operation is taking, such as opening a file or sorting a database. Progress indicators are often called *thermometer bars.* As an event progresses, the "level" of the thermometer rises until the entire bar is full, indicating that the event is 100 percent complete. Progress indicators can also be simple `percent complete` counts. "All the *progress indicator* does is keep you from falling asleep while your computer takes an incredibly long time to do something."

A progress indicator for this spot in the book.

PROLOG *(proh-log)* Short for *pro-gramming in logic,* a programming language of special interest to mathematicians and computer science researchers. In real life, it's useful in diagnostic-type applications and expert systems, where the procedure involves proving or disproving that something is or is not the case. "The timber industry uses *PROLOG.*"

PROM *(prahm)* Acronym for *programmable read-only memory,* a chip that enables a program to be written on it once — and only once — by the computer manufacturer. This type of chip sits in the middle of the spectrum between the two extremes: chips that come with the programming etched in by the semiconductor manufacturer, and EPROM chips, which can be erased (that's what the *E* stands for) and reprogrammed. See also *EEPROM, EPROM, ROM.* "Rather than let me go to the junior prom with Luke Perry, my dad made me finish assembling the *PROM* chips I had started."

prompt *(prahmpt)* 1. A little character that appears on-screen to let you know that the ball is in your court — it's your turn to start typing. In DOS, the prompt often looks like the greater-than symbol (>). In other programs, it may appear as a flashing underline or

DOS prompt.

flashing pipe (|) character. Sometimes, it's just a question mark. Whatever the form, a prompt tells you that the program is waiting for you to enter something. Usually, you must type something and then press Enter. "The DOS *prompt* has nothing to do with being on time." 2. The command used to change the appearance of the DOS prompt.

properties *(prah-puhr-tees)* The attributes and settings relating to some object or window in Windows 95 and later. You can usually change the properties by pointing the mouse cursor at the item and right-clicking the mouse. That action displays a shortcut menu, on which you find the Properties command. See also *right-click, shortcut menu.*

proportional pitch *(proh-por-shun-al pich)* A printing style in which each letter has its own size. The opposite of monospaced type. "Next time, I think that I'll pay the extra money and have our driveway done in *proportional pitch.*"

proprietary *(proh-prie-ya-tayr-ee)* Mine, all mine, and no one else's. Proprietary means that the company that developed the design owns the design and no one may duplicate it or distribute it without that company's permission. See also *open architecture.*

"The Macintosh System 7 is a *proprietary* operating system developed by Apple Computer, Inc. But then Apple considers everything it does to be proprietary. Apparently, it doesn't know how to share."

protected mode *(pro-tek-ted mohd)* 1. In 386 and later microprocessors, the operating mode in which a microprocessor can use all its memory and all its power. Otherwise, the microprocessor is operating in real mode, which merely makes it behave like a very fast 8086 chip. 2. Programs designed to take advantage of the full power of the microprocessor. 3. Operating systems that use the full power of the microprocessor. These systems include OS/2, UNIX, and Windows 95 some of the time. "Your computer cannot contract any diseases while it runs in *protected mode.*"

protocol *(proh-tuh-kol)* A common set of routines or methods by which information is transferred. If both computers know the protocol, they can send information quickly and reliably. Common protocols include Xmodem, Zmodem, TCP/IP, Ethernet, and other protocols too nerdy to write down. "It's important that the computers in a network use the same network *protocol.* Otherwise, no one nodes what's going on."

prototype *(proh-toh-tiep)* A model for later or more advanced versions of a piece of hardware or software. A prototype typically embodies the intentions of the

Prototype computer (with printer).

p

designer but hasn't worked out all the details. "My communications hardware is so difficult to use that I wonder whether the manufacturer just shipped me the *prototype*."

PrScr *(print skreen)* Another label for the Print Screen key. See *Print Screen.*

ps *(pee ess)* A UNIX command that shows you the *processor status*, or exactly what's going on in your UNIX computer at that time. Because a UNIX computer can be doing a number of things at a time as well as have several people using it at the same time, ps lets you know what's going on. "I just did a *ps* and discovered that Morgan is trying to break into the password file again."

PS/1 *(pee ess won)* Acronym for *Personal System 1,* the line of computers designed by IBM to succeed its original PC line for the home. It was the second attempt by IBM to enter the home computer market. See also *PCjr.* "I bought a *PS/1* computer to use at home. It's great for playing computer games, and it keeps the door open when it's windy out."

PS/2 *(pee ess too)* Acronym for *Personal System 2,* an IBM PC featuring a proprietary 32-bit expansion bus called the Microchannel bus. PS/2 computers are often shipped with the OS/2 operating system. The PS/2 was more of an odd duck than anything else. Today, IBM sells IBM PC clones, just like everyone else does. See also *MCA, OS/2.*

pseudo random numbers *(soo-doh ran-dum num-bers)* Because the computer is incapable of doing anything in a truly random manner, mathematical purists consider any random number generated by a computer a pseudo random number. For example, most programmers base their random-number calculations on the time of day (the number of seconds since midnight, actually). Because that value can be predicted, so can the random numbers. Hence, the guys who don't get out much ("mathematicians") claim that computers generate only pseudo random numbers. See also *random numbers.* "Oh, my! Take that *pseudo random number* away from me before I get ill!"

pseudocode *(soo-doh kohd)* The flow of a program expressed in fractured English — that is, part ordinary English and part programming language — so that the programmer can map it out without getting stuck in the details. See also *p-code.* "I wrote this program in *pseudocode* so that my mother could understand it. She's now a highly paid programmer in Silicon Valley."

PrtScr *(print skreen)* Another label for the Print Screen key. See *Print Screen.*

public domain *(pub-lik doh-mayn)* Software that has no copyright and can be copied and distributed freely. Hundreds of public domain programs are available through catalogs and PD distributors. Public domain is also called *freeware,* but it is not the same thing as *shareware.* Generally, public domain software is "at your own risk" stuff. If it makes your disk drive smoke and gives your computer a wet, hacking cough, that's your tough luck. See also *freeware, shareware.* "I got a great *public domain* program that lets me arrange my furniture on the computer. Now, if only I could take out the trash on the computer, I would never have to get out of my chair."

public key encryption *(pub-lik kee en-krip-shin)* A unique form of scrambling data that requires two separate passwords: a private key and a public key. The private key password can scramble and unscramble data that was scrambled with the public key. The public key password can only scramble data. If someone wants to send you a message, she must use your public key password, and only you can unscramble and read the message using your private key. This form of encryption is more secure than other forms of encryption that scramble data with only a single password. "To protect your privacy when you're using electronic mail, use *public key encryption.* The only hard part is scrambling and unscrambling your data all the time and remembering your private key password."

puck *(puhk)* A pointing device used on a digitizer pad. A sophisticated type of mouse. In addition to mapping an exact location, the puck sends direction information. It has a whole lotta buttons.

pull *(puhl)* To remove a chunk of data from a stack. The same as the *pop* command. See *pop, push.*

pull-down menu *(puhl-down men-yoo)* In a software application, a pull-down menu is a list of intriguing possibilities that appears when you select an option from the menu bar. To choose a command from the list, you drag the mouse down to it and let go of the button or use the appropriate keyboard strokes. The Macintosh popularized pull-down menus in its original operating system back in 1984. Now, pull-down, pop-up, and tear-off menus are commonplace. "I wish that *pull-down menus* worked more like window blinds; when you pull them down far enough and let go, they should flap around the menu bar a few times."

punched card *(punchd kard)* Old-fashioned, unwieldy style of data processing that used a separate heavy-stock card to transmit information. The computer translated a hole pattern punched in the card — or the light coming through the holes — into electronic signals. This author prefers to think that they're obsolete. "Many eons ago, when I went to college, we registered for our courses by using *punched cards.*"

purge *(perj)* To get rid of unwanted or unneeded stuff, preferably in an automated manner, such as with a global search-and-delete operation or a PURGE command. "After eating pizza, I feel the urge to *purge.*"

push *(push)* To place data on a stack for storage. Stacked data can be envisioned as a stack of dishes, and it refers to the way data is stored in a part of computer memory. To *push* a record onto the stack means to install it at the top of the stack, where it is the first one *popped* when the stack is addressed. See also *pop, pull, stack.* "When I *push* that data onto the stack, I get a `Stack Overflow` error, and the computer tells me not to be so pushy."

push technology *(push tek-nawl-uh-jee)* The capability of a server on the Internet to send you specific information, either requested information or something matching your profile or a selected list of options. For example, you may subscribe to some type of push news service, which sends you the news you want to read rather than your having to surf the Web to find it. See also *Internet, Web.*

p

Q

Q: *(kyoo koh-lon)* PC disk letter designation for some type of Q drive. Sounds like a secret weapon, though it could be a hard drive, network drive, CD-ROM, or some other type of drive.

QBasic *(kyoo-bay-sik)* A version of the BASIC language that Microsoft includes with MS-DOS Versions 5 and 6. The Q supposedly stands for *quick,* though *quirky* also comes to mind. "For people who want to learn to program their computer without spending a large amount of money, figure out how to use *QBasic* because it's already on your computer for free. Then again, if you like blowing wads of cash on stuff you'll never figure out how to use, buy a C++ compiler instead."

quad-speed drive *(kwad-speed driev)* A CD-ROM drive that runs at four times the speed of the original CD-ROM drive. Also known as 4X. The use of this type of drive has been eclipsed by the 6X, 8X, 10X, 12X, 16X, and 24X drives, with probably faster models on the way soon.

Quadra *(kwa-drah)* A model name for a Macintosh with a 68040 processor. Various types of Quadras have been marketed, beginning in the early 1990s.

query *(kwayr-ee)* To inquire of. To ask a database for specific information. For example, to find all records containing *Padlevski* in the Last Name field, you use a query such as this one:

```
Last Name = Padlevski
```

The database then searches every record until it finds a match. Database queries can become rather complex and intricate, such as in the following line:

```
Last Name = Padlevski or (ZIP >
80000 and < 99999)
```

This query, which makes no sense, queries the database to locate all records containing a Padlevski in the Last Name field or a zip code between 80000 and 99999. See also *database.* "That last customer started yelling when I couldn't find his record in our database, so I *queried* in the database for all records containing 'Jerk' and found him!"

queue *(kyoo)* 1. A collection of documents or files waiting in turn as patiently as they can for printing or some other form of processing. For example, a *print queue* is a collection of documents waiting to be printed. "My document is waiting in the network print *queue* to be printed. It's number four. And I'm still waiting.

Yessir. I'm waiting. Here I sit, waiting for that document. It's number four. Wait! Wait a sec. Look! Everything is moving up. Now it's document three in the queue. Okay. Pretty soon now. Just keep standing here patiently. Waiting for my document to print. Just waiting here. Looking at the queue on the screen. There's my document. It's number three now. Used to be number four. Waiting in the queue. . . ." 2. British: *A line,* such as a line of people waiting to buy tickets. They say, "*Queue* up and buy your tickets. Jolly good. Tut-tut."

QuickBASIC *(kwik-bay-sik)* See *QBasic.*

quick-reference card *(kwik-ref-er-ens kard)* A handy sheet of paper, often laminated, listing the most basic or necessary commands for an application. Like a Cheat Sheet, but one that gives only answers and not any of the questions.

QuickTime *(kwik-tiem)* A Macintosh standard for storing and displaying digital video, consuming lots of memory and hard disk space just so that you can see a brief five seconds of a movie on your computer screen. "As a joke, I stored a film clip from an X-rated movie on my boss's Macintosh using *QuickTime.* How was I supposed to know that his wife was in the movie?"

quit *(kwit)* 1. What to do if your company makes you work on a Macintosh Plus computer or on a 286 PC with 256K of RAM. 2. A command that exits a program and typically is found on the File menu. Quit. Done.

Kapiche. All finished. All gone. Going bye-bye. See also *exit.* "The *Quit* command is one of the first commands you should know how to use. Nothing is worse than getting into a program and not knowing how to get out again (total 'Hotel California')."

quote *(kwoht)* To list the contents of a previous message in your reply. Quoting makes answering messages quicker and easier. A quote is marked by greater-than (>) signs. See also >.

QWERTY *(kwer-tee)* The name commonly given to a standard keyboard layout. The name comes from the combination of the first six keys in the third row on the keyboard. See also *Dvorak keyboard, keyboard.* "Several attempts have been made to replace the old *QWERTY* keyboard with something more sensible. It's like trying to switch the entire United States to the metric system: Can't be done."

Q

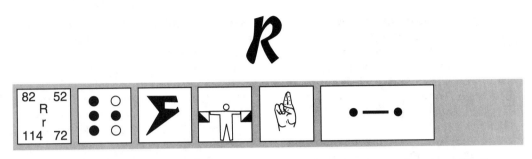

R: *(ar koh-lon)* A disk drive letter designation on a PC. Not every PC will have an R: drive, though, so it's probably a network drive or some removable drive or a drive on your cousin Melvin's computer because he has not only eight hard drives in his system but also a CD-ROM changer that holds six CDs at a time.

radiation *(ray-dee-ay-shun)* An invisible form of energy that kills nuclear power plant workers, blows up hot dogs in microwave ovens, and smacks you in the face every time you look at a computer screen. Completely harmless, just like all other invisible forms of energy. "Performing eye surgery with acupuncture is like treating hair loss with *radiation.*"

radio button *(ray-dee-oh but-un)* One of several buttons in a graphical user interface, only one of which can be selected at a time. The *radio* part comes from the type of buttons that used to be on car radios: Only one button could be pressed at a time; when you pressed a button to select a station, the other buttons all popped out. The same logic is applied to radio buttons, which are used to choose only one

Old keyboard radio button.

item from a group of options. Radio buttons are grouped together in arrays, or families. See also *button, graphical user interface.* "When I choose the Format⇨Tabs command in Microsoft Word, a set of *radio buttons* assaults me with several alignment options."

ragged justification *(rag-ed just-uh-fi-kay-shun)* An oxymoron which really means that text in a document has no justification. Ragged justification refers to both the left and right margins in a document not being lined up against anything. Specifically, justification is usually applied to either the left or right margins individually. Ragged-right justification, for example, refers to the uneven right edge of a paragraph of text. See also *justify.* "When I asked John why he took a two-hour lunch, he gave me a *ragged justification* for his actions."

RAID *(rayd)* Acronym for *Redundant Array of Inexpensive Disks,* a hive of several hard disks in one unit, each of which contains the same information. The idea behind RAID is to ensure that a backup copy of files always exists. Rather than store valuable data on a single hard disk that may fail at any time, RAID takes the opposite approach, by spreading data among two or more cheap hard disks on the chance that multiple hard disks are less likely than a single hard disk to fail. This technique is something used by large organizations, such as hospitals. "We lost all our data when our expensive 5GB hard disk failed. To prevent that from happening again, we use *RAID.*"

RAM *(ram)* Acronym for *Random-Access Memory,* a type of computer memory that can be written to and read from. *Random* means that any one location can be read from or written to at any time; it's not necessary to read all the memory to access one location. RAM commonly refers to a computer's internal memory, supplied by microchips and measured in kilobytes or megabytes. However, RAM can refer to any random-access memory medium, including magnetic disks and the human brain. RAM is usually a fast, temporary memory area where data and programs live until you save them or the power is turned off on your computer. See also *ROM.* "The best way to improve the performance of Windows is to increase the *RAM* in the computer. Follow this formula: Figure out how much RAM you can buy without going over your credit card limit. Then buy that much RAM and install it on your PC."

Sign of the RAM.

RAM disk *(ram disk)* A portion of a computer's memory (RAM) that is configured to behave like a disk drive. A RAM disk works just like any other disk in a system, though because it's electronic (made from memory), it's faster than any hard disk. RAM disks are given letters, just like regular disks, and can store files and programs. Because the disk is made from RAM, however, its contents disappear when you turn off or reset the computer. Under Windows 95, RAM disks are a waste of memory; that memory is best put to use for the massive memory appetite of Windows than for a tiny, fast disk. "The astrologer down the street says that it's best to create a *RAM disk* under the sign of Aries."

RAM drive *(ram driev)* Another term for a RAM disk. See *RAM disk.*

random *(ran-dum)* 3. Something in an arbitrary order. 1. Out-of-sequence or unexpected. 99. Not necessarily unpredictable; a random value can be anything. "You have been selected at *random* to be selected at random."

random access *(ran-dum ak-ses)* A way of reading information in any order. For example, telling a CD player to find a specific piece of music and play it is random access. With a cassette player, on the other hand, you have to fast-forward through earlier songs before reaching the song you want. In computers, random access lets you access any ol' information without having to read everything that comes before it. See also *sequential access.* "Those bureaucrats who have the information you need operate on a *random access* schedule."

R

random numbers *(ran-dum num-bers)*
Values generated randomly (with no particular aim, order, direction, or sequence), such as when you throw dice. These values are used in programming, especially in games in

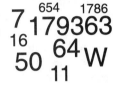

7 654 1786
.179363
16 64 W
50 11

Random numbers.

which unpredictable results make for a different game each time. See also *pseudo random numbers.* "Because of new theories about the nature of chaos and randomness, many people argue that there is no such thing as a *random number.* These people have not seen my checking account."

range *(raynj)* 1. A term used to describe a series of things, from a low-numbered thing to a high-numbered thing. A range can also mean a span of values, such as the range between 1 and 10. 2. A block of cells in a spreadsheet. See also *block, cell.* 3. A place where the deer and the antelope play. 4. Amana Radar.

raster *(rast-er)* A frame or pattern that an electron beam sends to the screen on a monitor. Scan patterns are sent to the screen continuously, one line at a time, to create the images and motion you see. The patterns displayed on the screen are sent by using an electron "gun" that wipes the inside of a monitor like a firefighter's hose. The patterns are sent from top to bottom, and each new pattern is sent before the last one is finished. This process creates "bands" of images, called raster images. If you look out of the corner of your eye at a computer screen, you can see a pulsating effect the raster images cause. "It's the *raster* scan line

you see when you look at a computer monitor on TV. Ugly, aren't they?"

RCA connector *(ar see ay kon-ek-ter)* A standard type of plug used for stereo headphones and speakers. It has a long, metal tip or prong surrounded by a plastic jacket that's a quarter-inch in diameter. This type of connector is used for some video systems, but mostly for computer audio equipment. "Nothing brightens a guru's heart like referring to the 'connector doohickey' properly as an *RCA connector.*"

read *(reed)* 1. To examine a value. 2. To transfer information from disk storage into memory. "My computer won't *read* the file from this floppy disk: It says, 'Cannot read from Drive A.' Maybe my computer needs glasses." 3. To transfer part of a file from disk storage into memory. 4. The programming language command that reads the next chunk of information from a file into memory.

read me file *(reed mee fiel)* A file that nobody reads. See also *README.*

README *(reed-mee)* A name given to a text file that contains up-to-date information about a program, such as changes to the documentation, information about last-minute additions, and explanations of errors that were not fixed before the product shipped. When a program differs from its documentation, software developers turn to the README file to explain what happened. Because README files are usually text-only files, they can be read with any text editor or word processor. They are also often named READ.ME, README.TXT,

R

READ_ME.TXT or README.DOC files. "I was having some trouble with a new software package. When I looked at the *README* file, it said that a last-minute change prohibited the software from working on my system. When the company sent me the bill, I sent them a copy of my SUEME file."

read-only *(reed-ohn-lee)* 1. A type of storage that can be read from but not written to. Most read-only stuff also can't be altered or erased. *"Read-only* media are used for information you would not want to change, such as your weight when you were 18 years old." 2. A type of medium from which you can read data but not write data to it. A CD-ROM disk is a read-only medium, which is where the RO in ROM comes from. See also *CD-ROM, ROM.* 3. A file attribute in DOS and Windows that protects files from being written to, modified, or erased. See also *file attribute, write-protect.*

read/write head *(reed/riet hed)* The mechanism in a disk drive that accesses and stores information on a disk. The "head" is usually a ceramic material that floats, or hovers, above the disk surface, creating a magnetic field that is charged by the magnetic impulses on the disk. When the read/write head writes information to the disk, the head changes the magnetic particles instead of being affected by them. This process is how information is read from and written to a disk. See also *head, head crash.* "A *read/write head* is a delicate thing; small particles of dust between the read/write head and the disk surface can cause errors. That's why you don't go slamming melted cheese sandwiches into your disk drives."

real mode *(reel mohd)* An operating mode of the 80286 and later microprocessors that behaves just like the 8088 microprocessor did in the first PC. DOS and all DOS applications use real mode no matter which microprocessor lives inside the PC. See also *protected mode.* "Abigail wasn't sure whether her virtual reality program would run in *real mode.*"

real number *(reel num-ber)* Any value, usually one that has some sort of fractional part. Contrast this type of number with an integer, which is just a whole number — no fractions and no decimals allowed. "I gave my accountant a copy of my income projection, and he told me that I should stop using imaginary numbers and try some *real numbers.*"

real soon now *(reel soon now)* A phrase commonly used by software companies in reference to the exact date they'll release a new version of their program that everyone is waiting for. This phrase is often leaked to the press to con people who haven't yet learned that every new version is usually full of bugs and not worth getting in the first place. "Many companies promise to release a new version of their program *real soon now* in a subtle attempt to keep you from defecting to a competing program."

real time *(reel tiem)* 1. A measurement of time based on actual time elapsed. For example, a simulation of two atoms colliding can take place in real time, or they can slow it down to observe things (in which case it would probably be fake time). 2. The immediate processing of input. For

R

example, a computer monitoring a nuclear power plant would respond to a radiation leak in real time (we all hope). "I'm sorry, Jenkins, but you can clock in only on *real time* here." 3. Analog time as opposed to digital time. See *analog, digital*.

real-time clock *(reel-tiem klok)* A computerized clock or timing device that tracks the accurate time. For example, when DOS used to start, it assumed that "today" was January 1, 1980, at midnight. In those olden days, people would have to set the time and date manually whenever DOS started — unless they bought a device called a real-time clock, which automatically kept track of the time and set the DOS clock every time the PC was turned on. All PCs sold today come with real-time clock circuitry on the motherboard. A battery maintains the proper time (more or less) when the PC's power is turned off. "The guy on the street corner told me that it was a *real-time clock,* but when I installed it, the faceplate came off, and a gum wrapper fell out."

Real-time clock.

reboot *(ree-boot)* To restart a computer. Starting a computer is called "booting" or "booting up." You can reboot a computer in two ways: You perform a cold boot by switching off the computer, waiting, and then turning it back on again. You perform a warm boot by punching a reset button. Although a warm boot is usually all that's required, a cold boot is occasionally necessary to clear memory completely. "When you *reboot* by pressing the Reset button,

be sure to make the "ka-chinka" noise out loud because modern computers no longer "ka-chinka" by themselves when you *reboot.*"

recently visited list *(ree-sent-lee viz-uh-ted list)* A summary of previous Web pages and other sites on the Internet to which a Web browser has taken you. From that list, you can pluck out a site to revisit it quickly. See also *history.*

record 1. *(rek-ord)* An individual unit of data stored in a database. A record consists of one or more related fields, which are the actual pieces of data being stored. Fields combine to create a record in the same way as blanks are filled in on a sheet of paper. The blanks are the fields, and the sheet of paper is the record. "When that annoying Mr. Smith called, I searched for his *record* and found 200 Smiths in the database. Perhaps we should sort our records by customer IQ?" 2. *(ree-kord)* To write information, usually applied in recording sound information and storing it in a computer file on disk. Normally, the word *write* is used when you record information to a disk or to memory (RAM).

recover *(ree-kuh-ver)* 1. To restore a deleted file. You can often recover deleted files by using an UNDELETE utility or command. See also *restore, undelete.* 2. A program's capability to continue operating after any errors that would normally send it crashing into outer space. "Our database program is pretty sophisticated. It can *recover* from serious errors, such as when I shot the computer with a bazooka."

recursion *(ree-ker-zhun)* An advanced programming concept in which the same function or routine is called from within itself, over and over, to complete some task. For example, consider the Chinese box. An example of recursion is an open-the-box function in a program:

```
Open the box
  If you find another box, then
"Open the box"
  Otherwise, remove the contents
of the box.
```

In this example, the "Open the box" function calls itself repeatedly to keep opening the Chinese boxes. Although something eventually will be found inside the smallest box, the program itself uses recursion to keep opening the boxes. The weird thing is that this type of programming concept actually works without blowing up the computer. "I tried to write a program that uses *recursion*. Every time the program called itself, however, it got a busy signal."

Recycle Bin *(ree-sie-kal bin)* The place where deleted files are sent in Windows 95. All delete commands in Windows 95 move deleted files into the Recycle Bin for storage. From there, you can undelete them by using the Restore command. See also *delete, restore, trash.*

redial *(ree-diyal)* 1. To dial something again, typically after getting a busy signal or no connection. Often used with online communications and a modem. 2. The command that directs the modem to dial a number repeatedly.

redirection *(ree-dur-ek-shun)* To send output or input to a device other than the standard device. Normally, output goes to the screen; you type it, you see it. Input normally comes from the keyboard. Using redirection, you can tell the computer where to send its output and from where to receive its input. This feature is in many operating systems, including UNIX, DOS, and OS/2. See also *input, output.* "I used output *redirection* to have the computer send all my network memos to the trash can."

redundant *(ree-dun-dent)* 1. See *redundant.* 2. Something that is repetitive, such as when two words that mean the same thing are used to describe something: "He was intelligent and had a high IQ." 3. A check made several times over just to ensure that everything is on the up-and-up.

reformat *(ree-fohr-mat)* To format something again. All disks must be formatted initially before they can be used. Reformatting a disk is formatting it again. This process erases the disk's contents, which is why it's something you should never do to your hard disk. See also *format.*

refresh rate *(ree-fresh rayt)* The speed at which a monitor redraws an image on-screen. The faster the rate, the less likely the screen is to flicker, which saves wear-and-tear on your eyeballs and brain. It also means that you pay much more for your monitor. See also *eyeball frazzle.* "Allan didn't pay much for his monitor. The *refresh rate* is so slow that it works more like a strobe light."

register *(rej-uh-ster)* 1. A tiny storage place inside a computer's microprocessor. A register is a memory location used by the microprocessor for various calculations. You never need to know about a

Early register.

register unless you program a computer at a very low level. See also *assembly language.* 2. What software publishers want you to do with your software products so that they can sell you upgrades through the mail. "Isn't it ironic that you have to *register* a software product before you can get customer service, yet you never have to register a gun?"

relational database *(ree-lay-shun-ul day-tuh-bays)* A method of tracking information that consists of several, separate files that "relate" to one another through key words or values. You can access information stored in one file through one or more of the other files because of the relations established in the database. For example, you may store customer address information in a Customer database and product order information in an Orders database. These two databases can relate to each other through the customer name. When you examine a customer record in the Customer database, you may, for example, be able to view all orders associated with that customer. Similarly, when you enter an order into the Orders database, you can type a customer name, and the entire customer record automatically

appears at the top of the order form. Another advantage of relational database design is that each field (type of information) in the database can be accessed individually (that is, you can search for an entry based on any field). See also *database, field, record.*

relational operator *(ree-lay-shun-ul ah-per-ay-ter)* A symbol used to compare two or more values. These symbols are used in programming languages to help the computer make decisions and evaluate results. See also =, >, <, *operator.* "I used a *relational operator* to calculate whether meat loaf was better than sushi for dinner tonight."

relative reference *(rel-uh-tiv ref-er-ens)* A cell address in a spreadsheet that relates to the addresses of other cells, rows, or columns. When a formula containing relative references is copied to other cells in the spreadsheet, the references are automatically updated to reflect cells that are relative to the new location of the formula. Relative references are applied only during pasting procedures. See also *absolute reference.* "When it comes time to tell spooky Halloween stories, we all use Aunt Shirley as a *relative reference.*"

release number *(ree-lees num-ber)* The second set of numbers in a software product's version. For example, MS-DOS 6.22 was Version 6 and release number 22. "Don't ever try to make sense of *release numbers.* They're not sequential, nor are they designed to have any relationship to earlier releases."

reload *(ree-lohd)* 1. To direct a Web browser to refresh the current Web page, as though you were visiting it again for the first time. The reload command causes the information on-screen to be resent from the Web site to your Web browser. This process enables you to see updated information as well as fix any broken pictures you may see. See also *broken picture.* 2. The button you click to reload the current Web page.

REM *(rem)* Abbreviation for *REMARK.* REM is a statement, or command, used in many programming languages (including the DOS batch file programming language) that lets you add a line to the program without affecting the program itself. In other words, it lets you enter remarks or comments to help explain what the program is doing.

remote *(ree-moht)* Something that is not within the near vicinity. A remote computer is one connected to a network from a distant location — such as from across the hall. Remote access means that you're using a computer that's not within arm's reach. "When I log on to our network from another location, my chances of making a connection are *remote.*"

removable disk *(ree-moov-uh-bul disk)* Any disk that can be removed from its drive or from the computer. "Uh-oh, there goes Fred down the hall with the jaws of life. We had better tell him that his hard disk isn't a *removable disk.*"

reply *(ree-plie)* To respond to a message, either an e-mail message or a newsgroup posting. You have the option of replying to the person who sent the message or including everyone else to whom the message was sent. "E-mail may be the fastest form of communications on the planet, but it seems like it takes forever to get a *reply* from some people."

ResEdit *(rez-ed-it)* Abbreviation for *Resource Editor,* a Macintosh utility that lets you access and edit system resources. ResEdit lets you mess with the various components of a Mac file. You can use this utility to rename menus, text in dialog boxes and buttons; copy or paste graphics; and so on. It's a fun tool, which implies that it's also quite technical and that using it is a sure key to goofing up your system. "That Johnson is such a card. He uses *ResEdit* to change all the error messages on the Mac to dirty limericks."

reserved word *(ree-zervd werd)* Any word or code used for a special purpose that cannot be used for any other purpose. Programming languages, operating systems, and some applications use reserved words. In DOS, for example, the words COPY, DEL, and REN are all names of DOS commands and are therefore reserved words. Other programs can't use these names, or else DOS will, well, get mad. "Around our house, block-head is a *reserved word.*"

R

reset *(ree-set)* 1. To restart the computer. "There. I just finished the final page of my speech, and I must admit that it's brilliant. Now I have a few idle moments to sit back and brain-relax and — hey? I wonder what this button labeled *Reset* does. . . ." 2. To restore previous settings. 3. (Capitalized) A key on some Macintosh keyboards that performs a warm boot when you press it. See also *warm boot.*

reset switch *(ree-set switch)* A button used to restart a computer, almost like turning it off and on again but without disrupting its power supply. Also known as the "panic button" because pressing the reset switch is often the only way to regain control of a computer run amok. See also *Vulcan nerve pinch, warm boot.*

resolution *(rez-uh-loo-shun)* A way of measuring the clarity of an image. Resolution involves the number of elements per inch — the number of pixels on-screen or dots a laser printer can produce — which indicates how clear and sharp an image is. For example, some laser printers produce 300 dots-per-inch (dpi) resolution. High-resolution printers display from 800 to 2,400 dots per inch. Video graphics resolutions are measured horizontally and vertically. A resolution of 320 x 200 indicates large dots to create an image; a resolution of 1,240 x 800 means smaller dots and a finer image and, therefore, a higher resolution. When you examine the resolution of an image, your naked eye can discern the dots in resolutions of less than 600 dpi. However, 300 dpi laser printers are considered to have an adequate resolution for most printing

needs. On color monitors, the resolution is also tied to the number of colors that can be displayed at one time. For example, a relatively low-resolution picture may be able to display several hundred colors at a time. It gives an illusion that the image has a higher resolution, but only because the eye is tricked by the multiple colors. Higher-resolution images generally use fewer colors. (Most computer games use a medium resolution as a trade-off.) Resolution may be abbreviated as *res* (pronounced *rez*); for example, "high res" or "low res" indicate high and low resolution, respectively. See also *pixel.* "I made a New Year's resolution that I'd get myself a high-*resolution* printer this year."

resource *(ree-sohrs)* Just as humans have natural resources, a computer has its own resources. A resource can be memory, disk drive storage, a printer, a monitor, and so on. In Windows and on networks, you always want to watch that your resources aren't running out. "We were getting low on *resources* and running out of disk drive space and memory, and then all of a sudden Al Gore shows up all hopping mad and everything. He made us go down to the computer store and buy more resources, but we can use only 50 percent of them because we have to save the spotted disk owl."

restore *(ree-stohr)* 1. To return to normal. "Yes, Mary is fully *restored* after her conniption fit." 2. The act of copying files from an archive or set of backup disks or a tape drive to their original locations on the hard disk. The opposite of backing up, this process is usually performed after something bad has happened. For example, after losing all your data, you restore your files from a recent backup disk. Or, if you delete a file, you can restore it from a backup disk. Needless to say, this process works only if you back up frequently. "Don't panic, Dave. You can *restore* the missing files from your backup floppy disks. You do back up, don't you?" 3. In DOS, the RESTORE command returns backed-up data to the hard disk. 4. To undelete a file from the Windows 95 Recycle Bin. See also *Recycle Bin, undelete*.

retrieve *(ree-treev)* 1. Fancy talk for accessing or opening a file, as in the Lotus 1-2-3 Worksheet Retrieve command. See also *open*. 2. The old WordPerfect command for opening one file inside another file.

Return key *(ree-tern kee)* The same as the Enter key, except that it gets its name from the carriage-return key on a typewriter. The key used like the Enter key on some Macintosh keyboards. "Both the Enter and *Return keys* generally perform the same function, but don't quote me on that."

reverse-engineer *(ree-vers en-juh-neer)* To decode hardware or software based on what the hardware or software does and how it affects things. Reverse engineering is performed primarily when engineers want to figure out how a black box gizmo works and they're either unable to take it apart or forbidden from taking it apart for legal motives. For example, the reason we all have "IBM-compatible" computers today is that someone somewhere

reverse-engineered the chips in the first IBM PC (the BIOS) and created a working counterpart without infringing on the IBM copyrights. "I'll bet that IBM really regrets that it didn't sic its legions of lawyers on the first company to successfully *reverse-engineer* the guts of the IBM PC."

revision history *(ree-vi-zhun his-toh-ree)* A list of the various versions of and corrections to a program. A revision history tracks what occurs in each revision. For example:

Version 1.0   Product introduced. They'll love this.

Version 1.1   Annoying "all files accidentally deleted" bug removed.

Version 1.2   Annoying "erased hard disk" thing fixed.

Version 2.0   Networking features added, flock sheared for $50 upgrade fee.

Version 2.1   Annoying "network not found" bug fixed.

Version 2.2   Support for tall people added.

Version 2.3   Support for left-handed people added.

Version 3.0   DOS 5 update, sheared flock for another $50.

Version 3.1   DOS bug fix.

"Obviously, most major applications don't include a *revision history* because it would prove to be a source of embarrassment."

RF *(ar ef)* Acronym for *Radio Frequency,* which includes a certain chunk of the electromagnetic spectrum that you would find terribly uninteresting. Mostly used with RFI. See also *RFI.* "Tune to KRUD; that's 1240 AM on your *RF* dial."

RFI *(ar ef ie)* Acronym for *Radio Frequency Interference,* the type of interference that occurs when two devices emitting electromagnetic waves interfere with one another. Computers, radios, TVs, and many other radio transmission devices emit waves that can interfere with other devices' waves, causing fuzzy noise, snow on the monitor, annoyed cats, and other anomalies. RFI is the reason that you can't use a mobile phone on an airplane and notebook computers undergo monstrous testing for FCC approval. Proper grounding and quality cables help to minimize RFI in computers. See also *Class A/Class B.* "This *RFI* is causing some strange effects on my computer. I could swear that I saw a fuzzy image of Bill Gates giggling on my monitor."

RGB *(ar jee bee)* Acronym for *Red, Green, and Blue,* the three basic colors of light (additive colors). Based on the mixture and intensity of these colors, you can produce many of the colors in the normal spectrum. TVs and computer monitors use RGB to produce color on-screen. You light individual red, green, and blue pixels to mix colors. "I have an *RGB* monitor, but in this case RGB stands for *r*andomly *g*oes *b*lank."

ribbon cable *(rib-un kay-bol)* Several computer wires bundled together to form a flat ribbon. Ribbon cables are often used for the printer and, inside the PC, disk drives. In the old Apple II days, the ribbon cables were multicolored — like rainbows. Today, they're usually all a pasty hospital-blue. See also *cable.* "Doris is so nice. She

A pretty ribbon cable with ugly connector attached.

thought that the office looked rather dreary, so she went around and tied bows in all our *ribbon cables.*"

Rich Text Format *(rich tekst for-mat)* A type of document file format that's readable by most major word processors. A Rich Text Format (RTF) file is basically a text file but with secret text instructions that describe the document's formatting. A document looks utterly gross when you see it in its raw, text-only format. Word processors that understand RTF, however, can read in the files and translate the ugly text into formatting codes, making the document look really nice. "The *Rich Text Format* was an attempt to create a common document file format compatible with all word processors and people living in Scarsboro."

right-click *(riet-klik)* To click the mouse's right button rather than the left button (which you normally click). You right-click in Windows 95 to bring up context (or shortcut) menus.

ring network *(ring net-wurk)* See *token ring network.*

RIP *(rip)* Acronym for *Remote Imaging Protocol,* a graphics language that lets modem users use their mouse to give commands to another computer through the phone lines. Many of the newest electronic bulletin board systems offer RIP so that users can use their mouse rather than type arcane commands. "Before bulletin boards started using RIP, you had to type commands to get anything done. With *RIP,* you can use the mouse rather than type to choose most commands. (Then again, have you ever tried typing a password by using a mouse?)"

RISC *(risk)* Acronym for *Reduced Instruction Set Computer,* a computer that runs very fast because the microprocessor can do only a limited number of things. The idea is that because those little things make the building blocks for larger things, its limited number of instructions doesn't hinder the RISC processor. See also *CISC.* "I don't care how fast it is. Putting something called *RISC* into my computer doesn't sit well with me."

RLL *(ar el el)* Acronym for *Run-Length-Limited,* an old type of hard disk controller that increases the capacity of the hard disk by using disk-compression technology directly from the hard disk controller. An RLL controller can increase disk storage capacity by as much as 50 percent. See also *IDE.* "Wow! Where did you get the antique *RLL* drive?"

 robot *(roh-baht)* 1. An automated mechanism that simulates or reproduces (or replaces) human activities, such as assembly-line work and deep space work. R2D2, from *Star Wars,* is an example of a robot. Robots are used in many applications, including computer assembly and testing. "Perhaps the most famous *robot* of all time is Robby the Robot from the film *Forbidden Planet.* He was charming and polite and a good friend, and he could crush your head like a grapefruit." 2. A program on the World Wide Web that searches the entire Web (or only part of it) for information you want. The robot then reports the results to you, typically in an e-mail message.

robotics *(roh-bah-tiks)* The study and application of robots. "My nephew studied *robotics* in school. Now he's working at Burger King. I suppose that he's experiencing what it's like to be a robot."

ROM *(rahm)* 1. Acronym for *Read-Only Memory,* any type of memory that can be read but not written to. For example, compact disks (CDs) are ROM media. 2. Chips inside a computer that permanently contain basic information. ROM chips are accessed like RAM chips, but their contents never change. See also *BIOS, RAM, PROM.* "I think that 'crash randomly' is a special instruction in my computer's *ROM.*"

ROM BIOS *(rahm by-oss)* Acronym for *Read-Only Memory Basic Input/Output System.* See also *BIOS.* "No, Mr. Pinkston, *BIOS* is not *ROM's* last name."

R

roman *(roh-man)* 1. A classification of type styles (fonts), including Times and many others. "A *Roman* man once said, 'Hello, my name is Gaius Julius Caesar, and I'm looking for a specific type of font, or do I need to ask?'" 2. The normal, nonslanted version of type, as opposed to italic type. See also *font.*

root *(root)* 1. The main user of a UNIX computer. Also called "root user," a special account that allows full access to all the commands, directories, and secret places on a computer. This is truly holy stuff. To be a root on a UNIX computer is akin to being a true computer god. "Bill keeps trying to log in as the *root,* hoping that someday the computer will be his. I don't like the grin on his face when he says that." 2. The first and often only directory on a disk. The root directory doesn't become important until you have subdirectories and a disk tree structure. Then, the other directories — the *subdirectories* — branch from the root, like a tree. In DOS, the symbol for the root directory is the single backslash (\ ). In UNIX, the symbol is a single forward slash (/). See also *directory, path, subdirectory, tree structure.* "I wrote this nifty program, DOG.COM, that instantly sniffs out the *root* directory of my hard disk's tree structure."

rounding error *(rown-ding ayr-or)* A one-cent error that occurs when a computer converts decimal numbers into binary code (for internal processing) and back again. Although this

error always happens, it's nothing to be overly concerned about — unless you're doing nuclear physics or thousands of lives are at stake, in which case you can use the "blame Microsoft" defense at your U.N. Crimes against Humanity trial. The reason for

Typical rounding error.

the rounding error is that certain numbers can only be approximated in a computer's memory as binary digits. As a result, a little bit of a fudge factor exists as a computer's approximations are mathematically manipulated. "I tried to explain that all the wrong answers on my math final were due to *rounding errors,* but the professor declines to believe that I'm a computer."

row *(roh)* 1. A horizontal array of data, as in a spreadsheet or table. Spreadsheets organize data into rows and columns to make totals and other calculations faster and easier. 2. A line of text in a word-processing document or just a line of text across a screen. "The typical PC screen has 25 *rows* of text, only four of which may make sense at any one time."

RPM *(ar pee em)* Acronym for *Revolutions Per Minute,* a measurement of the number of times something turns around. Disk drives and phonograph records (remember those?) spin at particular RPMs. Phonograph records spin at $33^1/_3$ or 45 RPMs. "I like CD players because I don't have to worry about the *RPM.*"

RS-232C *(ar es too-thur-tee-too see)* Acronym for *Recommended Standard-232C,* also known as RS-232. This term is not a Radio Shack part number. Instead, it's a standard

RS-232C connector thing.

method of transmitting data across serial cables and is used by modems, printers, and other serial devices. Lots of technical stuff surrounds this standard, and it can be boring, so that's all I'm going to say here. See also *serial, serial port.* "If *RS-232C* is the 232nd standard they came up with that year, I'd hate to have sat through the first 231 meetings."

RTF *(ar tee ef)* 1. See *Rich Text Format.* 2. The extension used with Rich Text Format document files.

run *(run)* 1. What to do when a computer starts to smoke. 2. To start a program. Other terms for *run* are *start, launch, execute, and initiate.* "The customer service operator told me to *run* my program, but I couldn't find a leash to fit it."

run-time *(run-tiem)* 1. The time spent while a program is running. 2. A special version of a program, such as a database or spreadsheet, that performs a specific task. For example, a run-time version of Excel would let you use your Excel worksheets but not let you use any Excel commands or options. *"Run-time* is a misnomer when you work with Windows. Then, it's more like walk-time."

R

S

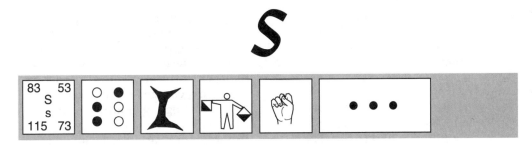

S: *(es koh-lon)* A letter designation for any of a number of different types of disk drives on a PC system. At this altitude, it's most likely a network drive, though it can also be a line drive late in the eighth inning, when it really counts.

S-100 *(ess won-hun-dred)* A type of expansion card and also the name of a CP/M computer from the late 1970s that used this type of expansion card. These systems are called *dinosaurs* today. See also *CP/M, expansion card.* "During their heyday, the *S-100* systems were the Cadillacs of PCs."

S-100 computer user.

SAA *(ess ay ay)* Acronym for *Systems Application Architecture,* a set of guidelines that IBM developed for standardizing the way computers work. Most people follow these guidelines and then add just enough "improvements" to destroy the whole purpose of a standard in the first place. See also *IBM.* "My computer follows the IBM *SAA* standard. That seems odd because my computer is a Macintosh."

sans serif *(sans sayr-if)* A typeface that lacks *serifs,* which are tiny, ornamental curves and such things that appear at the edges of letters. Believe it or not, serifs make letters easier to read. Sans serif typefaces (*sans* is from the French word for *without*) are harder to read but better suited for titles. Times is an example of a serif font; Helvetica is sans serif. See also *serif.* "A simple desktop publishing rule is to use *sans serif* fonts for headlines or titles and serif fonts for the text."

save *(sayv)* 1. To store data in permanent form, typically on a disk drive. 2. The command that saves data. Almost every program has a Save command to store work. "Use the *Save* command periodically to store your work."

save as *(sayv az)* To save a file to disk by using a different name or format.

scalable font *(skay-luh-bul fawnt)* A type of font that can appear in different sizes and still look good. Although nonscalable fonts can also appear in different sizes, at certain sizes they look as horrible as seeing your skin pores through a magnifying glass. "I use *scalable fonts* only in my desktop publishing work, just in case some customer wants to change the type size at the last minute." See also *font.*

scan *(skan)* To read text, images, or bar codes into a computer. Accomplished by a device called a *scanner.* See also *scanner.*

scan rate *(skan rayt)* The speed at which a monitor draws an image on-screen. Sometimes called the *refresh rate* and measured in hertz (Hz). The higher the scan rate, the more expensive the monitor. And, as anyone familiar with computers knows, the more you pay for it, the better it is. See also *refresh rate.* "My monitor has a *scan rate* of 72 Hz. Most clerks in the grocery store have a scan rate of about 18 items a minute."

ScanDisk *(skan disk)* A utility program that comes with DOS and Windows which identifies and repairs problems on floppy or hard disks. ScanDisk is a more advanced and easier program to use than the ancient MS-DOS CHKDSK command.

scanner *(skan-er)* 1. A device that can electronically "read" printed text or images into a computer. Scanners come in two sizes: flat-bed and handheld. Flat-bed scanners can scan an entire page at one time; handheld scanners can scan in widths of approximately four inches. 2. In 1981, Hollywood released a bad horror movie called *Scanners,* in which people could use mental powers to make other people's heads explode. See also *scan.* "While watching *Scanners* on TV and trying to concentrate hard enough to make my dog's head explode, I decided to buy a *scanner* so that I wouldn't have to retype newspaper articles into my word processor."

scope *(skohp)* 1. (Capitalized) A mouthwash typically not used by halitosis-happy computer programmers. 2. A term used by programmers to describe the area within a program in which a variable can be used. "While rinsing my mouth with *Scope,* I noticed that the *scope* of my subprogram's variables included my own subprogram and those subprograms written by Bob. But that subject is really beyond the scope of this book."

Scrapbook *(skrap-book)* A desk accessory on the Macintosh that stores frequently used graphics images or text for pasting into documents. See also *Clipboard.*

screen blanker *(skreen blank-er)* See *screen saver.*

screen buffer *(skreen buf-er)* An area of memory used to store the graphics or text image displayed on-screen. Also called *screen memory* or *video RAM.* "And all this time I thought that a *screen buffer* was this thing from Ronco for only $19.95 that you use to clean your monitor."

screen dump *(skreen dump)* A printout of an image that appears on-screen. The unflattering term *dump* is often used in computer lingo to mean the wholesale copying of information from one place to another. Although I could dwell on this subject for a long time and get very descriptive, the editorial matron at IDG Books Worldwide, Inc., Diane Steele, would doubtless frown on such verbosity. "Whenever my computer crashes for no apparent reason, I try to get a *screen dump* so that I can show the technician what happened and why his last solution didn't really work after all."

screen font *(skreen fawnt)* A bitmapped font that mimics the appearance of printer fonts. Because printers often print with a resolution of 300 dots per inch or more, the fonts tend to look better printed than they do on-screen. As a result, fonts displayed on-screen may look plain and simple compared to the fonts printed on a printer, resulting in confusion when you try to figure out what you're doing. "I hate *screen fonts* because you can never tell what they'll look like until you print them and waste paper in the process."

screen saver *(skreen say-ver)* A special program that periodically blanks out the screen and replaces it with utter darkness or often some form of graphic or entertainment. Screen savers prevent the same image from appearing on-screen and being "burned in" permanently. For example, many older PCs have images of 1-2-3 or WordPerfect permanently etched into their monitors. Some screen savers can be quite creative. Rather than just blank the screen, they show images of some sort, such as flying toasters, lightning flashes, or raindrops. See also *phosphor burn-in.* "If I don't touch my keyboard or mouse for five minutes, my *screen saver* shuts off my screen and displays fish in an aquarium to protect my monitor from burn-in."

scroll *(skrohl)* To move text or graphics vertically or horizontally on-screen as though the monitor were a

porthole, looking at a much larger image a little at a time. "With a 250-page document, a monitor can show only half a page at any given time. To see the rest of a document, you have to *scroll* up or down. Then again, you can just pretend that you saw only part of the document so that you can't be held responsible for the rest of it."

scroll bar *(skrohl bar)* 1. Where Plato went for drinks with Aristotle. 2. A horizontal or vertical strip that appears on the right or bottom side of a window and lets you use a mouse to scroll the image up and down or left and right.

scroll box *(skrohl boks)* A rectangular control living in a scroll bar that enables you to scroll the image in a window. You can drag the scroll box up or down (or left or right) or click around it to scroll the image. The scroll box also shows you the approximate position of the current screen display in relation to the beginning or end of the file. "Don't waste time pressing the Page Up and Page Down keys. Move the *scroll box* wildly up and down in the scroll bar and pretend that people are in there being slammed alternately into the floor and ceiling."

Scroll Lock key *(skrohl lahk kee)* 1. A key that appears on keyboards and seems to do absolutely nothing when you press it. 2. In some (but not all) programs, a key that changes the mode of the cursor keys on a keyboard. Normally, pressing the up-and-down cursor keys causes the cursor to scroll up or down. If you press the Scroll Lock key, however, and then press the up-and-down cursor keys, the cursor remains fixed on-screen,

S

and the text or graphics seem to slide up or down underneath. If you try this technique with a program and nothing happens, you know that your program ignores the Scroll Lock key. "Sometimes, I like to press the *Scroll Lock key* while I'm using different programs, just to see which programs actually use the Scroll Lock key."

SCSI *(scuz-zee)* 1. Acronym for *Small Computer System Interface,* yet another standard for connecting tape drives, hard disks, and scanners to computers. This acronym is truly whimsical and easily pronounceable, like WYSIWYG but not like GUI. With a SCSI interface in your PC, you can connect as many as six peripherals, including hard drives, CD-ROM drives, scanners, more hard drives, and more CD-ROM drives. See also *termination.* 2. A device that adheres to the SCSI standard. "Because this hard drive is a *SCSI* drive, you need to spend *another* $120 for a *SCSI* card inside your PC in order for it to work."

SEA *(see)* Acronym for *Self-Extracting Archive,* usually a Macintosh archive that was compressed by using the StuffIt program. Files with the SEA extension can automatically uncompress themselves on a Macintosh floppy or hard disk. See also *StuffIt.* "Sometimes, when I copy files from CompuServe, they have the SIT or *SEA* file extension. If they have the SIT extension, I have to use StuffIt to uncompress them; if they have the SEA extension, however, they uncompress themselves if I double-click them."

search *(surch)* To scan through a document for a matching bit of data. See also *find.* "Because the board can't decide who we should lay off, we're going to conduct a *search* of everyone's hard disk and fire all those who have the words *boss* and *toupee* in one or more of their files."

search and destroy *(surch and duh-stroy)* 1. A military term made popular during the Vietnam War, which is a nice way of saying to look for someone so that you can kill him. 2. A form of search and replace in which you replace what you found with nothing. Although the proper term is really *search and delete,* no one would turn to that entry in a dictionary. See also *find and replace.* "Someone told me that my computer program had bugs in it, so I spent the past few days on a *search-and-destroy* mission using pesticides long since outlawed by the government."

search and replace *(surch and ree-place)* To look for specific characters in a file and substitute them for another character or group of characters. See also *find and replace.*

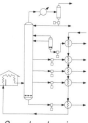
Complex drawing.

search engine *(surch en-jin)* A Web page designed to hunt down and locate information on the World Wide Web. Several types of search engines exist: Yahoo! is a catalog-type of search engine; it contains lists of Web pages by category — like a library. Web Crawler is a robot-type of search engine; it locates Web pages based on their content, which is the text or images that appear on the Web page. Excite is a content-type of search engine; it examines the content of a Web page overall and matches that content with the searches you perform. The nifty thing about all this is that the use of a search engine on the World Wide Web is free. See also *World Wide Web*. "I was able to look up an old girlfriend on the Web by using a *search engine*. She's making a million dollars a year selling pictures of her cats."

search path *(surch path)* See *path*.

search string *(surch string)* The group of characters a computer looks for when it's given the Find or Find and Replace command. See also *string*.

sector *(sek-ter)* A unit of disk storage, the smallest unit into which information can be written. A formatted disk is divided into tracks and sectors. A track is a ring of information encoded on the disk. Each track is divided into sectors. On a PC, each sector holds 512 bytes of information. See also *cluster, track*. "The technician told my mother that her hard disk had a bad *sector,* so she took it home and scolded it."

secure browser *(seh-kyoor brow-ser)* A Web browser that is SSL-compliant, which means that it can send and receive information and any eavesdroppers will be unable to decipher it. Browsers from Netscape and Microsoft are considered secure browsers. Other browsers — who knows? See also *SSL, Web browser*. "Using a *secure browser,* all residents of the United States

transferred their bank balances to offshore accounts in 2006, rendering the IRS extremely frustrated."

seek *(seek)* To move the read/write heads of a disk drive so that information can be read from disk, in much the same way as you might move a needle over a record on your grandmother's old turntable. This term is quite a religious one for a computer, don't you think? You'd expect a term such as Go To or Find or Search. Seek, of course, always implies that some chance of failure exists, which is probably why the computer gods selected it instead. See also *read/write head*. "I bought a Bible program and wanted to find the passage '*Seek* and ye shall find,' but I got a *seek* error instead."

segment *(seg-ment)* A portion or part of something. With worms, a segment is a new piece of the worm that makes it longer — a worm-slice, should the worm chance to crawl over an up-ended razor blade. In the PC, a *segment* refers to a 64K chunk of memory. "Programs generally run slowly under DOS because they must fit their parts into puny little 64K memory *segments*."

select *(seh-lekt)* To highlight and choose text or graphics that appear on-screen. A selected object can then be manipulated somehow by the program. Selected objects typically appear in inverse type (white on black) or inside a graphical outline. See also *cut, copy, paste*. "Before you can delete, copy, or cut anything off the screen, you have to *select* it first so that the computer knows what you want to delete, copy, or cut."

S

Select All *(seh-lekt ahl)* To select everything in a document, all text and graphics images, at one time. This command is a good one to use to erase everything at one time, adjust everything on-screen, or copy everything at the same time. If you use it carelessly, it's also a good way to delete four years' worth of work at the touch of a button. "I chose the *Select All* command, and everything in my room became highlighted."

selected *(seh-lek-ted)* Highlighted text or graphics images that show you which objects will be affected by the next command you give (cut, copy, or delete, for example). "I told my grandfather that I had to click the mouse button to make objects *selected*. He thought that I had joined a new cult or something."

self-modifying *(self-mod-ih-fie-ing)* When a program makes changes to itself while it's running. Many virus programs are self-modifying (also called *mutating*) to prevent detection by antivirus software. Many artificial intelligence programs are also self-modifying, to give the illusion of correcting themselves or adapting to outside stimuli like a living organism does. "I wrote a chess program that's *self-modifying*. It started out playing chess very well but eventually re-wrote itself into an accounting program."

semiconductor *(sem-ee-kon-duk-ter)* A material that is neither a good insula-tor nor a good conductor of electric-ity. Semiconductors are used to make transistors, diodes, integrated cir-cuits, and all the other neat stuff that makes up the parts of a computer. Silicon and germanium are two popular materials used for semicon-ductors. See also *germanium, silicon.* "Before he got a job designing *semi-conductors* in the electronics industry, George used to work part-time as a conductor on Amtrak."

separator bar *(sep-uh-ray-ter bar)* A thin line in a pull-down menu that helps group related commands. See also *pull-down menu.* "The File menu of my word processor has a *separator bar* between the Church and State commands."

Gymnast practicing on a separator bar.

sequential access *(see-kwen-shul ak-ses)* To scan information starting from the beginning, such as what you do with a tape backup or a cassette tape on a stereo. In comparison, random access lets you scan for information anywhere, such as on a CD-ROM. Sequential access is usually much slower than random access, although if you want to kill some time so that you can goof off for a while, it's a fine method for searching on a computer. See also *random access.* "Every time I want to play my favorite song stored on a tape cassette, I have to use *sequential access* by fast-forwarding or rewinding. If I had the song stored on a CD-ROM, I could use random access and start playing the song immediately."

serial *(seer-ee-al)* To transmit data, one bit after another. Each byte is split up into bits and sent along in single file, usually through a single cable. This term contrasts with *parallel,* in which data is sent eight (or more) bits abreast — like marching in a parade. The advantage of the serial method is that the information can be sent over longer distances. See also *data word format, parallel.* "Talking is a *serial* activity because you have to speak the words one after another. Arguing is more parallel in nature because nobody bothers listening to what the other person has to say before he starts shouting right back."

serial mouse *(seer-ee-al mows)* An input device (mouse) that plugs into a computer's serial port. This type of mouse is not as popular as it once was, considering how most PCs now come with special mouse ports. See *bus mouse.* A serial mouse also tends to interfere with a computer's modem, which is another reason to hate using them. "My *serial mouse* is doing 15-to-life for cheese theft."

serial port *(seer-ee-al port)* A connector on the back of a computer that allows data transfer, one bit at a time. Also known as a modem port, COM port, or RS-232 port. It comes in various sizes. See also *parallel port, RS-232C.* "Lois bought a *serial port* for her PC but was crushed to find out that a milk or sugar port wasn't available."

serial printer *(seer-ee-al prin-ter)* An oddball printer that plugs in to the serial port rather than to a computer's parallel (or printer) port. Serial printers were popular in the early 1980s, when some computers lacked parallel ports (or Centronics ports, as they were known then). Today, they're dinosaurs. "I decided to buy my boss the slowest printer possible, so I got him a *serial printer.*"

serif *(sayr-if)* Tiny, ornamental curves on letters to make them easier to read. Most typefaces have serifs. See also *sans serif.* "This book uses a typeface with *serifs* so that the printing doesn't strain your eyes and give you headaches while you're reading it. Too bad the same can't be said for legal documents, tax forms, and textbooks."

Omar Sharif.

server *(sir-ver)* 1. Usually the most expensive computer that nobody can use because it's busy controlling the entire network. You would think that the server would be the "slave" on the network, but that isn't so. The server is the "master computer," the one all the other computers hook into and beg for the use of disk drives and printers. This concept is the same evil concept that dominated mainframe computing during the past three decades. See also *client/server network.* "If you want to sabotage a network, don't bother wrecking each computer. Just unplug the *server,* and then the whole network will sink like the Titanic." 2. A type of computer sold as a server, usually a powerful PC with lots of hard disk storage and maybe an extra microprocessor or two. When the 486 was first introduced, it was sold as a "server" computer; today's high-end machines are also billed as servers. "Today's *server* is tomorrow's low-end entry machine."

S

session *(sesh-in)* 1. A 50-minute hour spent with a psychiatrist to help repair the mental trauma of having to use a computer. 2. An individual activity being carried out by a multitasking computer. See also *multitasking.* "Psychiatrists love multitasking computers. Because they charge $120 for an hour *session,* a computer running three sessions gets billed $360."

setting *(set-ing)* The configuration of a program that defines its appearance on-screen (color, window size, and memory usage, for example). "By the time the sun finished *setting* in the west, I had finished modifying the program's *settings* so that it wouldn't keep appearing as hot pink on purple every time you load it up."

setup *(set-up)* 1. The way a computer is configured. "Oops! Your computer doesn't know about your new hard disk. I guess you forgot that part of the *setup* process." 2. (Two words) To install new software. 3. The name of the program used to install new software. See also *configure, install.*

 SGML *(es jee em el)* Acronym for *Standard Generalized Markup Language,* a type of text formatting language that stores several different ways to present the same information. See also *HTML, Web page.*

sh *(shel*; *es aych)* 1. The Korn shell in UNIX. An interface that lets you use UNIX, which was what Microsoft modeled DOS after (in case you didn't know). See also *csh.* 2. The command you use to start the sh shell. "Dale uses UNIX all the time, and he thinks that the *sh* command is two letters too short."

shareware *(shayr-wayr)* Software you can legally copy and give away but must pay for if you use it regularly. Many shareware programs rival the features of commercial programs but cost much less. After you pay for shareware, you may get a printed manual, telephone support, and/or notice of future upgrades. See also *public domain.* "*Shareware* programs let you try before you buy, which is similar to asking your local Ford dealer whether you can drive around the latest Mustang for a few weeks before deciding whether you want to buy it."

sheet feeder *(sheet fee-der)* A tray that holds paper and gives up a page at a time to a printer. Sheet feeders let you use special stationery or letter-head that you may have lying around rather than use computer paper every time. "Every time my boss hands me a memo, I just flip it over, store it in my *sheet feeder,* and print on the other side, thereby saving valuable computer paper."

shell *(shel)* 1. An interface that's usually easier to use than the ugly program it's trying to cover for. For example, a DOS shell is a program that makes DOS easier to use. Windows is a type of DOS shell, even though shells exist for Windows (such as the Norton Desktop) that supposedly make it easier to use. Not all shells make things easier, however. Some shells make things more complex; if that's what the user wants, it's still considered a shell. 2. The name given to any program that someone uses to control a computer. In DOS, the shell is really a program called COMMAND.COM. That program displays the DOS prompt, interprets your commands, and runs other programs. In UNIX, the shell is sh or csh. See also *csh, sh.* 3. (Capitalized) The name given to the command that runs another program from a first program. For example, the Shell command in WordPerfect enables you to run a second program without having to quit WordPerfect first. When you quit the second program, you're back in WordPerfect. "Sue sells csh (sea *shells*) by the seashore, and she *shells* from csh (see *shells*) to see what she sells."

Shift key *(shift kee)* A modifier key used primarily to produce uppercase letters from a keyboard. You can also use Shift in combination with any key to generate a command or produce some wacky symbol. "Hold down the *Shift key* while tapping the F4 key once and then let both of them go. That's what Shift+F4 means when you see it printed in the manual. Shift+Tab means that you hold down the Shift key and press the Tab key."

A shift key.

Shift+arrow *(shift ayr-oh)* To hold down the Shift key, tap one of the arrow keys (up, down, left, or right), and then let both of them go. This command is often used for moving the cursor to highlight text in a word processor. "Press *Shift+left arrow,* and the cursor highlights all the text you

just wrote. If you then press Del, you wipe out all your valuable work in an instant."

shift+click *(shift-klik)* 1. To hold down either Shift key while clicking the mouse button at the same time. Shift-clicking is used to select two or more objects on-screen. See also *click.* 2. On the Macintosh, any click of the mouse when used with any modifier key on the keyboard. In addition to Shift, you can use the Command (Apple) key, Option key, or a combination of them. (Ted Nelson, the developer of hypertext, claims that the Macintosh mouse has *four* buttons, three of which are on the keyboard.)

 Shockwave *(shok-wayv)* An extension or plug-in for a Web browser that enables you to see animations or run programs over the Internet. See also *plug-in.*

shortcut keys *(short-kut kees)* A keyboard combination that serves the same function as a command on a pull-down menu. For example, Ctrl+S is the shortcut key for the Save command on the File menu.

shortcut menu *(short-kut men-yoo)* A pop-up menu associated with part of an application, icon, or window. A shortcut menu appears when you point the mouse at something and click the right mouse button. See also *right-click.* "Little Red Riding Hood clicked on Grandma's house to get the *shortcut menu,* but the wolf ate her."

S

shoulder surf *(shohl-der surf)* To look over another person's shoulder without being seen. Shoulder surfing is often used to see which keys someone types for a password or to read someone's telephone calling-card numbers at a public phone. "Be careful that no one tries to *shoulder surf* whenever you use your calling card at a public phone. They may be trying to inhale your cologne or perfume, or they may be trying to read your telephone calling-card numbers."

Show Clipboard *(shoh klip-bord)* A command that lets you see what's being held (the last item that was cut or copied) in the Clipboard. By choosing the Show Clipboard command first, you can see what will appear on-screen if you choose the Paste command next.

shrink wrap *(shrink rap)* The clear, plastic covering on most computer software sold in stores, giving it the illusion that it hasn't been touched by the grubby little hands of other people before reaching your computer desk intact and pristine. Most software is sold in shrink-wrapped boxes for that sanitized look, much like finding a "sanitized for your protection" paper loop for covering the toilet seat in a motel room. Most software stores do not accept returned software unless it's still shrink-wrapped, which makes you wonder how you would know to return it in the first place. "No, madam, *shrink wrap* does not make you thinner."

SHTML *(es aych tee em el)* Acronym for *Server-parsed HTML* (Hypertext Markup Language), a type of Web page document that contains special commands to enable a Web page to do more, run faster, jump higher, and so on. See also *HTML.*

shut down *(shut down)* 1. To turn off a computer. 2. The name of a series of commands that is executed whenever a computer is shut down. 3. (Capitalized) The Windows command used to quit Windows and optionally turn off the computer. "No, sir, a brick tossed into a computer's hard drive is not a proper *shut down* command."

sidelit *(sied-lit)* Additional illumination from the side of a liquid crystal display (LCD) to make the screen easier to read. See also *backlit.* "If it weren't for my *sidelit* LCD, I wouldn't be able to use my laptop computer on a dark plane ride. I'd really miss all those 36,000-foot games of Solitaire."

Sieve of Eratosthenes *(siv ov eer-uh-tahs-thuh-neez)* A programming concept for finding prime numbers (any number that cannot be divided by anything other than one and itself), named after that ancient Greek guy. Used in benchmark testing.

Some guy, probably not Eratosthenes.

SIG *(seeg)* Acronym for *Special Interest Group,* a collection of people who share the same interest in computers. For example, they may use a specific type of computer, such as an Amiga; use a specific type of program, such as dBASE IV; or specialize in a field, such as artificial intelligence or desktop publishing. "Cool people say that they belong to a *SIG*. Uncool people say that they belong to a special interest group because everyone knows that only cool computer people use acronyms whenever possible."

sign on *(sien on)* To call another computer, such as a local BBS, CompuServe, or Prodigy, and type your name and password so that you can start using the services. See also *log in*. "Before breaking in to the Pentagon computers, we put the 'Do not disturb' *sign on* the motel door and then plugged our portable computers into the phone jack so that we could dial out and *sign on* without anybody watching us."

signal-to-noise *(sig-nul too noys)* The amount of information versus idle chatter in a newsgroup posting or e-mail message. Refers to posters who tend to gloop up their messages with unnecessary quotes or topics not relating to the subject. From a communications term referring to how much of the signal is disturbed by random noise on the line. See also *noise*.

signature *(sig-na-choor)* A file containing information to be appended to (put at the end of) an e-mail message or USENET posting. These files typically contain your name, contact information, and — if you're a sophomore in college — about 4K of useless ASCII graphics and *Star Trek* quotes. "Howie was able to create a delightful

signature using only three lines of text. Obviously, he's Net-sensitive."

silicon *(sil-uh-kon)* 1. Sand. 2. An element used in making glass and the ceramic wafers out of which computer chips are punched. Do not pronounce this term as "silly con." "The hors d'oeuvres at any computer party wouldn't be complete without a tray of *silicon* wafers."

Silicon Valley *(sil-uh-kon vowl-ee)* The place in northern California that is world-famous for making semiconductors, microprocessors, and other computer electronic circuitry. They also have a few good pizza parlors and take-out Chinese restaurants. "We drove through *Silicon Valley*, up El Camino Real, to look for a job in the computer industry. With computers so prevalent, we wound up getting a job with a computer company in Fresno instead."

silicone *(sil-uh-kohn)* An element (Si) with the atomic number 14 and an atomic weight of 28.0855. It has little to do with computers. "You sound like a rube if you use the word *silicone* when you're referring to a computer."

SIMM *(sim)* Acronym for *Single In-line Memory Module*, a tiny circuit board that holds several memory chips. Several SIMMs plugged in to a computer look like headless cockroaches stuck face-first in the surface of a roach motel. See also *SIP*. "A *SIMM* makes it easier to install large amounts of memory. Rather than plug in individual memory chips in your computer, you can just plug in a couple of SIMMs."

S

simulation *(sim-yoo-lay-shun)* A program or device that mimics the operation of something else, such as real life. A flight-simulation program mimics the flying of an airplane (although how many airplane cockpits do you know use a keyboard to control a plane?), and a stock market simulation mimics the real-life rise and fall of stocks on Wall Street. See also *emulation.* "To give my kids an idea of what driving a real car is like, my computer has a driving *simulation* they can play with."

single-density *(sing-gul den-suh-tee)* The earliest form of storage on magnetic media that has been replaced with double-density and quad- or high-density. A single-density, 5¹/₄-inch floppy disk may contain 180K of data; a double-density, 5¹/₄-inch floppy disk may contain 360K; and a high-density, 5¹/₄-inch floppy disk may hold 1.2MB. See also *double-density, high-density.* "Don't buy *single-density* floppy disks because they're obsolete. Then again, everything else will be, too, in another month or two."

single-sided disk *(sing-gul-sie-ded disk)* A floppy disk that stores data on only one side. Along with single-density, another antique.

single-user *(sing-gul yoo-zer)* Equipment that only one person can try to use at any given time. A laptop computer is a single-user computer because if two or more people try to type on the keyboard

Barbara no longer wants to be a single user.

simultaneously, it may look obscene. Some database programs are single-user, meaning that only one person at a time can use them. Multiuser database programs let two or more people at a time use them. See also *multiuser.* "Lots of companies want to eliminate *single-user* computers and connect everything in a network. That way, they can watch what everyone's doing and keep people from playing games on their computers at work."

SIP *(sip)* Acronym for *Single In-line Processor,* a type of memory-expansion card that's similar to a SIMM. The difference between a SIP and a SIMM is that a SIP uses a row of tiny pins as a connector — like a cheap comb. SIPs aren't generally user-upgradable and are usually installed only at the factory. See also *SIMM.* "I need more *SIPs* because my PC gulps down memory."

SIT *(sit)* The extension given to a file that has been compressed by using the StuffIt program. "If you have a *SIT* file, uncompress it by using StuffIt."

site license *(siet lie-senz)* A software agreement that lets you legally use multiple copies of the same program on several computers at the same time. Site licenses are cheaper than buying multiple copies of the same program and are legal in comparison to software piracy. "Although we have a *site license* for WordPerfect and DOS, the folks who make the Space Zombies game want us to also have a site license for 500 copies."

S

Skipjack algorithm *(skip-jak al-guh-rithm)* The specific instructions for encrypting and decrypting files, used in the Clipper encryption chip that the government wants everyone to use so that it can read our e-mail. See also *Clipper.* "The *Skipjack algorithm* is classified as a government secret because if everyone knows how it works, they can figure out how to crack its code. If you want to find out how the Skipjack algorithm works, get a job with the government and then defect back to the people."

SLED *(sled)* Acronym for *Single Large Expensive Disk,* which is another way of putting all your eggs in one basket. Computers that use a SLED often have a multimegabyte hard disk that costs a fortune. "After we lost all our data because we bought lots of cheap hard disks, we decided to buy a *SLED* and get our money's worth. Then it failed anyway."

slimline case *(slim-lien kays)* A computer case that's short and narrow and perfectly suited for squeezing into tight spaces on desks that have no room. Slimline cases usually offer fewer expansion slots and disk drives than normal computer cases (referred to as *desktop cases*). If you have absolutely no plans to upgrade your computer in the future, get a slimline case. Otherwise, get a bigger computer case that offers more room for expansion. "I bought a *slimline case* because I didn't have much room on my desk to put a computer. Now I can't add a hard disk or another disk drive because the slimline case has no room. Wow, do I feel like I just got ripped off."

SLIP *(slip)* Acronym for *Serial Line Internet Protocol,* a method of hooking up a computer to the Internet by using a high-speed modem and standard phone line. See also *PPP.* "This is how we *SLIP* on the Net, SLIP on the Net, SLIP on the Net. This is how we SLIP on the Net, so early in the morning."

slot *(slawt)* A long, thin hole into which an expansion card is plugged. Usually called *expansion* slots, although in advertising you may see that a PC comes with "eight slots," which means that you can plug in as many as eight expansion cards. The term *slot* is the easy term. Nerds call all the slots *the bus* and refer to it by terms such as MCA, ISA, EISA, and NuBus. See also *expansion slot.* "Plugging things into your PC's expansion *slot* makes upgrading your hardware Tinker Toy simple. Just remember to turn off your computer before you do this, or else your PC's guts will smell like burnt toast."

small caps *(smal kaps)* A text attribute or style in which lowercase letters are replaced by capital letters of a smaller size. For example, the following title is in small caps:

BOSCO SLUGWORTH LANCES A BOIL

The first letter of each word is capitalized. That's called *initial caps.* The subsequent letters are still uppercase, but in a smaller size than the other letters. That's *small caps.* If all the letters were capitalized, it would be called *all caps.* "These three, charming, old ladies came into the computer store looking for *small caps,* so I told them to go to the milliner instead."

Smalltalk (*smal-tok*) One of the first object-oriented programming languages in the world. Originally developed at the Xerox Palo Alto Research Center, the Smalltalk interface has been responsible for the graphical user interface ideas of the Macintosh and Microsoft Windows. So now you know who to blame. "Blake thinks that he's cool because he programs in a pure object-oriented programming language such as *Smalltalk* rather than C++. I'd think that he was cool, too, if any of his programs ever worked the way they're supposed to."

smart terminal (*smart ter-muh-nul*) A computer, connected to a network, that can function independently of the network. Smart terminals are usually just personal computers with their own hard disk, disk drive, and memory. In comparison, *dumb terminals* are usually nothing more than a monitor and keyboard. See also *dumb terminal*. "*Smart terminals* scare most managers because they can't control them as easily. Who knows whether that employee is working on a report or his résumé? Managers who distrust smart terminals are called dumb managers, and managers who trust smart terminals are called smart managers."

smartcard (*smart-kard*) A type of credit card that contains a computer chip that remembers information. A special device can read the smartcard or write new information to it. This type of technology may one day replace the PCMCIA cards that are popular in laptops. Then again, it may not. See also *PCMCIA*.

smiley (*smie-lee*) An emoticon or ASCII "picture" that conveys a happy mood or something fun. It consists of a colon, a hyphen, and the right parenthesis, which looks like a face turned sideways:

:-)

People who use e-mail use this symbol to denote a light mood because expressions are often missed and jokes that would be taken lightly in verbal communications often lose their meaning when they're written down. "I would have busted you in the chops for that message, had you not appended a *smiley*."

SMM (*es em em*) Acronym for *System Management Mode,* a standard developed by Intel for automatically reducing energy consumption in its chips when the computer isn't being used. The idea behind SMM chips is that they conserve energy and prolong the batteries of laptop computers. "The latest Intel processors offer *SMM* to cut off power consumption by your computer if you're not using it. SMM is great for people too lazy to hit the on–off switch on their computers."

smoke and mirrors (*smohk and meer-ers*) Slang term describing special effects to make a product look and sound more enticing and powerful than it really is. Smoke-and-mirrors techniques are commonly used in advertising and sales. A great smoke-and-mirrors story has to do with the ancestor of the Macintosh, the ill-fated Lisa computer. (Although the Lisa was, in many ways, the "father" —

or is it mother? — of the Macintosh and Windows, in another way it isn't because it stole the idea from elsewhere.) When the original Lisa was demonstrated for the computer industry, it wasn't a computer at all! Instead, the designers had rigged — under the table — several Apple II computers, which actually controlled the Lisa. This example is classic smoke and mirrors. "The product demo had us floored. But then, a little dog pulled back the curtain on the left, and the computer said, 'Pay no attention to that nerd behind the curtain!' I suppose that the whole thing was just *smoke and mirrors.*"

SMTP *(es em tee pee)* Acronym for *Simple Mail Transfer Protocol,* the basic way text messages are exchanged on the Internet. See also *MIME, POP.*

snaf *(snaf)* The edges of tractor-feed paper — the row of holes the tractor mechanism grabs to push the paper through. Typically discarded after the paper has been printed on.

sneaker net *(snee-ker net)* A nonnetwork in which information is exchanged between computers by copying files to a disk and then walking (in your sneakers) to another computer to use the disk. "Believe it or not, I once worked at a 'high-tech' company that used *sneaker net* to transfer its files."

SNOBOL *(snoh-bal)* Acronym for *StriNg Oriented symBOlic Language,* a specialized programming language for processing character strings (text). Developed at Bell Laboratories in 1962, SNOBOL is rarely used today,

except as an answer for computer trivia questions. "*SNOBOL* isn't the Latin of ancient computer languages. No, it's more like Aramaic."

snow *(snoh)* Small, flickering dots and specks that sometimes appear on certain monitors, caused when the screen image changes too fast for a lame monitor to handle. Usually found only on CGA monitors or really bad VGA monitors. "Edna, this isn't *snow* on your monitor. I think that we need to go to the pharmacy and get you some Head & Shoulders."

Various snow.

soft hyphen *(soft hie-fen)* A word break in a word-processing document that appears only when a word hangs precariously close to the right margin, in which case a hyphen hyphenates the word. At times, the term may also apply to any hyphen character, which is used to split a word. This concept contrasts with hard hyphens, which are not supposed to split a word when that word is too close to the right margin or when the hyphen is used as part of a phone number or other piece of text you don't want to split. "No, if you poke a *soft hyphen,* you don't get gunk all over your fingers."

software *(soft-wayr)* Computer programs. Applications. Software generally refers to any type of computer program, from an operating system, such as DOS, to a utility to an application to a program stored on a ROM chip. This term contrasts with *hardware,* which is the physical side of computing. The software makes the

S

hardware go. Without software, the hardware is nothing but potential — like an uneducated kid minus the hyperactivity. See also *hardware.* "Og know difference between *software* and hardware. Hardware hard. Software soft."

SOHO *(soh-hoh)* Acronym for *Small Office/Home Office,* which hardly anyone uses except for computer magazines that are trying to create another acronym for everyone to remember. SOHO is often used to describe products that people think would be just perfect for a small office or home office, such as a computer desk that folds up into an aquarium or flower pot or a portable lamp that doubles as a food warmer. "If a big company buys a product, it's not considered a *SOHO* product. If a big company wouldn't be interested in a product, it's considered a SOHO product or something absolutely useless that nobody in their right mind would consider buying in the first place."

sort *(sort)* To organize according to some pattern or rule. The typical sort is alphabetical, though you can also have numeric sorts. Sorts can also be ascending or descending. An ascending sort goes from first to last, from smallest to biggest, or from *a* to *z.* Descending goes the other way. "Kinkaid should be busy for a while. I just told him to *sort* our list of Japanese clients — in Japanese."

sound card *(sownd card)* A PC expansion card that adds sound and music capabilities to a computer. See also *MIDI.*

SoundBlaster *(sownd-blas-ter)* A type of music and sound expansion card for a PC. The SoundBlaster card has become something of a standard in all PCs. Most games are compatible with SoundBlaster, and many PCs even have SoundBlaster circuitry on their motherboard.

source *(sohrs)* 1. A file being copied. 2. The location of the file being copied. The location of the copy is known as the target. See also *target.* "The first *source* for anything has to be your brain. Or it could be the devil, if you're possessed."

source code *(sohrs kohd)* Programming instructions. They're fed into a program called a compiler, which makes object code. A program called a linker then builds the final program from the object code. Source code is created by using a text editor. "Melvin is such a deft programmer that his *source code* reads like poetry. Okay, you have to be pretty weird to appreciate it."

space *(spays)* The character, or blank, produced by pressing the spacebar. ASCII code 32. Unlike the space produced on a typewriter, the space made by computers is actually a character on-screen, just like A or $ or the ~ thing. "I keep having to tell Tom that *alot* is really two words. I told him to insert a *space* character, so he drew a picture of Captain Kirk."

spacebar *(spays-bar)* The biggest key on a keyboard, the one that produces the space character. "Is it called the

The spacebar.

spacebar or the spacebar key? Is it a bar or a key? And, no, I won't make any tired and obvious outer space cocktail lounge jokes here."

spaghetti code (spuh-geh-tee kohd) A program written so sloppily that it has no flow or logic. It's said of this type of program that reading it is like following a noodle around on a plate of spaghetti. Spaghetti code programs are typically written by people who are new to programming or by a programming committee. "Well, I guess if Sergio Leone wrote a program, it could be called *spaghetti code*."

spam (spam) (Often capitalized) 1. An annoying e-mail message or newsgroup post, typically one containing an advertisement. From Spam, a spiced-ham, meaty kind of thing sold by Hormel. (Spam is short for spiced ham.) Also can be from a Monty Python sketch involving Spam. 2. A message sent to a group of people, via e-mail or in a newsgroup. The message typically isn't germane to the discussion topic or is trying to sell something. 3. Unwanted e-mail. See also *e-mail, newsgroup, spew.* "The only way to fight *spam* is not to respond."

SPARC (spark) Acronym for *Scalable Performance ARChitecture,* a RISC processor developed by Sun Microsystems for its line of workstations (SPARCstations). It must be cool; I've never seen one. See also *RISC.* "This Sun workstation is running kind of slowly. Maybe it needs another *SPARC* plug."

special character (spesh-uhl kar-ek-ter) 1. Any oddball or unusual character, one typically unavailable on a keyboard. For example, the trademark character (™) is considered a special character because it's not on a keyboard. 2. Characters that perform special functions, such as the * or ? characters that are used as wildcards to match filenames or text being searched for.

speed (speed) A measure of how fast something is. The speed of microprocessors is measured in megahertz (MHz). Disk drive speed is measured in access time by milliseconds. Generally speaking, the larger the number, the faster the thing operates (and the faster the money comes from your wallet). See also *MHz, millisecond.* "I wouldn't say that this new printer is fast. Its *speed* is probably one notch above stop."

spell-check (spel-chek) To run a command that checks the spelling of text in a document. See also *spell checker.*

spell checker (spel chek-er) A program feature or command that looks for misspelled words and suggests corrections. This feature is really necessary only in English, where spelling still remains a mystery some 150 years after Webster made up the whole idea. Although a spell checker does spot mangled English, it does not check words in context: "Eye yam deer two ewe" is spelled correctly but makes no sense. "Now I never have to learn to spell because my computer's *spell checker* does it for me."

S

spew (*spyoo*) A single message posted repeatedly to the same newsgroup. A spew can be spam, or it can be some doofus just repeatedly reposting the same message. Annoying. See also *spam.*

spike (*spiek*) A sudden, often lethal, increase in the power coming through the wall. Spikes, typically caused by nearby lightning strikes, can potentially fry electronic equipment but more typically do nothing other than cause the screen to flicker momentarily. Look out your window. Find a tall tree. If a bolt of lightning were to hit that tree, it would send a power spike through all the circuits in the room in which you're sitting, making your PC's guts go pop. See also *surge suppressor.* "I bought a surge suppressor to protect against power *spikes,* but I still unplug my computer during an electrical storm."

Spock (*spahk*) 1. The character Leonard Nimoy played on the original *Star Trek* television show. The computer-loving crowd admires Spock because he too enjoyed using computers. Some great Spock-computer *Star Trek* moments:

> "This computer here is the key. Destroy this one, and the whole planet goes."

> "Computer? Compute to the last digit the value of pi." (The computer starts screaming here.)

> "Landru is a computer."

> "The computer lied."

See also *Vulcan.* "Okay, *Spock.* It's your turn to wear a red shirt and beam down to the planet." 2. A real-life doctor, well-known for his expert advice about caring for babies and for blocking trains carrying nuclear waste.

spoiler (*spoy-ler*) An e-mail message or newsgroup posting that contains information about an upcoming event, such as a long-awaited movie or TV show. The spoiler message "spoils it" for someone who wants to see the show without knowing beforehand what will happen. USENET posters are typically very nice about this stuff, using the word *spoiler* in the subject line of their message to let others know that they should skip the message if they don't want to know what's coming up.

spoiler space (*spoy-ler spays*) Several blank lines at the beginning of a message. The lines "push down" the bulk of a message that contains a spoiler so that if someone accidentally views the message, they don't see something offensive, such as "Kosh is dead" or something like that. See also *spoiler.*

spool (*spool*) The process of sending tiny bits of information over time, usually while a user is off doing something else. For example, a print spooler stores files to be printed, sending a small amount of each file to the printer every so often so that the computer is bogged down waiting for the printer. Spooling is a feature of the Windows and OS/2 operating systems.

S

spooler *(spoo-ler)* The device that spools. See also *spool.*

spreadsheet *(spred-sheet)* 1. A program that mimics a calculator, with hundreds of displays all arranged in neat rows and columns. Each display is really a "cell," which can store text, a value, or a formula. The formulas are typical calculator formulas, often involving other cells. All this stuff works together to create interactive numeric information, enabling you to examine data, such as general ledgers, payroll accounts, loans, and other types of financial and numeric data. Accountants love spreadsheets, as do scientists, mathematicians, and people with nothing better to do on a Saturday night. See also *macro, number crunching, template.* "I told my mother that I'm using *spreadsheets* at the office, and she thought that I was demoted to a maid." 2. A document created by spreadsheet software. See also *worksheet.*

Teensy view of a spreadsheet.

sprite *(spriet)* 1. A moving element in a graphical display, such as in video games. 2. (Capitalized) A sugar-flavored, carbonated beverage with exaggerated claims of refreshment that two out of three hard-core programmers and computer users prefer over Coke, Pepsi, and Kool-Aid. "Whenever I get tired of watching *sprites* on my computer, I drink a Sprite."

SS/DD *(es es/dee dee)* Acronym for *Single-Sided/Double-Density,* an obsolete floppy disk format that stored 180K of stuff on a 5¹/₄-inch

disk. "We found an old *SS/DD* disk in the storage room the other day. Stood around for about an hour marveling at such an antique."

SS/SD *(es es/es dee)* Acronym for *Single-Sided/Single-Density,* another obsolete floppy disk format that stored only 90K of data on a 5¹/₄-inch floppy disk.

SSL *(es es el)* Acronym for *Secure Sockets Layer,* a protocol for sending and receiving information on the Internet in such a way that only authorized recipients can decode the information. See also *secure browser.*

stack *(stak)* A data structure that programmers use to store and remove data in a last-in, first-out (LIFO) order, used especially in assembly language. Information is placed on the stack by using a *push* command. Information is removed with a *pop* command (or a *pull* command). The most recent item pushed is the item that is popped, which is why the stack is known as a LIFO construction. Weird but useful in programming. See also *LIFO, pop.* "Programmers who like pancakes prefer using *stacks.*"

standard *(stan-derd)* 1. A word that produces uncontrollable laughter from any engineer in the computer industry. Something management takes seriously (especially the marketing types). 2. A stubborn, mythical belief held by Computer Bigwigs that they can define specific methods, appearances, or equipment that everyone else in the world will voluntarily follow. See also *ANSI, ISO,* and any of the other number of

S

standards defined by the computer industry that everyone either fiddles with or ignores. 3. A flag.

star network *(star net-wurk)* 1. A network configuration in which the central computer has a direct line (network cable) connecting it to every other computer on the net-work. The network map (topography) resembles a star, with the big, hefty file server in the middle and piddly old PCs sitting around it. See also *server, topography.* 2. CBS.

star-dot-star *(star-dot-star)* See **.**.

Star Trek *(star trek)* A science fiction TV show, with a rabid following among computer groupies. *Star Trek* tells the story of a spaceship sent from Earth to explore the galaxy so that its captain can find various women and engage in fisticuffs with strange, new aliens every week. Remarkably enough, the aliens all looked like human actors wearing lots of makeup and speaking perfect English. Known as ST:TOS on the Internet, for *Star Trek: The Original Series.* "I'm very thankful for *Star Trek.* Without it, we'd have to put up with lame *Voyage to the Bottom of the Sea* computer humor."

Star Trek: The Next Generation *(star trek the nekst jen-er-ay-shun)* The popular sequel to the original *Star Trek,* ST:TNG (as it's known on the Internet) has several beloved charac-ters, including an android named Commander Data, a Klingon named Worf, and the poised, sophisticated Captain Picard. Some two-year-olds know who these guys are before they even recognize Bert or Ernie. (I'm not even going to discuss Barney.) "If you don't watch *Star Trek: The Next Generation,* you may have trouble conversing with nerds, geeks, and gurus."

 Start *(start)* The name given to the Start button on the Windows taskbar. See also *Start button.*

start bit *(start bit)* The tiny chunk of information that signals the beginning of data transfer. "Before my wife starts yelling at me for spending too much time at my computer, she starts wringing her hands. To me, that's a *start bit* signaling that she's about to start nagging again."

Start button *(start but-tun)* A button on the far left side (or top) of the taskbar in Windows, used to display the pop-up Start menu to control various things in Windows 95 and later. You can also access the Start button by pressing the Ctrl+Esc key combination or the Windows key, if your keyboard sports one.

Start thing button.

start-up disk *(start-up disk)* The disk a computer's BIOS searches for in an operating system. The operating system is loaded from the start-up disk. On a PC, it's the first floppy drive (A:) and then the first hard drive (C:). "My hard disk is my *start-up disk.* When the hard disk starts acting flaky, I have a special floppy disk that I use for my start-up disk. If that floppy disk doesn't work, I cry."

S

static *(stat-ik)* Random electrical noise that garbles voice and modem communication through the phone lines. "Every time I try to dial in to the NASA computers, *static* interferes, and I have to hang up. Every time my mother-in-law calls, I make crackling noises with my mouth and pretend that *static* is preventing me from hearing what she has to say."

stealth virus *(stelth vie-rus)* A sneaky type of virus that tries to make itself invisible to antivirus programs that may kill it. "I'm sorry, Jay, but pointing that expensive Air Force radar detector at your PC just won't work. It may be infected by a *stealth virus* that our technology cannot detect."

stop bit *(stop bit)* The tiny chunk of information that signals the end of a successful data transfer. Hanging up the phone in the middle of a call is *not* an example of a stop bit. "Some communications programs let you choose between one or two *stop bits.* Most of the time, a one stop bit is fine, unless the other computer doesn't stop, in which case you need two stop bits."

storage *(stohr-edj)* A place to put valuable information in the hope that you'll be able to find it again. Common storage devices are tape drives, floppy disks, hard disks, and CD-ROM disks. Memory (RAM) is also storage, although it's temporary. See also *RAM.* "We use a special optical disk for *storage.* That way, our data will survive a nuclear attack, even though we may not."

storage media *(stohr-edj mee-dee-ya)* A disk on which you store information.

string *(string)* 1. A group of letters. Although humans call groups of letters *words,* computers call them *strings.* A type of variable, as opposed to values or numbers. Strings are text. Strings can include letters, numbers, symbols, spaces, and other characters. Often, strings are enclosed in double quotes. 2. A type of variable in a programming language that holds string information as opposed to a value. "Although I consider my name to be a representation of ancient history, when I type it in my database, the computer just thinks of it as a *string* of meaningless characters."

string variable *(string vayr-ee-uh-bol)* A symbol that a program uses to represent a group of characters. Most databases use the string variable NAME to represent a person's name. "Yes, you should store the word *yarn* in a *string variable.*"

structured programming *(struk-sured pro-gram-ming)* 1. A method of writing programs in small subprograms or modules so that the programs are easy to read and understand. Structured programming emphasizes that programs can be written using three types of statements: sequential, conditional, and loop. Sequential program statements run one after another; conditional statements are IF-THEN or CASE statements; and loop statements are WHILE-DO, DO-WHILE, FOR-DO, and REPEAT-UNTIL statements. If you have no idea what this stuff means, you probably don't need to know anything about structured programming, except for the

S

fact that it rarely works and that's why programs now have so many bugs in them. "The closest I've come to *structured programming* is building a little house from old issues of *TV Guide.*" 2. A myth pursued by computer scientists with the same vigor that early Spanish explorers had when they searched the New World for the Fountain of Youth and the Seven Cities of Gold.

StuffIt *(stuf-it)* A compression program for the Macintosh that can smash multiple files into a single file to take up less space. Most Mac shareware is distributed online in the StuffIt format. "My boss asked me how to decompress the files he downloaded from CompuServe, and I told him to *StuffIt.* Now I'm out of a job, and he still can't get to his files."

style *(stiel)* 1. Text formatting and character attributes all combined into one. Style refers to the way text looks. 2. The command used on some programs to format text. A collection of formatting and character attributes that can be applied to text all at one time. "I have two *styles* I use for my memos: Fancy Sycophant for writing letters to my boss and Ugly Automaton for writing letters to those who work for me."

stylus *(stie-les)* A long, pointy thing, like a pencil. A type of input device, such as a mouse. You use a stylus to draw on an electronic pad embedded with sensors. What you draw shows up on-screen. This thing is more expensive than a typical computer mouse but offers a higher degree of control. See also *puck.* "If Baron

Lytton had known about computers, he may have said, 'The *stylus* is mightier than the mouse,' but he would have run the risk of being locked up for that."

subdirectory *(sub-di-rek-tuh-ree)* The old term for a folder. A directory within, or "under," the current directory. All disks have directories, in which they store files. The directories can also store other directories,

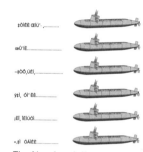

The Navy's subdirectory.

which are then called subdirectories. Technically, the term applies only to directories "beneath" another directory. Generally, any directory on a disk — except for the main, or root, directory — is called a subdirectory. See also *tree structure,* for more confusion. "I'm sorry, Private, if you want to find a *subdirectory,* you have to look on the navy's computers."

submenu *(sub-men-yoo)* A menu's menu. A menu contained inside another menu. For example, if you're presented with a menu of choices and choosing one of them displays another menu, you have a submenu. In a GUI, a submenu is often a secondary or tertiary menu that hangs on to the main menu like an ugly piece of gum. "Today's *submenu* offers several items: Ham, pastrami, turkey, Provolone, Swiss, Cheddar, and a variety o' fixin's."

subnotebook computer *(sub-noht-buk kom-pyoo-ter)* See *laptop.*

subroutine *(sub-roo-teen)* A miniprogram within a larger program. For example, a program may have a subroutine that displays text on-screen. The main program "calls" that subroutine whenever it wants to display text on-screen. "My son just can't seem to finish his homework. I think that his brain is missing some *subroutine.*"

subscribe *(sub-skrieb)* 1. To sign up for a newsgroup. You don't really "sign up" — you merely tell your newsgroup-reading software that you want to make one group part of your regularly visited places. That way, the subscribed group always appears in the application, showing any new or unread messages. See also *newsgroup.* 2. To sign up for a mailing list on the Internet. This is done by sending a mail message to a moderator or mailing-list host.

subscript *(sub-skript)* Text that appears smaller and below its surrounding text. A text-formatting attribute, available in word processors and other programs, that lets you manipulate text. The number 2 in H_2O is a subscript. See also *superscript.* "Jacob was trying to explain to me that the printer was broken, but it turned out that he accidentally turned on *subscript* mode and didn't know it. Ah, the joys of WordPerfect. . . ."

suite *(sweet)* A collection of applications, usually major applications such as a word processor, spreadsheet, database, and others that would cost more if you bought them separately. Theoretically, all programs in a suite are supposed to work together and use similar commands. Realistically, all programs in a suite are together simply because some company packaged them that way in an effort to sell more programs (especially when it comes time to upgrade). Ideally, after you understand how to use one program in a suite, you can quickly use the others. Also, after you create data in one program, you can effortlessly (supposedly) share that data within other programs of the same suite. "An integrated program is one program that offers a word processor, spreadsheet, and database. A *suite* is a collection of three or more separate programs that some marketing genius thought would look nice packaged together regardless of whether they work alike or share data."

suits *(soots)* The people who run a computer company. Derogatory term used by engineers and low-level employees for those who wear suits all the time and claim to know a great deal about computers but who are mostly MBA types who are just out for stock options and to play golf with their boss. The term *suits* comes in handy because these people's turnover rate is high, and often it really doesn't matter who's wearing the suit.

Suit.

S

Super VGA *(soo-per vee gee ay)* Faster than regular VGA. More powerful than EGA. Able to leap puny old CGAs in a single bound. Look, up on-screen, it's high resolution, it's colorful — yes! — it's Super VGA. IBM introduced its best PC graphics standard in 1987: the VGA. Other manufacturers liked it but offered an improvement called Super VGA, also known as SVGA. If you're buying a graphics card for your PC, Super VGA is the way to go. See also *VGA*. "*Super VGA* gives Phil the graphics horsepower he needs in order to see his naked-lady GIF collection at full resolution."

supercomputer *(soo-per-kom-pyoo-ter)* Faster than a regular computer, a very large, powerful, and fast computer. Supercomputers are used for important things, such as drawing dinosaurs in *Jurassic Park*. Unlike a mainframe, a supercomputer has an interesting design that makes it very, very fast. That's about all you need to know because you can't have a supercomputer in your house; turning it on would dim all the lights in the neighborhood. "I hear that the boys in the lab just love the new *supercomputer*. They bow to it every time they enter the room."

superscript *(soo-per-skript)* Text that appears smaller and above its surrounding text. Superscript is a text-formatting attribute that's available in word processors and similar programs that manipulate text. The number 10 in 2^{10} is superscripted. See also *subscript,* unless you've already come here from there. "Simon Nathaniel IV thinks that it's really nifty when he prints his name with a *superscripted* four: Simon Nathaniel[4]."

superstore *(soo-per-stor)* A large store that sells lots of different computer equipment, software, books, and furniture, except for the ones you really need. Most superstores give the illusion of offering the lowest prices for name-brand equipment but are often priced higher than competing stores that aren't part of a nationwide franchise. "Superman, Batman, Spiderman, and Wonder Woman all bought their computers at a *superstore.*"

supertwist *(soo-per-twist)* A type of laptop display that's much better than regular twist. "They call this a *supertwist* display because only Superman could twist the circuits that tight."

support *(suh-port)* 1. What you pay extra for when you pay extra. 2. What you don't get when you pay extra. 3. What you're supposed to get with every computer you buy, whether you pay extra or not. 4. Training or someone available for help with a new PC or a place to get the PC repaired. Support is the most important factor in buying a computer and one that many people neglect as a trade-off for a low price. Support includes service after the sale as well as phone help, classroom help, and other assistance. Software vendors offer support in the form of phone lines, toll-free or not, over which you can ask questions. Sometimes this process actually works. "The only *support* that comes from waiting on hold is support for the long-distance phone company."

S

surfer *(ser-fer)* A slang term that describes someone who spends an inordinate amount of time exploring an electronic network, such as the Internet, CompuServe, or local electronic bulletin-board systems. Often used with the slang term *Net,* as in *Net surfer.* "If you have questions about using the Internet, ask Ted because he's the local Net *surfer* around here."

surge *(serj)* An increase in the power level coming through the wall socket. Surges are gradual and build to a point where they may do some damage to a PC's components. Usually this damage is prevented by a circuit breaker, or sometimes — in an utterly unbelievable twist of altruism — the power supply may give up its life to save the rest of the PC's components. A surge is the opposite of a brownout, when the power drops to low levels and a PC may not even start. See also *spike, surge suppressor.* "Serge was expecting the power *surge* to make his computer run faster. However, the circuit breaker popped, and, though he lost my data, his computer is again saved from the perils of the electric company."

Serge Avogadro.

surge protector *(serj proh-tek-tor)* 1. A device that guards against power surges so that a computer doesn't blow up when the volts climb. See also *surge.* "Although a *surge protector*

is a good thing to have for a PC, it doesn't protect your computer against other power-line nasties, such as spikes, line noise, and people who trip over cords." 2. A device that protects you from Serge.

suspend *(sus-pend)* 1. To temporarily halt but not completely stop — more like freeze. "When I answer the phone, I must *suspend* my dot-matrix printer. Otherwise, I can't hear a darn thing." 2. A command in Windows 95 that puts a computer into an energy-saving sleep mode.

SVGA *(ess vee jee ay)* An acronym for *Super VGA,* a PC graphics adapter standard. See also *Super VGA.*

swap file *(swap fiel)* A chunk of a hard disk used to store information in memory. The operating system, in dire need of more RAM, simply copies a huge chunk of RAM to the swap file on disk. When the system needs to access that memory again, it loads the swap file from disk into memory. This is the reason that PCs with not enough RAM in them work sluggishly under Windows; a great deal of information is being copied back and forth to the swap file. See also *virtual memory.*

switch *(swich)* 1. A knob or lever that has two positions, usually On and Off. It can also be a graphical representation of a knob or button in a GUI. In IBM lingo, the Big Red *Switch* used to mean the on–off switch on a computer. "Back in the early PC days, the *switch* was really big and red. Today, on–off switches are no longer red, nor are they necessarily big."

S

2. A command option or parameter. For example, the /F switch in the DOS FORMAT command is used to tell FORMAT how big of a disk to format. 3. To move from one program to another in a multitasking environment. See also *multitasking.*

SX *(es eks)* A suffix, added to older Intel microprocessor numbers, which indicates that the chip is something less than a DX model. The 386SX was crippled by running at half its bit-width internally. The 486SX was crippled by its lack of a built-in math coprocessor.

synchronous *(sing-kroh-nus)* Happening at the same time, or in synch. Usually, this term applies to synchronous communications. In that mode, two computers communicate at a specific pace with each other, sending bits back and forth "on the beat." Microcomputer modems are asynchronous devices and do not send information at a specific pace. See also *asynchronous.* "No, Bob, *synchronous* communications doesn't mean that we have to sing to each other."

syntax *(sin-taks)* 1. A tax on beer, alcohol, or cigarettes. 2. The set of rules regarding the way a language is put together. It applies to programming languages as well as to human languages. "Computers are persnickety. Disobeying their laws of *syntax* is akin to telling your neighbor, 'Day nice outside hot not it is.'"

syntax error *(sin-taks ayr-or)* You have violated the rules of syntax, usually while writing a computer program. If you flip-flop words or

misspell something, the program compiler spits out a syntax error, and then you're left scratching your head to figure out what you did wrong. "Computers say 'Syntax error' because the people who programmed them are too lazy to make the message any more precise."

sysop *(sis-op)* Abbreviation for *system operator,* the head honcho in charge of a system. This term revolves primarily around computer bulletin boards (BBSs). The person who owns the computer and the BBS and in whose house it sits is the sysop. This position is an exalted one among the modeming crowd. Everyone wants to be a sysop or be in the sysop's favor. See also *BBS.* "I begged the *sysop* for advanced access to his system; finally, he gave me level-six access. The funny thing is, there's no one on level six."

Morgan was thrilled to be the sysop.

SysRq key *(sis-tim ree-kwest kee)* A key added by IBM to its PC-AT keyboards that doesn't do squat. In fact, it has been demoted to sharing the Print Screen key on most 101-key keyboards. Back in the PC-AT days, IBM was rumored to be planning a use for the SysRq key in some new-fangled operating system. When OS/2 came out, however, it used the Ctrl+Esc key combination rather than SysRq. "About the only thing the *SysRq key* is useful for is seeing how people try to pronounce it."

system *(sis-tim)* 1. A way of doing things. 2. The program that controls the entire computer. See also *operating system.* 3. The whole computer. 4. The network. 5. The Powers That Be. 6. What you can't fight. "Something has to be in charge, and that's the *system.* It rules the computer. Real life has a system too, but it doesn't rule anything. Instead, The Conspiracy is in charge. And it watches everyone through cable TV and listens to our phone calls. And there's a helicopter over my head right now, and they're watching me type this thing. And that gnat is a spy for a terrorist group."

 System 7 *(sis-tim sev-vin)* The operating system used on most Macintosh computers. System 7 is not the same thing as DOS on a PC. Most of the Macintosh operating system is encoded in its ROM. System 7 provides the Finder interface plus other extensions to the internal operating system of the Mac. "I upgraded to *System 7* because I thought that it would bring sanity to my Mac. Alas, the computer may be sane, but it's still as slow as ever."

System 8 *(sis-tim ayt)* The successor to System 7, soon to be supplanted by System 9, I suppose.

system clock *(sis-tim klawk)* An internal time clock maintained by an operating system. Used primarily to record the time when files were saved to disk. "I once reset my PC's *system clock* wrong on purpose to prove to the boss that I was getting work done way ahead of the deadline."

Thoth was thrilled to have upgraded to System 8.

system disk *(sis-tim disk)* A disk that contains all the programs required to start a computer. For most of us, the system disk is our hard disk, which starts the computer every time we turn it on. You can also start a computer from a floppy drive, which some people do just to kill time. "You can't start a PC without a *system disk.* For this reason, we recommend that everyone create an emergency boot floppy, with which you can start your PC in times of woe."

 System Folder *(sis-tim fol-der)* A special directory on a Macintosh computer that contains all the system files. Roughly equivalent to the Windows directory on a PC. In the System Folder, you put (or have already installed) all the files necessary to make Mr. Mac boot up properly and special files and programs, such as fonts, desk accessories, Control Panel thingies, and other stuff I can't think of. "The term *System Folder* makes it sound so neat and tidy. The truth is that the System Folder is perhaps the junkiest folder on my disk."

system font *(sis-tim fawnt)* A typeface built into an operating system or GUI. System fonts are the fonts that *must* be there. Text on menus and in dialog boxes is usually composed by using the system font. Yes, you can have more than one system font. "Truly, the *system font* is the most boring font you have. I recommend buying other, more exciting fonts and using them in your documents instead."

 system tray *(sis-tim tray)* An area on the far right side of the taskbar that contains the time,

S

volume control, and other tiny icons that control certain programs or certain aspects of Windows 95 and later. Pointing the mouse at an item on the system tray often displays more information about that item. Clicking an item activates it, usually displaying a dialog box or window offering more information. Items tend to come and go in the system tray; don't be alarmed if something disappears, because it usually means that you've stopped running a related program.

system unit *(sys-tim yoo-nit)* The IBM name for the computer box, also called the console. See also *console.* "Earl is such a card. He cleverly disguised his *system unit* in an old Philco TV box."

S

T

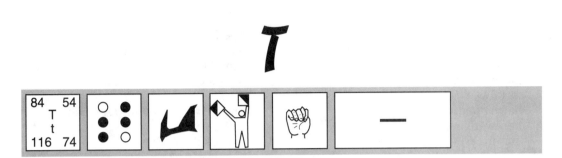

| 84 T t 116 | 54 74 | ○ ● ● ● ● ○ | | | — |

T: *(tee koh-lon)* The letter designation for what can be a network drive in your computer. You probably don't have a T:, but it can also be a hard drive, RAM drive, CD-ROM drive, removable drive, front-wheel drive, or any other type of drive in a C. Sheesh.

T1 *(tee won)* A high-speed communications line for Internet access, typically running at speeds of as much as 1.544 megabits per second. Only Internet providers, universities, and large companies typically have a T1 line, though that doesn't stop millions of Net surfers from dreaming about it.

T3 *(tee three)* A high-speed communications line for Internet access, providing speeds of 45 megabits per second.

tab *(tab)* 1. The character produced by pressing the Tab key. ASCII code 9. Also Ctrl+I. 2. A chunk of blank spaces created by pressing the Tab key. This chunk is treated as a unit so that if you want to delete the tab space, it deletes the whole thing, not one blank character at a time. "This is absolutely amazing — I pressed the *Tab* key, and this diet beverage rolled from my disk drive slot."

Tab key *(tab kee)* The key on a keyboard that produces the tab character. In most programs, when you write something, pressing the Tab key moves you forward one tab stop, whether that's a chunk of spaces in word processing, a field in a database, or a cell in a spreadsheet. In a dialog box, pressing the Tab key moves you to the next input field or gizmo in the dialog box. You can move backward through the fields or cells by pressing the Shift key along with the Tab key, known as a "back tab." "On most PCs, the *Tab key* has printed on it two arrows pointing in opposite directions, which leads me to believe that the key doesn't know which direction is which."

table *(tay-bul)* A way of organizing data or text in rows and columns, especially in a database context. You don't need a tablecloth for this kind of table, nor do you need good table manners. A data table is simply a way to store information or, in word processors, to present text in a neat and tidy manner. "A tax *table* lists income on the left side and tax categories along the top. In the middle, you can find out what outrageous amount the government wants you to pay."

Taiwanese *(tie-wan-eez)* Of or relating to the island of Taiwan; specifically, a computer or piece of hardware manufactured in Taiwan. Most no-name computers or hardware comes from Taiwan, where it can be reproduced reliably and at a reduced cost. Although it's sometimes used as a derogatory remark, some great innovations have come from Taiwan, particularly with regard to notebook computers.

Taiwan.

Taligent *(tal-uh-jent)* An object-oriented operating system developed by Apple, IBM, and Hewlett-Packard in a desperate attempt to wrestle the operating system market away from Microsoft. Did it work? I don't know. You don't see anything called Taligent on your computer, do you?

tape *(tayp)* A magnetic data storage medium (long, thin, brown stuff), essentially the same material as audio- and videocassettes. The advantages of this medium are its low cost and high density (capability to store lots of information). The disadvantage is that it offers only linear, or sequential, access, which means that you have to rewind or fast-forward through the whole tape to find what you're looking for. In contrast, disk drives offer random access so that you can get to any given point within a fraction of a second, with no re-winding or fast-forwarding involved. You generally use tapes only to store backup copies of data. See also *sequential access.* "Okay. Who's the joker who put the Scotch tape in the *tape* backup unit?"

tape backup system *(tayp bak-up sis-tim)* A tape drive and software designed to back up files from your hard disk. See also *backup, tape drive.*

tape drive *(tayp driev)* A machine in which you insert a tape cassette that records data. The machine is like a tape recorder and player, reading and writing information to the tape. This process is how sophisticated PC users back up their data. They buy

Early tape drive.

these backup tape cartridges, slam them into the tape drive, and then run special tape backup software. No swapping is involved (as long as the tapes can hold enough data), and the backup takes only a few minutes. Tape drives are about as expensive as new hard disks. Many formats are available: $1/4$-inch cartridge, 8mm VCR cartridge, 4mm audio, and nine-track. "I'm sorry about the demotion, Jason, but what you thought was a toaster oven was really our new $2,000 DAT *tape drive.*"

tar *(tar)* Abbreviation for *tape-archiver,* a backup and archiving program used on UNIX computers. In addition to obviously copying files to a tape backup, tar can also be used to clump together a bunch of files, slapping the TAR extension on them. Getting the files out again leads most people to madness (and, yes, if a simple solution were available, I'd offer it here). "Although Darryl was overjoyed to get FTP to work on the Internet, getting his files out of the *tar* proved to be messy."

T

task *(task)* A computer operation; something you do with a computer. If you're word processing, for example, the computer's task is word processing. The term *task* would be an utterly redundant thing if it weren't for multitasking, which is the capability of a computer to do several things — several tasks — at the same time. "Most of the time, my computer's main *task* is to ignore me."

task bar *(task bar)* See *taskbar*.

task switching *(task swich-ing)* The art of switching between several programs running at one time. In Windows, you can press Ctrl+Esc, Alt+Esc, or Alt+Tab or click a specific window that represents a program. When you move from one open application (task) to another, you are task-switching. "The boss told me that I was *task-switching* too often between Word and Solitaire."

taskbar *(task-bar)* A strip of buttons along the bottom of the Windows desktop. Each button relates to a window or task on-screen, enabling you to switch between the tasks by clicking the button. Also on the taskbar are the Start button and system tray. (You can move the taskbar to any side of the screen, but it appears mostly at the bottom.) "One of the most annoying things about Windows 95 is the disappearing *taskbar*."

TCP/IP *(tee see pee ie pee)* Take Caffeine Periodically/ Intravenously, Preferably. Har, har. Actually, it stands for *Transfer Control Protocol/Internet Protocol,* and it means that information can be

shared between two strange networks. TCP/IP is one of the ways in which information is sent back and forth over the Internet and nothing you need to concern yourself with, really. "I went for a job interview that asked for *TCP/IP* knowledge. When I asked what it meant, they said, 'We were hoping that *you* knew!'"

TeachText *(teech-tekst)* A simple text-editing program the Mac uses to read and display README files. "I don't think that the *TeachText* program is teaching me anything."

tear-off menus *(tayr-off men-yoos)* Menus you can tear off the menu bar (symbolically, of course) and place in any convenient location on-screen. For example, you may press Ctrl while clicking the File menu to tear it off. You can then drag the menu to any location on-screen. Tear-off menus are not widely used. "Baby Jonah accidentally got hold of the computer. He found the *tear-off menus,* and now they're all over the floor."

techno weenie *(tek-noh wee-nee)* Someone very, very into computers, often discussing them in cryptic and loving terms. Techno weenies may not lack social graces, like geeks, but they still tend to be overly absorbed by technology. See also *alpha geek.*

Techno weenie.

technology *(tek-nal-uh-jee)* A stone used to shape another stone (as in the Stone Age) can be considered technology. You may say, in a broad sense, that technology means the use of tools. Power tools. Big anti-torque drills. Large, dirt-moving vehicles. Ah, technology. More often, the word refers to "high" technology, which is characterized by being abstract and not accessible to the naked eye. If you open the hood of a vintage American car, you can tell exactly what's going on by seeing how the parts fit together and how they move. This process is not-so-high-tech. When you're talking about electronics, though, the relationships are not apparent. One silicon chip can have millions of transistors, and you may have no idea about the relationship of each one to its neighbors, nor where to fit the crescent wrench. "*Technology* comes from the ancient Greek term that roughly translates this way: 'If your VCR is blinking 12:00 all the time, you probably don't get any of this stuff.'"

telecom program *(tel-uh-kom prohgram)* Communications software.

telecommunications *(tel-eh-kom-yoo-nuh-kay-shuns)* The field of technology dealing with communicating at a distance. It includes, but is not necessarily limited to, telephony, telegraphy, consumer radio, broadcast television, cable television, satellite television, radar, ham radio, CB radio, two tin cans connected by a string, and data transfer. "*Telecommunications* enables you to get confused at greater and greater distances."

telephony *(tel-uh-foh-nee)* The art and science of making telephones work. (It could just as well have been called "telephonology," but an editor was on the loose that day, and the word got cut short.) Essentially what happens in the telephone process is that the voice — and all embarrassing or annoying background noises — get converted into electrical signals that travel through the wires and then get reconverted to sound at the other end. Imagine all this, even though Alexander Graham Bell used only two ordinary cups and a length of wire to make the World's First Telephone happen.

teletype *(tel-uh-tiep)* 1. The old, clunky, typewriter-like things that typed "by magic," thanks to remote wires that controlled a keyboard. In the early days of computing, teletype machines were used to communicate with the behemoth computers of the time. You would type, klunka-wunka, and then the computer would type back at you, klunka-wunka-faster. All this stuff was transcribed on a long sheet of paper that was fed into and out of the teletype machine. 2. In these exciting, carefree computer days, teletype is used to describe the dumbest and least sophisticated way to connect one computer to another. The teletype is nothing more than a keyboard and monitor (also called a dumb terminal) that enables you to send information to and receive it from another computer. It's abbreviated TTY because most computer nerds can't remember whether teletype has one or two *l*s in it. "In the early 1980s, I used to communicate with my friends on home computers using then-speedy 2,400 bps modems. At the same time, the hot line connecting the White House with the Kremlin was run on a sluggish, old *teletype* machine running at only 300 bps. That setup meant that in the time Ronald Reagan could send 'Ivan, kiss your *@# goodbye,' I could have downloaded Tetris."

telnet *(tel-net)* The closest thing UNIX has to a DOS modem program. Telnet is a command you can use to dial up another UNIX computer or, really, any computer on the Internet, and then log in and use that computer as though you were a terminal. "You can do little with *telnet* unless you understand UNIX."

template *(tem-playt)* A "master" document for a word processor, spreadsheet, or other application that is used as the starting point or rough draft for other documents. Because the template generally contains all the formatting, all you have to do is fill in the blanks. Some software packages come with numerous templates so that you really don't even need to understand how to use the software. You can create your own templates by performing the formatting and composing the text that will appear in every document of that type. Then, every time you need an invoice, for example, you open the template file, fill in the blanks, and print the document. Then, you can either save the additions to the file (as a new file, now, so that you don't mess up the template) or not. "I'm going to use a *template* to write a letter to Santa Claus this year."

tera- *(tayr-uh)* A prefix meaning trillion (the same prefix from which we get the word *terrible*, by the way). Usually heard in computer terms when someone is talking about terabytes, which are pretty close to a trillion bytes (which is the same as a thousand gigabytes or a million megabytes). The actual measurement of a terabyte is 1,099,511,627,776 bytes. "If you had one dollar for every byte in a *tera*byte, it would take Bill Gates 134 years to catch up with you if he made $8 billion per year (not including interest or subtracting taxes)."

teraFLOP *(tayr-uh-flop)* Acronym meaning one trillion FLoating-point OPerations (FLOPs) per second, a way to describe an *extremely* fast computer.

terminal *(tur-muh-nal)* A monitor hooked up to a mainframe computer. The term comes from the root of the Latin word for *death*, which makes you wonder why we board airplanes in terminals. Like people, terminals can be either smart or dumb, and the only way to find out how smart or dumb they are is to check how they relate to the computer. If a terminal has a mind of its own, it's a smart terminal, which means that it has some processors, maybe even a CPU, and maybe even a disk drive so that it can store its own data. With these types of capabilities, the terminal doesn't need to rely on the mainframe for all its operations. If all it has is a monitor and keyboard (or similar peripherals), it's pretty dumb. "People can get terminally ill from sitting at *terminals* their whole lives."

T

terminal emulation *(tur-muh-nal em-yoo-lay-shun)* The capability of an average, run-of-the-mill desktop computer to cleverly disguise itself as a certain type of terminal hooked up to a mainframe computer. This process can be done only with the right software, called terminal-emulation software. You need to worry about this stuff only when you actually *want* to be hooked up to a mainframe computer — a rare circumstance for most of us mortals. "They've finally perfected Macintosh *terminal emulation* for the PC. Everything works really slowly, and the system crashes just before you save your file to disk. (You think that I'm kidding.)"

terminate-and-stay-resident program *(tur-muh-nayt and stay rez-uh-dent proh-gram)* See *memory-resident program, TSR.*

termination *(tur-muh-nay-shun)* A requirement of SCSI devices that one of them must be the last one in the chain. It works the same way as stopping a leak: SCSI devices are all hooked together in a daisy chain. The last device on the chain, however, must be terminated (a special doohickey must be installed) to let the SCSI controller know that it's the last device. See also *daisy chain.* "If you don't do proper *termination,* your SCSI controller will appear dead to you."

text *(tekst)* Letters, numbers, and other characters or symbols on your keyboard. Just plain writing — no formatting or other fancy stuff. See also *ASCII.* "*Text* is boring."

text box *(tekst boks)* A box on-screen in which you can type text. Also called an input box. Oh, and you can edit text in the text box. What else? Nothing that I can think of right now. It's late, and *Star Trek* is on in three minutes. "Here's a good one: When you're searching for text, type **my brain** in the *text box.* Then click the OK button. The computer doesn't find the text, and it displays a message that says, 'Error: Can't find my brain.' Ha-ha."

text editor *(tekst ed-uh-ter)* A crude form of a word processor that lets you modify (or *edit*) text files. Programmers use text editors to edit program source code files. Text editors are handy because they don't use formatting or graphics or anything fancy. Programmers just want something in which to easily type their boring programming instructions without being bothered by the formatting. We mere mortal users can take advantage of text editors as well, even using them as word processors, if we like. They come in handy for working with small files. Indeed, this book was created using a text editor so that the authors had a common file format (plain text or ASCII) in which to work. (Eventually, we all moved up to Microsoft Word for Windows because IDG Books Worldwide, Inc., told us that we were working too fast.) See also *editor.* "My award for the worst *text editor* ever goes to the old, crummy EDLIN in DOS."

text file *(tekst fiel)* A file that contains only text or ASCII characters. Many word-processing, database, and spreadsheet programs give you the

T

option of saving your stuff as "text only" or as a text file: Not only do you lose all the formatting and special characters not associated with text files, but also the information can be easily digested by just about any other program on any other computer. See also *ASCII*. "A *text file* is the most common type of file format."

text mode *(tekst mohd)* The opposite of graphics mode. An operating mode in which a PC displays text, not graphics, on-screen. "DOS uses *text mode*. Windows uses slow mode."

thermal printer *(ther-mul prin-ter)* A computer printer that creates an image by burning a sheet of wax paper in a neat and tidy fashion. "Burning" is too harsh of a word. The wax paper is merely darkened by the printing mechanism,

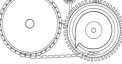

An interesting illustration.

creating text and graphics in a smooth, quiet fashion without wasting any ink. Unless your fax machine uses plain paper, it contains a thermal printing mechanism. Thermal paper is often waxy and turns all black if you leave it out in the sun. "My *thermal printer* has a reputation for having a smell as bad as a dot-matrix printer's noise."

thesaurus *(the-saw-rus)* 1. A collection of words and other words with the same meaning. 2. The capability of a word-processing program to come up with synonyms to match a word

you've chosen. You can highlight a word and ask the thesaurus for some synonyms, and the software then generates a list of alternatives or suggestions. The Murphy's Law of thesauruses says that the more certain you are that a synonym with exactly the right flavor exists, the more certain your thesaurus is not to even list the word you're referencing, let alone its synonyms. "What would the *thesaurus* offer if you looked up synonyms for 'molecular beam epitaxy'?"

three-dimensional spreadsheet *(three-duh-men-shun-el spred-sheet)* In spreadsheet technology, the practice of creating a group of spreadsheets and organizing them like pages in a book. They then have depth in addition to the usual rows and columns. Depth is the third dimension of the spreadsheet. "I started to learn how to work on a *three-dimensional spreadsheet,* but I got lost because I had only a two-dimensional brain."

tick *(tik)* 1. Another name for the apostrophe character. See also '. 2. A notch on the axis of a chart that denotes an increment. For example, if the Y axis represents dollars, every tick mark may represent $100. 3. A beat in your computer's internal clock-ticking, timekeeping thingamabob. PC computers generate 18.5 ticks per second. If you hear some nerd say, "How many clock ticks was that interrupt?," you know that a clock tick measures just about $1/_{18}$-second and can nod your head knowingly. "There was this German POW camp in World War II. One summer day, the commandant assembled all the prisoners out under the hot sun. He said, 'Today, we will

T

do special exercises. I want you to tilt your heads from left to right, left to right. When you tilt your head to the left, you will say "*Tick!*" When you tilt your head to the right, you will say "Tock!" Everyone!' All the prisoners started tilting their heads, tick-tock, tick-tock, out under the hot sun — with sweat just pouring from their faces. Everyone followed along except for one prisoner. He just tilted his head to the left over and over, saying, 'Tick, tick, tick.' The commandant walked up to the man, looked him over, and said, 'We have ways to make you tock.'"

TIFF *(tif)* Acronym for *Tagged Image File Format,* a bitmapped graphics file format used frequently for images read in by using a scanner. TIFF files are high-resolution dot images. "No, we don't support that graphics standard here. We support PCX, GIF, *TIFF,* and anything painted by Lichtenstein or Klee."

tilde *(til-duh)* See ~.

tiling *(tie-ling)* A technique for arranging various windows in a graphical user interface so that they're all nicely sized and organized, like a mosaic, without overlapping each other. The key here is *without overlapping.* Another arrangement possibility is cascading. See also *cascade.* "*Tiling* is a good choice when it doesn't matter whether the images in each window are chopped off and difficult to read."

time-sharing *(tiem shayr-ing)* A strategic use of resources (microprocessor, printer, disk drive) in mainframe or networked computers. The time that is being shared is the computer's processing time. Typically, it's being shared among several users and also may be shared among several programs. In a time-sharing situation, a computer is programmed to know how to use its processing resources to attend to a hierarchy of priorities. "Because our computer knows how to manage *time-sharing* so well, I think that I should have my own time-sharing program so that my time gets divided properly among my kids, my spouse, and my job."

time slice *(tiem slies)* Amount of processor time allocated to an application, usually measured in milliseconds. For example, if you're running several programs at a time in Windows, each program gets a "slice" of

A slice of time.

the computer's time. The size of the slice can be adjusted, enabling some important programs to use up more time than other, not-so-important, ones. See also *multitasking.* "Roy found this old film from the 1940s. It shows Albert Einstein creating *time slices* with a Ginsu knife."

title bar *(tie-tel bar)* In a GUI such as Windows or the Mac system, the, well, title that is prominently displayed on a long bar that stretches across the whole window. An especially effective invention because you always know where you are and don't need to call customer service to get you unlost. It typically includes the name of both the application you're using and the document in which you're working. Even when you haven't named the new file yet, the program provisionally calls the document something like Untitled or Document until you come up with your own name for it. "I was hopelessly lost until I looked up at the *title bar,* which said that I was working in Microsoft Word on the T.DOC document."

TLA *(tee el ay)* Acronym for *three-letter acronym.* The computer industry (and the government) is fond of them. "Nope, our manual just makes too much sense. Why not fill it with more *TLAs* and have Mr. Fujimori stick some raw Japanese in there, too?"

toaster *(toh-stur)* 1. A computer device that's so homegrown, so user-friendly, and so intuitive that it's almost like the toaster you use to toast bread. The original Macintosh design was fondly called "the *toaster*" by its fans. "The original Macintosh was fondly called 'the *toaster*' at the height of its popularity. Now it's often called 'the footstool.'" 2. A device called the Video Toaster is used in the Amiga computer to enable you to create studio-quality videos in your own home.

toggle *(taw-gul)* 1. A type of switch that alternates between two modes, typically on or off. An example is the button on your TV that turns it both on and off. When the TV is turned off, the button turns it on and vice versa. In a computer program, a toggle may be a graphical button or some other option that can be turned either on or off. Selecting the button once turns it on; selecting it again turns it off. "I keep *toggling* between slow and slower mode on my PC. I don't think that I paid enough money for this thing." 2. An option for a command or program that can be turned either on or off.

token ring network *(toh-ken ring net-werk)* A networking format in which PCs are connected in some way. They use this token thing, passed between the computers on the network hose, to decide who's on first. That's the most I can make out of this definition because it's heady, IBM stuff. Most people use Ethernet networks because they are easier to understand. I always think of bus tokens when I see *token ring network* in print. See also *network.* "No, sir, I don't think that you'll find a book about the *token ring network* in the fantasy section."

toner *(toh-ner)* The black, icky stuff laser printers print with. Technically, toner consists of highly carcinogenic, electronically charged ink particles, just like a photocopier has. Toner is used to form an image on paper. Actually, the laser printer "welds" the toner to the paper using heat and tiny laser beams manned by elves. "Marcia was changing the *toner* when it broke open. Now she looks like she works in a coal mine."

toner cartridge *(toh-ner kar-trij)* A box containing toner for a laser printer (or other type of machine, such as a copier or fax machine). This technology makes an unbearable job simply horrible. In older machines,

T

you had to fill the toner container with powdered toner, which had the advantage of enabling you to approximate the effects of six years' worth of cigarette smoking in a mere ten minutes. Today, toners equate themselves to just about a pack of cigarettes. "I told Phil about having his old *toner cartridge* recharged, but he misunderstood and tried to plug it into the wall."

tongue depressor *(tong dee-press-er)* A paper or plastic insert for a floppy disk drive, designed to protect it from damage during transport. Most of today's floppy drives are quite robust and no longer require the tongue depressors.

toolbox *(tool-boks)* 1. For software developers, a set of programs that can be used as building blocks for creating applications so that they can avoid the need for reinventing the wheel every time they write a program. "Using a *toolbox,* anyone can create a cool-looking program with only several weeks of intensive training." 2. For software users, a collection of tools that serve a common purpose. See also *tools.*

tools *(toolz)* A set of programs you can use within a given software application that have effects similar to the real-life tools they're named after. Bear with me on this one. As an example, in a paint program, you may have "brushes" of different diameters, a roller, and a spray can. You can use these tools in the program to get a specific job done. "I'm having such a good time playing with all these *tools* that I don't know when I'll get around to actually painting a picture."

top-down programming *(tahp-down proh-gram-ing)* Writing the larger parts of a program first and filling in the details later. "*Top-down programming* doesn't mean that you build the program's roof and then the foundation later. It's more along the lines of writing the overall feeling for the program first and then filling in the holes later."

topology *(toh-pahl-uh-jee)* 1. The configuration of a local-area network — how the network is physically laid out. The basic types are centralized and decentralized; the basic formats are the star topology (centralized) and the bus and ring topologies (decentralized). Understand this, and you, too, can earn massive sums working as a network coordinator. 2. The study of the actor Topol.

touch pad *(tuhch pad)* An input device for which all you have to do is touch a spot, and it registers as a signal to the computer. The "spots" are cleverly disguised keys or buttons, and the whole front of the touch pad display is a layer of soft plastic.

tower PC *(taw-er pee see)* A desktop computer on its side, but really a computer that was made to stand vertically (up and down). This type of computer usually has more room and tends to be more powerful than the mere mortal desktop model. "Because Kevin lives by an airport, the FAA told him to put little red lights on top of his *tower PC.*"

Kevin with his new tower PC.

TPI *(tee pee eye)* Abbreviation for *tracks per inch,* the amount of information that can be stored on a disk. The more tracks per inch on a disk, the higher the disk's "density" and the more data it can store. It's also a good way to tell some high-density disks from low-density ones. The lower-density disks use 40 or 80 TPI. High-density disks use 135 TPI. "I've been using computers for more than 12 years now, and no one I know uses the term *TPI* when they talk about a floppy disk."

track *(trak)* A "ring" of information on a disk. Most disks record information on disks by storing that information on several concentric rings, or "tracks," recorded on the disk's surface. This term involves complex, disk-formatting stuff. The track contains sectors that each usually contain 512 bytes of information — the stuff you save on the disk. Knowing about tracks and sectors isn't important in using a disk. The information may come up only when you use special disk utilities (disk repair and diagnosis programs) or when you format the disk. The term *cylinder* may also be used to refer to a track of information on a disk. "This disk is no good. I guess my AMTRAK file keeps jumping the *track.*"

trackball *(trak-bahl)* An input device that operates similarly to a mouse. Whereas a mouse has a ball you roll on your tabletop, on a trackball, the ball part is on top, and you rotate it by using your fingers. Trackballs are popular with artists, who find the large ball easier to manipulate than the clumsy soap-on-a-rope-like mouse. Trackballs are also common on notebook computers because they don't have this device hanging outside the case, nor do you have to roll them around on a flat surface, such as on your thigh. "This *trackball* is not only easier to use than a mouse, it also doesn't have a tendency to roll itself off the desk as much."

TrackPoint II *(trak-poynt too)* A tiny knob, embedded between the G and H keys on the keyboard, developed by IBM as an alternative pointing device that substitutes for a mouse. The TrackPoint II looks and feels like the red tip of a rubber eraser and is easy to use after you get the hang of it and realize that it won't rub pink stuff off all over your fingertips. "Tim tried to yank out the *TrackPoint II* from his laptop with a pair of pliers. That was until I told him that it was supposed to be there and that he could use it like a mouse."

tractor feed *(trak-ter feed)* A mechanism for feeding paper through dot-matrix printers. This kind of paper is what is commonly known as "computer paper," the stuff with the holes on either side. See also *snaf.* "I always have trouble lining up the little holes so that the paper goes through the *tractor feed* without getting overly perfed."

tractor food *(trak-ter food)* Your most valued documents, caught in the jaws of a tractor-feed mechanism. "I watched as my precious annual report became *tractor food* in a matter of seconds."

T

Transfer Load Files *(tranz-fer lohd fiels)* The hilarious name of the command used to open files for early Microsoft applications. Obviously, they stole the term *open* from somewhere else.

transparent *(tranz-payr-ent)* 1. A computer function that's close to invisible in its action. 2. Anything that happens without your being directly involved or requiring your input or attention. For example, a fax that's sent while you continue to work on another document is a transparent operation. "My communications software sends documents to other users *transparently*. They don't even see the document on the other end."

trash *(trash)* A special place to put unwanted documents and files. The trash icon on the Mac desktop looks just like a trash can, and all you have to do to dispose of your unwanted stuff is to click the item in question with the mouse and drag the item to the trash can. A handy feature of the Mac trash can is that its sides bulge out when it has discarded files in it, and it doesn't ultimately dump the stuff until you give it the command to Empty Trash — just like in real life! "The nicest thing about the Mac *trash* can is that the dogs don't knock it over every Thursday night."

tree structure *(tree struk-chur)* One of the more visual concepts in organizing files on a hard disk. Files are stored in "directories," each of which is connected to other directories like branches in a tree. The main directory on every disk is called the *root* directory. Other directories branch from the root, and still other directories branch from them, making the thing look like an electronic family tree. See also *path*. "I almost had a heart attack when Earl walked by with the pruning shears, claiming that he was going to fix his hard disk's *tree structure*."

trigonometry *(trig-uh-nom-uh-tree)* A branch of mathematics having to do with the relationships of the parts of a triangle. If you hear terms such as sine, cosine, and tangent, you can nod wisely and say, "Ah, trigonometry!" Trigonometry helps you figure out unknown measurements of a triangle (such as an angle or a side) based on known elements. "You can use *trigonometry* to figure out the height of a distant mountain, if you know how far it is to the mountain and what the angle of view to the peak is, and also if someone whispers its height in your ear."

Earth with large chunk missing.

trinary *(trie-nayr-ee)* 1. Three. For example, a solar system with three suns. 2. The name for the base *three* counting system. Supposedly, they're working on *trinary* computers, which shall eventually supplant binary computers. See also *binary*, *trit*. "Boy, if you thought that binary was rough, wait until you have to count in *trinary!*"

triple-click *(trih-pel-clik)* To click the mouse button three times in rapid succession to access weird and arcane functions. Triple-clicking is uncommon and is used only in programs whose designers could not figure out more effective means of accessing features. "When I *triple-click* this icon, I get a message telling me to stop drinking so much coffee."

trit *(trit)* A trinary digit. A trit can be 0, 1, or 2. "Binary is to bits as trinary is to *trits.*"

troglodyte *(trog-luh-diet)* From the Greek word meaning *cave dweller,* a special class of nerd that prefers to work in the dark recesses of computer rooms. People who have developed nocturnal feeding habits like those of bats and moles. See also *Morlock.* "The university cafeteria is keeping special hours — not to mention a special diet — for the *troglodytes* on campus."

Trojan horse *(troh-jen hors)* A nasty computer program cleverly hidden inside a legitimate program. It comes from a strategy used in the Trojan War, in which the Greeks pretended to give a gift of a huge, wooden horse as a peace offering to the city of Troy. As Troy slept, the many soldiers hidden inside the horse clambered out and attacked the city, which most historians agree was a sneaky thing to do. Sneaky computer programs that pretend to do one thing yet disguise a more nefarious deed are called Trojan horses. You are more likely to find a Trojan horse packaged inside shareware or freeware than in off-the-shelf commercial software. "There is argument behind the notion that Microsoft Windows is a *Trojan horse.*"

TRON *(tron)* 1. A BASIC programming language command that's a conjunction of *TR*ace and *ON.* The TRON command displayed information about the program as it ran, enabling a programmer to examine what was going on and hunt for errors. 2. A 1982 Disney film, most of which was created inside a computer — the first time that was ever done. Had a better script been written, *TRON* may have amounted to something nifty. See also *Cray.*

troubleshooting *(truh-bul-shoo-ting)* Tracking down an error or glitch, often through the process of elimination. "*Troubleshooting* is easy if all you ever do is blame your computer."

true *(troo)* 1. The opposite of *false.* It can also mean "yes" or "on." In binary math (also called Boolean math), true means a 1 or positive, and false means a 0 or negative. "Believing that a computer would save me time and effort proved too good to be *true.*"

TrueType *(troo-tiep)* A category of fonts, created jointly by Apple Computer and Microsoft, that bypasses the need for a page-description language or a utility that enables fonts to be displayed on-screen. Instead, the smarts that translate the font to the screen or to the printer are kept inside the font itself. In the olden days, you had to pay dearly for computer programs and printers that understood a multitude of fonts and displayed and printed them well. TrueType fonts take care of the details, making everything look and print swell. TrueType fonts are also called *scalable fonts,* which means that you can select any type size without having to worry about distortions. See *PDL, scalable font.* "Using these widely available and inexpensive *TrueType* fonts, I've been able to design a document that looks just as bad as my handwriting."

T

TSR *(tee es ar)* Acronym for *Terminate-and-Stay-Resident* program, a special type of program that always stays in RAM and can be easily activated by a keystroke or hot key. Also known as a *memory-resident program,* which is a better term, but TSR is the name the programmers called it (after the name of the internal DOS function), so the people in the marketing department (who love three-letter acronyms anyway) just followed suit. These programs became popular when the Borland SideKick program was introduced in the mid-1980s. SideKick gave you instant access to a slew of interesting little programs, all by pressing the Ctrl and Alt keys at the same time. SideKick would "pop up" right on top of whatever other program you were running. At the time, this feature proved to be immensely handy. Other programmers learned the SideKick secret, and soon dozens of TSRs and pop-up programs appeared. The problem was that because Borland cheated to get the pop-up effect, none of the TSRs would cooperate with each other. A TSR-laden PC would often crash, and the programs would conflict. The pop-up type of TSR program isn't popular anymore, thanks to multitasking programs, such as Windows. Popular TSRs include the mouse driver, CD-ROM driver, DOSKEY keyboard enhancer, and certain file-undeleting utilities. "Please, Mr. Cooper, don't get all upset just because the old folks' home has adopted *TSR* software."

TSTN *(tee ess tee en)* Acronym for *Triple-SuperTwist Nematic* display, a type of screen on high-end laptops.

 TTFN *(tee tee ef en)* Online acronym for *Ta Ta For Now.* Another way to say good-bye in an e-mail message or newsgroup posting. "I was worried when Ryan always signed his electronic epistles *TTFN,* until I found out that it wasn't anything dirty."

TTL *(tee tee el)* Acronym for *Transistor-to-Transistor Logic.* What is it? Who knows, who cares, why bother. TTL was listed as a type of computer monitor, typically the old-style monochrome monitors, and the acronym really bugged most PC users. Everyone always asked, "What's TTL stand for?" Now you know. "I feel so culturally enriched now that I finally know what *TTL* stands for."

A transistor and two sisters.

tty *(tee tee wie)* 1. A UNIX command that tells you which terminal you're using. "I typed **tty** on my laptop, and the computer told me that I was about to land at O'Hare." 2. Abbreviation for *teletype.* 3. A type of terminal emulation, usually meaning (and this is a secret) "absolutely no emulation whatsoever." See also *terminal emulation.*

Turing machine *(toor-ing ma-sheen)* A simple computer developed by A.M. Turing in the 1930s. By reading a piece of paper tape, it was supposed to be capable of diagnosing which problems could be solved by machines. Turing's machine could only move the tape forward, put a mark on it, erase the mark, or stop it in its tracks. Turing claimed that the machine could solve any problem that could be expressed as an algorithm. See also *algorithm*. "I don't think that I'd have a use for a *Turing machine*. I just want to solve the problems; I don't care whether they *can* be solved."

turnkey system *(turn-kee sis-tem)* A computer system all packaged and ready to go for a specific task. The system is complete with computer, monitor, keyboard, disk drives, software, and other peripherals. The term comes from the automotive industry — where you can put a key into your car's ignition, turn the key, and operate the vehicle without anything else to buy, install, set up, or learn. "I always thought that *turnkey system* had something to do with sardines."

tutorial *(too-tor-ee-el)* A training session that guides a student step-by-step through a procedure. Of particular interest are the tutorials packaged with many contemporary software programs. Generally, they are interactive so that you can play along and press keys to get the program to continue. "The *tutorial* for my accounting package comes with instructions for loading a gun."

TWAIN *(twayn)* Acronym for *Technology Without An Important Name,* a standard for acquiring graphics, such as input from a scanner, computer video, or something else that brings graphics into the computer. "Because Adobe Photoshop can gobble up a *TWAIN* image, we should buy a TWAIN scanner."

tweak *(tweek)* To customize, tailor, adjust, rearrange, cajole, or otherwise mess with. More specifically, to change settings on a piece of hardware or software so that your needs are more closely attended to. "I want to *tweak* my word-processing program so that it stops beeping when I misspell a word."

Twinkie *(twink-ee)* A staple in the diet of computer programmers and other nerds. Fits into most of the four basic food groups. Also, the consumption of Twinkies has been used as a defense in the most egregious crimes; if you need a scapegoat,

Eyeball frazzle affects this organ.

invoke the Twinkie defense. See also *M&Ms*. "Because I had some heavy-duty programming to do, I had some *Twinkies* for a power breakfast."

twisted pair *(twist-ed payr)* One wire that's secretly a pair of wires wrapped around each other. The kind of wire typically used in commercial telephone systems. The wire is "twisted" because you talk into the mouthpiece, and it's heard in the earpiece. If the wire weren't twisted, you would talk in the mouthpiece, and the sound would come out the mouthpiece. The term is also used in local area networks, especially those that use common phone wiring to connect the computers (common phone wiring is the same thing as "twisted pair"). The good thing about twisted pair is that it's cheap and ubiquitous; the drawback is that it doesn't carry nearly as much information as the thicker, coaxial cable (the stuff cable TV travels through). "Here come our network guru and his female companion. Jeez. Aren't they a *twisted pair?*"

T

TXT *(tee ecks tee)* 1. Abbreviation for *text.* 2. A file extension used for text files, generally in DOS-based computing. Examples include LETTER.TXT and GOFISH.TXT. "When I tell my word processor to save my files as 'text only,' it automatically slaps the *.TXT* extension on the filename."

type-ahead *(tiep-uh-hed)* A term for a buffer (a part of memory) that enables you to continue typing while the computer is busy doing something else; you type ahead of what you see on-screen. The stuff you type appears as soon as the computer is unbusy. "Because of the *type-ahead* buffer in Windows, I can enter several commands and wait for the computer to catch up. I seem to do that often."

typeface *(tiep-fays)* The design of characters in a font. Refers to the physical characteristics of a family of letters and numbers. Typesetting has grown into a major art form, and the number of available typefaces — even to personal computer users — is almost endless. The main division between the categories of typefaces lies in their use of serifs — the little hooky things at the ends of the letters. For that reason, they are called either *serif* typefaces or *sans serif* (without serif) typefaces. Other categories include display faces and decorative faces. "One of my favorite *typefaces* is Omar Serif."

typewriter *(tiep-rie-ter)* 1. A mechanical device used to print images on paper. Considered obsolete in the era of the computer. Heck, even IBM sold off its typewriter division years ago. 2. A typeface that resembles type-writer output. (So much for advances in technology!) 3. Of or referring to the layout of keys on a computer keyboard. The computer keyboard (the alphabet keys, at least) is laid out just like a typewriter keyboard. There is no reason for this because there are no moving parts in a keyboard as there are in a typewriter. See also *QWERTY.*

T

U

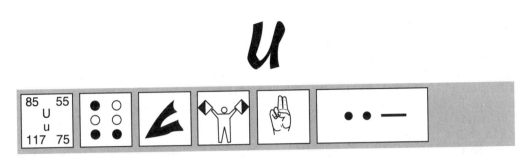

U: *(yoo koh-lon)* Oh, no! It's drive U on a PC! Run for the hills!

UART *(yoo-art)* Acronym for *Universal Asynchronous Receiver/Transmitter,* the gizmo (actually, the integrated circuit) in a computer that changes the parallel data stream inside the computer into the serial data stream (and vice versa). It takes the bits marching eight abreast inside your computer and lines them up single file for the serial port. This lineup is required for devices that use the serial port, such as a modem. See also *bit, modem, parallel port, serial port.* "Oh, my serial port, *UART* the port of my dreams!"

UMB *(yoo em bee)* Acronym for *Upper Memory Block,* an area of upper memory on a PC that can be "filled in" with real memory using some sort of memory-management magic that only the eggheads can comprehend. A memory device driver, such as EMM386.EXE in DOS, is required in order to create UMBs. Then, using other memory-management magic too mental to mention here, programs can be "loaded high" into those UMBs, which makes more memory available to your programs. It's magic! See also *conventional memory, high memory, low memory, memory, terminate-and-stay-resident program.*

undelete *(un-duh-leet)* To put something back the way it was before you deleted it. To restore a file after you have deleted it, to resuscitate it, to resurrect it. See also *restore, unerase.* "Just because you have an *undelete* command doesn't mean that you should be careless with the delete command."

underline *(un-der-lien)* 1. In word processing or desktop publishing, the attribute applied to text that makes it look under-

Underline character.

lined. Underlined text was once used in typed manuscripts to indicate that the typesetter should use italics. 2. The underline character on your keyboard. See _. "I knew a guy who tried to underline things by typing a word, backspacing (which erased the word), and then typing the *underline* character. Although that technique would work on a typewriter, with a computer you must use a special command that underlines the text for you."

underscore *(un-der-skohr)* Another term for underline, probably introduced by the more musical-minded among computer users. See *underline.* "Now that you're a power user, Michael, you need to stop saying 'underline.' It's *underscore.*"

undo *(un-doo)* 1. To put the situation back to the way it was before you messed it up. 2. A command in most applications that enables you to cancel the effects of whatever you just did. You can undo typing and formatting commands, but don't get careless about your work, because you can't undo everything. "I just hope that when I die and get to Heaven, God offers me an *undo* command."

undocumented *(un-dok-yoo-men-ted)* A feature of your hardware or software that is not explained in the user's manual. The explanation gets left out either because the manufacturer forgot, didn't think that it was important, hasn't figured out itself how the feature works, or wants to keep it a secret from you or its competition. Computer-book authors love to find undocumented features in software products; it's their life! "I stumbled onto an *undocumented* feature that makes Windows run 100 times faster."

unerase *(un-ee-rays)* Just like *undelete,* this term was coined by the DOS utility guru Peter Norton, when he first came up with the idea of undeleting files, in the early 1980s. Norton created a program called UnErase — the first of its kind — that recovered deleted files. He made tons of money and founded a complete category of computer software called *utility programs.* See also *guru, undelete, utility.* "All praise be to Peter Norton on high! Thank you, O Peter, for thy grace and thine *UnErase.*"

unformat *(un-fohr-mat)* 1. A command that undoes the damage when you accidentally reformat a disk. This command was wholly necessary in the early days of hard disks; the FORMAT C: command, which formatted hard disks, offered no warning! The unformat command enabled such a boneheaded maneuver to be easily repaired. 2. The process of restoring a disk that has been accidentally reformatted.

Unicode *(yoo-neh-kohd)* A new "universal" standard for sharing information among different programs and computers. Unicode is meant to replace the ancient ASCII standard and includes all the characters represented by the ASCII standard as well as additional characters for displaying languages such as Greek, Hebrew, Arabic, Russian (which uses Cyrillic), Chinese, Japanese, and Korean. See also *ASCII.* "Now that computers are being used all over the world, computer companies want to adopt the *Unicode* standard for sharing documents because it means more market share for them in countries such as Taiwan, Pakistan, and Greece."

unicorn *(yoo-ni-korn)* A mythical creature that looks like a horse with a single, spiral horn jutting from its forehead. According to legend, only a pure virgin maiden, who could tempt the unicorn to lay its head and horn in her lap, could

Unicorn fleeing a DOS program.

tame a unicorn. The origin of this legend obviously has sexual overtones that aren't polite to discuss in public. "Many girls love *unicorns* when they're growing up. Then, when they get older and start dating men, they realize that mythical creatures really have much more to offer than real-life human beings."

Uniform Resource Locator *(yoo-ni-form ree-sohrs loh-kay-tor)* See *URL*.

universal serial bus *(yoo-nuh-ver-sal seer-ee-al buss)* A new serial port standard that enables as many as 127 different devices to be connected to a single port. Known by its acronym USB, the speed of the universal serial bus is relatively slow, which limits the type of devices that can be connected. For most users, however, it provides an excellent solution for a PC that's running out of slots, interrupts, or DMAs. See also *DMA, expansion slot, firewire, IRQ.*

UNIX *(yoo-niks)* An operating system developed at Bell Labs in the late 1960s and refined throughout the 1970s and 1980s. Written in the C language (which was developed by the same folks at the same time), UNIX is a multiuser operating system, often running on minicomputers and workstations, though versions for the PC have existed since the early 1980s. You also can install UNIX on personal computers and

Typical UNIX user.

mainframes. UNIX is very popular on college campuses and in scientific communities. The entire Internet has its roots in UNIX. The advantages of UNIX lie in its portability from one system to another and in its support of a wealth of applications programs, many programmers' utilities, and programming languages, making it popular among the wizard and geek factions. UNIX is primarily a command-line operating system, similar to DOS but much more crude and cryptic. Several GUIs are available for UNIX, including X Windows, Open Look, and NeXTstep. Incidentally, the name UNIX is a pun of sorts: It's a takeoff on an operating system called Multics. Multi, Uni — get it? See also *C, DOS, Linux, operating system.* "When a programmer must protect his harem of PCs, he gets some *UNIX.*"

unsubscribe *(un-sub-skrieb)* To remove your subscription to a newsgroup or mailing list. The opposite of subscribe. See also *subscribe.*

UNZIP *(un-zip)* 1. To remove files from a ZIP archive. See also *archive, ZIP.* 2. The name of the program that unzips.

up *(up)* In the general direction of the sky or ceiling, unless you're in Australia (just checking to see whether you're paying attention). "Up" refers to the direction of the top of the document, even if the top is nowhere on-screen and is, in fact, just another happy electronic memory to your computer. See also *down arrow, up arrow.* "To scroll *up,* keep jabbing at the up-arrow key."

u

up arrow (*up ayr-oh*) 1. An arrow pointing upward, as on one of your cursor keys. Pressing the up-arrow key moves the cursor up in the document by one line of text. "You won't believe this: I pressed the *up arrow,* and my computer levitated." 2. A control at the top end of a vertical scroll bar in most graphical applications. Using the mouse to click the up-arrow key in graphical applications usually moves the contents of the window down a line or so. Yes, pressing the up-arrow key moves the contents down, but that's so that you can see "up" to the preceding line on-screen. Weird, backward, hard-to-understand — yes, this is how a computer makes life easier for everyone. If only the steering wheel on your car worked that way. . . .

upload (*up-lohd*) To transmit a file from your computer to another computer. If you're sending a file to another computer, you're uploading. That computer, on the other hand, is downloading the file from you. It doesn't matter who started the file transmission or which computer you're using. If you're sending a file, you're uploading it. See also *download.* "I often *upload* my word-processing files to CompuServe to send to publishers in remote parts of the world, such as Indiana."

upper memory (*up-er mem-o-ree*) Memory on a PC between the 640K mark and one megabyte — a 384K chunk. Upper memory was marked "reserved" by IBM in the original PC design. Although items such as video memory, expansion cards, and the BIOS were placed there, the memory

could not be used for running programs. (DOS runs programs in the first 640K of memory, called conventional memory.) See also *conventional memory, high memory, UMB.* "Every time Phil gets a haircut, he loses some *upper memory.*"

uppercase (*up-er-kays*) Capital letters. The terminology comes from the earliest days of typesetting, when the individual metal letters mounted on blocks were stored in trays. The typesetter would pick out the letters needed for the job and arrange them on a plate. The capital letters would be stored in the top (or upper) case, and the small letters would be stored in the bottom (or lower) case. See also *case-sensitive, lowercase.* "Text typed in all *uppercase* letters is hard to read. In fact, it almost seems as though the writer is SHOUTING AT YOU."

UPS (*yoo pee ess*) 1. Acronym for *Uninterruptible Power Supply,* a fancy term for battery backup — an emergency supply of power in case the power coming from the wall suddenly stops or when Jim, the dork from Marketing, trips over the PC's cord. Having a UPS often means that you have just enough time to save your stuff and turn off the computer while you're in the dark. You can't really work from the backup battery in the UPS. "This blackout is horrible, but there's Jim, sitting in his office with the only working PC hooked to a *UPS.* Let's unplug him and run something useful instead, like the Nintendo." 2. Acronym for *United Parcel Service,* a delivery firm that brings you computer goodies you order through the mail.

u

uptime *(up-tyme)* 1. The time that the computer is working and you can get stuff done, as opposed to downtime, when the computer isn't feeling well and nothing works. See also *downtime*. "The dog is lethargic, Doctor. How can we increase his *uptime*?" 2. A UNIX command that reports statistics about how long a computer has been running.

upward compatible *(up-werd kum-pat-uh-bol)* Designed with the future in mind. The item in question, usually a document or file created by some application or piece of hardware, will work with the next version of the product or with components not on the market yet. Software is generally only downward compatible, meaning that the newest versions of the application will work with files generated from previous versions, but the previous versions will not work with files created with the new version. See also *downward compatible*. "Wow! This new computer is really designed to be *upward compatible*. It has a plug in back marked R2D2 Connection."

URL *(yoo ar el)* Acronym for *Uniform Resource Locator*, a type of command that can fetch a variety of types of information from various corners of the Internet. Common URLs are *http* for Web pages, *ftp* for file-transfer protocol sites, gopher for *gopher* servers, *mailto* for sending e-mail, and *news* for accessing newsgroups. See also *Web browser*. "They'll think that you're a Net weenie if you pronounce *URL* as 'Earl.'"

Uruguay *(yoor-uh-gway)* The second-smallest country in South America. Mostly agricultural, Uruguay exports meat and textile products. Its capital is Montevideo, which has some lovely museums. See also *Montevideo*. "Our sojourn to South America just wouldn't be complete without a trip to *Uruguay*."

Uruguay.

USB *(yoo ess bee)* Acronym for *Universal Serial Bus*. See *universal serial bus*.

USENET *(yooz-net)* 1. Contraction of USEr NETwork, an Internet facility that offers a wide variety of newsgroups, bulletin boards, and public forums. 2. The same thing as a newsgroup, or the entire group of newsgroups. See also *Internet, newsgroup*. "Old-timers know Internet newsgroups as *USENET*."

user *(yoo-zer)* A person using the computer and software as a tool, as opposed to a programmer or hardware engineer. The term has nothing to do with the skill level of the person at the keyboard. Even nerds of the high programming priesthood are mere users when they sit at a computer. See also *user-friendly, user group, user-hostile*. "The computer industry is the only legitimate industry that calls its customers *users*."

user-friendly *(yoo-zer-frend-lee)* 1. Supposedly implying that the software or hardware is easy enough for even you or me to understand. Also called intuitive or idiot-proof. It means that you can easily figure out

u

what to do without having to look it up in the manual or the online help system. Yeah, right! See also *user, user-hostile.* "You know, the computer industry must figure that *user-friendly* means slow and plodding."

user group *(yoo-zer groop)* A club or gathering of computer users devoted to the study of a particular piece of software or hardware. User groups exist for the Macintosh, DOS, Adobe Photoshop, and many, many more. See also *SIG.* "*User groups* are a great source of information and a good place to ask questions about your computer or a software package. If you show up late, however, stick around and listen to the conversation. You might have accidentally stumbled on a meeting of the Older Guys with Pen Packs and Pot Bellies Society."

user-hostile *(yoo-zer-hos-tiel)* 1. The opposite of user-friendly. It means that no matter how well you treat your computer and the software installed on it, they never lift a finger to make your life any easier. The epitome of user hostility is the DOS prompt, a cursor blinking on an otherwise blank screen. "I worked on a computer that made me enter the code <pil4,69> whenever I wanted to print a plus sign. Now, *that* was a *user-hostile* machine."

user ID *(yoo-zer eye dee)* Yes, you can get "carded" by your computer. The user ID is a number or code word assigned to you by the system administrator or one you make up yourself. The ID is used to tell the computer who you

Olmec head.

are, often in place of your name. For example, Bill Gates' ID on the Microsoft internal mail system is "billg." Don't confuse the user ID with the password. The ID is something that identifies who you are to other people using a computer. In contrast, the password is secret and proves to the computer that the guy who logs in as billg is really Bill Gates and not some joker from the competition who's trying to find out all the Microsoft secrets. See also *password, user.* Recently overheard in the system administrator's office at a major software vendor: "No, I'm sorry, the *user ID* 'god' is already taken. You have to think of something else."

user interface *(yoo-zer in-ter-fays)* What you see when you turn on a computer. You interact with this set of prompts, cursors, and software devices to get something done in a program. The interface is what you see — in your face — and how you communicate with the computer and (you hope) get things done. See also *DOS, GUI, interface, Windows.* "The best *user interface* is on *Star Trek,* where they actually tell the computer what to do. Did you ever hear the Enterprise computer say, `Bad command or filename?`"

user name *(yoo-zer naym)* The same thing as a user ID. See *user ID.*

user profile *(yoo-zer proh-fiel)* 1. A little blurb about a member or user of a network that others can access so that they have a better sense of whom they're talking to. Users write their own blurbs that may include their name, age, geographic location,

u

the kind of computer they're using, and their interests as they relate to that specific bulletin board. "Fortunately, my *user profile* didn't include the fact that I have 12 designer pocket protectors."

utility *(yoo-til-i-tee)* Software intended to help you fix, tweak, or enhance your system. Unlike a true application, a utility generally doesn't produce any output or documents. Instead, utilities are designed to make working with a computer or an operating system easier. Utilities, once called software tools, were intended for use primarily by programmers to help ease programming drudgery. See also *backup, debugger, file compression, undelete, unerase, virus.* "At the time of the Michelangelo virus scare, sales of computer antivirus *utilities* went way up. It makes you wonder who thought up that Michelangelo thing."

UUCP *(yoo yoo see pee)* Acronym for the *UNIX-to-UNIX Copy Program,* an international wide-area network of all sorts of UNIX computers, all interconnected à la the Tholian Web. UUCP is a program used to copy information from one UNIX computer to another, which is sort of a backbone of the whole Internet system. "We've hooked up our top-security project on a computer with *UUCP.* This setup enables us to exchange mail with other UNIX sites and read USENET user groups, and it enables hackers to try to crack into the computer."

u

u

V

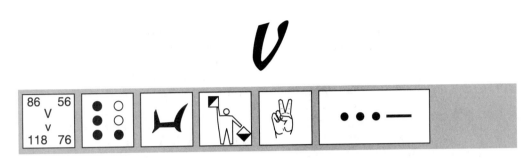

V: *(vee koh-lon)* The letter designation for what's most likely a network drive on a PC. See also *C:, D:, E:, F:, G:, H:, I:, J:, K:, L:, M:, N:, O:, P:, Q:, R:, S:, T:, U:, W:, X:, Y:, Z:.*

V.Fast *(vee-fast)* A (once) fast modem standard, set up according to the CCITT V standards (and many standards exist). These standards all start with V followed by a dot and a number. The number indicates how fast the modem can go (though there is no relation between the number and the modem's speed); other modems that share that standard can communicate with each other. Supposedly, a V.Fast modem toots along at more than 14,000 bps, and maybe even 28,000 bps. "After the *V.Fast* standard proves to be too slow, will they create a V.Faster and V.Fastest standard?"

vaccine *(vak-seen)* A utility that helps your computer fight computer viruses. It works by looking for the symptoms of virus activity, such as suspicious attempts to infiltrate relatively secluded areas of a hard disk, drowsiness, and high fever. The vaccine then removes the virus, making your PC infection free. See also *virus*. "So, let me get this straight, you tried to cure your PC of any possible virus by sticking a moldy orange into your disk drive? Why not just try a *vaccine* next time?"

vacuum tube *(vak-yoom toob)* An old-fashioned technology used in early computers. This device transmits information by controlling the flow of electrons, as semiconductor diodes and transistors do in modern computers. "A *vacuum tube* is something you can look for in a computer museum, such as the marvelous Boston Computer Museum, which, incidentally, is in Boston."

vandals *(van-dols)* 1. A type of Internet virus that visits unsuspecting Web page browsers. Using Java or ActiveX, a vandal invades a computer and can either destroy files or send sensitive information back to the host over the Internet. Not the same thing as a cookie, which is passive. See also *cookie, virus.* 2. (Capitalized) The University of Idaho football team, which usually gets chomped on by the Montana Grizzlies.

vaporware *(vay-por-wayr)* A type of product, whether hardware or software, that has yet to materialize on the market but is promoted as though it were about to revolutionize the computer industry. In many cases, people have plenty of good reason to believe that the product will never even make it to the market, at least not in the lifetime of its purveyors. See also *Microsoft.* "Anything you've

V

read about or heard about in the computer industry but have yet to see in a store is *vaporware*."

VAR *(vahr)* Acronym for *Value-Added Reseller,* an individual or business that integrates components provided by *Original Equipment Manufacturers* (OEMs) and gets them properly packaged and documented for end users who usually need all the bells and whistles. VARs often package hardware, software, training, documentation, and even custom software services for specialized industries. See also *bells and whistles, end user, OEM.* "We purchased a large medical system from a *VAR.* The advantage is that we can complain to one source for all our problems."

variable *(vayr-ee-a-bol)* In programming, a symbol that represents a numerical value or string of text used in a program. Using variables gives a programmer the flexibility to change the value at any point in the program, even if there seems to be no need for that kind of flexibility at the outset. See also *wildcard.* "The content of a *variable* can change at any time. This fact leads me to believe that Bill Clinton's brain contains way too many variables."

Typical variable.

VAX *(vaks)* A line of computers produced by Digital Equipment Corp. (DEC). In the olden days, the term VAX was often used to mean a large and cumbersome yet highly capable and powerful computer. The notion of "a VAX on your desktop" used to be thought of in science fiction terms. In 1988 or thereabouts, that concept became a reality as the microcomputers of the time reached the processing capabilities of the early VAX computers. "No, it's not true that the first Apple computer was the result of the engineers leaving a Mommy *VAX* and Daddy *VAX* alone overnight."

VBX *(vee bee eks)* Acronym for *Visual Basic eXtension,* but often just called a Visual Basic custom control. VBXs are reusable programs, written by other people, that you can add to your own Visual Basic or C++ programs so that you don't waste time writing part of a program that somebody has already written. VBXs first appeared in Visual Basic; just as their popularity has peaked, Microsoft plans to make them obsolete and make everyone use a new standard called OCX instead. See also *OCX.* "Visual Basic is so popular because you can buy loads of *VBXs,* paste them together, and make powerful programs quickly with almost no effort other than shelling out lots of money to buy *VBXs* from different companies."

VDISK *(vee-disk)* A DOS device driver used to create a RAM drive. See also *RAM drive, virtual disk.*

VDT *(vee dee tee)* Acronym for *Video Display Terminal,* otherwise known as a monitor (with a keyboard). The term VDT, however, is more likely to be used in talking about the negative health effects of these machines, which have been implicated in everything from eye strain to birth defects. VDTs produce a substantial amount of electromagnetic radiation, which may or may not be enough to cause the various maladies that monitors have been accused of causing. For protection, you can get screens that filter out these electromagnetic fields. Screens that polarize the visual output so as to avoid glare are even more widely available. See also *radiation.* "I like my *VDT,* but I'm worried about the EMFs it produces. I'm worried that I might get RSI or CTS from all that typing, too. It's the dangerous side of computing that gives me so many of life's thrills."

vector graphics *(vek-tor graf-iks)* Graphics drawn by using lines. The lines start at a certain point and go off in a certain direction for a certain distance. (Certainly, you knew that.) Vector graphics are fine for CAD programs, though don't expect to see many flower vases done that way. See also *bitmap, graphics.* "Victor loves *vector graphics* over bitmaps."

Victor Vector, discoverer of vector graphics.

verify *(ver-uh-fie)* To confirm the existence of something. In computing, the term often refers to the double-checking that takes place after a file is copied. The computer verifies that a duplicate is identical to its original. Although verifying makes the copying process take a little longer because the computer has to double-check, it ensures that no errors were produced during the duplication process.

"Because disk media is much more reliable than in the old days, most DOS users don't bother to *verify* file copies."

Veronica *(ver-on-eh-ka)* Acronym for *Very Easy Rodent-Oriented Net-wide Index to Computerized Archives,* a program developed at the University of Nevada to help you search through various Internet Gopher servers to find the information you need. Veronica, like her pals Archie and Jughead, were made obsolete by the World Wide Web. Also see *Gopher.* "The real *Veronica* probably would have nothing to do with any Gopher."

version *(ver-zhun)* An edition of a product. Versions are usually designated with a number, such as SlothCom 2.0 for Windows, in which 2.0 is the version number, second version, first release. Although you can't count on the numbers to be in numerical order (I don't know why this is so), 1 typically comes before 2, 2 comes before 3, and so on. The decimal portion of a version number generally represents a small enhancement or bug fix to the initial version release, so that Version 2.1 is always more reliable than 2.0. Intermediary releases have more digits following the decimal, such as Windows 3.1.1, which is really just the Microsoft way of avoiding the fiasco caused by releasing a whole new version. "*Version* 1.0 of any product — the first one out of the shoot — is generally the worst. Of course, the computer industry knows that we know that, so we can't recommend Version 1.1 either."

V

vertical *(ver-tuh-kal)* Relating to the up-and-down direction. With computers, you can talk about vertical markets, vertical centering, vertical columns, vertical justification, and vertical scrolling — all of which apply in some way to up-and-downness. "Charlie told me that he was feeling *vertical* today."

vertical market *(ver-tuh-kal mar-kit)* A group of relatively few consumers who need specific software. Most programmers who don't work for major software vendors create programs for the vertical market. For example, real estate agencies are a vertical market that needs specific software written for it — stuff you can't find on the shelf at Software-o-Rama. "Elevator software is a *vertical market.*"

vertical scroll bar *(ver-tuh-kal skrohl bar)* The gizmo on the right side of a window in a graphical application that you use to scroll a document up or down. By clicking the scroll bar with the mouse or pressing the arrow keys, you can move the contents of the window up or down in various increments. The little marker that travels along the bar is called the *elevator box.* It shows you how far along you are in the document. See also *horizontal scroll bar.* "To get to the end of my document, I put these little people in the *vertical scroll bar's* elevator box. Then I say, 'Free fall!' and drag the elevator box quickly to the bottom of the scroll bar. It may scare the little people, but I get to the bottom of my document quickly."

VESA *(vee-za)* Acronym for *Video Electronics Standards Association,* an organization devoting its existence to setting video standards for computers. The most prominent standard set by VESA has been the development of the VESA local bus, designed to make IBM computers run graphics faster. The VESA bus was succeeded by the PCI bus, which does the same thing and more. See also *PCI.*

VGA *(vee jee ay)* Acronym for *Video Graphics Array* or *Video Gate Array,* a color graphics display standard that was an improvement over its predecessors in terms of color selection, resolution, and accuracy of image. A VGA monitor can display as many as 256 colors at one time. The resolution (image sharpness) of VGA is 640 pixels horizontally by 480 lines vertically. Super VGA monitors are even more impressive, with resolutions reaching 1,024 x 768. See also *CGA, EGA, graphics, monitor, resolution, SVGA.*

video *(vid-ee-oh)* Anything visual in a computer. More specifically, it can refer to the display function of a computer (that is, video display) or the act of incorporating video devices (VCRs and video recording equipment) with computer technology. Video standards established by the Video Electronics Standards Association (VESA) help to ensure that computer components work together in such a way that you can actually see something on-screen (which is nice). That's the kind of video that's common to all computers. "I got my father some *video* software for his birthday. Now he sits around all day in dark glasses in front of his computer yelling, 'Cut!' into a megaphone."

video adapter *(vid-ee-oh uh-dap-ter)* An expansion card that enables software and a PC's monitor to talk with each other. Also called a *video card*. See also *CGA, EGA, expansion slot, SVGA, VGA*. "The graphics on your PC consist of two elements: the monitor and the *video adapter*. The monitor you see. The video adapter lurks inside your PC's guts."

video board *(vid-ee-oh bord)* See *video adapter*.

video card *(vid-ee-oh kard)* See *video adapter*.

video memory *(vid-ee-oh mem-oh-ree)* A special part of the computer's RAM in which images displayed on-screen are stored. "Frank must have a huge amount of *video memory*. He remembers seeing the old *Gary Moore Show* live on TV."

video mode *(vid-ee-oh mohd)* The various resolutions and number of colors available for the different types of graphics adapters used by IBM-compatible computers. Several video modes now exist, ranging from 0 to whatever. Characteristics include graphics or text-only display, color or monochrome, number of colors, resolution (height and width in pixels), and, in text-only mode, number of columns (the number of characters you can fit on a line). See also *mode*. "Jane pasted some flowers on her monitor to help cheer up its *video mode*."

video RAM *(vid-ee-oh ram)* The chips used to make up video memory. They're built into high-end video

adapter boards. "The Megalons used a *video RAM* to break into Captain Video's secret fortress."

videotext *(vid-ee-oh-tekst)* Words and numbers that come to your computer (or your TV, for that matter) over the wires. Types of videotext commonly transmitted include news, weather information, and stock quotes. In Europe, a videotext system was designed for use with cable television there. Using a special type of computer, you can hook into the system and access information right at home on your TV. Americans must have thought that this idea was too dumb because they never bothered with it. "*Videotext* is an appropriate format for up-to-the-minute news whose value depends on being transmitted quickly — stuff such as, 'Hey! Some guy just broke into your house. Go check the bedroom window.'"

virtual disk *(vur-choo-uhl disk)* A make-believe disk that doesn't exist in reality, like most flying saucers. A fancy term for a RAM disk, a disk created from the computer's memory. See also *RAM disk*. "Father Matthew wants to put all his sermons on a *virtual disk*."

virtual machine *(vur-choo-uhl mah-sheen)* 1. A software simulation of another computer. Useful for testing software on large computers, such as mainframes. For example, a group of engineers typically create a new computer on a larger mainframe and then run tests to see how the computer performs. All this testing is done before the first real machine is created, primarily to work out the

V

bugs. New microprocessors are created in a similar manner. 2. On 386 and later PCs, a special operating mode, the V86 mode, in which the microprocessor can pretend that it's actually several 8088 computers all running at the same time. This concept is the reason that operating systems such as Windows and OS/2 can *multitask* (run more than one program at a time).

virtual memory *(vur-choo-uhl mem-oh-ree)* The use of disk drive storage to simulate RAM. Some operating systems borrow parts of the disk drive and swap out massive chunks of memory to a file on disk — a *swap file.* That way, true memory (RAM) is made available for programs that need it. The memory saved on disk can be put back into real memory when it's needed later. See also *hard disk, memory, RAM.* "You can tell when your computer uses *virtual memory* because your system slows w-a-y d-o-w-n."

virtual reality *(vur-choo-uhl ree-al-uh-tee)* An oxymoron that describes a brave new world of computer technology that creates a simulated multidimensional environment. A user is encased in the environment, or can be, with paraphernalia that can include a helmet, goggles, gloves, and a belt, all used as input devices. Getting "inside the space" makes you feel as though you're trapped in a dream world. Within a virtual reality environment, you can see, hear, and feel your way around a software application. The main uses of virtual reality are games and design/engineering. Game arcades already offer virtual reality setups in which you can hunt down and kill your opponent in a place called Cyberspace, which is not far from downtown Los Angeles. More significantly, virtual reality is used for engineering because it enables an engineer or designer to simulate any view of a product being worked on. For example, in designing a car, you can simulate being inside the engine. See also *artificial intelligence, expert system, knowledge base.* "Sometimes I think that my whole life is one big *virtual reality* machine — especially when the cat talks to me."

virus *(vie-ruhs)* 1. A nasty type of program created by nasty people. A virus is capable of replicating itself and doing severe damage to the contents of other users' systems. To protect your system against viruses, you should get your software only from reputable places, run an antivirus utility, and religiously back up your hard disk so that lost data can be quickly and reliably replaced. See also *vaccine.* "If you can't cure your computer of a *virus* it has caught, you should at least let it rest and feed it plenty of chicken soup." 2. Another term for a Trojan horse, though it's inaccurate. See also *Trojan horse.*

VisiCalc *(viz-uh-kalk)* Trademarked name for the first spreadsheet software, originally developed for CP/M and the Apple II computers. VisiCalc is short for "*Visi*ble *Calc*ulator," which is how its designer envisioned it: a grid of cells, each of which works like a calculator. The concept was refined by Lotus in its 1-2-3 application.

Microsoft Excel now dominates the spreadsheet market. Even so, a VisiCalc user would feel right at home using 1-2-3 or Excel.

VisiCorp *(viz-ee-korp)* The company that developed the once popular VisiCalc program. VisiCorp died the painful death of many of the early computer software developers: It announced a wonderful, new program that just took too long to develop. People grew old waiting for the company's much praised VisiOn *(vizee-on,* though I always pronounce it "vision") software. Besides, at that point, Lotus was winning over the IBM world with its easy-as 1-2-3 spreadsheet.

Visual Basic *(vizh-yoo-el bay-sik)* A Microsoft dialect of the BASIC language that lets you create programs by drawing your user interface on-screen and then writing BASIC commands to make the program do something worthwhile. Microsoft also uses Visual Basic as a common language for all its business applications, such as Excel, Word, and Access. Theoretically, in the future, you will be able to write Visual Basic commands to make Excel or Access easier to use; realistically, most people will probably never attempt to do so unless they want to drive themselves crazy. "*Visual Basic* is so popular because it makes programming a whole lot easier than using an arcane language such as C++ or Pascal. The only thing Visual Basic doesn't make easier is figuring out why you want to write a program in the first place."

visual programming *(vizh-yoo-el proh-gram-ing)* A way of creating software by making menu choices with the mouse and cutting and pasting items so that typing and linear thought are minimized. The plus side is that you don't have to know much about programming to be able to work with this technology and produce results. The minus side is that many of your choices are made for you, and you often have no way to customize certain options. See also *programming*. "*Visual programming* makes it possible for someone such as Uncle Ralph to create custom applications. Remember his spice rack? Doesn't the thought of Ralph programming make you cringe?"

VLB *(vee ell bee)* Acronym for *VESA Local Bus*. See also *VESA*.

VL-Bus *(vee el buhs)* Another term for a VESA Local Bus. See also *VESA*. "Boy, my computer has VESA, VLB, and *VL-Bus,* and it has only one slot!"

Various squiggly lines.

VLSI *(vee el es ie)* Acronym for *Very Large-Scale Integration,* a technology that refers to semiconductor chips. The chip is engineered so that it can accommodate a large number of transistors and can do more. See also *CMOS, MOS, semiconductor.* "*VLSI* circuits are not larger than other chips; they just contain more information."

VMM *(vee em em)* Acronym for *Virtual Memory Management,* a hardware or software device that controls virtual memory. See also *virtual memory.*

voice recognition *(voys rek-uhg-ni-shun)* Technology that can recognize and work with the spoken word. It translates sound signals into digital signals that can be processed and analyzed by a computer. The prospect offers a whole new world of opportunity for computers: being able to talk to your computer as you talk to your friends (or, more appropriately, to your children) and being able to repot your plants or remodel your kitchen while you're doing your computer work. Voice recognition technology is in a constant primitive state. See also *voice synthesis.* "The first thing I'd do with *voice recognition* technology is tell Windows exactly what it can do with the `General Protection Fault` error message."

voice synthesis *(voys sin-thuh-sis)* The opposite of voice recognition. In voice synthesis, a computer can create something that sounds like speech from text that it reads from a hard or floppy disk. Voice synthesis is much easier to create than voice recognition, which is why computers talk like computers. "I had always imagined that my computer was female. When I plugged in that *voice synthesis* expansion unit, however, it sounded like Arnold Schwarzenegger on a slow day."

volatile memory *(vol-uh-tiel mem-oh-ree)* Another term for RAM. Computer memory is often called volatile because it requires a constant flow of electrons to maintain its contents. Turn the power off, and — poof! — there goes memory. See also *RAM.* "Walk gingerly around the computer. You don't want its *volatile memory* to go off."

volume *(vahl-yoom)* 1. Another name for a disk, whether it's hard or floppy. Comes from the old computer days when, rather than have a disk inside a computer, lab technicians mounted a tape volume on a high-speed tape machine. The term works for computer storage in the same way that a volume is a single book in a larger collection of works. See also *disk, floppy disk, hard disk.* "I got an error message that said, `No volume in drive A`, so I turned up my stereo." 2. The control in Windows that sets how loud the computer's speakers play.

volume label *(vahl-yoom lay-bol)* A disk's name. See also *label.*

von Neumann *(vahn noy-man)* The father of all modern computers. John von Neumann invented an architecture that created a data bottleneck named after him. Although it involves an extremely fast CPU and fast storage, the processing is slowed down to the rate of the transmission of the data from one place to another. Yes, his name is von Neumann, but you pronounce it *von Noyman.* "Yes, Dr. *von Neumann,* and not two guys named Steve, really started this computer revolution."

V

voodoo *(voo-doo)* Tried-and-true technology to apply when all else fails. Rather than press keys and click a mouse, you can chant invocations, perform ritual dances, or feed weird concoctions of exotic herbs to your computer in an effort to get it to cooperate. "If your PC worked fine yesterday and for some reason it doesn't today — even though you didn't change a thing — it's *voodoo.*"

 VRAM *(vee-ram)* Another term for video memory, often applied to the actual RAM chips. See also *video memory.*

VRML *(vur-muhl)* Acronym for *Virtual Reality Modeling Language,* a 3-D version of the standard HTML Web page document. "To see a *VRML* document on the Web, you need a Web browser that understands *VRML.*"

Vulcan *(vol-kan)* 1. A planet in Epsilon Eridana. 2. Name for a person from the planet Vulcan. From Mr. Spock, on *Star Trek.* 3. A computer wizard, such as Mr. Spock from *Star Trek.* See also *Spock.*

Vulcan nerve pinch *(vol-kan nurv peench)* 1. A manipulation of the neck or shoulder that renders someone blissfully unconscious. Used by Mr. Spock on *Star Trek* to contrast with Captain Kirk's coldcocking some alien. 2. Nickname for the Ctrl+Alt+Delete key combination that renders a PC unconscious (by rebooting it). See also *Ctrl+Alt+Delete.*

v

W

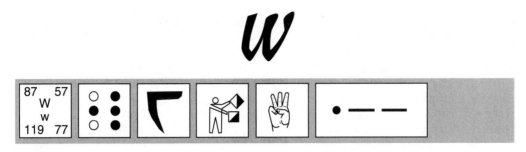

W: *(dub-ohl-yoo koh-lon)* A disk drive letter designation, probably representing some disk drive on a network as opposed to a disk drive in your system. Really, it would have to be the 21st hard drive, the 20th CD-ROM drive, the 14th removable drive, or the 19th RAM drive, or something else so utterly nuts that it doesn't deserve mentioning here. (Honestly, most high-letter drives are network drives.)

 WAIS *(ways)* Acronym for *Wide-Area Information Server,* a valiant attempt by the Internet to make it easy to search for specific types of information. Made obsolete by the World Wide Web.

wait state *(wayt stayt)* A short delay that occurs when a microprocessor accesses data from memory. Because a microprocessor is generally faster than a memory chip, the microprocessor waits for the memory chips to "catch up" by sitting around and having a cup of coffee for the duration of one wait state every time it accesses the memory. A *zero wait state processor* is much faster and takes advantage of faster memory chips. How long is a wait state? It depends on how fast the processor is. In any case, it's a slice of time way too fast for a human to experience. See also *zero wait state.* "I had to call tech support yesterday about my laptop. They said that it had only one *wait state;* when I took it to the post office, however, it suddenly gained about 40 wait states!"

wallpaper *(wahl-pay-per)* A graphical image placed on the desktop, or background, of a GUI. If you close all windows in a GUI, you see the wallpaper underneath. Although wallpaper serves no particular purpose, it can be interesting and amusing to your friends. "My favorite *wallpaper* is the Nagel painting called *Sushi.*"

Wambooli protocol *(wom-boo-lee proh-toh-kahl)* A complex algorithm for data transmission that means nothing whatsoever. From the non-sense word *wambooli* and the non-sense term *protocol.* "Yup, I'd bet that the new *Wambooli protocol* will smoke out that RARP thing that Karl's working on."

WAN *(wan)* Acronym for *wide area network.* See also *wide area network.*

wapro *(wah-proh)* The Japanese term for *word processor.* I just thought that I'd throw it in here because it's one of those terms you usually don't see in a computer dictionary. "The proper response to the question *'Wapro?'* is 'Wa-kari-mas-en,' or 'I don't understand.'"

Yoshi is waiting for his Microsoft Word wapro to load.

WarGames *(woor gayms)* A 1983 film starring Matthew Broderick about a teenage hacker who gains access to a top secret military computer. As is always the case in this type of situation, the computer attempts to initiate World War III. Yet another example of Hollywood's fascination with modems and nuclear weapons.

warm boot *(warm boot)* The process of restarting a computer by pressing Ctrl+Alt+Delete or an equivalent reset button. A warm boot occurs when you restart a computer without turning it off. Warm booting is much faster than cold booting, which occurs when you turn the computer off and then back on. See also *cold boot, Ctrl+Alt+Del, reboot.* "After I install certain software on my hard disk, the programs tell me to restart the computer by pressing Ctrl+Alt+Delete, which *warm-boots* the computer. That seems so much cozier than the cold-boot approach."

warp coils *(warp koy-els)* 1. The massive hoops of metal that enable a starship to glide through space at high speeds without any chiropractic injuries to the crew. 2. Any sufficiently advanced or mysterious thing you don't understand that's inside a computer. "The PC won't boot! Why doesn't someone check the innertubular couplers, quantum phase adjustment wing nuts, and the *warp coils?*"

watch icon *(watch ie-kon)* A mouse pointer that looks like a tiny watch. The watch icon, indigenous to the Macintosh computer, tells you that the computer is thinking and that you have to wait. In the early days of the Macintosh, the watch's little hands did not move. Today's watch icons are much more sophisticated. See also *beachball pointer, hourglass icon.* "Spacelab, this is Houston. You'll have to wait on that emergency meteor collision avoidance program. We're still getting the *watch icon* here."

watt *(wot)* A unit of measure for power consumption. Watts equal volts times amperes. Hence, a 10-volt, 10-amp power source puts out 100 watts of power. It helps if you think of watts in terms of a lightbulb. A 100-watt lightbulb is much brighter than a 60-watt bulb. TV studios use 1,000-watt K bulbs to light their sets, which are terribly bright. A typical PC uses 250 watts of power, just like a 250-watt lightbulb. See also *amp.* "I use 50-*watt* lightbulbs in my computer room, so I don't get much glare on the screen. Also, I'm a troglodyte, so it reminds me of my cave-dwelling forefathers."

WAV *(wayve)* 1. A type of sound file in Windows. 2. The extension of a file that contains a WAV sound.

Web *(web)* 1. Nickname for the World Wide Web. See also *World Wide Web.* 2. Prefix for any of a number of things having to do with the World Wide Web.

Web browser *(web brow-zer)* Software designed to view documents written in HTML, which includes all pages on the World Wide Web. There are two popular Web browsers: one from Netscape and the other from Microsoft. Web browsers display information from the Internet by using text, graphics, sounds, and all sorts of interesting distractions. The browsers can also display Gopher, FTP, and newsgroup information. See also *plug-in, World Wide Web*. "The spider asked whether I was going to kill her, and I said that I was just a *Web browser*."

 Web catalog *(web cat-uh-log)* A page on the World Wide Web that contains listings of other Web pages, organized by topic or subject. A Web catalog is similar to a library card catalog, listing Web pages by subject or topic. See also *search engine*. "The most popular *Web catalog* is Yahoo!."

 Web page *(web payj)* A document on the World Wide Web. The term *page* has nothing to do with the length of the document; some pages are short, and some are very long. Any single document is still merely a page.

 Web server *(web sir-ver)* A computer or software program that runs on a computer and answers requests for Web pages on the World Wide Web. Web servers are usually part of an Internet service provider's array of computers. Or a business may have a computer that works as a Web server, answering HTTP requests from the Internet and sending Web page information to other computers.

Web site *(web siet)* A collection of Web pages closely linked to each other. A company's presence on the World Wide Web. A Web site is merely the entire collection of Web pages relating to a specific topic or owned by a business, group, or individual. For example, your own personal Web site may consist of several Web pages dedicated to your cat's recovery from chemotherapy. A Web site is not the same thing as a Web server. See also *Web server*.

Web space *(web spays)* Disk storage space that can be used to hold Web pages. Typically offered as a service of an Internet provider. You can store HTML documents in your Web space, which makes them available to anyone on the Internet. You have to follow certain rules, of course, about filenames and locations in your Web space, and, for a hefty fee, you can get someone to tell you what those rules are. "Every Internet service provider should offer you some *Web space* as part of its monthly fees."

Web TV *(web tee-vee)* Another stupid attempt to get computer users to watch the TV. Seriously, a type of computer that uses the TV as an output device for viewing information on the World Wide Web. Computer owners from way back know that TV sets make for lousy computer monitors. While you're viewing the Web TV stuff, it looks okay; if you visit anywhere else on the Web, however, you suffer the perils of eyeball frazzle. See also *eyeball frazzle*.

 WebCrawler *(web-crah-lur)* A robot designed for searching the World Wide Web. WebCrawler displays its results based on how many Web pages contain words similar to those you're searching for. See also *robot*.

WFWG *(win-dohz for werk-groops)* Acronym for *Windows for Workgroups* and one that's very hard to say as an acronym, so no one does anyway. See also *Windows for Workgroups.* "I told my mom that I was working on *WFWG,* and she thought that I had become a professional wrestler."

what-if *(wot-if)* A term used for testing a spreadsheet with various values to generate different results for analysis, such as, "If I made a gazillion dollars, what percentage would my house payment be?" Then you can enter another value, such as, "Now, what if I worked at McDonald's? Hey, can this thing deal with negative numbers?" What-if testing is commonly used in spreadsheets, in which you can enter different values in cells, and the formulas recalculate their results based on the different scenarios. See also *spreadsheet.* "Jimmy used a spreadsheet to calculate various *what-ifs* for the money he embezzled. Now he's doing 5 to 10 but is trying to get the judge to work out a what-if for good behavior."

wheel mouse *(weel mows)* Another name for the Microsoft IntelliMouse. It's like a regular mouse but with a wheel-like button between the two standard PC mouse buttons. See also *IntelliMouse.*

Whetstone *(wet-stohn)* The name of a program used for testing the speed of a microprocessor. The Whetstone is used as a standard test for microprocessor speed. See also *microprocessor, MIPS.* "Hey, my computer can do 1,500 *Whetstones* — and that's with one cable tied behind its back!"

wide area network *(wied ayr-ee-uh net-werk)* A network of computers that spans a large distance, as opposed to a local area network, which involves computers in the same building. See also *LAN, network, network operating system, node.* "Realtors can access a *wide area network* that provides multiple listings and other services for a computer. That way, they can send messages, such as 'Hey! Mr. and Mrs. Turkey looking for duplex — completely real estate ignorant. Be on the lookout!'"

widow *(wid-oh)* 1. The last line of a paragraph abandoned at the top of the next page while the rest of the paragraph sits at the bottom of the preceding page. See also *orphan.* "Sometimes, if a document is full of *widows,* simply writing about a bunch of elderly bachelors makes the *widows* disappear." 2. A computer widow is a female spouse who is abandoned by her husband who spends way too much of his time in front of his computer.

widower *(wid-oh-er)* The male version of a computer widow. See also *widow.*

wildcards *(wield-kahrds)* Characters or symbols used in place of a number of possible combinations. Wildcards represent one or more characters that "could be anything" in a search or command. For example, if the * symbol is a wildcard, the search text *s*ing* matches any word or item that starts with an *s* and ends in *ing.* See also **.*, ?.* "*Wildcards* come in handy when you search for text and don't know how to spell, when you search for files and don't know their whole names, or when you play Shanghai with the in-laws and have a lousy hand."

WIMP *(wimp)* A disparaging acronym for *windows, icons, menus, pointing device.* It's the wimpy GUI way of using a computer as opposed to using the command line. See also *command line, icon, menu, mouse, window.* "Don't show me that *WIMP* interface! I'm a real man! Give me the DOS prompt any day!"

Win *(win)* 1. A prefix applied to any product, device, or program that has anything remotely to do with Microsoft Windows. 2. The old DOS command used to start Windows. "Is it a coincidence that Windows starts with *'win'?*"

Winchester disk *(win-ches-ter disk)* A hard disk. For years, hard disks were called Winchester disks. This term had nothing to do with any company named Winchester that made hard disks. Instead, it referred to the first IBM hard disk that stored 30 megabytes of information on each side. Because the drive was a 30-30, people dubbed it a Winchester disk after the famous Winchester rifle. Until the mid-1980s, hard disks were often called Winchester disks. This term drove everyone nuts because they assumed that some person or company named Winchester made the disks. It just wasn't so. Today they're called hard disks, plain and simple. See also *hard disk.* "Yes, ma'am, our hard disks come in three sizes: *Winchester,* Colt, and Daisy."

WinCIM *(win-sim)* Acronym for *Windows CompuServe Information Manager,* a graphics front-end for using CompuServe in Windows. Believe it or not, CompuServe is a text-based online service. By using a front end such as WinCIM, however, you can use pull-down menus and the mouse to wade through all the various menus. See also *CompuServe, front end.*

window *(win-doh)* An area on-screen that displays data, programs, or information. A window can be moved, resized, opened, and closed, enabling you to organize the data on your computer screen. In most GUIs, you can open numerous windows at the same time and juggle information on-screen. You can switch between windows by simply clicking the window you want. However, you can work in only one window — called the *active window* — at a time. See also *active window, GUI.* "Sometimes I get carried away and open 20 or 30 *windows* at the same time. This number usually results in the building inspector's coming in with a worried look on his face and muttering something about earthquakes."

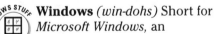 **Windows** *(win-dohs)* Short for *Microsoft Windows,* an operating system for PCs. Windows began its life in 1983 as a shell (graphical user interface) for DOS computers. Windows/386 was a custom

A typical alpha geek.

version of Windows for the 386 computer that had more power than the original version. Windows 3.0, which appeared in 1990, became a rival of DOS, with advanced applications and programs that made it almost an outright replacement. Finally, Windows did become its own operating system in 1995, with Windows 95. Today, almost every PC sold comes with a copy of Windows 95 on it, which may have more to do with sneaky Microsoft licensing habits than any desire on behalf of the computer-using community. Even so, Windows is useful because it provides a common way of using programs, which makes them easier to learn how to use. Windows also manages the way a PC works and takes care of common chores, such as working with a printer and the disk drive. For example, when you set up a printer in Windows, that printer is automatically available in all your Windows programs. This capability lets us poor users concentrate on our work rather than on fussing with the computer and printer drivers or some such. See also *GUI, Microsoft*. "*Windows* can be a fun place in which to work. And then there's now."

Windows for Workgroups *(win-dohs for werk-groops)* A special version of Microsoft Windows designed for a local area network. Its features were melded into Windows 95.

Windows keys *(win-dohs kees)* Three special keys on a 101-key keyboard (which actually makes it a 104-key keyboard) that perform special functions in Windows. Two of the keys are the Windows key, which pops up the Start menu (the same as pressing Ctrl+Esc). The shortcut menu key displays the shortcut menu for whichever item is highlighted

on-screen, which is the same as pointing the mouse at that item and right-clicking. "No, you don't need *Windows keys* to use Windows."

WIN.INI *(win in-ee)* The configuration file for Windows, though its importance is diminished under Windows 95 and later. This file contains commands that determine how Microsoft Windows looks and behaves on a computer. Because the WIN.INI file is an ASCII file, you can edit it by using a text editor. If you ever lose or modify your WIN.INI file, Windows may not work properly on your computer. "Every time you install a new program, it automatically updates the *WIN.INI* file. For the fun of it, I copied my WIN.INI file to my boss's computer, so now his computer refuses to work properly."

WinMark *(win-mark)* A measurement unit used to determine the speed of a computer when it's running Windows-based programs. The two most common WinMark measurements are Graphics WinMark, which measures the speed of displaying graphics, and Disk WinMark, which measures the speed of accessing a hard disk. The higher the WinMark value, the faster the computer. "My computer is better than your computer because *PC* magazine scored mine at 21.8 on its Graphics *WinMark* test and yours at only 17.4. Nya, nya, nya."

Winsock *(win-sock)* Short for *Windows sock*ets, a set of programs designed to help Internet software programs access and use the Internet on a Windows PC. Essentially, Winsock is included with your Internet dialer program.

The dialer program makes the connection to the Internet and activates the Winsock software. Other Internet programs you run then use Winsock to access the Internet. "Nope, unless your flight-simulator program is on the Internet, you won't need a *Winsock* to fly."

winsock2 *(win-sock-too)* The latest whiz-bang version of the Winsock standard. See also *Winsock*.

Winstone *(win-stone)* A benchmark test of a computer's capability to run Windows. See also *benchmark*. "*Winstones!* Meet the *Winstones!* They're a way to measure your PC! When you're running Windows, it will see just how fast fast can be!"

Wintel *(win-tel)* An adjective describing a computer with an Intel processor that is capable of running Windows. Wintel essentially describes what's commonly called a PC. Same thing. "I assume that if we rename *PCs For Dummies* to *Wintel For Dummies,* few people would buy it."

wiz *(wiz)* A computer user who is sharp and fast and looks good at the computer. A wiz is not quite as adept as a wizard. See also *guru, hacker, wizard.* "Thank you for writing and calling me a computer *wiz*. Please note that *wiz* does not contain an *h*. That means something else entirely."

wizard *(wiz-erd)* A computer user of high caliber. Not quite a guru, a computer wizard can solve most problems in most cases without assistance of any kind. See also *guru, hacker, wiz.* "No, Amy isn't quite a guru. She's a *wizard,* one who knows

how to solve a problem but just can't quite explain how."

WMF *(dub-ohl-yoo em ef)* Acronym for *Windows MetaFile,* a special graphics file that was once used in earlier versions of Microsoft Windows. It was yet another attempt at a common file format. "Whenever you see a graphics file with the *.WMF* file extension, it either is really old or was created by someone who doesn't know that the .WMF file format is obsolete."

word *(wurd)* 1. A collection of data bits processed as a unit. On the PC and with most microcomputers, a word is 2 bytes of data that are 16 bits "wide." Sometimes, a word is as little as a byte (8 bits). The size varies, which is why I'm being vague here. 2. (Capitalized) The name of a word processing program created by Microsoft. 3. A unit of the English language, such as *duh.* "Yes, Microsoft *Word* can write whole documents, which makes us wonder why they didn't call it Microsoft Document."

word processor *(wurd prah-ses-er)* An application that lets you write and edit documents. Word processors generally have the capability to copy and move text in a document (by individual words, phrases, or paragraphs), search for specific words or phrases, insert and delete text, format (including margin settings, fonts, and character styles), and, of course, print. Popular word processors include Microsoft Word and WordPerfect. See also *text editor.* "My *word processor* has features that let me create tables and columns. Hey, you'd almost think that this was a construction project rather than a memo."

W

W

WordStar *(wurd-star)* One of the first word processors ever sold and also one of the first to lose its dominance in the market because of mismanagement and a failure to upgrade for three years. Because WordStar existed in the days when computer keyboards lacked function keys and cursor (arrow) keys, it defined certain keystrokes that are still used by many programs. These keystrokes are usually referred to as "WordStar commands."

WordStar Keystroke	What It Does
Ctrl+S	Moves cursor one character to the left
Ctrl+D	Moves cursor one character to the right
Ctrl+E	Moves cursor one line up
Ctrl+X	Moves cursor one line down
Ctrl+A	Moves cursor one word to the left
Ctrl+F	Moves cursor one word to the right
Ctrl+Y	Deletes a line

"Although hardly anyone uses *WordStar* anymore, lots of programs still use WordStar commands because they're based on ancient computer history. With Windows becoming more popular, WordStar commands may finally fade from memory like a bad dream."

word wrap *(wurd rap)* The way a word processor automatically determines whether the word you are typing fits within the right margin

and, if not, places that word on the next line. When you use word wrap, you don't have to press the Enter key at the end of each line, as you once had to do on a typewriter. You just continue typing. Text editors do not have word wrap; you have to press Enter at the end of each line. See also *hyphenation.* "*Word wrap* used to be considered a bonus feature in early word processors. Today, a bonus feature is the built-in space shuttle simulator and advanced physics calculation module."

worksheet *(wurk-sheet)* A document created by a spreadsheet program. Not all spreadsheet programs refer to their data files as worksheets; some call them spreadsheets, others call them pages or sheets, and some even call them documents. In any event, a worksheet can be saved as a file on disk. See also *document, spreadsheet.* "I saved my Budget *worksheet* on disk as BUDGET-A and then saved the Budget I show to the IRS as BUDGET-B."

workstation *(wurk-stay-shun)* A nebulous term used to describe a powerful computer generally used for scientific or engineering applications, such as CAD. A workstation usually has tons of RAM, gobs of disk storage space, a high-resolution graphics adapter and monitor, and a powerful microprocessor. Although workstations often use the UNIX operating system, some high-end Macintosh, DOS, and OS/2 machines qualify as workstations. See also *mainframe, network, PC.* "At work, I have a Pentium Pro *workstation,* and at home I have a Pentium MMX playstation."

World Wide Web *(wurld wied web)* The fun part of the Internet, often abbreviated WWW or just "Web." The World Wide Web is a way to access the information on the Internet using text and graphics, like you'd read in a magazine. Each document on the World Wide Web — a Web page — can contain links to other Web pages displaying additional information. Those links make the Web resemble a giant spider's web: All Web pages are interlinked and related to each other somehow. The Web is now the "hot topic" or "next big thing" to hit computerdom. For that reason and because the computer industry is so into the Internet, the Web is given much more attention than it deserves. See also *hyperlink, Internet, Web browser.* "The *World Wide Web* is just another valiant attempt to make the Internet easier to use and navigate."

WORM *(wurm)* 1. Acronym for *Write Once Read Many*, a disk medium to which you can write data only once but read the data as often as you like. Most optical disks are WORM media: MO disks, DVDs, CD-R, and so on. Plain CD-ROM disks, however, are not WORM media because only the manufacturer can supply the information on the disk. You do not "write to" a CD-ROM; they have read-only memory (ROM). See also *CD-R, DVD, MO, ROM.* "The best two acronyms in all computing are SCSI and *WORM.* It's entirely possible to have a SCSI WORM drive. If you do, constantly refer to it that way because it's bound to upset someone somewhere." 2. A type of virus that infects system after system, like a worm chewing through soft earth. The most famous WORM virus was the one released by a college student that shut down the entire Internet in only three hours. (He expected that it would take 24 hours and was rather surprised at what he had done.) See also *virus.*

WPG *(dub-ohl-yoo pee jee)* Acronym for *WordPerfect Graphic,* a special graphics file format that gives WordPerfect the capability to display pictures in documents. WordPerfect comes with several .WPG files for you to play with, although none of them is useful when you want to get some real work done. "If you're going to draw a picture of me with a clueless look on my face, at least store the graphic as a *.WPG* file so that I can display it in my WordPerfect document."

wristpad *(rist-pad)* A foam-rubber pad that fits in front of the keyboard and is designed to elevate your wrists as you type. This placement supposedly cuts down on some nasty injuries that can take place if you type with your wrists slouched down below the keyboard, which is the way we all type anyway. "Since Mrs. Levitt isn't around to whack your wrists with a ruler, like she did in typing class, you had better get a *wristpad.*"

wristwatch pointer *(rist-wach poynter)* See *watch icon.*

write error *(riet ayr-or)* An error that occurs in attempting to save data to a disk. Write errors can occur because of glitches on the disk surface or not enough space on the disk or in trying to save to a write-protected disk. A good user interface "traps" the write error, provides some clue about the exact problem that occurred, and, maybe, if the computer's in a good mood, tells you how to fix it. Otherwise, the system may crash. "Nothing induces computer panic like having a beautiful document created in memory but not being able to save it to disk, thanks to a *write error.* Try another disk."

write protect *(riet proh-tekt)* To modify a disk or file so that others are unable to edit or erase its data. You can write-protect a disk by activating the write-protect tab, a doohickey that makes the disk unwriteable. On $3^1/_2$-inch disks, you flip the write-protect tab so that it exposes (or opens) the hole in the disk. On ancient $5^1/_4$-inch disks, you placed a piece of opaque tape over the write-protect notch on the side of the disk. Write protection is useful when you are copying disks and want to protect the originals. "When I gave my files to a coworker to examine, I *write-protected* the disk so that she couldn't change the files. Just in case, I also made a backup copy. And I'm holding her husband and children hostage."

WWW *(dub-ohl-yoo dub-ohl-yoo dub-ohl-yoo)* Acronym for *World Wide Web.* See also *World Wide Web.*

WYSIWYG *(wiz-ee-wig)* Acronym for *What You See Is What You Get,* the ability to view information on-screen as it should appear when it's printed. Although degrees of WYSIWYG are displayed in computerdom, most people agree that the Macintosh and Windows environments offer true WYSIWYG. WYSIWYG is so common now, in fact, that the term is quickly falling out of common usage. "If this page-layout program offers a *WYSIWYG* display, why does it need a Print Preview command?"

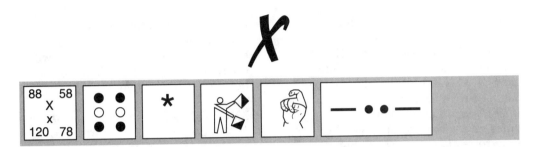

x *(eks)* 1. Something that is unknown. 2. A placeholder for what could be any other number. For example, MS-DOS 6.*x* refers to all the releases of MS-DOS Version 6: 6.0, 6.1, 6.2, 6.22, and so on.

X: *(eks koh-lon)* A letter for some type of disk drive in a PC. Drive X: sounds kind of mysterious; *Viruses from Drive X* would be a great title for a creepy David Cronenberg movie. Most likely, drive X: would be a network drive. See also *map*. "Drive *X* is where you keep the X files."

X.25 *(eks-twen-tee-fiev)* A communications protocol for arranging data in packets that includes identification of the recipient and sender of the data. This protocol is mostly advanced network stuff, not required knowledge unless you plan to bring in the big bucks someday by being a network guru. See also *network*.

x86 *(eks-ay-tee-siks)* A designation for the Intel family of microprocessors used in the IBM PC and its ilk. "The *x86* designation replaced 80x86, probably because it's easier to type."

Xanadu *(zan-uh-doo)* 1. A mythical city in Kubla Khan, known for its incredible beauty and romance. It's also rumored to be an advanced network and information system available to all PCs all over the world. Someday. Soon. See also *network*. "To Melvin, *Xanadu* is any computer superstore." 2. A bad 1980s movie starring Gene Kelley and Olivia Newton-John. "*Xanadu!* Xana-doo-oo!" 3. An information storage and retrieval project founded by hypertext developer Ted Nelson.

xBase *(eks-base)* A generic term for any program that can read, write, edit, modify, and otherwise destroy database files compatible with the dBASE program. Some popular xBase programs are Microsoft FoxPro, CA-Clipper, and Alpha Four.

XCMD *(eks see em dee)* An external command available for the Macintosh HyperCard programming language. Accessing the XCMDs means that a HyperCard programmer has more functions and pizzazz available than when using HyperCard alone. See also *HyperCard*. "Josh used a bunch of cool *XCMD*s to spice up his fungi HyperCard database."

XENIX *(zee-niks)* A version of the UNIX operating system that was adapted by Microsoft to run on personal computers. In the old days, you couldn't buy a

Typical XENIX user.

copy of UNIX like you could buy DOS or System 7 or OS/2, so Microsoft packaged its own version of UNIX, which it called XENIX. Now people use SCO XENIX or SCO UNIX from the Santa Cruz Operation, Inc. See also *UNIX, Linux.* "Lauren had the computer science club rolling with her repertoire of archaic *XENIX* puns."

XGA *(eks jee ay)* Acronym for *Extended Graphics Array,* a type of video adapter that provided a higher resolution than previous adapters. Utterly failed as a standard; like PGA, it was too expensive, and not enough software supported it. "When a computer acronym contains the letter *X,* as in *XGA* graphics, it typically means that the marketing department has already used the II, Turbo, Pro, Gold, and 2,000 monikers."

Xjack *(eks-jak)* A registered trademark for a pop-out phone cord connector typically found on laptop computers. Also written in all caps: XJACK. "Most of the better PCMCIA modem cards have an *Xjack* connector on them, which makes hooking up a phone line easier than using some of the dorky methods of the past."

XMODEM *(eks-moh-dum)* 1. A communications protocol for transferring files between computers (often across phone lines) and catching errors that occur during transfer. This protocol ensures that the file that's sent is identical to the file that's received. See also *checksum, CRC, error-free protocol, Kermit, YMODEM.* 2. The name of a program that included the XMODEM file-transfer protocol. XMODEM, written by Ward

Christensen, is often called the "Christensen protocol" by some old-timers. "Oh, Charles, darling, get with the times! No one uses plain old boring *XMODEM* anymore."

XMODEM-1K *(eks-moh-dum won-kay)* A variation of the XMODEM protocol in which 1K packages were sent rather than 128-byte packages. It was faster than plain old XMODEM.

XMS *(eks em ess)* Acronym for *Extended Memory Specification,* a memory-management standard for enabling DOS applications to access extended memory. XMS memory-management software provides access to the extended memory through the XMS standard, a set of rules developed by Microsoft and other industry bigwigs. Windows 95 uses an XMS memory manager called HIMEM.SYS. See also *expanded memory, extended memory, extended memory specification.* "I'm going to need a new *XMS* manager on my PC. All my extended memory is threatening to go on strike."

XON/XOFF *(eks-on/eks-awf)* Signals for stopping and starting the flow of data during transmission between computers. XON/XOFF lets the receiving computer stop the flow of information so that it can be processed as it comes in. The XON character is Ctrl+S. That stops data from being sent and also enables you to catch up and read the screen. The XOFF character is Ctrl+Q. On some systems, only the Ctrl+Q character gets things moving after being frozen by a Ctrl+S. See also *flow control, pause key.* "We used *XON/XOFF* signals with our walkie-talkies."

XOR *(zor)*
A logical opera-
tion, otherwise
known as
Exclusive OR
or sometimes
EOR. See
Exclusive OR.

Exclusive OR

1 XOR 1	=	0
1 XOR 0	=	1
0 XOR 1	=	1
0 XOR 0	=	0

Exclusive OR operations.

X-ray *(eks-ray)* An electromagnetic
radiation of a short wavelength (less
than 100 angstroms, if your tape
measure is handy) that can pass
through walls, bodies, and other solid
objects. Computers don't produce
X-rays (but don't quote me on that
one). "Airport *X-ray* machines do not
damage your computer or laptop PC."

XT *(eks tee)* Acronym for *Extended
Technology,* a model of the IBM PC
computer that extended the architecture of the original 8080; extra expansion slots and a hard disk were
added. See also *AT, boat anchor, PC.*
"Let's put it this way: If your hot-air
balloon were leaking, the first thing
over the side would be that old *XT*
computer."

X

Y: *(wy koh-lon)* The letter name for some disk drive in your PC, a drive you probably don't have. Because a PC is capable of having a drive Y:, however, the term has to be in this dictionary. Most likely, a Y: on your computer is a network drive. I'm serious: It's a network drive. See also *network drive.*

Y2K *(wy too kay)* Acronym for the *Year 2000 problem,* where 2K represents 2000. See *2000 bug.*

Y adapter *(wy uh-dap-ter)* A cable with one end on one end and two ends on the other end — like the letter *Y.* This arrangement enables two devices to be connected to a single port; only certain kinds of devices, however, allow the use of Y adapters.

yacc *(yak)* Acronym for *yet another compiler compiler,* a UNIX tool used to create other languages and compilers. See also *UNIX.* "I know that the letters are *cc,* but does *yacc* really have to stand for *yet another compiler compiler?*"

A Yak delivering software and poultry to monks in Tibet.

Yahoo! *(yah-hoo)* A large catalog of information stored on the World Wide Web, at www.yahoo.com. See also *Web catalog.*

Year 2000 bug *(yeer too-thow-sand buhg)* See *2000 bug.*

yiblette *(yib-let)* A small piece of something, usually a long, skinny piece. A wee little chunk of cable. The plural is *yiblettes.* "One piece of spaghetti is a *yiblette,* not enough to get fat on."

YMODEM *(wy-moh-dum)* A communications protocol based on the XMODEM standard. Although YMODEM allows faster data transmission than XMODEM, it was soon eclipsed by ZMODEM. See also *XMODEM, ZMODEM, protocol.*

V

Z

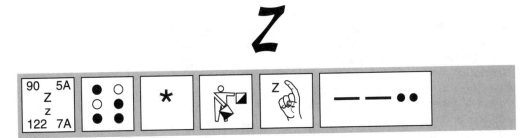

Z: *(zee-koh-lon)* Name for the last disk drive in a PC. Whew!

Z80 *(zee-ay-tee)* The name of an old, 8-bit microprocessor used in the days of the CP/M. The Z80 microprocessor was developed by an ex-Intel employee to mimic the Intel 8080. See also *CP/M*. "Nary 20 years ago, the *Z80* was considered the cutting edge of technology. Today, that and $2.25 will buy you a tall double latté."

Zamboni *(zam-boh-nee)* 1. The machine used to clean the ice in an ice skating rink. 2. The act of cleaning the ice using a Zamboni machine. "Our hockey team is so bad that the best part of the game is watching the Zamboni."

Avogadro Zamboni, not the developer of the Zamboni ice machine.

zap *(zap)* 1. To remove a file permanently from a disk. Unlike deleting a file, zapping a file removes it without the possibility of its being undeleted. See also *undelete*. "The first thing any 3-year-old learns how to do on a PC is to *zap.*" 2. To zero out the contents of memory; to write the value zero (or some other value) to every location in memory, perfectly erasing whatever was there. 3. To accidentally erase a disk drive. "Oops! Nothing on this disk. You must have accidentally *zapped* it." 4. To touch something and experience a static electrical discharge.

zero wait state *(zee-roh wayt stayt)* A condition in which the microprocessor does not have to wait until it can read information from RAM. See also *wait state.*

ZIF *(zif)* Acronym for *Zero Insertion Force,* a type of socket for plugging in chips, usually the CPU, such as the Pentium. Unlike other types of chip sockets that force you to push a chip into place, a ZIF socket lets you blithely drop the chip in the socket and then close a lever to cinch the chip securely in place. "If it weren't for the *ZIF* socket, we would be putting microprocessor chips into our motherboards with the same force and zeal as a toddler shoves a building block into the VCR."

ZIP *(zip)* 1. A suffix applied to files that have been compressed with the PKZIP utility. A ZIP file can be anywhere from 5 to 95 percent smaller than the original file (or group of files, if more than one was compressed at a time), which is useful for transferring files over a modem or for saving disk space. 2. The act of creating a ZIP file. "Dolores always *zipped* her files twice. She was afraid that they might accidentally become unzipped on the hard disk and embarrass themselves." 3. A type of removable disk (and drive) — like a super floppy drive. ZIP disks can store 100 megabytes of information. And they're fast, like a hard disk. These disks are descendants of the old Bernoulli box (made by the same company, in fact). See also *Bernoulli box.*

ZMODEM *(zee-moh-dum)* The most popular and efficient communications protocol, used by almost every communications program to send files back and forth. A successor to the XMODEM, YMODEM line (so ZMODEM was the obvious name for it), this file-transfer protocol enables information to be sent over the phone lines quickly and reliably. Also, ZMODEM sends the file's name and other information, automatically saving the file to disk for you. This protocol was a massive leap in convenience over the clumsy, older XMODEM method of doing things. See also *XMODEM, YMODEM.* "When I asked Klaus how he wanted me to send the file, he kept saying *"ZMODEM, ZMODEM."* I thought he was saying 'the modem, the modem,' so I kept asking over and over."

zoom *(zoom)* 1. To enlarge or reduce an image, typically a document displayed in a window. To "zoom in" enlarges the image. To "zoom out" reduces the image. This process is a boon to some users with large monitors, enabling them to display information large enough to be seen by the naked eye. 2. The command that zooms in or out, changing the way a document is displayed in a window. "I tried using the *Zoom* command to make my computer go faster, but it made my text bigger instead."

zoom box *(zoom boks)* An area or button on a window that increases the window size to full-screen proportions. "Arnie, get your ear away from the monitor; it's a *zoom box,* not a boom box."

Notes

Notes

Notes

Notes

Notes

Notes

BEST SELLERS ON EVERY TOPIC...

INTERNET

Internet For Dummies®, 5th Edition
0-7645-0354-5
Includes one
CD-ROM
$19.99 US
$26.99 Canada

Netscape Communicator 4 For Dummies®
0-7645-0053-8
$19.99 US
$26.99 Canada

Internet Explorer 4 For Windows® For Dummies®
0-7645-0121-6
$19.99 US
$26.99 Canada

The World Wide Web For Kids & Parents™
0-7645-0098-8
includes one
CD-ROM
$24.99 US
$34.99 Canada

E-Mail For Dummies®, 2nd Edition
0-7645-0131-3
Includes one
CD-ROM
$24.99 US
$34.99 Canada

America Online® For Dummies®, 4th Edition
0-7645-0192-5
Includes one
CD-ROM
$24.99 US
$34.99 Canada

Internet Directory For Dummies®
0-7645-0217-4
Includes one
CD-ROM
$24.99 US
$34.99 Canada

Internet For Teachers™, 2nd Edition
0-7645-0058-9
includes one
CD-ROM
$24.99 US
$34.99 Canada

Internet Games For Dummies®
0-7645-0164-X
$19.99 US
$26.99 Canada

#1 Bestselling Computer Book Series

"More than a publishing phenomenon, 'Dummies' is a sign of the times."
— The New York Times

30 MILLION

NEW!

THE INTERNET FOR DUMMIES® 5TH EDITION

A Reference for the Rest of Us!

by John Levine, Carol Baroudi, & Margaret Levine Young

Get the Information You Really Need The Fun and Easy Way™

Your First Aid Kit™ for Fast Relief and Stunning Results

What to Do When Bad Things Happen™ — Explained in Plain English

IDG BOOKS

OPERATING SYSTEMS...

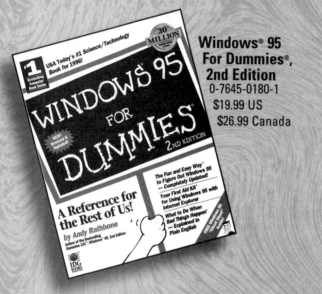

Windows® 95 For Dummies®, 2nd Edition
0-7645-0180-1
$19.99 US
$26.99 Canada

Windows® CE For Dummies®
0-7645-0260-3
$19.99 US
$26.99 Canada

Dummies 101®: Windows NT®
0-7645-0167-4
Includes one CD-ROM
$24.99 US
$34.99 Canada

DOS For Dummies®, Windows® 95 Edition
1-56884-646-0
$19.99 US
$26.99 Canada

Windows® 3.11 For Dummies®, 3rd Edition
1-56884-370-4
$16.95 US
$22.95 Canada

PC GENERAL COMPUTING...

PCs For Teachers™, 2nd Edition
0-7645-0240-9
Includes one CD-ROM
$24.99 US
$34.99 Canada

Upgrading & Fixing PCs For Dummies®, 3rd Edition
0-7645-0129-1
$19.99 US
$26.99 Canada

PCs For Dummies®, 5th Edition
0-7645-0269-7
$19.99 US
$26.99 Canada

PCs For Kids & Parents™
0-7645-0158-5
Includes one CD-ROM
$24.99 US
$34.99 Canada

Modems For Dummies®, 3rd Edition
0-7645-0069-4
$19.99 US
$26.99 Canada

Year 2000 Solutions For Dummies®
0-7645-0241-7
Includes one CD-ROM
$24.99 US
$34.99 Canada

Great Software For Kids & Parents™
0-7645-0099-6
Includes one CD-ROM
$24.99 US
$34.99 Canada

Mobile Computing For Dummies®
0-7645-0151-8
$19.99 US
$26.99 Canada

DATABASE...

**Approach® 97
For Windows®
For Dummies®**
0-7645-0001-5
$19.99 US
$26.99 Canada

**Access 97
For Windows®
For Dummies®**
0-7645-0048-1
$19.99 US
$26.99 Canada

**Access 2 For
Dummies®**
1-56884-090-X
$19.95 US
$26.95 Canada

**Filemaker® Pro
3 For Macs® For
Dummies®**
1-56884-906-0
$19.99 US
$26.99 Canada

SPREADSHEETS/FINANCE/
PROJECT MANAGEMENT...

**Excel For
Windows® 95
For Dummies®**
1-56884-930-3
$19.99 US
$26.99 Canada

**Excel 97
For Windows®
For Dummies®**
0-7645-0049-X
$19.99 US
$26.99 Canada

**QuickBooks® 5
For Dummies®,
3rd Edition**
0-7645-0043-0
$19.99 US
$26.99 Canada

**Microsoft®
Project 98
For Dummies®**
0-7645-0321-9
Includes one
CD-ROM
$24.99 US
$34.99 Canada

**Quicken® 6
For Windows®
For Dummies®,
4th Edition**
0-7645-0036-8
$19.99 US
$26.99 Canada

**Microsoft®
Project For
Windows® 95
For Dummies®**
0-7645-0084-8
Includes one
CD-ROM
$24.99 US
$34.99 Canada

**Microsoft®
Money 98
For Dummies®**
0-7645-0295-6
Includes one
CD-ROM
$24.99 US
$34.99 Canada

**Quicken® 98
For Windows®
For Dummies®**
0-7645-0243-3
$19.99 US
$26.99 Canada

OFFICE SUITES...

**Microsoft®
Office For
Windows® 95
For Dummies®**
1-56884-917-6
$19.99 US
$26.99 Canada

**Microsoft® Office 97
For Windows®
For Dummies®**
0-7645-0050-3
$19.99 US
$26.99 Canada

**Microsoft®
Works For
Windows® 95
For Dummies®**
1-56884-944-3
$19.99 US
$26.99 Canada

**ClarisWorks®
Office For
Dummies®**
0-7645-0113-5
$19.99 US
$26.99 Canada

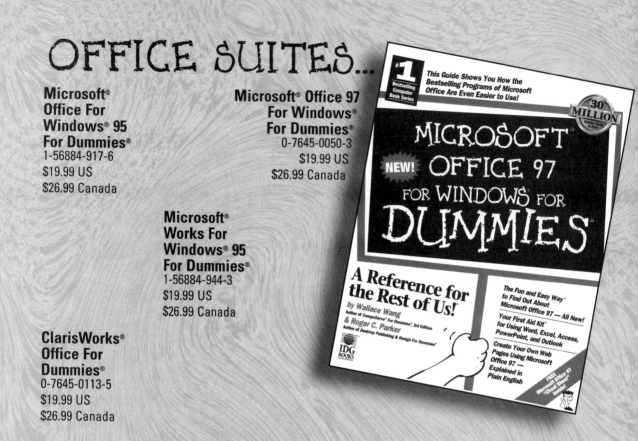

WORD PROCESSING...

**Word 97
For Windows®
For Dummies®**
0-7645-0052-X
$19.99 US
$26.99 Canada

**Corel® WordPerfect® 8
For Windows®
For Dummies®**
0-7645-0186-0
$19.99 US
$26.99 Canada

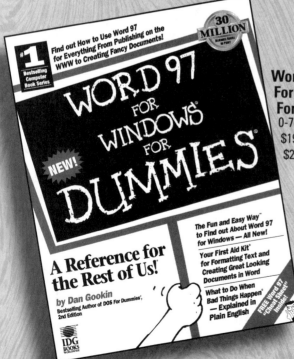

**Word For
Windows® 95
For Dummies®**
1-56884-932-X
$19.99 US
$26.99 Canada

FOR A COMPLETE LISTING OF ALL OUR DUMMIES BOOKS™, VISIT OUR WEB SITE AT.
www.dummies.com

There are 4 easy ways to order

1) CALL: 800-762-2974
(24 hours a day, 7 days a week)

2) FAX: 317-596-5295

3) VISIT our Web Site

4) MAIL THIS ORDER FORM TO:
IDG Books Worldwide, Inc.
attn: Order Entry
7260 Shadeland Station, Ste 100
Indianapolis, IN 46256

QUANTITY	ISBN	TITLE	RETAIL PRICE	TOTAL

SHIP TO:

Name_____

Company_____

Address_____

City/State/Zip_____

Daytime Phone_____

Shipping & Handling Charges	Description	First Book	Each Additional Book	Total
Domestic	Normal	4.50	1.50	$
	Two Day Air	8.50	2.50	$
	Overnight	18.00	3.00	$
International	Surface	8.00	8.00	$
	Airmail	16.00	16.00	$
	Overnight	17.00	17.00	$

Payment ❑ **Check to IDG Books (US Funds Only)**
   ❑ **Visa** ❑ **Mastercard** ❑ **American Express**

Card #_____ Exp._____ Signature_____

***Price subject to change
without notice.***

Promo Code: BOB

CA residents add applicable sales tax	
IN, MA, and MD residents add 5% sales tax	
IL residents add 6.25% sales tax	
RI residents add 7% sales tax	
TX residents add 8.25% sales tax	
Shipping	
TOTAL	

IDG BOOKS WORLDWIDE™

IDG BOOKS WORLDWIDE BOOK REGISTRATION

Register This Book and Win!

We want to hear from you!

Visit **http://my2cents.dummies.com** to register this book and tell us how you liked it!

- ✔ Get entered in our monthly prize giveaway.

- ✔ Give us feedback about this book — tell us what you like best, what you like least, or maybe what you'd like to ask the author and us to change!

- ✔ Let us know any other *...For Dummies* topics that interest you.

Your feedback helps us determine what books to publish, tells us what coverage to add as we revise our books, and lets us know whether we're meeting your needs as a *...For Dummies* reader. You're our most valuable resource, and what you have to say is important to us!

Not on the Web yet? It's easy to get started with *Dummies 101®: The Internet For Windows® 95* or *The Internet For Dummies®,* 4th Edition, at local retailers everywhere.

Or let us know what you think by sending us a letter at the following address:

...For Dummies Book Registration
Dummies Press
7260 Shadeland Station, Suite 100
Indianapolis, IN 46256
Fax 317-596-5498

BUSINESS AND
GENERAL
REFERENCE
BOOK SERIES
FROM IDG

COMPUTER
BOOK SERIES
FROM IDG

WWW.DUMMIES.COM

Discover Dummies Online!

The Dummies Web Site is your fun and friendly online resource for the latest information about ...*For Dummies®* books and your favorite topics. The Web site is the place to communicate with us, exchange ideas with other ...*For Dummies* readers, chat with authors, and have fun!

Ten Fun and Useful Things You Can Do at www.dummies.com

1. Win free ...*For Dummies* books and more!
2. Register your book and be entered in a prize drawing.
3. Meet your favorite authors through the IDG Books Author Chat Series.
4. Exchange helpful information with other ...*For Dummies* readers.
5. Discover other great ...*For Dummies* books you must have!
6. Purchase Dummieswear™ exclusively from our Web site.
7. Buy ...*For Dummies* books online.
8. Talk to us. Make comments, ask questions, get answers!
9. Download free software.
10. Find additional useful resources from authors.

Link directly to these ten fun and useful things at
http://www.dummies.com/10useful

WWW.DUMMIES.COM

For other technology titles from IDG Books Worldwide, go to
www.idgbooks.com

Not on the Web yet? It's easy to get started with *Dummies 101®: The Internet For Windows®95* or *The Internet For Dummies®*, 4th Edition, at local retailers everywhere.

Find other ...*For Dummies* books on these topics:
Business • Career • Databases • Food & Beverage • Games • Gardening • Graphics
Hardware • Health & Fitness • Internet and the World Wide Web • Networking
Office Suites • Operating Systems • Personal Finance • Pets • Programming • Recreation
Sports • Spreadsheets • Teacher Resources • Test Prep • Word Processing